Will Rogers
A BIOGRAPHY

Books by DONALD DAY

Backwoods to Border, Edited with Mody C. Boatright
(A Texas Folklore Society Publication)

From Hell to Breakfast, Edited with Mody C. Boatright
(A Texas Folklore Society Publication)

Big Country: Texas
(American Folkways Series)

The Autobiography of Will Rogers, Editor

Franklin D. Roosevelt's Own Story, Editor

Will Rogers on How We Elect Our Presidents, Editor

Woodrow Wilson's Own Story, Editor

Uncle Sam's Uncle Josh, Editor

The Autobiography of Sam Houston, Edited with Harry Ullom

The Evolution of Love

Sanity Is Where You Find It, Editor

Will Rogers

A BIOGRAPHY

by DONALD DAY

DAVID McKAY COMPANY, INC. New York

WILL ROGERS

PUBLISHED SIMULTANEOUSLY IN THE DOMINION OF CANADA

Seventh Printing, February 1969

LIBRARY OF CONGRESS CATALOG CARD NUMBER: 62-16719

MANUFACTURED IN THE UNITED STATES OF AMERICA

VAN REES PRESS • NEW YORK

To KLARI

"America's Most Complete Human Document"

SHORTLY AFTER WILL ROGERS CRASHED TO HIS DEATH with Wiley Post on August 15, 1935, at Point Barrow, Alaska, Carl Sandburg commented: "There is a curious parallel between Will Rogers and Abraham Lincoln. They were rare figures whom we could call beloved with ease and without embarrassment." Another Lincoln authority, Robert Sherwood, added: "The impact upon the people of America at the death of Will Rogers was similar to that produced by the death of Abraham Lincoln."

"Rare figures whom we could call beloved with ease and without embarrassment." A poetic concept that could have come only from a man who occupies a similar niche in the people's affection, and one which with Sherwood's statement supplies for the heart a full measure of understanding. And yet the mind is teased for a fuller comprehension.

Perhaps for Will Rogers a statement by Damon Runyon contains the best clue: "Will Rogers was America's most complete human document. He reflected in many ways the heartbeat of America. In thought and manner of appearance and in his daily life he was probably our most typical native born, the closest living approach to what we like to call the true American."

If this be so, the comprehension the mind seeks must emerge out of a study and appraisal, an unfolding, literally "a reading," of that "complete human document" against the times, events, and in relation to the people that produced it.

DONALD DAY

New York
February, 1962

Acknowledgments

IT IS DIFFICULT TO SINGLE OUT A FEW OF THE MANY WHO helped me with this book over the years. To all of you who gave your time and counsel I offer my profound thanks. I owe much to Mrs. Paula McSpadden Love, niece of Will Rogers and curator of the Will Rogers Memorial at Claremore, Oklahoma, and to her husband, Robert Love, Director of the Memorial, without whose cooperation my books on Will Rogers could hardly have come into being. By their untiring work, their love for Will Rogers, they have collected and preserved material that would otherwise have been lost.

I also gratefully acknowledge the unfailing and generous cooperation of Will Rogers, Jr. and his brother Jim, as well as that of Mrs. Rita Aurand.

Sources have been acknowledged throughout. Where material is not identified, the source in almost every case is Will Rogers' original manuscripts.

Contents

Illustrations

(between pages 242 and 243)

1

"There's a Lot of Mule in Willie"

"ANCESTORS DON'T MEAN A THING IN THE HUMAN TRIBE," Will Rogers once commented. "They're as unreliable as a political promise. A western range mare is liable to produce a Man o' War. You won't know what will happen. You just raise 'em and then start guessing. They no more take after Father and Mother than a Congressman will take after a good example."

Nevertheless, Will was fantastically proud of his Indian blood and it may well have been the dominating force in heredity's contribution to his make-up. "My ancestors met yours when they landed," he told a *Mayflower* group. "In fact, they would have showed better judgment if they had not let yours land."

Will was part Cherokee Indian from both his paternal and his maternal side. The original home of the Cherokees was in the valley of the Tennessee River, some 40,000 square miles, extending from the headwaters of the Kanawha and Tennessee rivers southward to the Appalachian foothills and westward to the Tennessee River, including portions of North Georgia, North and South Carolina and Tennessee.

An intelligent, industrious and peaceful people who loved their mountains and rivers and wanted nothing more than to make a pleasant, prosperous world for themselves, they were, from the beginning, outrageously victimized by the whites. Against this avalanche pouring in on them in constant pressure, they were understandably divided on what to do. In the end they were totally destroyed as a nation. "The manner and method of their destruction wrote the last and saddest chapter of Indian life east of the Mississippi. For they were not destroyed by war; the white man simply removed them from the land, as the English had moved the Acadians. There was no Evangeline to immortalize their tragedy, but their story remains one of the best known in American history, perhaps because it epitomizes everything that happened to the red man in his long battle against white supremacy." [1]

There was absolutely no justification for the removal of the Cherokees beyond greed and avarice. They were not a savage, warlike people who had inflicted a long series of brutalities on the white man. Their only fault was that, in living in peace, they wanted to live in their ancestral home, the country that they loved.

The majority of the Cherokees had allied themselves with the British against the French and then with the United States in the War of 1812. Most members of the tribe had adopted the white man's ways of living. Gone were the wigwams. Instead, the majority lived in houses, some of them sumptuous, and were farmers, ranchers, millers, smiths and traders. They had their own school system, read books, perused American and English newspapers, and had a newspaper of their own. A Cherokee, Sequoyah, devised an alphabet for the tribe that revolutionized their schooling.

In 1826 the tribe held a convention and drafted a written constitution modeled after that of the United States, something no other Indian tribe had ever done. It was adopted the following year by vote and under it the tribe became an independent nation. This ran counter to the claims of the state of Georgia, which maintained that instead of owning their lands the Cherokees were merely tenants of the state. In 1829 a removal bill was introduced in Congress. In the meantime the state of Georgia, acting independently, had divided up the land and deprived the Cherokees of practically all their civil rights. The tribe took the case to the Supreme Court, which at first ruled against it on the grounds of no jurisdiction as the Cherokees were an independent nation. The following year, however, the Court reversed itself.

[1] John Tebbel and Keith Jennison, *The American Indian Wars* (New York: Harper & Brothers, 1960), p. 222.

"John Marshall has made his decision," President Jackson remarked, "now let him enforce it."

President Jackson proceeded with the plan to move the Cherokees to the west regardless of the Court's decision. This travesty is as dark a blot on American history as exists. The bodily removal of over 15,000 Cherokees from their ancient home was accomplished by a military force of 7,000 under the command of General Winfield Scott beginning in May, 1838. Before this many Cherokees, sensing the inevitable, had gone west voluntarily, among whom was Will Rogers's great-grandfather, Robert Rogers, who settled with his family in the Arkansas Territory and later, when the other Cherokees were forced to move, joined them in the Going Snake District of the new Cherokee Nation.

The grandfather of Will's mother, John Gunther, was a mixture of Welsh and English. He settled in the Cherokee country where as a powdermaker and trader he accumulated considerable property. One holding, a salt flat, adjoined the territory of the Paint Clan of the Cherokees. Its chief visited Gunther to barter for salt and brought his fifteen-year-old daughter, Catherine, with him. One glimpse of her and bachelor John offered the clan salt "while the grass grows and the rivers run" in exchange for her in marriage. The chief accepted his offer.

A shy, timid girl, Catherine was never at ease in her husband's big log house. When children came, Gunther refused to let her care for them, and when they reached school age sent them to boarding schools. Catherine spoke no English and the children were not allowed to learn Cherokee, so she could not communicate with them. As the years passed, she would disappear for weeks to live with her own people. Then, drawn back by the desire to see her children, she would slip into the big house for a short time, almost unnoticed by her husband and children. One of these, Elizabeth, married Martin Schrimsher, of whom little is known except that he had a trace of either German or Dutch blood. Shortly after their marriage, they went west over "the trail of tears."

It was springtime, the trees were greened out, and everything seemed propitious for a great harvest. To these people who had lived in these beloved surroundings for countless centuries, probably before

Greece attacked Troy in the name of a fair woman but really over trade routes, the threat of expulsion held over them was as unreal as most of the white man's ways. This was a believing people who had made peace with the stern forces of nature and with themselves. The crops were planted and the young corn, with a good seasoning in the ground, was knee-high when the soldiers, without warning, appeared on the scene, with wagons to haul the Indians and their possessions to a stockade. Any belongings left behind were stolen or burned by a frontier rabble that came on the heels of the soldiers. Those herded in the stockade suffered from dysentery and fevers and were the prey of white jackals attempting to fleece them out of their last money.

Herded into flatboats on the Tennessee, they began the journey into the fearful West, from which, according to their mythology, blew the sere wind of death. They feared the dark country more than the journey, but in this they were mistaken. It was the journey that became the real horror. Out of the 15,000 who began the trek more than 4,000 perished. Eventually, they reached their new lands, most of them impoverished, and members of their families left in shallow graves along "the trail of tears." There was nothing to do except start a new life under new promises that were to prove as untrustworthy as had those of the past.

After the main body of the Cherokees arrived in their new home, promised to be theirs by treaty as long as the grass grows and the rivers run, an autonomous government was set up with the capital at Tahlequah, schools were established, and the members of the tribe got down to the business of their individual affairs. Martin and Elizabeth Schrimsher settled on the Verdigris River and it was there that a baby daughter, ironically named Mary America, was born on an unknown date. In another part of the Nation, on January 11, 1839, there was born to James Rogers (the son of Robert) and Catherine Vann Rogers a baby boy. He was named Clement Vann. Intermixed in them was Indian, Irish, English, and either German or Dutch blood. Will's father was probably one quarter Cherokee and his mother three eighths.

Clem's father died when he was young, and upon reaching school age he was sent to a boy's seminary at Tahlequah. It was there that he met Mary America Schrimsher, now "a tall, slender girl with dark hair and flashing black eyes." So pretty and witty was she that Clem had eyes only for her. The most popular girl in school, she let him know that she approved, but she was not going to make a final decision until she had looked around a bit. A new land and new conditions had changed things since John Gunther had bought a bed companion with salt.

With the impetuosity of a sixteen-year-old boy, Clem stormed home to prove himself. There he found intolerable conditions. While he had been at school his mother had remarried, and in a few days it became apparent to her that her husband and her high-spirited son could not get along. With rare wisdom and confidence she gave Clem two Negro slaves, 200 head of cattle, and a dozen ponies and sent him forth to make it on his own. In doing so she passed on to him an injunction from his father: "Tell Clem to always ride his own horse." Clem began ranching near the present town of Oolagah, Oklahoma.

Under the Indian law, all the land was held in common by the tribe, and thousands of acres beckoned to anyone with the enterprise to make use of them. Clem not only had the enterprise but had invaluable help in his two slaves, Rabb and Houston, who were reliable and industrious. "There wasn't any man better to be owned by than Mister Clem," Rabb commented many years later. "When he said a thing he meant it, and you didn't trifle when he give you an order. But he treated us good." As soon as the ranching operation was organized, Clem turned it over to Rabb and Houston and opened a trading post. By "hard work, perseverance and taking advantages of his opportunities" (a formula Will was to take many a crack at later as it was exploited particularly in the pages of the *American Magazine*) in a couple of years Clem had a flourishing business and an expanding ranch. In the meantime he had seen to it Mary heard about his progress and when he proposed marriage she accepted. They set up housekeeping in a log cabin he had built near the trading post. A year later a baby girl was born whom they named Elizabeth. At almost the same time the Civil War began.

Most of the influential and wealthier Cherokees owned slaves, and tremendous pressure was brought on the Nation to go with the Confederacy. A prominent Cherokee, Stand Watie, recruited a mounted rifle regiment and twenty-one-year-old Clem became a first lieutenant. Everything was in doubt and confusion. Fighting broke out among the Cherokees and open warfare with nearby tribes. Clem's trading post and ranch were in the midst of it, as well as adjacent to the Kansas border where Union troops were stationed. Mary and Elizabeth were first removed to Fort Gibson, where the baby sickened and died. As the fighting became more bitter, Clem took Mary to Texas, where other relatives had fled for safety, and at Bonham in 1863 another baby girl, Sallie, was born.

By the time of General Lee's surrender, on April 9, 1865, the Cherokee country was, with the exception of Virginia, the most ravaged section of the strife-torn land. Brigadier General Watie's regiment had covered itself with glory and was the last to lay down its arms. With his surrender, on June 3, 1865, the last pure Indian government in the United States passed away. A new treaty had to be negotiated with the United States, and the Cherokees, having picked the losing side, had to be content with a territorial status and the loss of much of their land to other tribes that had fought with the North.

The moment that Clem was mustered out as a captain, he hurried to Texas for Mary and the baby to begin life anew. Back in the territory destruction and desolation awaited them. Clem's cattle had long ago vanished into hungry stomachs and his improvements at the trading post and on the ranch were piles of weed-covered rubbish. To get a small stake he worked as a common laborer at Fort Gibson, but this definitely was not "riding his own horse." After a few months he began freighting between St. Joe, Missouri, and Dallas, Texas. Although he had built up a prosperous business, with the coming of railroads he realized he could no longer compete. On his last trip he carried a stock of goods into the Choctaw and Chickasaw Nations, and traded for cattle which he drove to the Verdigris River bottoms across from where he had first ranched. He brought Mary and the baby there and began ranching in earnest. In the next decade he fenced in thousands of acres of rich grassland, the first man in the region to use barbed wire. In addition, he brought in herds of cattle, fattened them on unfenced range, and shipped them over the railroad to the Kansas City and St. Louis markets.

As Clem became enormously successful, the small log cabin gave way to a large, two-story house with open halls and porches upstairs and down. Broad stone chimneys flanked both ends and there were open fireplaces in four of the seven rooms. The walls were of heavy walnut logs cut in the river bottom and the structure was weather-boarded outside and plastered inside. In addition to his private activities, Clem became judge for the district in 1877 and senator in 1879, the year Will was born. Known far and wide as Uncle Clem, he was one of the richest and most influential men in the territory. Everyone was welcome at his house, although Kansas people were not looked upon with affection. "As a young boy I didn't know a Republican from a Democrat," Will said, "only in one way; if some man or bunch of men rode up to the ranch to eat or stay all night, and my father set me to watching 'em all the time they was there—what they did and what they carried off—why, I learned in afteryears that they was Republican; and the ones I didn't spy on—why, they were Democrats. For the Democrats were loyal that way—they never took from each other."

By the time Will began his verbal protests, November 4, 1879, his mother had given birth to eight children. Sallie, Maude, Robert and May were alive, the others having died at birth. Will was named Colonel William Penn Adair in honor of a prominent and influential Cherokee leader. At seven his name was entered on the Authenticated Rolls of the Cherokee Nation as No. 2340.

"I am the only known child in History who claims to Nov. 4th as my Birthday, that is election day," Will wrote. "That's why I have always had it in for politicians." [2] His appearance on the scene was not auspicious for a career in the *Ziegfeld Follies,* if a contemporary witness may be believed. A bashful cowboy came to see him a few days after he was born. He shuffled from one foot to the other.

"Barney, I know exactly what you are thinking," Mary said, a smile crinkling the corners of her eyes.

"What do you mean, ma'am?" Barney asked.

"You're thinking this is the ugliest baby you ever saw," she said.

"You know, Sam," Barney later told another cowboy, "Mrs. Rogers sure is a mind reader."

[2] *Autobiography of Will Rogers* (Boston: Houghton Mifflin Company, 1949), pp. 1-5. There is Will's own account of his entry into the world here.

Many years later Will and Barney met at Claremore and chuckled over this.

"There was something else mighty peculiar about that first time I saw you," Barney recalled.

"What was it, Barney?" Will asked.

"You was speechless."

The "speech" may not have been there yet but the other elements were—both in inheritance and in environment. In the baby there was a mixture of slightly more than a quarter Cherokee Indian, much Irish, a sprinkling of English, Welsh, Scotch, and either Dutch or German.

The country that Will opened his eyes to was "a fragment of earth unlike any other in the whole world because it somehow gave realization to a spirit," in the words of Noel Kaho. It was not, as some claim, because it "held the last flare of the Anglo-Saxon spirit, that here was the last frontier." It was something else, something indigenous, "too well blended with Osage and Delaware and Cherokee to carry an alien tag." It was a way of life peculiarly Indian, "a spirit of gaiety and laughter at work" that "somehow got distilled and poured into the heart of a little boy." [3]

Aristocrats of the American Indians, the Cherokees were a lively, intelligent people, fond of jokes and extremely gregarious. Yet beneath the lively exterior they had solid character. Over and over the victims of white diplomacy, their chiefs made bad bargains, but the Cherokees kept their part of the bargains. Sustained by their saving grace of humor, they had over the years grown tolerantly cynical of white civilization. Their religion—which had such an appeal for Sam Houston—was poetic, dramatic and couched in much pageantry. For untold centuries their gods had protected their ancient hunting grounds and given them a good life in which time was marked not by clocks and calendars but by the change of seasons, by birth, life and death. It is not difficult to understand that the white man's religion would be looked upon with suspicion since it preached one thing and practiced another. Missionaries on the Arkansas unsuccessfully tried to convince them that Christianity was a better safeguard against evil

[3] Noel Kaho, *The Will Rogers Country* (Norman, Okla.: University of Oklahoma Press, 1941).

spirits than their own pagan religion. The hell-fire that went with Christianity seemed infinitely worse than the minor discomforts of witches and hobgoblins.

Regardless of whether their way was better or not, something more powerful overwhelmed it and most of the beliefs and mores of the Cherokees were pushed into the background. Nevertheless, they were not, and never will be, completely eradicated. The mixtures of blood in Will Rogers, particularly the Indian racial instincts and memories, never ceased their tug of war. Nor did the call of this land that gave him birth ever cease, although it could not contain completely his restless spirit.

There were the times also. The Civil War seemed to have drawn the United States into itself as a coiled spring which at the war's end pushed the nation to the Pacific in one tremendous surge. This movement was checked for a while in the territory because it had been assigned to the Indians. But only so long as there was other free land to settle on. This somewhat held back the changes taking place in the rest of the country but not for long. The first decade of Will's life, the 1880's, saw his father's ranch and farm operations expand to their fullest and then gradually decline. They were to change sharply when once again under pressure from the land-hungry whites the Indians were to have their lands taken from them.

Most important for Will's development was the family life surrounding him in contrast to that outside. Within it the boy lived in an atmosphere of warmth, love and security. Outside, quite a different situation prevailed. Because of the difficulty of extradition, the Indian Territory became a haven for criminals of all kinds, a situation not of the Cherokees' making or willing. Eventually the situation became so desperate that the United States courts began handling murder cases rather than leaving them to the Indian courts. "In the old days in the Indian Territory," Will recalled, "there were so many United States marshals and so many whiskey peddlers that they had to wear badges to keep from selling each other." Many train and bank robbers hid out in the territory. "Most of us boys knew these outlaws by sight," Will commented, "but that was about all we wanted to know about them. We sho' didn't ask too many questions. In the glorious old State of Oklahoma a rope is not only an implement; it's tradition. Our history has been built on citizens dangling in the air by a rope and some escaped the dangling that would have made better history if they hadn't."

Men living in a violent land must tread more softly, but when they act it must be with firmness and decision. Such a one Willie (as his family called him) had in the person of his father, whom he greatly admired and wanted to please, although he seldom could do so. But it was his mother that he adored and her influence went with him the rest of his life. She had suffered the death of three of her children in infancy and when Willie was not quite four the older boy, Robert, died of typhoid fever. Will's only memory of his brother was seeing him astride a brown horse named Kaiser on his way to help the cowboys with cattle work, and he envied him the horse even then. With the knowledge that there would be no more sons, Mary hovered over Willie with tender care and was happy to see him grow into a healthy, sturdy youngster. The two became boon companions. Always Will recalled her in her rocking chair, smiling at him and lifting her hand to the gray-streaked, black hair, which she wore in a knot at the back of her head. "Mama's name was Mary," Will wrote, "and if your mother was an old-fashioned woman and named Mary you don't need to say much for her, everybody knows already."

Proud of her home, Mary kept the big house neat and spotless. Invariably, when she returned home from visiting neighbors she brought seeds and cuttings, and people came from miles around to see the yellow jonquils and white and lavender hyacinths planted inside the white picket fence that enclosed the yard. On frosty nights, Will would help her cover the tender young plants she had been growing in tomato cans in the house for early spring transplanting. Her voice was calm and soft in contrast to Clem's, which was loud and blustery.

"Although I was quite young," said Miss Gazelle Lane, long the librarian at Claremore, "I still remember Will's mother. She had a buckboard and drove a white horse. She and Willie would go visiting together. I have always thought this was where he got his interest in going to see people. When anybody in our section saw a buckboard and white horse coming, they knew they were in for a good time."

In line with many frontier women, Mary wanted her son to become a preacher. Uncle Clem did not argue too openly about it, although he growled that "there is damn little money in it." On the other hand, he did not encourage such a course for his son by example. He gave in to Mary on asking blessing at mealtime, but as if ashamed of himself for his weakness, the next moment he might pour out a string of cuss-words "as thick as a hoe handle." One of his favorite tricks, especially when there was company present, was to take Willie's nursing bottle away from him so that the boy would rip out some cuss words he had taught him. "Stop that, Clem," Mary would say. "Why, it makes me sick to hear it." On the question of working on Sunday, which Mary deplored, Clem turned a deaf ear. Work was his religion and Sunday was no exception. In another way, also, Willie emulated his father. Even when Uncle Clem did not profane the blessing by cuss words, he mumbled through it as fast as he could so that he could get at his food. He had an enormous appetite, as did Willie, who never lost his taste for the food he ate at home.

It was "beans cooked plenty soupy like, just old plain white navys, cooked in plenty of ham or fat meat. Got to eat 'em with a spoon." And then ham, fried ham, cured on the ranch, "smoked over an old hickory log fire, then salted away for a long time. Then the cream gravy. You know there is an awful lot of folks dont know much about eating gravy. Why, not to be raised on gravy would be like never going swimming in the creek." Ham gravy was the last word for Will, although "good beefsteak gravy" was a close second. But it had to be made after the beef had been cut thin and fried hard. "Do you know all this eating raw, bloody, rare meat, like they order in those big hotels, and City people like, that aint it," he commented. "That old raw junk goes for the high Collars in Cities, they are kinder cannibalistic anyhow." Along with the beans, ham, steak and gravy went corn bread. "Not the corn bread like you mean," he hastened to say. "I mean corn pone, made with nothing but meal, and hot water and salt. Then for dessert? Dont have room for any dessert. Had any more room would eat some more beans."

Willie's mother was in poor health after his birth, and much of his daily care was left to a Negro woman, Aunt Babe Walker. She was the soul of kindness, an extremely religious woman who read the Bible when she had nothing else to do, or sang religious hymns. "Come here, Willie," she would call. "The good Lord say, 'suffer little children to come unto me.' " Years later Will admitted that this frightened him because he did not want to suffer.

As Will grew older and spent more time outside, Aunt Babe's husband, Uncle Dan Walker, took charge of the boy. It was he who first interested Willie in roping and made him practice until every throw was perfect. "Naw, naw, Willie," he would grumble, "that ain't the way to do it. Hold yo' rope thisaway." Perhaps to keep the boy out of mischief, Uncle Dan had him practicing hours on end, most of the roping being done on an old elm stump in the yard which Will later said he wore to the ground. Gradually, as the boy improved, Uncle Dan permitted him to rope at moving objects. "I could rope turkies at four," Will said, "and I caught 'em, too."

Uncle Dan's son, Mack, and daughter, Charlotte, were Willie's earliest playmates. "Charlotte could catch a goat with a lariat before I could get my loop made," Will admitted. "After roping a nanny goat, she would milk it while we looked on." Willie and Mack practiced riding on the goats until their mounts learned they could be dislodged by butting into a rail fence. After this Will would get down on all fours and let Mack cinch a saddle on his back. Then Mack would climb on the saddle and Willie would start bucking around the yard while imitating the sounds of a horse's hoofs. "Sounds jes like a stampede coming," Uncle Dan growled. After a few rounds Willie would flatten down on the ground and with one huge lunge, his hands held high in the air like the front feet of a horse, would buck off his playmate.

"Now it's my time to be the hoss," Mack would say.

To this Willie shook his head stubbornly. Ordinarily, he took his turn at anything without complaining, but neither now nor in the future did he like to get bucked off a horse, although he took many nasty spills playing polo. Actually, Willie liked roping better than anything, and it nearly resulted in his being seriously injured or killed.

Willie and his sister, Maude, were walking across a pasture when, suddenly, they heard Uncle Clem yelling at them to run for their lives. They glanced around to see him galloping toward them on horseback and pointing to one side. Startled glances showed a great bull tearing at them, its horns lowered. Maude began to run, holding onto Willie's hand. He jerked loose, planted his feet firmly apart on the ground, and measured out a loop on a small rope he had been carrying.

"Run, Willie, run," Maude screamed from the safety of the fence.

As the bull was almost on Willie, Uncle Clem reached down from his speeding horse and scooped him up to safety. Out of danger, Uncle Clem stopped the horse, laid Willie across the horn of his saddle and gave him a good spanking. The boy clamped his lips shut and did not make a sound.

"Why didn't you run?" his father demanded.

"Didn't need to," he said while trying to keep the tears back. "I'd have caught him with my rope."

"Willie's awful brave," Maude bragged later.

Uncle Clem shook his head with the same stubborn look Willie had in his eyes.

"Well, I guess there isn't much to do," he confided to Mary. "There's a lot of mule in Willie."

This stubbornness had in it a stoical acceptance that was Indian in its origin and nature. Long past the normal time for weaning, Willie refused to give up his nursing bottle. All pleas were met with clenched teeth and a shake of his head. One day he and Maude were crossing the Verdigris River in a boat during floodwaters. Willie had his bottle in his hand. A log struck the boat and jarred the bottle out of his hand. In stunned silence he watched the bottle float out of sight, and he never asked for it again.

Another stubborn acceptance indicates a different characteristic. When Willie was seven or eight the family went to visit relatives at Christmastime. The boys were outside shooting off firecrackers. A cousin, Spi Trent, noticed a package of firecrackers hanging out of Willie's back pocket, and set them off. As they began to explode Willie made a running dive into a snowbank. The seat of his pants was burnt off and he was scorched so badly that he had to be doctored with lard and put to bed. Months later he and Spi were riding together.

"Willie," Spi said, "did you suspect who set off those firecrackers?"

"I knowed, Spi."

"Why didn't you tell who done it?"

"Well, Spi," he said, "the seat of my pants was already burnt off and I didn't see no sense in havin' the seat of yours whipped off."

Willie's beloved rope often proved a nuisance to others. When he was six he roped a big turkey gobbler as it took flight, breaking its neck.

"I'll never do it again," he promised, as hat in hand, his grin flashing, he handed it to its owner, "but I'll stay until you eat it."

In addition, he paid for the bird out of his weekly allowance.

Tolerant in most things, Willie's constant roping of everything in sight, particularly inside the house, annoyed his mother. One day when a neighboring woman was visiting her, Willie kept roping various objects in the room.

"If you don't quit that, Willie," she threatened, "I'll spank you."

Willie kept right on roping. Mary got to her feet and started toward him. Instantly his loop flashed out and, as it settled over her head, he drew it tight, pinning her arms to her sides. As she still moved toward him, he backed away as he had seen good roping horses do. Finally she stopped, shook her head, and burst out laughing.

"If you'll promise not to spank me," Willie offered, shaking a warning finger at her, "I'll turn you loose."

In addition to teaching Willie how to rope, from the time he could toddle outside, Uncle Dan, with Clem's enthusiastic approval, was accustoming him to the back of a horse. At first he would put the boy on the back of a gentle old animal and lead it around the corral. As he grew older he would ride up front on the saddle when cowboys were working the cattle. Willie's curious eyes studied the way the men got on their horses, turning the horse's head with the rein so it would not start off before they were in the saddle, and how they swung up in one quick, graceful movement, then handled the reins lightly so as not to injure the horse's mouth. More than anything else in the world, Willie wanted a horse of his own, and his father had promised him one as soon as he was old enough. When Willie was five, his father told him he thought the time had come.

"When do I get him?" Willie asked.

"Tomorrow."

All of Willie's pleas to learn more about the horse met with a shake of the head from Uncle Clem. Willie was up at daylight, prowling the barns and corrals, but there was no sign of a pony that might be for him. At the usual time, Aunt Babe called him to breakfast. This morning there were hot biscuits, big slices of hickory-cured ham with red-eye gravy, a huge platter of fried eggs, fresh-churned butter, and a big goblet of milk for him.

Willie glanced around the table to see if anyone was watching him. His father sat at the head of the table, a big, impressive-looking man with heavy eyebrows and drooping mustache. As usual, he had on a white shirt, collar, tie, coat and vest. An important man in the territory, he dressed the part. Mary sat at the foot of the table and although almost fifty, her face still showed traces of the pretty girl she had been. Next to Uncle Clem sat Sister Sallie. She was a young woman now, tall and pretty, and would blush if Tom McSpadden's name was mentioned to her. Across from Sallie sat Maude and May. Willie was between Sallie and his mother. It was a tight-knit family in which there was a great deal of warmth, affection and love. As he looked them over proudly, Uncle Clem thought that all of them made too much fuss over Willie. Then he did exactly the same thing by giving him everything he wanted.

"Papa . . ." Willie said hesitantly, when his father had finished the blessing.

"Yes, son."

"Do you remember what day this is?"

"Wednesday, I think."

"Don't tease the boy, Clem," Mary said. "I think he is too young, but you did promise him a pony."

"Pshaw!" Uncle Clem snorted. "Nothing grows a boy up into the right kind of man like a good horse, and I am a man of my word. Eat your breakfast, Willie."

As Willie gulped his food he kept one eye on his father. Suddenly there was a cowboy whoop outside. Uncle Clem pushed his chair, wiped his mouth on his napkin, dusted off his vest and stood up.

"Come on, Willie," he said.

The boy raced outside, followed by his father and the rest of the family. There stood Uncle Dan holding the reins of a small sorrel mare with an arched head. She had on a little saddle. Uncle Dan handed the reins to Willie. He took them, held them tight, placed a foot in the stirrup and tried to swing up. As he did so, he slackened the reins and the pony started forward.

"Watch out, Clem, he'll get hurt," Mary called out.

"Try again, Willie," said Uncle Clem, motioning Mary to be quiet.

This time Willie pulled the reins too tight and the pony circled on him.

"Please, Clem . . ."

"Try again, Willie."

This time he made it. With a touch of the rein he turned the pony, rode out the open gate and down a lane toward the river, waving to them as he passed out of sight. A wonderful feeling of exhilaration came over him. He had a horse under him and he was on his way. Never was he to feel so much at home, so much a complete being, as when on a horse. "There is something wrong with a man who doesn't love a good horse," he always maintained, and he was never to see a good one that he did not want to own. Actually, a horse could not have lived with a better family than Uncle Clem's, and it was to be the same when Willie had a family of his own.

His rope, his horse, his doting family, a lust for living, and certainly one of the grandest playgrounds in all the world. Willie would have been content for time to stop, but things have a way of changing and the boy helped them to do so.

"If it wasn't for my pony and my rope," he said to his mother, "I might grow up to be famous."

Mary raised an eyebrow and that night had a talk with her husband. By now Sallie had married Tom McSpadden and moved across the river near a school. It was determined that Willie would live with Sallie when school opened and begin his education.

2

Dry Grazing in Academic Pastures

WILLIE PUT ON A REAL BUCKING ACT WHEN TOLD THAT he was to leave home to be corralled within the four walls of a schoolhouse. He finally agreed, since he was to live with Sister Sallie, but only on condition that his pony, Dandy, go with him. As an additional inducement, Uncle Clem bought him a special handmade saddle like his own with W.P.R. tooled on the side of it.

Life with the McSpaddens was pleasant enough, but the one-room log cabin schoolhouse with uncomfortable split-log, backless benches was a nightmare. Most of the pupils were full-blood Indians. "I had just enough white in me to make my honesty questionable," Will said. Life inside the schoolroom was unbearable. Willie was always ready to go to a spring for a bucket of water to pass around, and the teacher was glad to get the fidgety boy outside under any pretext. Only at recess and noon play periods did he really come alive. The boys raced their ponies and played games. Willie was nicknamed "Rabbit" because of his big ears and speed in running. "A person that gabbed as much as I did had to be fast," he admitted.

As the redbud and dogwood bloomed in the spring and the grass turned green, Willie barely managed to stick it out until school closed. When he rode up to the house at home, with a whoop of joy, he had improved his roping and riding, knew how to cure hiccoughs by swallowing oil of cloves, knew that if a fox barked he must bark back at it, but the report card he carried indicated he had learned little else.

This made not the slightest dent in his high spirits. A year older and Dandy under him, he ranged farther afield, spending much of his time with the six sons of Rabb Rogers, one of Clem's former slaves. They rode and roped, picked berries and swam in Rabb's creek. Although the other boys did, Willie would not fish or hunt. "There must be a lot of pleasure in it," he wrote later, "but I just dont want to be shooting at any animal, and even a fish, I haven't got the heart to pull the hook out of him." When a cousin of his came in one day and proudly displayed a fawn he had shot, Willie took one horrified look. "You oughtn't to have killed it," he said.

When another year at this school produced the same results, Uncle Clem enrolled him the following fall in a girl's seminary at Muskogee along with Maude and May. Willie was to room with the principal's son, and it was hoped that the more serious atmosphere might awaken his interest in learning. Furthermore, Dandy did not accompany him. It was a grave miscalculation. The girls were at the "giggling" age, and Willie liked nothing better than to get them started. It might be by the slow, lazy way he got out of his seat, or the manner in which he peeked out from under his forelock, like a shy little brown pony, or when he would let one eyebrow climb to the top of his forehead. He could mimic, also, and as he talked he would let his voice go from a deep bass to a falsetto in one sentence. He was such a funny, homely little boy, with mischievous gray eyes, a lock of brown hair that was always hanging down into his face, that he had little trouble keeping them giggling.

It was not a happy time, though. "I felt just like Old Custer did when he was surrounded by Indians," he described the year there, "as I was an island completely surrounded by petticoats."

The summer that followed was the unhappiest of his life. It began by an attack of measles, with a relapse that kept him in bed for several weeks. Then Sallie lost her first baby. While he was still in bed his mother came down with typhoid fever. Although relays of wagons hauled ice from Coffeyville, 40 miles away, Mary's fever could not be controlled and she died. When they buried her in the little family cemetery, with its twisted cedars and crape myrtle bushes enclosed by an old-fashioned iron fence, Willie was too sick to attend the services.

"My folks have told me what little humor I have comes from her," he wrote. "I can't remember her humor but I can remember her love and understanding of me." He was ten when she died.

The following fall Willie was sent to the seminary at Tahlequah that his father had attended, but he did not last until Christmas. He became extremely untidy in his dress, let off Indian war whoops in the hall, and refused to obey orders. Earlier in the fall Uncle Clem had bought 3,000 cows in Texas and on the drive to the ranch a number of them had died, leaving motherless calves. There were about fifty of these and he gave them to Willie to tend. The boy taught them to drink milk out of a bucket and branded them with his own brand—shaped like the front end of a dog iron.

But life at home was not the same with his mother dead, Sallie married, and the other girls off at school. Uncle Clem was gone from home much of the time in connection with his various enterprises and public duties. Willie was alone in the big house at these times except for a woman, Mary Bible, who had been hired to help when his mother was sick. When fall came Uncle Clem packed him off to Willie Halsell College (actually what might be designated as a junior high school today) about 20 miles from the ranch. The boy remained here for four years in what were perhaps his happiest schooldays. This was due partly to many of the neighboring boys and girls being there, and also because home was less pleasant than ever as his father had married Mary Bible.

Years later, long after the school had closed, Will attended a homecoming of its alumni. "We are celebrating the passing of Willie Halsell Institute," he said. "Well, there were guys went there that would have put Harvard and Yale out of business. I studied art at Willie Halsell. I also took elocution. I stopped just in time or I would have been a Senator."

In the summer of 1893 Willie accompanied Uncle Clem to Chicago with a trainload of cattle, riding in the caboose. After the cattle were sold, they took in the World's Fair. In the Streets of Cairo they ate Turkish, Hungarian and Egyptian dishes, Oriental johnnycake, hot zelabiah and Arab's loaf, which they broke in imitation of a Bedouin in the desert. Willie rode a camel and a giant Ferris wheel, the first one built. It carried 2,260 riders at one time and from its 300-foot height the city and Lake Michigan spread out before his eager eyes.

As it reached the top, he instinctively dug his spurs into the wooden bench on which he sat.

The most exciting part of the trip was Buffalo Bill's Wild West Show. It opened with the great showman making the Grand Entry atop Old Duke, "the grandest parade horse on earth. Behind him rode Uhlans, Arabs, Russian Cossacks, French Chasseurs, British Hussars, Japanese and American Cavalry." As Buffalo Bill (Colonel William F. Cody) swept off his big black hat and in a dramatic voice boomed, "Permit me to introduce the Congress of Rough Riders of the World," Willie took in a deep breath, closed his eyes, and sighed as he let the air out.

A dizzy whirl of fast-moving acts followed: the pony express riders; the Fifth Royal Irish Lancers riding at full gallop as they picked hats off each other; an Indian act with 150 Sioux; a prairie watering hole to which wild buffalo came close to where Buffalo Bill and an emigrant train were camped with lighted fires over which supper was cooked and eaten, followed by a Virginia reel on horseback.

All this faded into insignificance, however, when the Mexican *vaqueros* began their roping routine. These colorful performers were headlined by a man in "an embroidered jacket, buckskin trousers ornamented with brass buttons, a red sash and a hat trimmed with gold braid" by the name of Vincente Oropeza who was billed as "the greatest roper in the world." And he proved so to Willie. He did "fluent spins, leaped lightly in and out of his whirling loop and snared a racing horse by its front feet, back feet, all four feet, the saddle horn and, finally, by its tail." As a closing stunt, he wrote his name, one letter at a time, in the air. This brought tears to Willie's eyes, and as accurately as Oropeza spelled out his name he spelled out the future course of the boy's life.

In the summer of 1895, sensing that the future of the territory was no longer in agriculture, Uncle Clem helped organize a bank in Claremore, bought extensive property there, and moved there to live. As farmers flocking in on the railroads had taken up the free grazing land, his holdings had shrunk to a fifth of their former size. In the same summer, carried away by admiration for the horse and buggy of the traveling representative of Scarritt College, at Neosho, Missouri, Willie had enrolled for the fall term.

The first day on the campus Willie met a woman with two daughters who had attended Willie Halsell with him.

"Why, Willie Rogers," she exclaimed, "it looks like you're just following my girls around."

"Yes'm," he agreed, "where they go I go, an' what they learn I learn."

"I hope not," she replied.

Willie managed to stick it out at Scarritt for a year and almost until Christmas of the second year. An old mare owned by one of the teachers ambled out on the campus, followed by her colt. Willie was standing toying with his rope with a group of boys.

"Rope her, Willie," one of them said.

Willie's lasso shot out and caught the mare around the neck. She bolted, jerked the rope from his hand, and stampeded, with her colt following, across the tennis court, tearing the net down, and then disappeared down one of the streets of the town. Along with this news, and a bill for five desks Willie had whittled up, came a report that the boy was at the bottom of his class in grades. He was requested not to return after Christmas. Uncle Clem decided on sterner measures. A military school with its discipline might succeed where the others had failed.

On January 13, 1897, Willie enrolled in Kemper School, Boonville, Missouri, in what would roughly be the sophomore year of high school. Eighteen years old at the time, on arrival he created a sensation with his ten-gallon cowboy hat, flaming red flannel shirt, fancy vest, and a red bandanna handkerchief knotted at the throat. His trousers were stuffed into high-heeled red-top boots with jingling spurs. A number of ropes of various sizes were coiled around his suitcase.

At first the showmanship of the school appealed to him. He enjoyed parading in his uniform with its brass buttons and high, ornamented collar. For a few weeks he kept his rifle immaculate, the brass on his uniform shined, his bunk neat and orderly. But then he lapsed into his old careless ways. In his studies he excelled in the "talking subjects" where he could "bull" his way through or where his phenomenal memory served him well. "He glanced through a list of the books of the Old Testament once," a classmate recalled, "and rattled them off like an alarm clock." He excelled also in "elocution," where the teacher who usually emphasized the correctness of gesture and pronunciation, realized that Willie was an exception to the rule. He soon became known as the school wit. "Just think of it," a classmate said later, "there's Will Rogers getting big money for saying the same things over the radio he got demerits for saying in the mess hall at Kemper."

The cadets were not permitted to attend the performances of traveling shows and vaudeville that sometimes came to the little Ozark town. Willie seldom missed one. He would borrow an old suit from the janitor, pad his front with a pillow, black his face and hands, put on false hair, and in this disguise slip by the guard. In the local opera house he would go to the gallery for Negroes. He was not reported by his classmates perhaps for selfish reasons. He would repeat the performances, acting them out and giving the routines word for word as he had heard them.

It was at Kemper that Willie first flaunted his pride in his Cherokee blood. Many of the cadets came from other sections of the country and some of them openly made fun of anyone with Indian blood. In one class an instructor referred to an Indian as a thoroughbred.

"A horse is a thoroughbred," Willie protested, jumping to his feet. "An Indian chief is a full blood."

At another time he was standing in the local bank gazing at a print of the painting, "Custer's Last Stand."

"You know, I like that picture," he said.

"Why?" another cadet asked.

"It's the only time my people got the best of it."

Before returning to the ranch for his first vacation Willie wrote that he was going to teach the cowboys the cadet manual of arms. To prepare for the instruction he sent along a chart so that the grounds could be properly marked off. A score of cowboys and neighboring boys gathered for the exhibition.

"Here he comes a-struttin'," his cousin, Spi Trent, described it. "There was no regulation rifle on the ranch and he was usin' a short, sawed-off saddle gun. He had on his blue uniform decorated with brass buttons . . . every one fastened. On his head was a cute little military cap. We had a peacock on the ranch, but on this day that dressy bird sure dragged his tail feathers when he got a look at Willie, all buttoned up an' rarin' to go. He came a-stompin' stiff-legged up to the marked-off place, giving orders in a high-toned voice way down in his throat like he was a general. Ten-SHUN!ARMS Right! He came to a halt right in front of where the boys were standing. Order ARMS!" Then he let the butt of his rifle drop to the ground. The jar caused the gun to go off and the bullet grazed his forehead and knocked his cap off. Although blood was running down his face, Willie went on with the show. He put his hand to his heart, rolled his eyes, and staged a pretty good death scene.

"Maybe we better bury him out on the Lone Prairee," one of the cowboys drawled.

This brought Willie out of his act laughing.

In the fall of 1898 Willie saw Vincente Oropeza perform his roping act again, this time at Springfield, Missouri. By observing closely he managed to memorize most of the tricks. After this, as one cadet put it, "his rope was in motion at Kemper more than his tongue." If he could not persuade a new cadet to stoop over, run down the hall "and beller like a calf," he would pay an old one to do it for him. As the boy ran, Willie would lasso his right or left foot, both feet, either arm, or pin his arms to his sides. For hours he would hold the cadets in a trance as he put on a one-man act with his lasso, twirling it vertically and horizontally, stepping in and out, then making it do all sorts of curlicues. If he was not doing this, he was putting on amateur theatricals from what he had seen at the local performances or from his own improvisations.

More and more reports and stories about Willie's doings at Kemper filtered back to Uncle Clem at Claremore.

"I'm awfully worried about Willie," he told one of his partners at the bank. "It looks like he isn't interested in anything except showing off. I'm afraid he wants to go into the show business."

"Well, Clem," his practical-minded friend said, "there ain't no use to worry. All you can do to stop it is knock him in the head."

"Yeah," Uncle Clem agreed, "I reckon you're right."

Shortly after this Sallie and Maude, who was married now, received identical letters from Willie asking each to loan him ten dollars.

"I could not understand why Willie needed extra money as papa gave him a generous allowance," Sallie recalled. "I got in my buggy and drove to Maude's. Both of our husbands advised us not to send it. So did the postmaster. 'Willie gets too much already,' he said. But we sent it. Next thing we knew Willie had left Kemper and was in Higgins, Texas. A friend of his at Kemper had told him about a ranch there and he had gone to it looking for a job as a cowboy."

Will always said that he and Colonel Johnston, the commandant at Kemper, could not agree on how the school should be run, and being "an accommodating boy" he got out.

Anyhow, his "academic grazing" was at an end.

3

Greener Grass Beckoned

LATE IN THE WINTER OF 1898 WILL LANDED IN HIGGINS, Texas, and learned that the ranch his friend had told him about was eight miles across the state line in Oklahoma. He made his way there afoot and found no one at home except a cook and two or three "old broke-down cowboys." This provided him with food and someone to talk with until the owner, W. P. Ewing and his son, Frank, came home from buying cattle. Mr. Ewing, who knew Uncle Clem, wrote that Willie was there and asked what to do with him. Uncle Clem wrote back and told him to get any work out of him he could, which was more than he could do, and if he did not earn his board he would pay the difference. There seems to be a question as to whether he did so.

Congressman Percy Gassoway from Oklahoma, a cowboy on the ranch at the time, gave one version. After being away for a couple of weeks he came in one day and saw a tall, gangling youth sitting on the corral fence cracking jokes.

"Why is he around?" he asked Ewing.

"In the first place," Ewing said, grinning, "he's so funny I can't let him go, and in the second place, I'm just wondering if he can do anything. I can't fire him until I find out."

In spite of this confirmation that Will was not "workbrittle," he did a man's work in helping to drive 600 cattle from the ranch to Medicine Lodge, Kansas. At the end of his first month, Ewing made out a check for $30, top wages at the time.

"I can't take it, Mr. Ewing," Willie said, handing it back. "The fun I'm having is pay enough."

"He was a whiz with a rope and he didn't care what was on the end of it," Ewing said later. "He was all right at bustin' broncs, but he didn't like it. The other men would play cards and gamble but he wouldn't."

After four months, Will decided to move on for more adventurous activities. Ewing singled out a stout little Spanish pony.

"Ride it into Amarillo and sell it," he said.

"I just want something that will get me there," Will replied, pointing to a broken-down old nag. "I'll take Grey Eagle."

"You'll rename him Creeping Turtle before you get there," Ewing warned. "If you make it, turn him out on the range."

The next day, Will waved good-by to the Ewing family (destined to be his close friends for life), and prodded Grey Eagle into Higgins, where he spent the night. There an event took place that furnished him material for a weekly column in 1932. A cowboy who had driven in from a nearby ranch with four mules hitched to a wagon to get supplies went on a roaring drunk. After his drinking companions were under the table, in the wee hours of morning, he hitched the mules to a plow he had brought in to have repaired. Then he went to work plowing up the wide, unpaved black-loam main street, and several side ones. The startled inhabitants of Higgins woke up the next morning to find their houses and places of business surrounded by plowed land. The cowboy was rounded up and haled before an angry local magistrate.

"Shore I did it," he confessed. "She wasn't much good to anybody like she was, an' I thought I'd plow her up and sow her in grass."

In some roundabout way, Will maintained in 1932, President Hoover had heard about this remarkable happening and extracted from it the idea that "the grass would grow in the streets of America" if the Democrats won the Presidency.

After Will had had a good laugh over the incident he climbed aboard Grey Eagle, who picked his way out of the plowed ground to the open range. It was a good 150 miles to Amarillo, and it took him almost a week to make it. He passed only three ranch houses on the way, and at each the cook permitted him to cook up biscuits and dried beef to eat on the way. "One night I staked the old skate out," he wrote about the trip, "and hit the old sougans, as I was dead tired. During the night a thunder storm come up. I'd never seen such lightning and heard such noise in my life. A big bunch of range horses got frightened and run smack into that rope I'd staked my old horse out with. When another flash of lightning come, I couldent see him and thought he'd been killed. I was wet as a drowned rat and hit out back for a line camp I'd passed and hadn't gone in. I knocked and yelled, 'Hello! Hello!' and nobody answered. I went in and as my matches was wet—fumbled around in the dark till I found a table and went to sleep on it. When I woke the sun was shining bright and there just six feet away was a good, warm bunk with blankets and everything. There was coffee and a side of bacon and I made a fire in the stove and cooked up a bait."

After Will had "the wrinkles out of his belly" he set out on foot and at the top of a little hill saw Grey Eagle grazing, as good as ever.

One of the first things Will saw after getting to Amarillo was the recruiting office for Colonel Theodore Roosevelt's Rough Riders. This appealed to him as the adventure he wanted. He opened the door with a shaking hand, and faced a grizzled old recruiting sergeant.

"I'm Willie Rogers from Oklahoma Territory and . . ."

"Son . . ." The sergeant looked him over with a crooked grin and spat a stream of amber in the general direction of a cuspidor. "Son, what we want is men, not boys. We ain't aimin' to ask mamas and papas for consent."

Willie spun on his heel and slunk out. There were to be other setbacks. He could not eat like old Grey Eagle out on the range. He must find work as a cowboy.

Dozens of trail herds dotted the prairies waiting for railroad cars to haul them north and east. Willie hit up every trail boss he could find, but most of them were laying off men. After a week in which his belly protested louder and louder, he heard of a trail boss who needed a hand. Another cowboy was already talking to him when Willie arrived. "Right there I seen a feller talk himself out of a job," he wrote, "telling the boss what a good hand he was. The old cowman listened to him till he had had his say, then he told him, 'I'm in need of a hand all right, but I think you'd suit me too well.'" After the other man had gone, Willie asked for the job, giving Mr. Ewing as a reference.

"I think you'll do," the man said, giving him an appraising glance.

"Them was the happiest words I ever heard," Will commented. "I got to the chuckwagon just in time for dinner. The boys setting around grinned as I stowed away helping after helping of beans."

Willie wrangled horses for several days until the cattle his employer had brought to Amarillo could be shipped, and then the outfit moved to Panhandle City, crossing the Canadian River at the old LX Ranch where Frederic Remington had painted some of his most famous pictures. From there they moved to the boss's ranch near Woodward, Oklahoma, where Willie worked through a roundup and helped brand the calves. He was becoming a seasoned cowboy but, like everything else, the monotony of ranch life soon caught up with him.

An opportunity came to go with a trainload of cattle to California, and after the steers had been delivered Willie and another cowboy went on to San Francisco, where the end of the trail almost came for them. Willie turned in early at their hotel and was asleep when his companion returned. He must have blown out the light, which Willie had left lit, without turning off the gas. "They dug us out of there the next morning and hauled us to a hospital," Will wrote, "and believe me I didn't know a fighting thing until late that night and that was just bull luck. The main doctors gave me up, but a lot of young internes, just by practicing on me, happened to light on some nut remedy that no regular doctor would ever think of and I come alive. Well, I landed back home pretty badly buggered up. This stuff was located in my system. I went to Hot Springs to boil it out and when I would get in a hot room they would all think the gas was escaping some place."

It may have been fright at the close escape Willie had had or it may have been a wild hope that the boy was ready to settle down. Anyhow, Uncle Clem took a gamble. "You're the only child I have at home now, since May married, and if you're bound to punch cows, there's no need for you to leave," he told Willie. "I'm going to give you this Dog Iron Ranch, lock, stock and barrel. It's yours and you can run it the way you want to. There is a farmer and his wife there now and you can keep them if you want to."

It was exhilarating to have the ranch and to be his own boss. But Willie soon found that there were drawbacks too. Running a ranch carried with it responsibility and worries that a hell-for-leather cowboy did not have. Nor was it pleasant to have strangers in the old ranch house, particularly when the farmer's wife was from Illinois and knew nothing about the kind of food he liked to eat. But Willie was not the kind to mope over details and soon he was busier manufacturing ways to amuse himself than in working at ranching. He built a platform where open-air dances were held. He raced horses when he could arrange a match. Once when he was soundly beaten he traded his horse and $10 for a little yellow pony named Comanche that had beaten him. It was one profitable venture and this pony was to be the best horse he ever owned.

Willie sang tenor in a quartet that serenaded the Indian girls on moonlit nights. "I have what is called a fresh voice," he later described it. "It's got volume without control. It's got resonance without reason. It's got tone without tune. I got a voice that's got everything but a satisfied listener."

With Comanche under him, Willie went to every dance for miles around. In August, 1899, he attended a "tacky" party in Claremore. "An important feature of the evening," the Claremore *Progress* for the 19th reported, "was the 'cake-walk.' The prize, a generous-sized ginger cake, was awarded to Vic Foreman and Willie Rogers." Will later claimed that he was the first in the territory to do the cakewalk, as well as to own a rubber-tired buggy. When he stepped out in style in this, a high-prancing horse named Robin was between the shafts. Willie was so proud of the buggy that he suspended it by ropes from the beams under a shed to keep the rubber tires from wearing out.

To help break the monotony, as well as to keep from eating the food prepared by the farmer's wife, Willie persuaded Spi Trent to join him in building a log cabin. It was great fun for a while, but the problems of getting provisions, of cooking three meals a day, and of countless other irritating chores soon palled on them. After sticking it out for several months, it was a relief to both of them when Comanche, tied to a corner of the cabin, reared back in fright and the structure came down in a heap of logs.

While they lived there, a nearby farmer killed one of Willie's steers that had wandered onto his place, broken down a flimsy fence and eaten his young corn. According to range custom, he should have told Willie about it. Flaming with a mighty wrath, when he heard of it, the young rancher and his "hired man on horseback" rode forth to punish the farmer. On the way a cold rain blew up and soaked them to the skin. When they arrived at the farmer's cabin, he was not at home and his wife invited them to come in and get dry by the fireplace. She was thin and emaciated and five scrawny children of various ages huddled as near to the fire as possible. Later the farmer came in. He was a giant of a man with a deep, booming voice and a long red beard. His wife told him they had come out of the storm and as it was still raining he invited them to supper. "You'll have to eat beans," he apologized "as the storm has kept me from finishing butchering my steer."

It was still raining when supper was over, and the farmer insisted that they spend the night there. The next morning his wife sent them on their way with a hot breakfast in their stomachs. As they rode back to the ranch Spi gave Willie a wicked look.

"I thought you was going to tear that nester apart for killing your steer," he reminded.

"When I saw how little those poor folks had," Willie said, slow and quiet-like, "I wished they had killed two steers. Spi, I didn't lose that steer. I traded it for a little human happiness. There are millions of steers in the world, but human happiness is kinder scarce."

On July 4, 1899, Willie entered a steer-roping contest at Claremore and won first money. "It was the first one I ever was in," he wrote, "the very first thing I ever did in the way of appearing before an audience in my life. Well, as I look back on it that had quite an influence on my little career, for I kinder got to running to 'em, and the first thing I knew I was just plum 'Honery' and fit for nothing but show business. Once you are a showman you are plum ruined for manual labor again."

After winning this contest Willie heard that there was to be a big roping and riding shindig at St. Louis, put on by Colonel Zach Mulhall as a part of the fair for 1899. He sent in his name and "the next thing I knew I was getting transportation for myself and my pony." This time Willie did not win. "I made the mistake of catching my steer," he explained, "and he immediately jerked me and my pony down for our trouble."

In addition to the contestants, Colonel Mulhall took along a cowboy band of sixty pieces, all resplendent in ten-gallon hats, jackets, chaps, boots and spurs.

Later in the fall Willie planned to enter a roping contest at Oklahoma City. He and Spi were practicing on a steer that had strayed onto their range from a neighboring ranch, and in doing so killed it. They did not want this to become known, as it might embarrass Willie at Oklahoma City, and in an attempt to conceal the dead animal dragged it into a ravine and covered the carcass with brush and dirt. Of course in a couple of days the buzzards flying overhead gave them away. Nevertheless, they decided to bluff it out. For a couple of days, when they rode into Oolagah for their mail, nothing happened. Then one day they saw the rancher who owned the steer talking to some men and all of them were laughing. There was nothing to do but join them.

"Howdy," Willie said, as they did so.

"Hear you boys are figgering on winning the big money in Oklahoma City," the rancher said.

"Yeah," Will said, a sickly grin on his face.

The rancher kept talking about the contest, patting Willie on the back and offering encouragement, as the men about were obviously trying to stifle their laughter. Willie got more and more nervous. Finally, he caught the rancher by the arm, took him to one side, and confessed what had happened.

"The joke's on you and Spi," the rancher said. "I knowed who killed the steer all the time. All them fellers I was talking to knowed it and they was chuckling while I was ribbing you."

"What's the steer worth?" Willie asked.

"Nothing," the rancher said. "I've had my money's worth in fun."

Willie turned on his heel, went to a store and cashed a check for $50, ten more than the steer was worth. With the extra money he bought two boxes of cigars: one he gave to the rancher along with the $40 to pay for the steer; the other he opened and passed the cigars around to the crowd.

"I feel $500 better," Willie said. "I'll practice on my steers after this. I wouldn't have that on my conscience for anything. It felt like a whole herd of steers was stampeding around in my head."

The nineteenth century went into the ashcan of history as Willie reached his majority. As the first decade of his life had been one of expansion and growth for the country and for his father, the second decade, the 1890's, had been a watershed in which the country, as had Uncle Clem, changed from rural emphasis to urban, from agricultural and ranching to business and industry. Actually, the most important change was what had happened to the cowboy as a part of American life. During a period of roughly a quarter of a century, during which he was greatly shaped by the tradition, the cowboy had come into existence, reached the apex of his usefulness, and was already on the decline. Amazingly enough, though, he was to leave a profound influence. In the future he, like the knights of feudalism in their romanticized form, was to go through a similar process so that the original (which Will had been) was to bear as little resemblance to the synthetic process (which Will was to make use of) as the boots worn on the range bear to those worn by Texas oilmen. In the best sense of the word, Will was to become a link between the old and the new. Summed up as he went into manhood (without losing his "boyishness"), he was friendly but did not run with the pack; he was brimful of energy and enthusiasm but not "work-brittle" merely for the sake of working; he was talkative but not confiding; he was curious and at the same time careless in nonessentials; he was "a wanting man" but not ambitious as his father was; he was shrewd and intelligent but not as a businessman or a scholar; and, above all, he had "to ride his own horse," no matter where the journey took him. Will definitely needed direction and it could come in only one guise if he was to reach the heights: it must come in "gingham."

A strange loneliness had possessed him since the death of his mother. His sisters were married and had problems of their own; his father's remarriage, plus an obvious disappointment in his son's accomplishments, placed a barrier between them; his fiddle-footing it to dances and scurrying from one roping contest to another satisfied only surface needs. He needed something peculiarly his own and so far no one meeting the need had appeared. The first girl he had proposed to, as a teen-ager, had screamed: "I wouldn't marry you, Willie Rogers, if you was the last man on earth." The father of a girl at Neosha had set his dog on him and Willie had lost the seat of his trousers as he raced downhill. The daughter of the local hotelkeeper at Oolagah, Kate Ellis, was a good friend, but he knew that her parents disapproved of his irresponsible, helter-skelter ways, and certainly did not look upon him with enthusiasm as a potential son-in-law.

The answer to his needs came in the form of "the visiting girl."

4

"The Visiting Girl"

NOTHING IS FEARED MORE BY THE GIRLS IN A SMALL TOWN than "the visiting girl," particularly if she is pretty and vivacious. In the fall of 1900 when Betty Blake, convalescing from typhoid fever, came from her home in Rogers, Arkansas, to visit her sister whose husband was station agent for the Missouri Pacific Railroad at Oolagah, no one thought much of importance would occur. She had been warned. "I am afraid you won't like Oolagah," her sister wrote. "The only young people in town are the two daughters of the hotelkeeper, and one boy, Willie Rogers, who lives a few miles out on a ranch."

In truth the treeless, drab little village had been a disappointment to the high-spirited girl from the beautiful little Ozark town with its great oaks and breath-taking scenery. Aside from the railroad station and its stockpens, there were the two-story frame hotel, a livery stable, a church that doubled as a schoolhouse, and a few crude business buildings with rickety board sidewalks in front of them. The residential houses were small, most of them unpainted, and all crudely constructed. Main Street was a welter of dust in the summer, or a sea of black, sticky mud when it rained, and in the winter frozen into rough ruts.

Betty's sister and brother-in-law had quarters adjoining the station, and when she had nothing else to do, she sat on the telegraph table at the bay window facing the tracks. On a cold evening, as the eight-o'clock train from Kansas City puffed in, a lithe figure swung to the platform before the train stopped, grip in his hand. He strode briskly into the waiting room and she hopped down from the table to go to the window to ask what he wanted. One glance at her and he spun on his heels and left the room. A few moments later her brother-in-law came in with a banjo addressed to Will Rogers and asked where he had gone. She shook her head in amazement.

Early the next morning she heard the sound of horse's hoofs on the frozen ground outside, jumped from her bed and ran to the window to see who it was. It was Will Rogers riding out of town on Comanche, his overcoat collar turned up against the cold wind, the reins in one hand, a grip in the other, and a derby perched on top of his head. She watched him ride out of sight where the road snaked its way across the prairie. As he did so, she wondered how he would get his banjo and regretted that she had not spoken to him.

During the day Kate and Lil Ellis, the daughters of the hotelkeeper, excitedly told her that Will had brought back a bundle of popular songs from Kansas City. "He's coming back tonight and is going to sing them for us," Kate said. "Mother said for you to come for supper and stay afterwards, so you can hear them."

Will ate in embarrassed silence but, afterward, sitting in a low rocking chair before the fireplace in the living room, he lost all trace of shyness as he went through the repertory of songs imitating the way he had heard them on the stage in Kansas City. The one that impressed Betty most was "Hello, My Baby, Hello, My Honey, Hello, My Ragtime Gal." Later, they popped corn over the kitchen stove and pulled candy.

On leaving Will gave Betty the songs and asked her to learn to play them on her sister's piano. He promised to come back to hear them in a couple of days. "I am afraid I showed off a little that second evening," Betty confessed, "for I could see he was impressed by my musical accomplishments. I played the piano, then paraded my talents by stringing and tuning the banjo. Will made a few attempts at playing, but finally gave up and handed the banjo to me. He sang while I played, and I am quite sure that I outdid myself in fancy plinking and plunking."

Before returning home Betty's brother-in-law drove her and her sister out to the ranch. Will was away at the time and she was disappointed in what she saw. The house was cold, ill-kept, almost bare of furniture. Everything seemed neglected and run down. She did not see Will again, but shortly after New Year's she received a letter from him. Here is part of it:

Miss Betty Blake
Rogers Arkansas

My Dear Friend:

No doubt you will be madly surprised on receipt of this Epistle. But nevertheless I could not resist the temptation and hope if you cannot do me the *great* favor of dropping me a few lines you will at least excuse me for this for I *cant help* it.

Well I know you are having a great time after being out among the "Wild Tribe" so long. Well I have had a great time this Xmas myself. Have not been at home three nights in a month. Taken in every Ball in the Territory and everything else I hear of. I was in Fort Gibson again last week to a Masque Ball, and really had a time.

Say you people never did come out home as you said you would and see us "Wooly Cowboys" rope wild Steers. I have some pictures of it and if you want them I will send them to you if you will send me some of those Kodak Pictures you had up here of yourself and all those girls. Now isn't that "a mammoth inducement for you" to have your picture in a lovely "Indian Wigwam."

If you will come back up here we will endeavor to do all that we can to make you have a time—Dances, Skating, Sleigh Riding, Horse Back Riding (of which you are an expert), and in fact every kind of amusement on the face of God's Footpiece.

Well I guess you have an ample sufficiency of my nonsense so I will stop. Hoping you will take pity on this poor heartbroken Cow pealer and having him rejoicing over these bald prairies on receipt of a few words from you. I remain your true friend and

Injun Cowboy
W.P.Rogers

Somewhat surprised and taken aback by the tone of this letter, Betty waited several weeks before answering. Almost immediately Will fired back what she called her first "love letter" from him. It left no doubt of his feelings or intentions, even though he could not keep from dressing it up with showmanship:

Hillside Navy
Headquarters, Dogiron Ranch
Oolagah, Indian Territory
March 14, 1900

My Dear Betty:

Now for me to attempt to express my delight for your sweet letter would be utterly impossible so will just put it mild and say I was *very very much* pleased. I was also surprised for I thought you had forgotten your Cowboy (for I am yours as far as I am concerned).

I know you had a fine time when your Sweetheart was down to see you. Oh! how I envy him for I would give all I possess if I only knew that you cared something for me, for Betty you may not believe it or care anything about it but you do not know that you have made life miserable for one poor boy out in I.T. But you did for I think of you all the time and just wish that you might always have a remembrance of me for I know that I cant expect to be your sweetheart for I am not "smoothe" like the boys you have for sweethearts. But I know you have no one that will think any more of you than I do although I know they may profess to. Now Betty I know you will think me a Big Fool (which I am) but please consider that you are the one that has done it. But I know you dident mean to and I ought not to have got so broken up over you. But I could not help it so if you do not see fit to answer this please do not say a word about it to any one for the sake of a broken hearted Cherokee Cowboy.

Now Betty if you should stoop so low as to answer this please tell me the plain truth for that is what you should do and not flirt with me for I would not be smoothe enough to detect it.

I have some new Songs to send you also those pictures I promised. I was very glad to get your pictures and *thank* you very much for them. I have had lots of compliments on them, especially yours. I am going to Fort Smith some time soon and if you will permit I can probably come up but I know it would be a slam on your Society career to have it known that you even knew an ignorant Indian Cowboy. I still have lots of pretty ponies here if you will come out I will let you pick the herd.

Well Bettie please burn this for *my* sake. Hoping you will consider what I have told you in my undignified way and if not to please never say anything about it and burn this up.

I am yours with love
Will Rogers

The flaming pride hidden behind a false modesty, the impetuosity, the great craving for love and affection in this letter appealed to but also frightened Betty. She was quite right in having serious second thoughts. She did not burn the letter but she did not answer it either.

The next time Will and Betty saw each other was at a rodeo in Springfield, Missouri, later in the spring where he performed as a part of Colonel Mulhall's troupe. Will rode Comanche all over the arena, whooping and shouting in his exuberance that she was in the stands, not realizing that he was "loading the guns" of those who would both warn and tease her. Once again Betty was "the visiting girl" and Will definitely was not the only boy in town.

Despairing of Betty and needing excitement to keep up his flagging spirits, Will joined Colonel Mulhall's show as a regular trouper. It toured the Middle West, showing at state fairs, then headed south. The band was one of the big attractions. "Most of the members could not ride in a wagon unless their shirttails were nailed to the floor," Will said. "So Colonel Mulhall added a number of cowboys. He did this for a purpose. I held a slide trombone on which I could not play a note. The Colonel advertised that he could pick out boys in the band that could ride any old outlaw horse produced or could rope and tie a steer in less time than any challengers." This, of course, was the old come-on game.

At one place, San Antonio, Texas, the cowboys met some real opposition but came through. "It wasn't like it is now," Will said in 1934, "runty little calves—you roped steers. Them big boogers was given a hundred foot start and when the flag dropped, your rope was tied to your saddle. All you had to do was to take down that rope, build a loop, rope the steer, throw him and tie his legs. When you finished, you held up your hands. In ten minutes, the judge would look at that steer and if he was still tied properly, you got your time.

The judge was old John Blocker, who knew more about a calf than its mother did."

The spectators at San Antonio liked the performance so well that a big barbecue was given in their honor. Will was called on to make a speech, much to his surprise and bewilderment. He scrambled to his feet, blinked a few times and scratched his head.

"Well, folks," he began, "this is mighty fine grub, *what there is of it.*"

This produced a roar of laughter.

"Well, there is plenty of it," he started over when the laughter had subsided, *"such as it is."*

He got no further nor needed to. His first after-dinner speech had been a success.

In the fall Will saw Betty again at a street fair in Fort Smith, Arkansas. She was with friends and they exchanged a few words. He knew as he left her that she would be teased by her companions. A mammoth ball on the night of the last day closed the fair. Betty kept looking for Will during the evening, hoping to dance with him. But he did not come inside. As she danced past a window, she saw him standing alone outside watching the dancing. Two years passed before she was to see him again, and by then he had fiddle-footed his way around the world during which he did not write or communicate with her in any way. His pride would not permit it.

5

Grazing in Foreign Pastures

MANY TIMES IN LATER YEARS WILL ADMITTED THAT TWO pictures seen in a simple geography book had influenced his career more than all the rest of his schooling. One pictured a tremendous expanse of grazing land in Argentina and the other was of wolves chasing a sleigh in a howling Siberian blizzard with the obvious intention of devouring its passengers. The first was now to be the lure that drew him away from his dejection at not being able to have Betty for his own. Not for his life, though, would he have admitted it, and a ready excuse was at hand.

Although Will had been given enough land and stock by his father which if farmed and ranched profitably would have made him a good living, his basic justification for not doing so was that it did not offer enough possibilities. He remembered the time when his father's cattle had grazed thousands of acres, when it took half a dozen threshers to take care of the wheat, and when five full trains of cars stood on the sidings to haul off the steers. Such a situation, he reasoned, would have satisfied him, and of such he was to dream many times in his life. There were many others who thought and talked the same way, and envious and eager eyes were turned toward Argentina and magnified were the stories about huge fortunes that could be made there by ranching.

Responding to the lure of adventure and dreams of great wealth, perhaps to lay at Betty's feet to show how wrong she had been, Will proposed to his father that he sell the ranch and the cattle and go to

Argentina. Unable to talk him out of the notion, Uncle Clem bought the cattle but would not permit him to dispose of the land. The absurdity of Will's dream soon revealed itself. The extent of the knowledge about that country manifested itself when nobody in the Indian Territory could tell Will how to get to Argentina!

Early in 1902, with $3,000 in his pocket from the sale of the cattle, accompanied by a friend, Dick Parris, whose expenses he was paying, Will headed for New Orleans as being *in the right direction.* They were informed that no boats sailed from there to Argentina, and were advised to go to New York, which they did, only to learn that "the one boat a year" had already sailed. After two weeks of sightseeing in New York, they shipped for England because they had been told that a regular line plied between Liverpool and Buenos Aires. "I lasted just long enough to envy the Statue of Liberty for being in a permanent position," Will wrote. "Oh, Doctor, I sho was sick. This boat cut some capers. A bucking horse, why this thing did every thing but rare up and fall back. My diet consisted of a small part of two lemons on the whole trip. When I landed in England my sole purpose was to become a naturalized citizen until some enterprising party built a bridge back home."

While in London Will visited the Houses of Parliament in session, not a likely place for a Cherokee Indian cowboy to spend his time. In Westminster Abbey "a curious sort of sensation" crept over him although he had "personally" known few of the men buried there. The Tower of London intrigued him but, although Piccadilly Circus "was billed larger than anything" on the buses, it turned out to be "not much of a show." He admitted it was "a good location if they ever want to put on a show." The transportation system was a disappointment. "Hitch a thresher engine to a string of covered wagons and you have an English train—as fast, as comfortable and as handsome." He had a glimpse of King Edward, whose coronation ceremonies were in preparation, but he doubted if "the king recognized him." He made an interesting comment on the guards posted outside Buckingham Palace. "Can you imagine a flock of these located in front of the White House with Teddy Roosevelt there? But different nations have different ideas of humor."

After a week in London the two young men shipped for Argentina and landed in Buenos Aires on May 5, 1902. They registered at the expensive Phoenix Hotel, where English was spoken, and soon learned that no great expanses of free land were awaiting their coming. Nor were there demands for American cowboys at fancy wages. Will toted up what was left of his roll and found that after "paying dividends to steamship companies" it had shrunk alarmingly. To complicate matters, Dick had had enough traveling and was homesick for the Indian Territory. There was not enough money left for both to return, even if Will had swallowed his pride and agreed to do it, so he paid his companion's passage home, sending along gifts he had bought for members of his family.[1]

Not ready to give up so easily Will made a trip 800 miles into the interior to inspect a ranch. "I was sorter itching to show those gauchos how we could rope and tie a steer," he wrote, "so one day they wanted to catch one to pick the brand on him, so I takes me down my little manilla rope, and I even goes so far as to pick out the exact bit of earth where I would lay the brute down. Well I hadn't even got close enough to start swinging my rope when I heard something go whizzing over my head. A guy running about twenty feet behind me had thrown clear over my head and caught the steer. I couldn't speak much Spanish outside of asking for something to eat and cussing, but I took off my hat to that hombre and took my rope and tied it all up against my saddle with knot after knot, to give the impression that I didn't have any more use for it down there. They *savvied* the humor all right. They can rope a steer further than I could hit him with a rock."

On the other hand, Will was upset at the way the gauchos handled the cattle. "They drive them in a run," he wrote, "and I asked the boss if it did not take off too much fat. He gave the horse laugh and said, 'Why, they fill right out again.' In cutting out there are from three to five men to each animal. They would not believe that a horse knew enough to cut out a cow without guiding and one man to the head. They don't think of rounding up a herd of cattle with less than

[1] Mrs. Walker Milam, Sallie's daughter, wrote that Will sent gifts of "beautiful Brazilian lace collars for his three sisters. My own sisters and I wore my mother's on our graduation and wedding dresses. For grandpa there were bridles, quirts, and other presents." "Will Rogers as I Knew Him," Chelsea *Star*, Chelsea, Okla., Dec. 5, 1935.

thirty men. There is no chuck wagon. Yours is right on the saddle with you." The pay of the gauchos ranged from $5 to $8 a month, and Will had trouble getting their food down. Argentina, he decided, was "no place to make money unless you have at least $10,000 to invest. I don't expect to make any money here, but I would not take a fortune for the trip. You don't know what a good country is until you have seen others. Marry and stay home, boys," he advised, "for this country is overrated."

Instead of the hope of making money, by the time Will returned to Buenos Aires his big worry was whether he would eat or not. His habit of reading newspapers helped solve the problem. He found a notice in one he had used as cover while sleeping in a park that a shipload of stock was to be shipped to South Africa, and hurried to the stockyards to see if he could get work. Evidently the gauchos here were not so skillful as the ones on the ranch. "There was an old gaucho trying to rope a mule and missing every lick," he wrote. "I grabbed that rope and slipped the noose over that old hardtail's neck. The boss offered me 25¢ for every one I roped. Say, I stayed with 'em without any time off for breakfast and dinner. Then they offered me a job on that boat chaperoning them mules and she cows to Africa."

Will flipped a coin as to whether to wire his father for money to come home or take the job, and Africa won. Before sailing he wrote an illuminating letter home:

I never cared for money, *only for what pleasure it was to spend it,* and I am not afraid of work, and so, as I am now, I feel better than I ever did in my life, am in good health, so don't you all worry about me. I have spent a world of money in my time and I am satisfied, *as someone else has got the good of some of it.* It has not been all on myself and if you will only give me credit for just spending my own, as I think I have, I will be as happy as if I had a million. All that worries me is people there all say, 'Oh, he is no account, he blows in all of his father's money,' and all that kind of stuff, which is not so. I am more than willing to admit that you have done everything in the world for me and tried to make *something more than I am out of me* (which is not my fault) but as to our financial dealings, I think I paid you all up and everyone else. I only write these things so we may better understand each other. *I cannot help it because my nature is not like other people,* and I don't want you all to think I am no good because I don't keep my money. I have less than lots of you and I dare say *I enjoy life better than any of you, and that is my policy.* I have always dealt honestly with everyone and thing in the world and all of you and all the folks, and will be among you all soon, as happy as any one in the world, as then I can work and show people that I am only spending what I make.

Seasick all the way, the 32-day trip to South Africa was a nightmare to Will. The ship was a modern Noah's ark with horses and mules below, cows on the deck and sheep up where the crow's-nest should have been. Most of the crew were German, except an Irishman who was the veterinarian ("who spent most of his time working on me") and the Englishman who owned the stock. "I couldn't wrestle a bale of hay and seasickness at the same time," Will reported, "and they couldn't fire me, so I was appointed night watchman to the cows." After he had got to where he could eat "without a return ticket," the supply of food on the boat ran low and the Englishman saw to it none of the cows were slaughtered. "I finally figured out a way to land some extra nourishment," Will said, "since some of those cows had calves. I tied off the calves and when it got dark milked those old wild cows. They was harder to get to than the back end of a six floor loft. After bearfighting them old snaky heifers and getting kicked over till pretty near daylight, I would get my little pint cup ⅔ full. Well, I haven't drank milk since I was a papoose, so I would take it up to the cook who would load me up with everything this Englishman couldn't eat the night before."

Although the ship almost went down when it struck the tail end of a storm as it approached the coast of Africa, it managed to limp in to Durban, Natal. Will was allowed to land, as the Englishman gave him a job to help drive the stock 200 miles inland to his stock farm. He worked for him for several weeks doing everything from riding blooded horses for inspection of buyers to cleaning the stables and helping the blacksmith shoe the beasts. Soon tiring of this he drifted down to Ladysmith, where he got a job breaking horses for the British army. Although the Boer War was in process of being "diplomatically" settled, sporadic fighting kept breaking out. "You know these American and Australian horses killed and crippled more soldiers than the

Boers," Will commented. "Why they were Western Broncos that had never been broke and then they expected some of the yeomanry that had never rode anything worse than a 'Ansom Cab to crawl up in the middle of these old snuffy Bronks in a little Pancake Saddle. Why it was nothing less than suicide. When a whole company would get new horses and they would holler, 'Company Mount,' in ten seconds you could see nothing but loose horses and Tommies coming up digging the dirt out of their eyes. They had as much chance staying on top of some of those Renegades as a man would have sneezing against a cyclone. But you have to slip it to those old Tommies for nerve, they would come right up clawing mud out of their eyes and want to take another fall out of the Blooming Bleeder, but sometimes nerve can be taken for darn foolishness."

In December, 1902, Will made a 600-mile cattle drive to Johannesburg and on arrival learned that Texas Jack's Wild West Show was performing in the city. Homesick for the sight of people from the United States, he made his way to the show grounds. A lean, kind-looking man wearing American boots and spurs, greeted him.

"Howdy," the man said in a friendly drawl. "Anything I can do for you? I'm Texas Jack."

"I'm lookin' for a job," Will said, a big grin spreading across his face. "Got anything a feller might do?"

"Jus' might have. Where do you come from, son?"

"I'm Will Rogers from Indian Territory."

"Maybe you can ride and rope?"

"I can rope some," Will said, "but probably not good enough for the show." Texas Jack studied him for a moment. "I guess I'm a little longer on the ropin' than on the ridin'," Will added.

"Can you do trick roping?"

"Tricks? . . ." Will ducked his head. "A few, but they don't amount to much."

Texas Jack took up a huge coil of rope, made a loop in it, and began to spin it over his head, feeding out the rope as he did so until the loop became larger and larger. Will moved back to give the loop more room. Soon it was whizzing on the breeze, ninety feet of rope out, as the loop made an extended circle like the bottom of crinoline hoop skirts women once wore. This was usually the closing trick of a rope act, and needed much room. As it reached its full spread, Texas Jack let it fall to the ground.

Instead of taking the rope, Will took a smaller one from his grip, played it out in a loop and soon it began to writhe and jump as if alive. Then he danced through it vertically and horizontally. After going through this routine, without a word, he took the rope which Texas Jack still held in his hand, and let it play out as the showman had done. Its movements became long and smooth as the loop widened and a pleased smile came to Texas Jack's eyes as he realized this young stranger with his deft wrists exceeded him in skill.

"You're hired," he said, as the loop hit the ground, "an' you'll go on tonight."

Will was an instantaneous hit. "We have the best show in South Africa," he wrote home, "about 23 horses and 35 people and only 8 Americans with it. The play is partly a circus act and then they play blood-curdling scenes of Western life in America, showing Indians and robbers. I was an Indian but I screamed so loud that I liked to scared all the people out of the tent. Then we have riders of bucking bronchos, roping and fancy shooting and a little of everything. I am called 'The Cherokee Kid' on the program and do all the roping." He was paid $20 a week and had a car to sleep in. "Jack is the finest old boy I ever met and seems to think a great deal of me. He is a much better shot than Buffalo Bill. . . . This is a civilized crowd for he allows no gambling and drinking. I'm billed as 'the champion lasso thrower of the world.' "

Early in 1903 Will had some hopes of going home as Texas Jack was considering taking the show to the States. "I am going to learn a lot while I am with him," Will wrote, "that will enable me to make my living without making it by day labor." He also wrote that at matinee performances Texas Jack gave a medal to the boy who could throw a rope best. "I am their ideal," Will proudly wrote about the boys. "They see me rope in the show and follow me around to get me to show them so they can get the medal. They applaud until their little hands are sore."

For amusement Will roped wild zebras, the first man in the world to do so. In chasing one down a slope his horse stepped on a rock, stumbled and fell, rolling over Will several times. The horse broke two legs and had to be shot. Will was knocked unconscious and had a ragged gash on the back of his head that had to be sewed up. In spite of this, he missed only one performance.

He was not so proud over his boast that if a tiger used in an animal act got out of his cage he would rope it. "One afternoon in the middle of the show," he confessed, "Mr. Tiger busted out of his cage and started walking around. The people in the tent sat still, either from fright or thinking it a part of the act, but the performers sure were panicky. A couple of acrobats beat me up the center pole and I dived into a harness box. A clown was already in there and we held the lid down. Somebody kept yelling for 'The Cherokee Kid' to come out and rope the tiger. Finally, the tiger got tired and went back into his cage. Then the clown and I come out of the harness box. I kept still about roping tigers after that."

Texas Jack became increasingly fonder of Will as the days passed. "I like you," he told him one day. "You stick with me and you can take the show by yourself, and run it. I'll furnish the capital." Will seriously considered accepting the proposition, but the pull of the Indian Territory and home was too strong. "I've seen it all," he wrote, "and if I stayed much longer I might get buried in the life here and never be able to leave." When he did so he determined to go by way of Australia and around the world. When he left he had in his pocket a letter from Texas Jack to the Wirth Brothers who had a circus in Australia. It read:

"The Cherokee Kid" has performed with me during my present South African tour and I consider him to be the champion trick rough rider and lasso thrower in the world. He is sober, industrious, hard working at all times and is always to be relied upon. I shall be pleased to give him an engagement at any time should he wish to return.

Will's praise for Texas Jack was boundless. "He was one of the smartest showmen I ever met," he wrote. "It was him who gave me the idea for my original stage act with my pony. I learned a lot about show business from him. He could do a bum act with a rope that an ordinary man couldn't get away with, and make the audience think it was great, so I used to study him by the hour and from him I learned the great secret of the show business—*learned when to get off*. It's the fellow that knows when to quit that the audience wants more of."

Will's sea journey across the Indian Ocean was "20 days of agony," as "it sho' was on the warpath," and then the ship bypassed Australia and went on to New Zealand, which took five more days and then five days back. He landed in Sydney in time to see the Australian Derby, after which he went to work for the Wirth Brothers circus. Once again he was an immediate hit and toured the country with the show. There was no performance on Sundays and when he could get a booking Will made appearances to pick up extra money toward paying his passage home.

At a racing meet he hooked his toes around the saddle horn and with his pony "hitting the breeze leaned back over the horse's rump and picked up three handkerchiefs spaced at intervals on the ground." The governor general of the province was in the audience and sent a messenger asking him to do it again.

"I'll do it for $150," Will replied.

"But it's for the governor-general . . ."

"If he'll do it cheaper," Will drawled, "I'll loan him my pony and handkerchiefs."

Although the governor-general did not put up the money, it was raised by the crowd and Will repeated the performance.

After touring Australia the circus jumped to New Zealand, with an additional five more days of seasickness for Will. Will fell in love with New Zealand. "The best system of government in the world," he commented, "and the greatest scenery and natural resources."

By the time the New Zealand tour was over Will had enough money to book third-class passage home. When he reached San Francisco he had been gone from home nearly three years and had traveled over 50,000 miles—most of it seasick. "I started out first class, dropped to second class, and come home third class," he summed up. "But when I was companion to those cows on that perfumed voyage to Africa it might be called no class at all. George Cohan's trademark, Old Glory, sho looked good when I sighted it outside the Golden Gate." He made it home from San Francisco by freight train.

"When Willie got back home," Uncle Clem told a friend, "he was so broke he was wearing overalls for drawers."

6

"No Business like Show Business"

IF UNCLE CLEM HAD THE SLIGHTEST HOPE THAT WILLIE'S hardships on his jaunt around the world would turn him to more sober pursuits it was soon dispelled. For one thing, the spirit of the times was against him. Theodore Roosevelt's ebullient personality crackling out of the White House made for excitement and challenge. In spite of the dour and generally accurate warnings of the muckrakers and sober thinkers like Woodrow Wilson, a brash young nation fresh from the successes in Cuba and in Manila Bay did not have time to listen to howlers of doom. We were rich, weren't we? We were powerful, weren't we? President Roosevelt not only waved the Big Stick; he also spoke jingoistically and chauvinistically—and the country loved it. What was the use of being rich and powerful if you did not flaunt it? For another thing, Will came home a celebrity who must maintain his aura. In a region where few had gone beyond the nearest "blind pig," a man who had played in a circus in Africa, Australia and New Zealand, and had then come home by going around the world, was a hero who must not lose his halo. And yet Will already knew, as he was later to state, that being a hero is "about the shortest-lived profession on earth."

Fortunately, to escape from the monotony that soon boiled up around him, Colonel Mulhall was putting together a show at his ranch to take to the St. Louis World's Fair in the summer of 1904. When the Colonel learned about Will's return, he offered him a spot in the show, and Will moved his activities to the Colonel's ranch.

When he was not practicing roping Will banged away on an old piano. "He nearly drove my poor mother crazy," Lucille Mulhall, "America's first cowgirl," recalled. "He played a tune entitled 'I May Be Crazy, But I Ain't No Fool' over and over." Spi Trent maintained that when Will played it, his listeners were inclined to disagree with the title.

In April, 1904, Will went to St. Louis with the troupe. Colonel Mulhall was to furnish the stock and the riding and roping acts for a much larger show. Almost immediately arguments broke out. "Mulhall and the boss stable man got into a scrape and after the night show last night, they met out at the front when all the people were coming out and got to shooting," Will wrote Uncle Clem. "A boy that was standing near was shot in the stomach and it is doubtful if he will get well. A cowboy trying to stop the scrape was shot through the side. Mulhall did most of the shooting and if had hit the fellow he was shooting at, it would have been all right. He is no good." [1]

This unfortunate happening broke up the main show, and because of his loyalty to the Colonel, Will withdrew and took a job with a smaller one. "The riders had their quarters over the stables," Charley Tompkins, its manager, wrote. "Every morning, as soon as daylight would come, Will Rogers would be up and down in the Arena practicing with his ropes, trying out new tricks. He did this while the other Cowboys lay in bed until breakfast was called. I have at times sat and listened to some fellow pop off as to how he taught Will Rogers all that Will knew about roping. Mark it down from me: No one taught Will anything. He got it the hard way by hard work." [2]

Later in the summer Colonel Mulhall promoted a steer-roping contest at the Delman Race Track, in St. Louis, and on Sunday afternoons, when not performing at the Tompkins show, Will, Charley and others competed. It was while performing here that Will received a note that set his heart skipping faster than his rope. Betty Blake was visiting another sister in St. Louis and taking in the fair. She overheard an Indian girl say she had seen Will perform in the Wild

[1] Colonel Mulhall was sentenced to three years' imprisonment, appealed the case, and on a new trial was acquitted.

[2] Charles H. Tompkins, "My Association with Will Rogers," *Old Train Drivers Convention,* San Antonio, Texas, Oct. 1, 1953.

West Show, so she wrote saying she would like to see him. Will dashed off a reply asking her to meet him before the contest and he would take her in. "Come this eve *sho* and we will have a time tonight."

Betty was somewhat doubtful at first, but finally she, her sister and a girl friend decided to go. "The girls, of course, were curious about my circus friend and made no secret of the fact that they thought the occupation an undignified one for a young man with Will's advantages," she wrote. "Though I wanted to see Will very much, I had a wide streak of conventionality in me, and I was not particularly thrilled about Will's profession. But I hid my misgivings and tried not to hear the teasing and joking." [3]

Will could not meet them outside but he did leave tickets for them. When he entered the arena for his roping act Betty's misgivings were justified. He glistened in a tight-fitting red velvet suit, crisscrossed with gold braid. She was so embarrassed at the sidelong glances of her companions she did not hear the applause at the end of his act or realize he had put on a superb performance for her benefit. Later she learned the story of the costume. Since he was billed as "The Mexican Rope" artist in the Wirth Brothers circus, Mrs. George Wirth (whom Betty was to meet many years later) had made it for him. "Will was proud of the suit," she wrote, "but he never wore it again."

Overcoming her embarrassment, Betty met Will after the show and they had their first full evening alone. They had dinner on the Pike, strolled through many exhibits, and finally ended up at the Irish Village where they heard John McCormack sing. As they listened, it would have been fantastic to have peered into the future and foreseen this gawky cowboy appearing on the same stage with the famous tenor and with Will the featured attraction.

It had been Betty who broke off with him when she received his "impetuous" love letter; it was Will this time who broke a date they made *to go to Claremore for a horse!* As may be imagined, Betty did not relish this.

Actually Will was far from satisfied with the way things were going. Plenty of applause greeted his performances, but he had had that in

[3] Betty Rogers, *Will Rogers* (Indianapolis: Bobbs Merrill, pp. 82-83).

Africa, Australia and New Zealand. "Is there anything down there to do or that I could get into? I have seen the *fair?*"

A minor break came when he was given a week's engagement to do rope tricks at a St. Louis burlesque theater. A theater owner from Chicago saw his act and recommended it to a manager. Will was offered a week's engagement in the "Windy City." When he got there he found he had been canceled out because he "had failed to send Billings and Photos. I figured that was about the limit of orneriness when I dident have any pictures and dident know what billing was," he complained. "He didn't need much billing for thirty dollars."

Will's curiosity and love for all sorts of shows stood him in good stead. He was buying a ticket to a show at the Cleveland Theatre on Wabash Avenue when he heard the manager telephoning an agency for a substitute act.

"I have an act," Will spoke up.

"How long will it take you to get ready?" the manager asked.

"Just as long as it will take me to go to my hotel and return," Will replied.

Will opened the show with his act and went over well enough to be hired for the rest of the week. During one of his performances a speckled pup from a dog act ran across the stage and he was "lucky enough to land a loop on him as he breezed past." It got his biggest laugh but, infinitely more important, reminded him of Texas Jack's suggestion that he rope a live horse on the stage.

When Will had written Betty telling her he could not keep his date he had asked her to write him at Claremore. He did not receive a letter there. One she had written was forwarded from there and caught up with him in Chicago. She let him know in no uncertain terms that she did not care to play second fiddle to a horse, and that he was only one—and not at the top of the list—of her admirers. Will fired a letter back confessing no surprise at how she stood "with all those Railroad Gisables," but what did concern him vitally was that she had not married one of them. "You know according to form we both should have matrimonied long ago," he said in one of the most fantastic proposals in history, "and it wouldent do for this young gang *to look at our teeth* you know. But if you are not contracted for, *please file my application*." He then assured her he had not "had a girl since I left on that trip. On the tour I had all I could do to live, much less sport a damsel," and by the time he returned he was "so out of place and behind the times" that he now had a reputation as a girl hater. "I could just love a girl about your caliber," he added. "I am yours any old time." Although Betty reprimanded him severely for his language, she let him know that if he changed his occupation—became a good solid farmer or rancher or opened a place of business—she might look favorably on his application. Will was tempted but that "little bit of mule" in him prevailed.

Filled with enthusiasm for using a live pony in his roping act, on the way home from Chicago Will stopped in St. Louis and bought from Colonel Mulhall a little white pony that he thought might be trained for the act and shipped him to the Colonel's ranch. After spending Thanksgiving at home, he went to the ranch and began training Teddy, named for President Roosevelt. Hour after hour and day after day he worked on his act in a ring the size of an ordinary vaudeville stage. In about the same proportion, he banged away on the old piano. Colonel Mulhall was putting together a show to take to Madison Square Garden in New York for the following summer, and Mrs. Mulhall insisted that he must take Will along or she would go stark, raving crazy listening to his playing. At the same time she smiled tolerantly when he stole her fresh baked pies. "He's just a big, spoiled boy," she said.

At Christmas Will journeyed to Navata, Missouri, to a party that Betty was going to attend. When he unfolded to her his plans to go to New York with Colonel Mulhall's troupe and while there try to crash vaudeville with his live pony act, she let him know that in such a case she definitely preferred her "Railroad Gisables." When he got back to the ranch, his face set and a cold glint in his eyes, he tore into his practicing with even more determination. With such boon friends as Tom Mix and the two lively Mulhall girls there, he was soon back in "joshing" humor.

In April, 1905, Will shipped Comanche, for his riding in the Mulhall Show, and Teddy, in case he got a vaudeville engagement, on ahead to New York. He and J. H. Minnick, of Seymour, Texas, who had done some riding for him in his act, stopped off at Washington,

D. C., for a visit to the White House. The Washington *Times* reported:

Mr. Minnick was here during the inauguration and is remembered as the cowboy in the red shirt who did such wonderful tricks with his pony and rope on the Avenue as the parade passed by . . . Will Rogers is perhaps the finest ropeman in the world, doing a number of fancy tricks with a rope. This morning the two Westerners, attired in their cowboy boots and hats, went to the White House, and did some of their choice tricks for the entertainment of the children of the President. Rogers showed the children how a cowboy jumps the rope . . . They will come back from New York through Washington and say they will be here when President Roosevelt arrives. It is their intention to give a special performance for his benefit.

It was in the Madison Square Garden performance that Will got the most important break of his life in show business. A big steer that had come out of the chute to be roped jumped the barriers and ran amuck among the spectators. "The Indian, Will Rogers," an item in the *New York Times* on May 8, 1905, reported, "ran up the Twenty-seventh Street side and headed the steer off. As it passed the corridor again into view of the spectators he roped the steer's horns. Alone and afoot, he was no match for the brute's strength, but he swerved it down the steps on the Twenty-seventh Street ring. Immediately the ropes of a dozen cowpunchers fell over it from all sides, and it was brought down with a quick turn and led from the track."

Will took advantage of this in two ways. First, he enclosed a clipping in an envelope without a word and mailed it to Betty. Second, he used the publicity to get a hearing from vaudeville managers in regard to his act. Both seemed to fail. Betty did not write and the managers would not believe that a live horse could be roped on a stage. Nevertheless, when Colonel Mulhall's engagement at the Garden ended, Will, much to the Colonel's displeasure, remained in New York. Finally a manager (who growled that he had given Will a chance to get rid of him), put him on the "supper show" at Keith's old Union Square Theatre. "It was 6:30 on a hot afternoon," Will recalled, "and with Jim Minnick riding Teddy, a 'supper show' audience, one of the toughest to please in the show business, laid their afternoon papers down and kidded us into a pretty good hit." Will did not take chances. He had "Laughing Fred" Tejan, a famous claquer, in the audience to keep the laughs going. "Will was a scream that first night," Jim Minnick, who rode Teddy for the first week, commented, "and for a long time he said 'Laughing Fred' had more to do with the success of the show than I did."

At the end of a week the act was moved to Hammerstein's ("the greatest Vaudeville theatre of that and all time") and Buck McKee, a former sheriff of Pawnee County, Oklahoma, and a performer who had also been in the Garden, rode for Will (Jim Minnick had to return to his ranch). The show was a bigger hit here than at Keith's. "Will P. Rogers, the sensational lariat thrower is making his first appearance at the Paradise Roof, and has proved a sensation in every way," the New York *Herald* reported. "The novelty of his act lies in the dexterity and the oddity of what he does, and the whole makes a charming specialty well out of the ordinary run."

After the act was held over for the second week, one of Will's fellow performers tipped him off that he should ask for a raise. After mulling it over for several days he hesitantly asked for $10 a week more, which was instantly granted as Arthur Hammerstein had expected him to ask for double what he was getting. Joshed about it later, Will grinned, and said: "Boy, I've learned better and have made 'em pay since."

Will's act remained on the Hammerstein Roof for the rest of the summer and, as he was making personal appearances elsewhere, he had plenty of clippings to send to Betty. Eventually she wrote suggesting that they be "good pals." Will was not interested in this. "I wish to God I could look at it as you do but I cant," he wrote. "I got to love someone and it dont take me many guesses to tell who it is. I am on a fair road to success and have met some pretty big men here and stand pat with them." Will knew instinctively, as Voltaire found out the hard way, that "you better have some kings up your cuff."

As the summer of 1905 came to an end Will had an extra inducement which he thought might sway Betty. He had an offer to play an extended engagement in Europe. "So go to piling up your doll rags," he wrote, "and prepare to see the world as the *wife* of Rogers, the Lariat Expert. I go about Nov. 1st if I take it. Play several weeks in Paris, then London and Berlin." To his great disappointment she turned it down. "I have always had about what I wanted and it breaks my heart when I think I'll never get it," he wrote in a most revealing statement. "I am ordinarily a good loser but I guess my nerve is failing me this trip. I don't know how long I will stay at this. I might leave it any day and go back to the ranch. I have made a success and that's all I wanted to do. I want home offul bad and I am going to stay there too."

Will might have done so for a while, at least, if engagements had not kept him busy. "I want to send you a little token which I prize highly," he wrote Betty at Christmastime, enclosing a handkerchief. "It is supposed to be very fine work done by the Paraguay Indians. The old Indian Lady I bought it from asked me if I was married. I said, No. She said then give it to your wife when you do marry. I have kept it. Carried it all through Africa at times when I dident have a cent and was actually hungry, then to Australia, most of the time in an envelope in my locker, then back home and on all my travels. I did intend always to do as the old woman said, but I guess there's nothing doing for me."

In truth there was much novelty to Will's routine. Billed as a "dumb act," it was organized to show his skill with a rope. He would come on, shuffle down to the center of the stage, a coiled rope in both hands, as the orchestra played "Cheyenne":

> Cheyene, Chey-an-an-an,
> Hop upon my pony,
> There's room here for two, dear,
> Till after the ceremony . . .

Buck McKee astride Teddy would come galloping out of the wings across the stage and in the twinkling of an eye Will's lariats would dart out, roping both the rider and the horse. He would follow this with an amazing variety of trick roping, and close by doing the big crinoline astride Teddy who would back up as the loop widened.

The double-roping act had to be done so quickly that often the audience failed to recognize the skill employed. An actor on the same bill suggested that Will announce it. At the next performance, Will shuffled down front, took off his hat, scratched his head, and motioned for the orchestra to stop playing. "I want to call your sho nuff attention to this little stunt I am going to pull on you, as I am going to throw about two of these ropes at once, catching the horse with one and the rider with the other. I don't have any idea I'll get it, but here goes."

Before the orchestra could strike up again, a roar of laughter came from the audience. After Will had completed his act, he stormed off the stage "mad as a hornet."

"I'll never open my trap again," he told the manager.

"But, why?" the delighted manager protested. "You got a big laugh, didn't you?"

It took strong medicine to convince Will. "One day all the ghosts of the dead Indians over whose graves I let out whoops must have caught up with me," he explained, "because one night unseen fingers grabbed my rope and began to do all sorts of things to it, pulling it this way, that way, the other way, and both ways and sorely perplexing me. I commenced to get red in the face and the audience was gettin red in the eye. In my agony I said to myself, 'words, come to me!' and they came I don't know from where, but they came. 'Swinging a rope is all right,' I remember saying, 'when your neck ain't in it. Then it's hell.' I heard some faint titters. I went on. 'Out West where I come from they won't let me play with this rope. They think I might hurt myself.' Well, that audience started to laugh and forgot to look at the rope and I was saved."

Will's ability to think and act in a flash saved many bad situations. On one appearance he followed a comic barber routine that had left the stage covered with lather. When Teddy dashed out on the stage his feet slipped from under him and he went down, sliding toward the orchestra pit with Buck McKee's leg pinned under him. Fortunately, Teddy stopped with his head hanging over into the pit, which had been cleared in a flash. Will roped Teddy's head in a twinkling and pulled him up tight with one hand as he seized Buck with the other and dragged him from under the terrified animal. Together, they pulled and hauled until Teddy was on his feet.

"No cause for alarm, folks," Will drawled, as he patted the trembling animal to reassure him. "Just a little something extra we put in today to see how you'd like it."

After stagehands had mopped up the lather, Buck rode out again and Will made his catches perfectly.

Will gave much of the credit for the success of the act to Buck McKee. "He had that horse trained so well he was almost human," Will explained. "He's about one of the best with horses I'd say. Teddy would come tearing out on the stage and when I'd rope him, he would prance right out to the edge of the footlights over the drummer's head. Many a time I've seen a drummer mopping the sweat off his forehead after that stunt. They all thought Teddy would plunge right over into the bass drum—but he never did."

For his part Buck claimed he had the best part of the act because if an audience got after them he had a horse to get away on. "If that happens," Will retorted, "I'll give you and Teddy half a mile start and pass you. Teddy's boots is to help him stop fast. Mine is built to help me go fast."

Will caught on to the tricks of showmanship fast. He had a purple saddle blanket made for Teddy with "Will Rogers" embroidered on it in gold. Before showtime Buck would walk from the stable to the theater along the busiest streets, and Teddy would follow without a rope on him. Before doing the big crinoline Will would have an usher take one end of the rope to the back of the theater to let the audience see it was 90 feet long. Then there was his chewing gum, a habit he had picked up from shagging flies with the local baseball teams in the towns that he played. On the stage he might park it on the proscenium arch or over the W on the card announcing his act so that it came out Ill Rogers.

As patter became more important in his act, he began studying the routines of those on the bill ahead of him and making remarks about them. In doing so, he looked at his rope rather than the audience, thereby creating the illusion that what he said was impromptu and not carefully thought out, which it was. He also began roping those backstage who gathered in the wings to watch his act and dragged them out on the stage. Will laughed about this. "They'd get so mixed up they wouldent know their way off the stage. Sometimes I'd get a chorus girl in her kimona or something else."

With his experiences in Africa, Australia, New Zealand and in following the rodeo circuit, Will soon became a seasoned vaudeville trouper. He could sew on a button, darn a sock, press his own trousers, fry an egg over a gas jet, and turn out a tasty concoction of steak, gravy and biscuits in a dressing-room chafing dish. He could travel for twenty-four hours in a day coach, duck his head under a water tap, and go into his routine without a rest. "He could grumble as much as anyone and play practical jokes," someone commented. "Get a kick in the pants from a witty acrobat at Podunk and return it months later at Peoria. He could stand a man a drink, share a bed, make his overcoat serve double, and play a bit in another act when one of the cast was off on a toot."

Will could do all these things but he could not make Betty change her mind. In the spring of 1906 he took his act to Europe without her. His first billing was in Berlin, and on the way he stopped for a few days in Paris. "It is a wide open place," he reported to Betty, "and seems to have no laws especially of morality." The stage women he had encountered "ain't one to 11 with these for paint and make-up. Oh, how they strut." The men "just curl their mustache and put on all they got." The city had New York "whipped to a whisper for continuous performances," and he let Betty know that he lived at "one of the swellest hotels where Champagne flows like water."

The act was a big hit in Berlin but the city made a bigger hit with him. "I never get in till 8 or 9 or 10 in the morning," he wrote Betty. "Everything is wide open all night and we just go from one café to another. There is quite a bunch of English girls and a few of us boys, and I didn't think it was possible to go such a clip. N. Y. sleeps more in one night than Berlin in a week." Will was learning that a little competition might help.

Several times when riding in the Tiergarten Will met the Kaiser on the bridle paths, and failed to salute him, which caused no trouble at all. But when he roped a fireman stationed in the wings and dragged him out onto the stage the audience almost mobbed him. "The manager had to come out and explain that my rope slipped," he explained. "In Germany they have cultivated everything they got but humor." Nevertheless, Will's act was a tremendous success and he was offered an extended engagement but his schedule did not permit him to accept.

The act went over even better in London at the Palace, its leading music hall. He was paid more than he had ever received before and was offered three or four more weeks of work. While there he appeared before the exclusive Raneleigh Club, and learned later when presented with a beautiful silver cup that King Edward VII had been in the audience. It had taken him only a short four years to be "recognized" by the King!

Back in the States, riding the crest of the wave of his foreign success, Will invited Betty to join him in Oklahoma to meet his family. He seemed almost a stranger to her. There were parties, horseback riding, dinners and picnics, but always as a group. "Even in our moonlight rides," Betty wrote, "we both rode up in front with the rest. He never came around where I was unless we were playing and singing at the piano. I just could not understand it." She understood him less when on his way back to New York he stopped at her home and asked her to marry him at once. She frankly told him she could not accept a life of trouping over the country in vaudeville. "Our parting was a sad one," she commented, "but we promised to write."

In the spring of 1907 Will organized a Wild West troupe and took it to London, hoping that being a producer might appeal to Betty more than being a mere performer. Although his own act, which was billed for a couple of weeks before the larger troupe arrived, was a sensational success, the big show proved a dismal failure. It was top-heavy and slow-paced and, bogged down in managerial duties, Will's act lost its appeal. He was forced to tour the cities outside London by himself to raise the money to send the troupe back home, and he followed them a few weeks later, broke and discouraged. It was back on the vaudeville circuits for him.

During the next year and a half he played most of the cities of the United States and southern Canada on the various circuits, and during this time he and Betty kept up their correspondence. She would not consent to marry him, and yet she would not let him go. There was a spat over a girl he occasionally took out for a bite to eat or a beer after the show that he told her about. "She was such a nice lady-like smart kind of a kid," Will explained, "and she got a bit stuck on me."

He sent along a letter from her to him that proved it had not been serious. Betty was not satisfied. Then as the panic of 1907 made it more difficult to make a living, Will became more and more irritable. "If I act queer don't think of it," he wrote. "I ain't treating you right and I know it but I will later on. I am in wrong and will tell you all about it when I see you which might be Xmas . . . When you still refused me last spring—*we both will regret that*—for we could of been happy and a thousand times more prosperous. Still you was so *wise* you couldent be showed. I have not been worth a *dam* since, and you are the direct cause of it. I don't blame you, only I wish you had not been so *bullheaded.*" Will ended by taking some of the bite from his criticism by assuring her "I love you more than anything."

Not satisfied to wait until he saw her for an explanation, Betty insisted on being told all at once. Will sent her a letter from a woman he had been having an affair with begging him to see her again. Instead of appreciating his honesty and forthrightness, which was certainly not expected, she countered with some of her own activities. "So you snared you a *promising* lawyer," Will wrote. "What all did he promise you, and you him? Now you better slack up on *that stuff* for it gets you in bad and I will be getting sore." But he was not "sore" enough not to want to see her nor to tell her that he loved her.

As the routine of his life began to build up, Will considered seriously going back into ranching, and might have done so if the backwaters of the panic had not hurt that business. "One more year will let me out of this," he assured Betty, and then, as if afraid of being a weakling, berated himself. She had only hinted to him about her "Dearest Friend, T.H., the promising lawyer" but he, "like a big *rummy,*" had been a fool and told her "a lot of stuff that I had never ought to of told anybody in the world." But since he had done so he determined "to live life as she comes" and not have "much confidence in anything. We all make mistakes," he added, "but as long as we live the best we know how they can't be considered against one." After this rather philosophical approach, he then "playfully" admitted that he had got even with her "for I have fell in love with an *Actorine* and *gone plum nutty.*"

Betty blazed back, thanking her good fortune she had learned the sort of life he was leading before it was too late. Will at once dropped his playfulness. He chided her for thinking any other girl was considered in the same breath with her, and he was no longer sorry for telling all. "I told you I had always been a bad boy and guess I will continue to be one till you are with me and then it is all over. I will put all of this old life behind and I think I am man enough to do it too. I have had a lot of girls, not *sweethearts* or girls when it comes to settling down I would consider for a minute. I kinder always thought I knew about where my love and affection lay, and I gave you credit for not being a jealous girl. Now I am the jealous one of the two, and I took what you put in your letter as it was meant and come back at you with the actor gal one. But you size it up all wrong and write that offul letter. If I wanted to break off, I think I could do it in a great deal more gentlemanly way than that. I wouldent beat around the bush trying to save your feelings but out with the whole truth." He then took her to task for saying he had made "unpleasant insinuations," and called it the worst thing she could say. "It would be the last thing on earth I would do," he assured her. "Why I would fight any one that would insinuate as much to me as that you acted the least bit unladylike at any time. Why Girl that's why I love you. That's why you are different from the rest."

Will considered closing his act and going to Rogers, Arkansas, to talk with her. But better judgment prevailed and, instead, he asked her to "cut out all this foolish talk for when I tell you you are the only girl for me I mean it regardless of how I act sometimes."

After a few more months of verbal sparring, one morning early in November, between bookings, Will appeared in Rogers unannounced, and told her to start packing as they were getting married. They would go to New York for a few weeks after which as a honeymoon they would make a tour of the Orpheum Circuit, then back to Claremore to live. Betty said "yes" this time.

Will left her to break the news to her family and went to do the same for his. "Back to the scenes of our childhood," he wired her from the Oolagah railroad station. "Wish you was at the old depot. Love, Billy."

They were married at Betty's home in Rogers, Arkansas, on Wednesday, November 25, 1908, thus ending a fantastic courtship and beginning what Gene Buck, Ziegfeld's man Friday, called, "the most perfect mating I have known." On their twenty-fifth wedding anniversary Will wrote: "The day I roped Betty, I did the star performance of my life."

How true that was! When Will told Betty that he had to have someone to love he revealed his most vital need. There had been no one since his mother's death whom he could completely relax with, be himself, to whom he could reveal his innermost desires and longings. Betty filled this compelling need to perfection.

7

"Two for the Money"

AS WILL HAD PROMISED, THINGS WERE DIFFERENT— different for both of them. For him life was more relaxed and less lonely, and for Betty more exciting. In St. Louis, on their way to New York, they watched Pop Warner's Carlisle Indians scalp their opponents in a Thanksgiving football game. That evening at dinner Betty drank her first champagne. Afterward they went to the theater to see Maude Adams in *What Every Woman Knows.* This was to be Betty's introduction to a New York star and she was trembling with excitement when the curtain went up soon after their entrance. The theater was jammed and it seemed terribly hot and stuffy to her. In a few moments her head began to swim and when the brightly lighted stage began to tilt she became alarmed.

"Please take me out," she whispered to Will.

Will quietly hustled her out and walked her back to the hotel, where she fell into bed and was asleep as soon he could get her undressed. She did not understand what had happened until the next morning.

"From the way you drank champagne," Will said, "I wondered what kind of a girl you were. I decided champagne-drinking must be an 'old Arkansas custom.' "

Will hustled Betty over New York at a mad pace, showing her the sights from the Aquarium to the zoo in Central Park. They climbed to the top of the Statue of Liberty and of the Singer Building, forty-one stories and the tallest in the world. The bells of old Trinity rang out the old and rang in the New Year for them. Betty wanted to see the opera. "I hustled around and got two seats from a Spec," Will wrote. "I noticed him laughing and thought it was at me. I dident know he was laughing at the seats. I dident know a seat could be so far away and still be in the theatre. We could just see the drummer. My wife was worried about how we could tell Caruso and I told her he would be the one that sings. My Lord, that's all all of them did. Well, I stuck it out till intermission and then went up to Hammerstein's to see the three Keatons and a good show. I don't think that show Caruso was in was much of a hit as I passed there next day and they had a different show billed."

Betty watched Will's routine for the first time at Proctor's Theatre in Newark. Although the applause was tremendous, she was not impressed. A few days later when she told a friend of hers from Arkansas, Mrs. W. H. ("Coin") Harvey about meeting Battling Nelson at the Metropole, a hangout for newspapermen, gamblers, sportsmen and actors, the old lady was shocked. "Betty, what will your mother think of you meeting a prizefighter?" she asked. Betty had no answer.

At the end of Will's two-week engagement in the New York area, they headed out on their honeymoon over the Orpheum Circuit. In every city where Will had billing, it was a repeat of the New York experience. He seemed determined to show her everything she had missed by not being with him on previous trips. When she protested at being routed out at daylight, he would brush it off. "Let's do it now, then we'll have the afternoon free for something else." Truly, these were days he had dreamed about and he did not want to lose a second. It might be a sightseeing trip or a horseback ride in a city park, or it might be a trip into the country on which they would take sandwiches and beer for a picnic. Then after his performance, which was usually last on the bill, it would be a snack in a quiet little restaurant. By the end of the tour, Betty had begun to like the carefree life and when Will was offered an extended engagement in the Percy Williams theaters back east, it was her decision to accept it. On another question he made the decision in a peremptory manner.

"I will be glad to help you correct the mistakes you make in grammar," Betty offered soon after they were married.

"Never mind," he snapped, "that's our bread and butter."

As they settled down in their New York headquarters, Betty more and more relieved Will of little nagging duties such as taking care of his correspondence with his family. Will turned over to her some rent property he owned in Claremore and she proudly opened an account in Uncle Clem's bank. "I'll surprise Billy with a big balance," she wrote.

Late in July, 1909, Will's sister May died suddenly, and he was unable to go to the funeral. "All of us children have been wonderfully fortunate in having such a kind and loving Father," he wrote, "not only financially but by word and action. I don't know what arrangements you all will make about May's children but I want to pay for the schooling for at least one of the boys."

As Will became more successful, Uncle Clem's disappointment in his son changed to pride. His second wife had died and he had moved to a corner room over the bank in Claremore. Will kept him supplied with clippings from the various newspapers in the cities where he appeared. "At the drop of a hint" Uncle Clem would whip out a particularly laudatory clipping. If the praise came high enough and his visitor was in to see about a loan, Uncle Clem was known to shave down the amount of security demanded or go on the note himself. Past seventy now, he could not ride as in his younger days, but when he hitched his high-stepping Kentucky-bred, Roger K, to his rubber-tired buggy he could raise as much dust as anybody in the region. "I'd hang on to my New York hat with one hand, and cling to the seat with the other," Betty wrote, "when Uncle Clem took me out on, as he said, 'a spin around the town.' " As for the newfangled automobiles just making their appearance, he had the deepest scorn.

At first Uncle Clem had been frankly suspicious about the amount of money Will was making. "Looks like something is wrong somewhere," he confided to a friend when Will's pay was $250 a week. But after going to New York with Sallie and Maude to watch Will perform he changed his mind. He stood up and by pointing his pencil counted the house. Then he sat down and did some figuring on an old envelope. "I tell you, girls," he complained, "that manager is making a lot of money off Willie." He attended every performance while in New York and would station himself outside to hear the comments after the show was over. If any of those coming out expressed doubts that Will had once been a cowboy, he would promptly correct them. Then he would identify himself and offer to introduce them to Will. Invariably, when Will joined him his father would have a crowd for him to meet.

Although Will was a recognized success, he was not a headliner. To achieve this he needed a big act with top performers. He ignored his failure with such a show in England, and in the summer and fall of 1910 hammered together an even more elaborate show built around glamorous women on dancing horses doing fancy roping and riding and on cowboys riding bucking horses on the stage. It did fairly well on the larger New York stages but was too unwieldy for most of the theaters on the circuits. Once again Will had to disband a show and once again he ended up broke. But in the meantime with the help of Betty and a theater manager he had learned something that prepared him for the next big step in his career.

At a performance in Philadelphia Betty was standing backstage with the manager watching the performance. "Tell me, Mrs. Rogers," he asked, "why does Will carry all those horses and people around with him? I would rather have Will Rogers alone on the stage than the whole bunch of them put together, and I know a lot of other managers who feel the same way about it."

Betty had been thinking the same thing, and she told Will about it.

Harried by managerial problems that he was not fitted to handle, Will thought it over.

"What would I do?" he asked the manager.

"Take that white horse and tie it out in the alley, tell Buck McKee and the rest of 'em to take the day off, then take that rope of yours and go out in Number One ["the Street" in front of the big drop curtain] and give 'em eight minutes of patter along with your rope tricks."

"What'll I tell 'em?"

"I'll stand at the first entrance and you can talk about me, about the mayor, about the other acts, about anything that comes into your head."

The manager had to shove Will out the first time he tried it. "If Buck McKee hadn't taken the day off," Will admitted, "he and Teddy would have been out there with me."

Most of the cast of the big show were either in the wings or down front and the rounds of applause that brought Will back time after time told them their "pink slips" were in the offing. The greatest wrench of it all for Will was in parting company with Buck McKee and Teddy. The horse was shipped to Oolagah, put out to pasture, and lived to old age with only one mishap. He broke out of the pasture and was found months later by Will's nephew, Herb McSpadden, hitched to the plow of a full-blood Indian. Although he seemed to enjoy this as much as appearing in the leading vaudeville theatres of America, the music halls of Europe and before the King of England, he was returned to a well-earned life of leisure.

Life became much more enjoyable for Betty and Will now that he had only himself to look after for the act. There was more money for them also as Will received as much for his own performance as he had for the old act. Buck's salary and the expense for Teddy had cut deeply into his earnings. Will's act as a "single" usually went on last so that it would give him a chance to watch the other performers so he could comment on them. "The house seems to kind of like it—but sometimes the actors don't."

Will's comments must have pleased the critics as well as the audience. He was seldom without a booking and as Betty went with him most of the time he was at his best. In Chicago, for the second time in the history of the Majestic Theatre, he was held over for a second week. His performance, which was a typical one, brought this comment from Richard Henry Little, critic for the Chicago *Tribune*:

> The accomplished Mr. Rogers not only delights the audience with his amazing dexterity with the lasso, but even more with his running fire of small talk. The great beauty of Mr. Rogers' conversation is that he never is quite through. He makes a remark and apparently marks a period by doing some trick with the lasso and the part of the audience that sympathized with his statement applauds madly. Then Mr. Rogers drops another remark that is diametrically opposed to his first statement and starts another section of the audience to great applause. But as this tumult drops down he makes still another comment along the line of his original thought that is a trifle more pertinent than either of the first two and differs widely from them.

Little ended his criticism with a most illuminating conclusion: "The remarks of Mr. Rogers when published properly look something like an extract from the Congressional Record because of the 'applause,' and 'great laughter,' and 'long continued demonstration' that must be scattered through the published text."

Will was soon to have less worries over his act as he was to have more responsibilities. There was to be an addition to the family. "I have about all my baby clothes made," Betty wrote Uncle Clem on August 21, 1911. "I am expecting the youngster about the fifteenth of October. Billy wants a boy of course, but I do not care which it is. If it is a boy, I am going to name it after Billy. I would name it after you, but there are so many Clems in the family I'm afraid they would get mixed up."

In her next letter Betty excitedly announced that they had seen "an airship" at Syracuse and had taken an apartment at 551 West 113 Street. "I can hardly wait until *he* comes. My mother came last Thursday. She is so well and I'm so happy and glad to have her here. We can get anything we want close to the apartment. We buy potatoes by the quart and peaches too. I wonder what the grocery man out there would think if one should go in and call for a quart of potatoes?"

The baby was born on October 20, 1911, and was a boy. It was named William Vann, for Will and for Uncle Clem. A package came from Clem containing three pairs of little black wool stockings with pink-and-blue toes and heels, and a pair of tiny beaded Indian moccasins. Will wrote his father to thank him. "We are doing fine," he stated. "Betty will write you. She sat up today."

Uncle Clem did not receive her letter nor see his newborn grandson. Within hours after the package arrived a telegram informed them of his death. He had spent the weekend in Chelsea at Maude's and had died in his sleep.

In the spring of 1912 Will appeared in his first regular show, *The Wall Street Girl,* starring Blanche Ring. He and Betty rode to the opening on the subway, both so nervous they could not talk. She sat down front in the orchestra section and shortly after the curtain went up there were excited whisperings around her and a number of people got up and left. Will came out on the stage, stopping the action of the play, and announced that the *Titanic,* the largest ship afloat, on her maiden voyage to the United States had struck an iceberg and had gone down with a shocking loss of life (1,517 dead, 53 of them children). This tragic news unquestionably hurt the show.

If the critics may be believed, the short run was not the fault of Will, nor of Blanche Ring for that matter. "Will Rogers, the lariat thrower, produced the only real humor of the evening" (the *Tribune*). "Rogers is more than a cowboy—he's an artist. . . . He threw a rope over 'The Wall Street Girl' and dragged off the first honors of the performance. Aside from his skill, Rogers displayed a sense of humor as fresh as a breeze from the Western prairies. Without betraying the slightest effort he 'roped' the house" (the *World*). "There were two high spots in 'The Wall Street Girl.' One of them was the 'Deedle-Dum-Dee' song of Blanche Ring herself, and the other was that extraordinary performer, Will Rogers, who did his regular vaudeville act, but who undoubtedly scored the success of the evening" (Charles Darnton). "There was a poet with his lariat who had come out of the West and inserted himself right in the middle of the play who was worth his weight in Gold to the management" (Acton Davies, *Evening Sun*).

After *The Wall Street Girl* closed Will went back on the vaudeville circuits, touring for almost a year by himself, while Betty lived at Rogers, Arkansas. The chief reason for this was another addition to the family, a baby girl born May 18, 1913, and named Mary Amelia after Will and Betty's mothers. Will was playing in Houston, Texas, when he received the telegram announcing her arrival.

While going it alone Will's prize possession was a scrapbook filled with pictures of Betty and the children. "I like being a successful and popular actor," he told a reporter, "but when it comes to being a matinee idol—gee whiz, these people in this scrapbook are the only ones I want to be an idol to. How could I be interested in them matinee girls with kids like these out home? That Bill, Jr., of mine is learning to throw a rope and has a hobby horse he rides all the time. He insists on being an actor like me—he thinks I am an actor—but watch me make a farmer out of him. He and his kid sister and their mother are going to meet me in Syracuse next week." Actually, Will's itinerary can be fairly well traced by the postcards he sent home to the children.

In late spring of 1914 Will told Betty to leave the children with her mother at Rogers, Arkansas, and to meet him in Atlantic City as he had big plans on the fire. When she joined him she learned that he had booked passage to Europe for them on the new German superliner, the *Vaterland,* that was to return from its maiden voyage. She had to gather a wardrobe in a few days but by now was used to doing things in a hurry. It was her first trip on a ship and she saw to it that they were dressed very carefully for dinner the first evening aboard. They were the first in the dining room and as it filled up, Betty's face reddened in embarrassment as the other passengers came in dressed as they had come aboard.

On the trip over Will's curious eyes noticed that the ship had unusually wide decks. "They said she was built to transport troops in case of war," he commented. "Her wide decks were to drill on. It didn't do our boys any good after we seized her when war was declared. Both of their days training was done over here. The boat and cooties were all we got out of the war."

Although Will had no bookings in England, where they first landed, he had been there only a few days when Sir Alfred Butts, for whom he had worked before at the Palace, offered him a part in *The Merry-Go-Round,* starring Nora Bayes, at the Empire. Will was doubtful about accepting. The theater was a large, noisy music hall, and there was constant activity and turmoil in the lobby centering around a huge bar. During the performance, people in the audience would go out to the bar for a drink or be served in their seats by "hostesses" or "percentage" girls. Will was afraid the activity, noise and confusion would crab his act. Sir Alfred insisted that he have a try at it. The result was amazing. When he was on, the lobby emptied and the girls stopped selling drinks. At the end of the week Sir Alfred wrote out a check for $400 and offered him an unlimited engagement.

While Will worked, Betty and friends toured the Continent, sightseeing and shopping chiefly in Berlin and Paris. When she returned to London Will saw to it that she kept hopping.

As the days passed, Will became increasingly anxious about the tense situation shaping up in Europe. Although everyone assured him that the world had "outgrown war," Will did not believe it. Over Sir Alfred's protests, he left the show and he and Betty sailed for the

United States on the German *Imperator*. By the time it docked in New York hostilities had broken out.

Will returned to his old bread-and-butter vaudeville, but not happily. The time had come for him to find a more stable spot in show business or go into some other line of work.

"Can you imagine when I die and St. Peter asks me what I did on earth to qualify for heaven," he said to Jack Lait, "and I answer, 'I spun a rope and kidded myself so's other people wouldn't kid me first'?"

"You're crazy," Jack argued, "with your ability the show business can be steady enough. All you have to do is to find the right spot. Then there is no limit to where you can go."

Fred Stone, one of his closest friends and the famous dancer and star of many Broadway productions, gave the prescription. "Stay in New York, even at less pay, Bill," he advised, "so that you can be in the right spot when the big opportunity comes."

Betty gave her "amen" to this.

8

"The Real Follies Are Out Front"

ACTING UPON FRED STONE'S ADVICE, WILL ACCEPTED vaudeville engagements only in and around New York. When there were not enough bookings at the major theaters to meet his expenses, he played smaller houses under an assumed name for as little as $75 a week. His friendship with the press proved invaluable, since his secret was not revealed, as did his ability to disguise himself and mimic.[1] In the summer of 1915 he took a house at Amityville, Long Island, across the road from Fred Stone, and here their third child, named James Blake, was born on July 25, 1915. In the same month another member joined the family, by the name of Dopey, a little round-bodied, coal-black pony, with glassy eyes, "the gentlest and greatest pony for grownups or children anyone ever saw. I don't know why we called him Dopey," Will recalled. "I guess it was because he was always so gentle and just the least bit lazy. Anyhow we meant no disrespect to him."

Horseback riding was a ritual in the Rogers family. The children had their first lesson on their second birthday, and Dopey was perfect for this. "He helped raise the children," Will wrote. "During his lifetime he never did a wrong thing to throw one of them off, or a wrong thing after they had fallen off. He couldent pick 'em up, but he would stand there and look at 'em with a disgusted look for being so clumsy as to fall off. I used to sit on him by the hour (yes, by the

[1] In later years, for a joke, he would impersonate Bill Hart and Spencer Tracy so perfectly that people asked for autographs.

year) and try new rope tricks, and he never batted an eye. Dopey and Dodo, another pet pony we got for Mary, rode in the best palace car by express."

This was a happy summer for Will and Betty. For companionship, in addition to Fred Stone and family, there was his brother-in-law, the famous novelist Rex Beach, and his family. The three men sailed on Great South Bay in Fred's boat, rode horseback and roped, picked up a smattering of polo, and swam. Rex was a superb swimmer and diver and, of course, Fred and Will, competitive and cocky as fighting roosters, tried to surpass him. On one dive Will hit his head on a rock on the bottom and was dragged out half-conscious.

"Didn't you know the tide was out?" Rex asked when Will could talk.

"There wasn't any tides in Rabb's Creek where I learned to swim," Will replied.

This accident could have had serious consequences as Will's right arm was paralyzed from it and he had vaudeville engagements coming up. By hours of practice he learned to do his rope tricks with his left arm. "I sho had to do a mess of tall talking those first weeks," he admitted. Eventually he regained the use of his right arm and later he would surprise his audiences by switching from his right to his left arm for his tricks.

"My earliest recollection of Will was as a thrilling figure on horseback who would come trotting along, swoop down, pick me up in his saddle, and then to my huge delight, whirl his lasso in ever-widening circles," said Dorothy Stone, whom he was to play with in *Three Cheers* when her father was injured in a plane accident. "I can remember his booming laughter, and how I would climb to the pommel of his saddle, with his arm resting me in his lap."

During this summer Will took his first airplane ride at Atlantic City in a "flying boat" made by Glenn Curtiss. For several days he and Betty had gone out to watch the flights and it was only on the last day that he developed enough nerve to go up. He was carried out to the plane on the back of another man and when it landed brought to shore in the same manner. "As the plane left the water," Betty wrote, "Will waved at me as he was to do so many times in the future. He was nervous but vastly pleased."

Will's next chance in a regular show almost proved disastrous. It was in a musical *Hands Off,* and his act was spotted between two full-stage musical numbers. This meant he had to work in Number One and did not have enough room for his tricks. Twice he tried the big crinoline and twice the rope hit the backdrop and fell to the stage. He was preparing to try again when the manager rang down the curtain. This meant failure, even disgrace that might blight his entire career. The audience came to his rescue. It resented this highhanded action. Led by his loyal first-nighter friends, wave after wave of applause shook the theater. When the curtain went up for the next number, it was hooted down. In desperation the manager asked Will to go back on. He refused to do so until the producer, Mr. Shubert, asked him as a personal favor. As he ambled out, grinning his appreciation, he was given a standing ovation. Once again, although Will received good critical notices, the production ran only a short time. Most important, though, one of the telegrams congratulating him for his performance came from Gene Buck.

Early in the fall Will had another opportunity in *Ned Wayburn's Town Topics* in the ill-starred Century Theatre on Central Park West, and this also had a short run. Back in vaudeville, he played two weeks at the Palace, and then moved to the Forty-fourth Street Theatre.

In all these appearances Will received top critical acclaim and yet his "rope of words" neither lengthened nor became strong enough to lasso anything permanent. Most of his comments were on other acts or on members of the cast. If he wandered afield, it was on subjects thought to be of general interest to a theatrical audience. His performance had been good enough and his comments pertinent enough, however, to plant an idea in the fertile brain of Gene Buck. He came up with the madcap conclusion that Ziegfeld needed this irrepressible cowboy to add humor to his productions.

When Buck first broached the idea Ziegfeld was almost hysterically opposed to it. It was inconceivable that this uncouth cowboy with his dirty, sweat-begrimed clothes, ungrammatical drawl, and shuffling walk could help "glorify" the most beautiful girls in the world bedecked in the most gorgeous costumes imagination could devise in a fairyland setting! If it had come from anybody except Gene Buck, Ziegfeld would not even have listened, and if anybody but Gene Buck had thought up such an absurd notion it would have been dismissed as a daydream.

At the time Ziegfeld had two productions at the New Amsterdam Theatre. Downstairs, since 1907, the *Follies* had flamed across the theatrical world. Nobody spoke of the extravaganza in comparison with other shows but as better or worse than the previous year. Its performance ended at 11:15 and Ziegfeld's other production, *The Midnight Frolic,* began on the roof at the stroke of midnight. "The *Frolic* was the start of this Midnight and late style of entertainment that has degenerated into a drunken orgy of off-colored songs, and close formation dancing," Will wrote. "It was the first midnight show. It could have 50 or 75 people in the cast, bigger than all modern day shows given at regular hours. It had the most beautiful girls of any show Ziegfeld ever put on, for the beautiful ones wouldent work at matinees for they never got up that early."

It was on the roof that Buck finally browbeat Ziegfeld into giving Will a spot. A typical routine in his first appearances went like this:

Hello, you Roof Roosters . . . you ain't missed a night or drink all year. . . . Some of you buy one drink and have one laugh in your system and try to conserve both of them. . . . You leave your wife at home, get a front table, light up a cigar, get a bottle of wine . . . of course the more wine you drink, the farther you can reach with your cigar to burst a balloon on one of the girls. . . . It adds up to about $10 a balloon . . . I am going to stick with this fellow Ziegfeld . . . I am off all the shows that go in for art . . . That fellow knows just how to drape 'em so you don't know just what they have on or haven't . . . You keep coming back and then you don't know . . . Somebody has got to do something while the girls change even if they don't have much to change . . . The reason Mr. Ziegfeld keeps me here is the people seem to drink more after watching my act. . . .

Actually, Ziegfeld saw no reason for keeping Will. True, at first he got laughs, but with an audience that had close to 50 per cent as "repeaters" and "plenty of insomnia" Will was having a nightmarish struggle to maintain its interest. Ziegfeld definitely was not amused. His genius turned toward the selection of girls and an impeccable taste for costumes and settings. Furthermore, Will's references to prominent men in his patter frightened him. Buck was able to talk him out of firing Will at the end of the first week, but halfway through the second, his face flaming from a reference Will had made to him, he called Buck into his office.

"That damn cowboy has to go," he ordered. "I am leaving for a couple of weeks and when I return I don't want him around here."

Gene had no choice but to call Will in and give him the bad news. As Will came up to his desk, he busied himself with some papers, wondering what to say.

"I'm glad to see you, Mr. Buck," Will said before Gene spoke. "I've got to have more money."

Buck gulped and blinked. "Why do you think you deserve more money?" he asked.

"I have a wow of an idea my wife gave to me," Will said. "She says I ought to talk about what I read in the papers every day. It would give me a brand-new act every night. I could talk about all sorts of things and people in the news."

"You would get us sued," Gene hedged.

"Not if I talked about public figures," Will argued. "They'd eat it up."

The idea appealed to Buck. If it worked, it might appease Ziegfeld, whose second look, after the girls, was at the box office and the cash register.

"Try it," he gambled, "and if it works, then we can talk about more money."

Buck was on hand that night to see what happened. Will ambled out and started his rope spinning. "See where Henry Ford's peace ship has landed in Holland . . ." he punctuated this with a spin of the rope as all eyes turned to him . . . "Got all them pacifists on board . . ." another spin "Holland's welcome to 'em, they ain't much good to us . . ." another spin "Ford's all wrong, instead of taking a lot of them high-powered fellers on his ship . . ." another spin . . . "he should've hired away all these Ziegfeld pippins . . ." another spin ". . . He'd not only got the boys out of the trenches by Christmas . . ." another spin ". . . but he'd have Kaiser Bill and Lloyd George and Clemenceau shootin' craps to see which one'd head the line at the stage door."

As the roof rocked with laughter and applause, Gene knew that if Will kept this up even Ziegfeld would be convinced. It was the proper time for doing so. Under the whiplash of the war, Americans were gradually crawling out of their shell of localism and isolationism, and news was taking on more vital meaning and pertinency. Will's long experience in reading newspapers from front to back coupled with his shrewd insight permitted him to dig to the heart of things. After doing so he was able to restate it in such a way that perked up ears and irrigated minds.

When Ziegfeld returned, the first thing he did was to call in Gene Buck.

"How did your cowboy friend, Will Rogers, take it when you fired him?"

"I didn't," Gene replied.

"What do you mean?" Ziegfeld's face flushed with anger. "You mean you didn't obey my orders?"

"Come hear him on the roof tonight," Gene said, "and then if you want to fire him, do it yourself."

Ziegfeld did not fire him but it was the cash register and box office that kept him from doing so. He would pace up and down, muttering to himself and tearing his hair, as Will unmercifully jabbed his verbal pitchfork into the "most sacred cows."

"I might be kiddin' an Archbishop and Ziegfeld would be worried for fear I was gettin' beyond my depths." Will chuckled. "But Flo didn't know what I knew—that I was holding up a grand boost for the Archbishop at the end."

As the war provided vivid and dramatic material in both events and leaders, Americans became more conscious of news and its reporting in various media. On the domestic scene, Woodrow Wilson, as president, was a dramatic figure who even as a college president had made news. A scholar and an intellectual, a visionary and an idealist, he was at the same time an astute, hardheaded and resourceful leader. In an incredibly short time as president he had pushed through more reforms under his New Freedom than had taken place since Lincoln. Tariff schedules had been reduced for the first time since the Civil War; the currency, particularly through the Federal Reserve Act and the banks established, had been made more flexible thereby partially breaking the control by Wall Street and the bankers over money; the Clayton Antitrust Act had struck out against monopoly and helped labor unions by exempting them from its provisions; and the financial distress of the farmers had been somewhat alleviated. This program had been achieved by dedicated help in Congress and not through the help of President Wilson's Cabinet, most of whom were appointed because of political demands. One of them, Secretary of State William Jennings Bryan, lent himself admirably as a subject for Will's satire. Bryan's knowledge of foreign affairs and the role the United States must play was on a par with his fundamentalist views on evolution.

Typical comments in Will's routine might be like this: "Bryan is against every public issue that comes up . . . About the only thing he is pleased with is himself . . . When Ford's peace ship sailed I went over to see it off . . . I got there just in time to hear Bryan say, 'God bless you' . . . That's the only thing he says for nothing . . . Well, you have to give him credit . . . He held out for more money . . . I thought for a while it might be a success . . . Bryan didn't go . . . President Wilson says a man has a right to change his mind and should, but Bryan has been doing the same act for 14 years . . . Bryan is really in earnest about preparedness . . . He is going to make a few free talks on it. . . . If Bryan and Billy Sunday were to lose their voices this wouldn't be such a bad old world to live in after all. . . . Now they have some of Bryan's speeches on phonograph records . . . in sections . . . They also have records of some guy reciting Gunga Din . . . listening to them would be my idea of an exciting evening."

Henry Ford, one of "the kings that Will kept up his cuff," was one of his best sources of humor: "I see where Ford just said he would send a bigger peace ship over . . . He is a glutton for punishment . . . I'll bet Bryan don't hold out for more money this time . . . Ford was mistaken when he says the people looked for a lot of highbrows on the Peace Ship and were surprised to find ordinary people . . . He said he could have sent thousands of them . . . He could, like hell . . . Why, Barnum couldent have gotten a collection like that . . . Why, he could of made money just showing them over here . . . Ford will go down in history as the man who shoved the mother-in-law joke into the ashcan."

Subjects and events, as well as men, furnished grist for his grinding: "They got Panama Canal fortified with guns pointing out to the oceans . . . Now they have discovered you could come up behind it on land . . . They never thought of that . . . We are prepared all right . . . Have the Panama Canal, Nicaragua, the Philippines and the North Pole . . . If we would take Cape Horn then we would pretty well have traffic tied up. . . . See where we lost two airplanes. . . . Lucky the other two couldent fly or we would have lost them also. . . . A man in the Virginia Legislature introduced a bill to protect the men . . . A woman can only be naked from the top of the head to three inches below the neck . . . then they must be covered with stuff you can't see through from there down to four inches of the ground . . . Nothing was said about going barefooted, which is a frequent occurrence in Virginia. . . . I read in another paper that skirts are to be shorter next year . . . If they keep on I want the Lord to let me live 2 more years . . . Of course our girls don't seem to have on much . . . but they're all wrapped up in themselves."

In the fall of 1915 the Friars Club of New York sponsored a show to make a week's whirlwind tour of principal cities in the East. Baltimore was on the list and great excitement prevailed when it was learned that President Wilson planned to attend. Most of the acts in the revue were based on skits written by George M. Cohan and right down to bit parts everyone was a star with a big reputation. Will was included to do his "specialty with a Rope and telling jokes on national affairs." It was a particularly good time for him as President Wilson was at the height of his much ridiculed note writing to the Central Powers in Europe and the United States and Mexico were feuding over Pancho Villa's raids into this country.

Will described his state of mind as he waited to go on: "Well, I am not kidding you when I tell you that I was scared to death. I am always nervous. I never saw an Audience that I faced with confidence. For no man can tell how a given Audience will take anything. Furthermore, I was to kid about some of the policies with which the President was shaping the Destinies of Nations. How was I to know but what the audience would rise up in mass and resent it? I had never heard, and I don't think any one else had ever heard of a President being joked personally in a Public Theater about the Policies of his Administration."

Will kept a copy of the act he had prepared (as he did for most of his appearances): "I am kinder nervous here tonight . . . I shouldn't be nervous, for this is really my second Presidential appearance . . . The first time was when Bryan spoke in our town once, and I was to follow his speech and do my little Roping act . . ." He heard the audience laughing, so he took a sly glance at the presidential box and President Wilson was laughing too. "As I say, I was to follow him, but he spoke so long that it was so dark when he finished, they couldent see my roping . . ." a long wait ". . . I wonder what became of him?" This went over great. As yet Will had made no direct reference to the President, but he was about to. "I see where they have captured Villa . . . Yes, they got him in the morning Editions and the Afternoon ones let him get away." Everybody in the theater was watching for the cue when to laugh, and Wilson was laughing. "Villa raided Columbus, New Mexico. . . . We had a man on guard that night at the army post . . . But to show you how crooked this Villa is, he sneaked up on the opposite side . . . We chased him over the line 5 miles, but run into a lot of Government Red Tape and had to come back. . . . There is now some talk of getting a Machine Gun if we can borrow one." Wilson was being criticized on all sides for lack of preparedness, and yet he led the laughter. "The one we have now they are using to train our Army at Plattsburg. . . . If we go to war, we will just about have to go to the trouble of getting another Gun." At this time there was talk of forming an army of 250,000 men. "We are going to have an army of 250,000 men . . . Mr. Ford makes three hundred thousand cars a year . . . I think, Mr. President, we ought to at least have a man to every Car . . ." President Wilson howled at this. "We are facing another Crisis in Europe tonight . . . but our President here has had so many of them lately that he can just lay right down and sleep beside one of those things . . . President Wilson is getting along fine now to what he was a few months ago . . . Do you realize, People, that at one time in our negotiations with Germany that he was five Notes behind! . . ."

President Wilson not only enjoyed this, but told many of his friends that it was the best satire pulled on him up to then. Will called this appearance his "proudest and most successful night." It meant something very personal to him. "A great many Actors and Professional people have appeared before him, on various occasions in wonderful high-class endeavors," he explained. "But I don't think that any person met him across the footlights in exactly the personal way that I did. Every other performer did before him exactly what they had done before many audiences, but I gave a great deal of time and thought to an Act for him, most of which would never be used again and had never been used before."

This was the ultimate secret of Will's success in his appearance before any group. President or policeman, prince or pauper, His Royal Highness or hobo, Will made every listener feel that he was being talked to personally.

Another forum opened for Will in 1916. The *Follies* edition of that year was the most spectacular and extravagant revue produced up to that time. As it began to shape up, Gene Buck realized that it was top-heavy and unbalanced with big numbers. As a constrast, he thought that Will's patter would add needed lightness and pace. Ziegfeld shuddered at the thought. Although a crowded Roof convinced him of Will's drawing power, he wanted none of him in his pet production. Nevertheless, before opening night it was obvious something had to be done. Grudgingly he offered Will a part. As usual he would not agree until he had talked it over with Betty. She shook her head. The additional salary offered, she felt, would not justify the extra work. The "repeaters" on the Roof from the *Follies* would mean two different routines. "Besides," she reminded, "the *Follies* go on the road."

This was a telling argument with Will. They were now living in Forest Hills, twenty minutes from the theater by subway, and the children were old enough to join him and Betty in their favorite sport—horseback riding and roping. Yes, he decided, Betty was right. For the first time everything seemed just right. He had a loving wife, adorable children, enough income to pay his overhead and buy a few more acres of land at Oolagah. What more did he want?

Will's first doubt came when he saw a flicker of relief spread over Ziegfeld's face when he turned down the offer. On the other hand, Gene Buck was glum about it and told him he had made a mistake.

Will bought four tickets for the opening at $12 apiece and he and Betty took a couple of friends from Arkansas to see it. As the revue unfolded, spectacle after spectacle, it was intolerably boring. Will squirmed in his seat, nudging Betty every few moments. "See, Blake" —he called her this when irritated—"what did I tell you? Boy, boy, I wish had had a crack at this."

After a couple more performances, even after some major surgery, the revue was still unwieldy. Ziegfeld waylayed Will in his dressing room one afternoon when he came in with a roll of newspapers to prepare his act for the Roof.

"I want you for the *Follies,* Rogers," he said.

"When do you want me to go on?" Will asked.

"Tonight."

Will dashed out to Forest Hills to break the good news to Betty.

"We'll spend the night in New York," he said.

"But your act?" she gasped.

"I'll use the stuff I prepared for the Roof, and then get more material for that out of the later editions. Hurry up, I have to get back in time to practice a dance routine."

For once Betty was ready to shed tears when the curtain in the theatre went up—tears of joy that, after all, Will was to have his chance that she had argued him out of and at what she saw there. The New York *American* for January 6, 1916, reported:

> Against a sky of Egyptian blue, glimpsed marble pillars bathed in calcium moonlight, two pretty girls in satin slippers and rather extreme riding breeches pirouetted after a polo ball. From the wings peeped out a bevy of girls in costumes possibly meant to approximate full dress in the South Sea islands. Came a pause: the polo players scurried off. A gorgeous creature in a Paris ball gown sauntered down the marble steps and across the stage nonchalantly. Then of a sudden a young man in shirt sleeves and other habiliments to match materialized right in the scandalized spotlight. The newcomer said something to the orchestra, which began to play "Finnegan's Wake." The young man had a rope in his hand, and the rope suddenly became alive and described strange circles in the air about him. A small girl (her name is Sybil Carmen) in white woolly chaparejos and a red skirt, bobbed into the circle and the oddly assorted pair began to waltz. The rope danced with them, hemmed them in, slipped under their feet skillfully and came up on the other side still whirling. Nothing that they could do embarrassed that rope. They played hop, skip and jump with it, but it always kept just out of the way.

Will made another appearance on the show, commenting on people and events. "Never had he gone over so well," Betty wrote. "It was a big and exciting evening and when he went upstairs to do his midnight performance, his magic stayed with him. After the performance on the Roof, we sat in our little hotel room, and over sandwiches and beer discussed the triumphs of the evening. We waited for the morning papers, and all of them gave Will excellent notices—the best, most important he had ever received."

The *Follies* was a better forum for Will than the Roof, where the audience was composed chiefly of tired businessmen looking for amusement. "I can't depend on New York jokes for the *Follies,"* Will said, "because such a large percentage of the audience is transients." Doing both shows, as Betty had warned, really kept him stepping. "I get my jokes out of the newspapers," he explained, "not out of the funny columns, but out of the latest news. At the matinee I pull stuff based on the noon editions of the afternoon papers. Well, before the evening performance all the matinee stuff is too stale for the audience, so I use the sporting editions, finals and home issues. But by the time the *Midnight Frolic* starts, these late evening jokes are also stale, so I get the first edition of the *Morning Telegraph* and make my monologue out of that. I buy more newspaper extras than any man in the world, because I've made up my mind no joke can get over after it is six hours old. A lot of clever writers have tried to fix me up with acts, but I can't get away with them. The public just won't allow me to learn a part. I've got to make it up as I go along. I'm going to try some day-old gags in Philadelphia, though, just as an experiment."

Although politics was the staple article for Will's routines, he was careful not to let the act become dull: "They say that a shark won't bite a leg that has a stocking on it . . . These theater goers must think they're sharks, the way they strain their eyes to determine whether stockings are being worn or not. . . . People think I can't be a real cowboy, or I wouldn't work in a show where there's nothin' but calves . . . The boys that are back from the Mexican border say the reports were wrong that it was 115 in the shade down there . . . They say that's a lie . . . There wasn't any shade there. . . . I'd like to be a millionaire, but I'd hate to be telling how I got it all the time."

The manner in which Will got over his humor was tremendously important. At one time within a few days a number of people committed suicide by jumping off Brooklyn Bridge. "They'll have to condemn Brooklyn Bridge . . . It's been weakened by suicides jumping off." The audience howled at it. "If I had told it," W. C. Fields remarked, "they would have mobbed me. He can get away with anything." At another time Will came on the stage laughing, as he thumbed back over his shoulder, then leaned over the footlights confidentially. "Fannie Brice was just telling us a grand story, and I'm laughing yet."

"Tell it to us . . ." the cry went up.

Will twirled his lariat, chewed on his gum, and scratched his head thoughtfully. "Lemme see, folks—" he winked—"today's Tuesday, isn't it? Well, I'll tell you that story about Thursday . . . It'll take that long to launder it."

In the *Follies* even more than on the Roof Will began lengthening his "rope of words" in another way. "I started picking the 'follies' out of the audience," he explained, "joshing the celebrities who came to the show." They liked it and so did the audience. Actually, this took on a "snob" appeal. Not to have been joshed by him was a blot on the escutcheon of the famous, the near famous and the self-important. To be introduced or roped by him either in the *Follies* or on the Roof was like owning a Rolls-Royce or belonging to the Union Club. Often Will would purposely ignore some celebrities who expected to be noticed and it was a rare treat to watch one of them fidget and become nervous as he glanced in their direction. If he wanted to play a joke on a friend or cut down to size someone he thought needed it, he would have the spotlight played on his victim, perhaps glance in his direction, and then not mention his name. "Ziegfeld was scared but it was a safe and simple game to follow," Will explained. "Your big butter-and-egg man, your author, baseball player, and especially your politician—like attention. They eat it up. And the folks who pay the tariffs at the box offices like to realize they are in prominent company. They go home and brag about sitting next to so-and-so even if they were ten rows away."

Will's way of doing this was not a hit-and-miss proposition. He was furnished a list of all the prominent people who had bought seats and their location. He found out from the newspapers each day who was "running *for* President or away *from* the police," as he expressed it.

Actually Will had discovered an unlimited source of humor ("fresh-laid jokes are the best") based on a simple formula: he might be working in the *Follies* but the real "follies" were out front, in the audience, in New York City, in New York State, in the United States, and in the world. No matter where or when, if observed closely and long enough, humor would crop out, and the bigger the man or the event the greater the "folly." It had to be separated properly from the trappings behind which it reposed, must be personal, political, social, economic or religious. Will had definite ideas and methods for this: "I use only one set method in my little gags, and that is to try to keep to the truth. Of course you can exaggerate it, but what you say must be based on truth. Personally, I don't like the jokes that get the biggest laughs, as they are generally as broad as a house and require no thought at all. I like one where, if you are with a friend, and hear it, it makes you think, and you nudge your friend and say, 'He's right about that.' I would rather have you do that than to have you laugh—and then forget the next minute what it was you laughed at." Will was at his best when things were happening in the world. Three or four thousand jokes would pass through his hopper in one season. With the coming of World War I his humor was to meet a crucial test.

9

"What We Laughed At during the War"

DURING WORLD WAR I, MOST HUMOR WAS PROVIDED BY magazines like *Judge,* the old *Life,* and in humor departments of magazines or books. There were performing comedians but they were, as Will pointed out, doing the same act over and over. Will was the only one using "fresh-laid" jokes. "I traveled for 4 years with the *Follies,*" he pointed out in the preface to a book he envisaged but never published, "the biggest stage show on the road, and all I had to do was to tell the audience new things to make them laugh each night. My little stunt consisted in talking on what I had read in the papers every day. Well, when the war commenced to get serious for us, I thought here is where you will have to change the style of your act. You can't keep kidding people." The year before the United States entered the war he could hit out at everybody and everything. "There was Villa, and neutralists, and note-writing and Bryan—dozens of heads aching to be hit." But after the country got into the war there would not be "a villain in the papers." All his friends confirmed his judgment on this.

"It only showed how little we understood the American people," he admitted later. "Why, they laughed better during the war than any other time, and the more serious the situation, the better they laughed if you happened to hit the right angle of it. There is nothing yet so serious that an American audience won't see something funny in it. All you hear is, 'Who won the war?' Well, the American sense of humor didn't do the cause any harm. *The people's funny bone developed in proportion to their backbone*. If Germany had had a sense of humor, there would have been no Kaiser, hence no war."

Will illustrated this. At the time the New York, New Haven and Hartford Railroad had a series of bad wrecks. In the fighting in France much emphasis was placed on "spring drives" when the weather improved. One day in the spring of 1918 the New Haven had a wreck in which fifty people were killed. That evening in his act Will said: "I see where the New York, New Haven and Hartford have started their spring drive." The audience yelled at this. The next day an official of the railroad sent word for "that alleged Comedian at Mr. Ziegfeld's to kindly eliminate any reference to the New York, New Haven and Hartford Railroad." That evening Will said, "I see where one of our Railroads have started in on their spring drive." This went over as big as it had the night before. "You see I did not mention the name of any Railroad in that," Will went on. "Last night I did and today Mr. (I gave his name) called up and told me not to mention his railroad's name, so you see I did not say a word about New York, New Haven and Hartford." This received the biggest laugh of all.

A bigger test came when Will played before President Wilson again in Washington. Did he dare kid the President now that the country was at war? "I took a peep at the President in his box, and said that Colonel House was the only man that ever 'listened' himself in. Northcliffe had that day refused the ministry of air, and I said the British had never heard of Bryan or he'd have got the job; and the President didn't seem to dislike that either. Then I went on and said, 'I guess Lord Northcliffe figured it's easier to tell how to run the war in his newspapers than to run it.' Mr. Tumulty, Wilson's secretary, told me that the President quoted that remark next day at a cabinet meeting."

Published speeches were Will's chief source of humor during the war. "If a man makes a speech he takes a chance on saying a damfool thing," Will said, "and the longer his speech the greater the thing. I read where Vice-President Marshall had said, 'Right will win.' That night I said, 'Right might win, but it would win sooner if we had a few more machine guns and uniforms.'" Even more ridiculous, the Crown Prince of Germany said that "God will help us to victory." This was Will's opening. "It's always struck me as funny that none of these Crown Princes, none of these Royal Guys have got hurt in the war since it was started by that guy that was heir to the Austrian throne getting killed . . . It looks like the only way we can get some of them Royal guys killed is to declare peace . . . Well, if the Lord's with the Crown Prince, the Lord's never been near enough to the firing line to know there is a war."

Good laugh producers during the war were the "dollar-a-year" men whose chief activities consisted in getting "10% plus cost" contracts for their companies; profiteers; draft dodgers; Hog Island and the wooden ships; the government management of the railroads; the airplane program that turned out more "air" than planes. His comments would make a gag history of the war. "The Guy that made the bullets was paid five dollars a day and the man that stopped them fifteen dollars a month. . . . When you see a lot of chaplains getting ready it's most time for the charge. . . . The chief army maneuver was to turn the shirts each day . . . that kept the Cooties marching and countermarching till it broke their hearts . . . Sergeant to Private looking through field glasses: 'How many men in that trench?' 'Thirty men and one officer.' 'How can you tell there's one officer?' 'All the rest are working.' . . . One girl in Paris figured in more engagements than the Legion of Honor."

Shortly before the end of the war Will appeared before President Wilson again, this time at the Metropolitan Opera House in a program honoring Enrico Caruso. The President was negotiating behind the scenes in an attempt to end the war. Will made some pertinent remarks. "The note from Germany had the only true thing in it that any of them had . . . It said, *anything we do at the Peace Conference will not be binding.* . . . Now Bulgaria has quit . . . They been in all these Balkan Wars and when they got in this they found out they was shooting with real bullets. Turkey wants to quit . . . They'll quit if the Allies will give them the Massacreeing privileges . . . One thing Pres Wilson asked Germany that I am surprised at, for as smart a man as he is . . . That was, we will not deal with you as long as you occupy invaded Territory . . . The Kaiser came back and says, 'If you can show me how I can give it up any faster than we are, I wish you would tell me . . . We are going out in high now . . . Germany dont know how we could get troops over there and get them trained so quick . . . They dident know that in our manual there is nothing about retreating, and when you only have to teach an army to go one way, you can do it in half the time."

President Wilson later quoted this last statement as coming from "an American humorist" ("I was only a comedian until then") and called it the most pungent comment made during the war. "Will Rogers' remarks are not only humorous," President Wilson said, "but illuminating."

Although Will was painfully honest in not using other people's material, he so loved a quip made by fiery old "Uncle Joe" Cannon, long-time Speaker of the House, that he used it several times. "All the officers in Washington wore spurs," Will said, "and there was no cavalry. People wanted to know why and 'Uncle Joe' gave them the answer. It was to keep their feet from slipping off their desks."

This comment may have been responsible for one of Will's most popular routines—on how to get a commission in "fighting the war in Washington." It went like this:

The only experience necessary is the danger of being drafted by your own board . . . Then pick out the branch of service whose office hours are the shortest . . . Then get your home Senator's address . . . Wait your turn in line and if you draw only a Captain, don't feel discouraged . . . You may meet a Cabinet officer and be promoted before night. . . . The next most important thing is the uniform . . . Unfortunately, our uniforms are mostly alike . . . When we have had as many wars as the European countries we can remedy that to the satisfaction of our officers . . . There would be no time to have it ready made as you have a date with a photographer at four . . . The clerk at the store can tell you what insignia to put on your shoulder and which end of the puttees to go on top . . . If you decide on boots buy spurs without rowels . . . It will be easier to put in the clutch and to shift gears . . . Also, the clerk for a small fee will show you how to salute . . . Otherwise you might go out and meet a cadet who has only been in West Point three years and you, as a superior officer, must return his salute . . . At this point you are a full-fledged American Officer in the Great War of Washington, and ready to go into operation. . . .

Your first act will be to call some humble, unpatriotic friend who you knew before you entered this awful conflict who is toiling trying to make enough to pay his taxes and meet his payments on his Liberty Bonds and ask him to dinner . . . You must go to the best place as you may be humiliated by being next to a lot of non-com officers . . . After dinner take your friend to the *Follies* who happen to be in town. . . . Now its perfectly proper for a Washington army officer to admit ignorance of the war but it's gross negligence to admit he is not acquainted with at least five of the girls . . . When the usher comes back and says there is no answer, bawl him out before your friend and tell him you guess he gave it to the wrong girl and was he sure he told her it was Captain Jasbo? . . .

On the first day the hardest task is to find a place to park the car . . . But the most important consideration is to make certain of the assignment. . . . The saddest case that has happened in this war was a fellow dident notice how his appointment read and he found he had been put with a regiment that was to go to the European War where real bullets were shot. . . . The rest of the day would be spent in meeting the secretaries . . . After that it was time to go to the hotel to dress for dinner in the uniform the tailor had made . . . Make for a café and sit in a prominent place to watch the new officers who had just been commissioned that day. . . .

That night the military training started . . . It consisted of twelve lessons to learn how to dance with a girl without catching your spurs in her dress . . . It was a good idea also to carry a French book in your pocket. . . . You know you are not going to use it but it lends a certain amount of atmosphere. . . .

By now you are facing a crisis . . . The next day you will have been in long enough to commence figuring on a promotion and nearly long enough to get the papers from home . . . That's one of the most anxious moments of your entire military career, wondering how the picture will turn out and if it's on the front page. . . .

Now you are ready to face the dangers. . . . Why, the casualty list in one day out of a million and a half officers in Washington was ten wounded getting in and out of taxicabs . . . two choked through their collars being too tight . . . 61 hurt through typewriters choking up . . . 500 prostrated when they heard the war was over and they would have to go back to work. . . . The hardest part of it will be trying to look like an officer, and how to act in the presence of someone who has been across . . . Most of them will have their hardest jobs trying to make their uniforms look worn somewhere else besides the trouser seat. . . .

In the fall of 1917, with the coming of the Russian Revolution, Will did his first newspaper writing. "I can write about Russia for I know that my readers don't know any more about it than I do," he commented. "There is always this to look forward to with Russia. *Pick up the morning paper and look for Russian news and have a fear of reading the worst. You won't be disappointed.* I will give the Russians credit for one thing: They dident sign a peace treaty with Germany. They said: 'What's the use of signing something? We just quit.' You see, Germany was willing to treat for peace as long as Russia did all the treating. Now they have given 'German freedom' to some province called Ukrainia which sounds like ukulele. I doubt if it lasts as long as that short-lived instrument. The ukulele had this advantage: not even a trained musician could tell if you were playing on it or just monkeying with it, but the Ukrainia liberty don't fool anybody. Those poor independents have 'Made in Germany' stamped all over them. You see the Kaiser has the dope on it this way: It is better to be surrounded by a lot of small nations than by a couple of regular ones. They come in handier to go through. If Russia's land holds out long enough, Germany should be able to make a very generous peace with her eastern foes. Russia was handicapped by not having a national anthem to fight by . . . If we had only known it, we could have loaned them 'Poor Butterfly,' but only on one condition, they keep it."

Although Will had a wife and three children, which exempted him from the draft, he seriously considered going into the armed services. He had opposed our entry into the war, but once in, the only thing to do was to fight it to a successful conclusion as soon as possible. Certainly, his friends and his draft board were right when they persuaded him that he could do more good for the cause by helping to keep up the morale of the country through his humor than he could have done as a fighting man. He and Betty put every cent they could spare into Liberty Bonds and Will gave freely of his time in raising money for the Red Cross. William Fox was general chairman for the drive among theatrical people, and Winfield Sheehan, later Will's boss at Fox Studios, was his captain. When the drive first opened Will wrote this letter:

May 21, 1917

Dear Mr. Fox:

I have tried hard during the last week to figure out what I personally consider my duty in the amount that I should contribute to the Red Cross fund. While not a wealthy man, I earn a very good salary. I am pleased and grateful, therefore, for the opportunity to contribute ten (10) per cent of my next year's income to the Red Cross, and put me down on the books for $5,200.

I wish I had greater wealth so that I could give a larger amount, and were it not for the fact I owe an obligation to three little children at home, I certainly would have been over there myself.

Yours truly,
Will Rogers

P.S. I pray to God this terrible war will be over in less than a year, but if not I hereby pledge myself to continue my subscription of $100 a week for the duration of the war.

In addition to contributing 10 per cent of his income, Will also more than "time-tithed" by working many benefits. His speeches, bringing laughs one moment and tears the next, kicked off the weekly meetings for the theatrical groups. The $2 million raised on Broadway, however, represented only a part of his efforts, as he appeared before any group that asked him to and when his schedule permitted.

In the fall of 1917 the entire Rogers family played a benefit at the Polo Grounds to raise money for the soldiers' "Tobacco Fund." "New Yorkers will remember the amazement the little tykes created when they came galloping out," a reporter wrote, "yipping and sticking to the leather like regular cow men. Their pa wasn't any prouder of them that day than he is every day, because whenever he thinks of, talks to, or sees, those kids, he just naturally throws his pride into high and breaks all speed laws on the statute book." Will himself wrote the captions for a picture spread of the show: "Youngest cowboy in the world, age two, and he can ride. If you want to start a Civil War, just try to take him off that pony. He eats there . . . All mounted on their own ponies . . . The youngest cow terrors in the world . . . Bill, six, and Mary, four. . . . Here we come, all in a dead run, and nobody holding on. They won't ride unless they can ride in a run. I'm riding the only opposition in a Ford... The Home Defense League on parade. The tough little bird on the end is not holding his gun right, but none of us had the nerve to tell him so. That's Roosevelt Rogers..."

The war ended in an uneasy armistice on November 11, 1918. The great cry was to get the boys back home and out of the army. "The most popular joke I had after the war in New York, and the Boys were coming back and parading every day was, 'If we really wanted to honor our Boys, why don't we let them sit on the reviewing stands and make the people march those 15 miles?' They don't want to parade, they want to go home and rest. But they wont discharge a Soldier as long as they can find a new Street in a Town that he hasent marched down yet. If the money spent on stands and Parades, and the high prices people paid for the seats, had been divided up amongst the soldiers they would have had enough to live comfortably on until the next war." He warned a cheering *Follies* audience that "this is only a rehearsal... Wait till the real thing comes." He had in mind the coming Peace Conference which would have a lot to do if the world was to be "made safe for democracy."

Will was going to describe what happened there as he saw it. Nothing could illustrate this better than what he told Albert D. Lasker, advertising executive and assistant to Will Hays, chairman of the Republican National Committee. Lasker interviewed Will at the request of Colonel Theodore Roosevelt. "The man has such a keen insight into the American panorama and the American people that I feel, in the course of time, he is bound to be a great factor in the political life of the nation," the Colonel had told Lasker. "I want you to meet him, because his good will can prove a great asset to the party."

Will listened to what Lasker had to say. "I'll be glad to talk to you at any time," Will said, "but I want you to know that I must hold myself as an unbiased commentator on public affairs."

The war had been the "great folly" and it was followed by the Peace Conference which "seemed to offer a better field for Humor provided you stick to the *Facts*."

10

"The Peace Feast Follies"

THE PEACE CONFERENCE AT PARIS FOLLOWING WORLD War I produced Will's first book. It was a compilation of what he had used in his *Follies* routines and in his day-by-day comments on what was taking place there, and was called *The Cowboy Philosopher on the Peace Conference.*[1] Will stated on the dust jacket: "I made this book short so you could finish it before the next war" and warned that "you can't tell peace from war without this book." In a dedicatory statement he said that "in the five times I have appeared before President Wilson I have used dozens of these same jokes about him, and he has the best sense of humor and is the best audience I ever played to. Which bear out the theory I work on, That you can always joke about a big Man that is really big, but don't ever kid about the little fellow who thinks he is something, cause he will get sore."

Will's first satire was on the "facts" on which he was to base his statements. They were "procured from the most reliable source. Here's how I got it. There is a fellow I know, Who has a friend, And this friends Sister had a sweetheart and he was a Soldier in France and his cousins pal was a Bunkie of Col Houses Chouffer, The Col told his Chouffer. So you see my information comes from the same place Pres Wilsons does." Not much different from the "lowdowns" passed on as coming from "unimpeachable sources!"

The "Peace Feast" came "when the Armistace was signed and Germany agreed to quit running at eleven o'clock on a certain day."

[1] New York: Harper & Brothers, 1919.

The United States was "bunked" in even this as it "got word a couple of days early making everybody have TWO DRUNKS where one would have done just as well. . . . It was delayed because the German Generals whom they sent out to sign it, had never been to the front and dident know just where it was." Everybody at the time was wondering what to do with the Kaiser. Not Will. "He should have been made to clean the streets after that first Armistace day."

Will noted that the signing of the Armistice almost coincided with our election day so that "the Germans and the Democrats learned their fate" at the same time. Actually, this had a profound bearing on the fate of the world.

In the off-year elections of 1918, President Wilson appealed to the country to return Democratic majorities in both houses of Congress, especially in the Senate, so as not to block his efforts to achieve a just and lasting peace that could be kept through the instrumentality of an international organization. Under the hammerings of the Republicans led by Colonel Theodore Roosevelt and Henry Cabot Lodge, aided by isolationists in both parties such as Senators Jim Reed and William Borah, joined by the tariff-Republicans interested chiefly in profits and the garden-variety politicians who wanted jobs, the country rejected Wilson's plea. Despite this agonizing setback, President Wilson went ahead with his plans. Regardless of politics, he could not envision anyone so craven as to risk the fate of the world for such selfish reasons. He had outlined his program to Congress the past February in his Fourteen Points that later became the Covenant of the League of Nations. He had unquestionably brought the war to a quicker conclusion by appealing over the heads of the leaders of the Central Powers to the people, and he hoped he could do the same thing in this country. In doing so he grossly misjudged both the temper of the people of the United States and the actual war aims of the Allied countries. Before the Armistice was signed, Theodore Roosevelt sent identical telegrams to Senators Henry Cabot Lodge, Miles Poindexter, and Hiram Johnson that the peace must be "dictated by the hammering of guns and not the clicking of typewriters" and that unconditional surrender of the Germans and not an Armistice must be the American policy. Then after the Armistice had been signed Roosevelt warned both our allies and our enemies that "Mr. Wilson has no authority to speak for the American people at this time."

As the constitutional elected chief magistrate of the country, with two years to serve, if President Wilson did not speak for the country on such an important consideration, who did? Certainly, it may be argued that Wilson erred deeply in not taking a prominent Republican with him on his peace mission, but who can doubt that if he had taken a man like Lodge or Roosevelt the arguments that defeated the League in this country later would have been used at the Peace Conference itself and resulted in even greater injustices?

No one in this country saw clearer than Will Rogers the troubles that were boiling up and the need to approach them with a sense of humor. He called President Wilson's journey "the Number 2 Peace trip," the first of course having been Ford's effort, and complimented Wilson on using "better judgment than the first one as it waited until the war was over."

Before the conference opened Wilson made a tour of England, France and Italy, lining up support of the people so that if he had to he could go over the heads of their rulers to get his League of Nations into operation. Will made some pertinent comments. "Can you imagine how sore these Republicans got when they read about a Democrat sleeping in Buckingham Palace? . . . In Paris, President Wilson got an earful from Col House . . . The Pres had a letter of recommendation from Caruso so he met some of the best people in Italy . . . The King of Italy and also the King of England have agreed with him up to now . . . But neither one will be at the Peace signing . . . England is orally in accord but there has been nothing signed. . . . See the Peace Feast is about to begin . . . Hope the Turkish delegation dont bring all their WIVES or we never will get Peace . . . All will go well for the first week or so when they're just complimenting each other . . . But watch out when it comes time to divide something! . . ."

The conference met in an atmosphere of fear, hatred and greed—fear of bolshevism, hatred for the enemy, and grasping hands reaching for colonies and money reparations. Only by refusal to give in was President Wilson able to get his Fourteen Points into the preliminary treaty. "There is to be no more wars. . ." Will remarked about this ". . . then there is a paragraph a little further down told you where to get your Ammunition in case there is one."

President Wilson had barely overcome the opposition he had to meet in Paris when he realized that to save the League he had to do the same thing in the United States. "Pres grabbed his old commuting boat, the *George Washington,* and come back to explain The League of Nations to Congress . . . You know those guys cant read anything and understand it. . . . After eating out of 15 million dollar Gold Plates and hobnobbing with Kings and Dukes can you imagine how Congress looked to the Pres when he come back . . . ?"

The President was making some headway with Congress, unfortunately a "lame duck" one, when warning rumblings reached him from Paris. Wilson rushed back there. "America dident know till they got over there that those European Nations had a disease for years called Gimmes . . . England and Japan had a secret Treaty where England was to get everything south of the equator and Japan everything north of it. . . . Everybody at the Table wants a second helping . . . And Germany, the cook, hasent got enough to go around . . . They agreed on one of the Fourteen Points . . . That was that America went in for *nothing* and expects *nothing*. . . . They are all UNANIMOUS . . . WE GET IT . . . *The best time to have formed the League was during the war when all these Nations needed each other*. . . . All those Nations claim they were fighting for freedom . . . But a little more land would make a little more FREEDOM. . . . I wonder if we quit fighting too quick and dident sign peace quick enough? . . . *But then it has been just this hard at the end of every war to try and prevent another one*. . . . Japan's claims are sorter novel . . . They want pay for capturing part of China, one of our Allies. . . . If Japan gets all of her Claims, China will pay more indemnities than Germany who lost the war . . . you know China has one of the best Japanese Armies in the World."

President Wilson was able to get the League of Nations back into the treaty, but he could not keep out many inequities. He accepted them because he thought an active and strong League might iron them out in the future. On the other hand, his concept of self-determination for small nations in the creation of Czechoslovakia, Finland, Poland and Yugoslavia, brought with it almost as many inequities as were cured. Geographers may outline theoretical boundaries but this does not correct the wrongs suffered by racial minorities. Furthermore, the treaty fixed the total war guilt on Germany, thereby whitewashing "some gray if not black" conduct of other nations. Germany's colonies were taken from her, slices of her territory lopped off, and huge indemnities imposed. "I thought the Armistice terms read like a Second Mortgage," Will commented, "but this reads like a foreclosure."

"If he puts this thing through and there is no more wars," Will said about Wilson, "His address will be WHITE HOUSE WASHINGTON D C till his whiskers are as long as the Peace Treaty. If it should be a Fliv (which it wont), why, then a letter would reach him at ALABI NEW JERSEY. So all Credit to Pres Wilson. It took a Game GUY to go through with it."

As hundreds of billions of dollars in debts and hundreds of millions of dead eloquently point out, President Wilson failed to make the League of Nations a saving force in the world. He could have forced acceptance of it in this country if he had yielded on Article X, which gave to the organization authority and means to enforce its decisions. In his opinion, without this authority it would have been "little more than an influential debating society.[2] In order to capture the White House in 1920, the Republican party made the League the chief issue of the presidential campaign, and in doing so capitalized strongly on the isolationist feeling prevalent in the country at the time.

In September, 1934, Will was sitting in his room in the Athenee Palace Hotel, Bucharest, worrying about another World War that he saw in the making in this "powder keg of the world," as the Balkans were called. In the ensuing years he had been over most of the world several times and spent countless hours studying politics. This was his judgment on what had taken place since the Treaty of Versailles:

I am a great believer in letting every country run itself. Heretofore, we been a terrible old busybody, jumping around over the world advising folks. Trying to make Babtists and Methodists out of Chinamen that have got the most perfect and satisfying religion in the world,

[2] In the late summer of 1919 President Wilson made a swing around the country appealing for the League. In September, he dramatically warned the country that, unless the League was made operational, in twenty years the world would have another general war that would make the first one seem like child's play. He missed the coming of World War II by less than two weeks!

and have had it when we was hanging by the tails throwing cocanuts at each other. We have fought wars to keep Spain from taking all the sugar out of the Philippines. We made Cuba so free that our own Ambassador cant stay there without being shot at. We made the world "safe for democracy," then everybody went "dictator" on us. We fought a war to stop wars, then sold enough ammunition to start a dozen wars. We fought to make self-determination of small nations at the end of the war. We give every people that had ten signers a country. It will take forty wars to get back the original countries that were taken away from each other after the last war. Every nation was supposed to go into the last war to fight for its liberty and its homeland. But at the Versailles Conference they were dividing up islands and captured countries like a remnant sale. Austria come out with nothing but 200 yards of the Danube River and a half dozen Strauss waltzes. Hungary went in hungry and come out starved to death. Italy was signed up with one side, saw they had picked the wrong horse, run and made a bet on the other side. Went in to make the world safe for Romans and come out with Trieste and Fiume, and an everlasting hatred of Jugo-Slavia.

Japan had no more business in it than an Esquimo has in an Upton Sinclair election. But they went in and come out with all Germany's possessions in the Far East. Not only dident lose money and men, dident lose any time. All the expense they had was sending the Allies a cablegram saying, "We are in too."

So you can see we are really maby not much worse than the rest of 'em. But somebody should take our entry blanks away from us so we cant enter into any of them. Wars would be great things if they would make 'em closed corporations. Nobody allowed to enter but those directly interested.

11

The "Folliest" of All: Prohibition

THE UNITED STATES DISREGARDED PRESIDENT WILSON'S advice on another question too—Prohibition. Most laws had in them an "element" of a "joke" to Will, but the effort to legislate as to what a person drank or did not drink was the most absurd "joke" of all. His comments made to "the follies out front" from the rostrum of the *Follies* were brought together in his second book, *The Cowboy Philosopher on Prohibition,* published in August, 1919.[1] He warned on the cover that "you won't find the country any drier than this book," and in a foreword admitted "the more I can keep my readers away from the title" and on the other side (about 95 proof) "the more chance I got getting away with it." He also had to admit, regretfully, that it was "not subsidized by any Liquor Concern." His thanks went to "Professor Lowell of Harvard for the English translation" and to "the Writers of the Old and New Testaments for furnishing facts for some of my strongest arguments against Prohibition." He looked forward with dread to the future because he liked to play to "an audience who have had a few nips, just enough so they can see the joke and still sober enough to applaud it." He also predicted empty galleries for the Congress that had voted for it, for no one could listen to a representative or a senator "without a certain amount of liquor in him."

The thing that disturbed Will the most was the way Prohibition

[1] New York: Harper & Brothers, 1919.

came into being. It had been fobbed off on the American people by crusaders, backed chiefly by business interests who thought that a man worked better when sober, at a time when millions of men were in the army, many overseas and unable to vote. The Volstead Act, passed before the 18th Amendment to the Constitution had been ratified, paraded itself as a war measure. Will took sharp issue with this. "Now France fought quite a bit in the war and trained on Wine . . . England did her part on Scotch and Polly and Ale . . . Canadian Club furnished its Quota in Canada . . . Italy Chiantied over the Alps into Austria . . . Women's clothes and Scotch Whiskey didn't keep the Highlanders back much . . . Guinness's Stout kept the Irish fighting as usual . . . The American Troops didn't retreat any further than you can run your hand in a Paper Bag, and they had been used to Old Crow and Kentucky Bourbon . . . Russia was doing fine till some nut took their Vodka from them and they went back to find it. . . . Germany, the Country with the smallest percentage of Alcahol in their National drink (which is beer), and Turkey who are totally prohibition, why, they lose the war . . . Looks to me like if Germany and Turkey ever wanted to win a war they better start drinking a MANS SIZE DRINK . . . Prohibitionists ought to be arrested for treason since treason means anything that gives annoyance to your own people, thereby giving aid to the enemy . . . Outside of profiteers, I can't think of anything that has given more annoyance . . ."

Actually, parading Prohibition as a "protection" of our fighting men, an effort to keep them as pure and innocent as William J. Bryan himself, was a smoke screen. The real reason the measure was pushed through came from a fear by the vested interests of what might happen when millions of men were released from the armed services without jobs. A little alcohol in desperate men's stomachs, especially those who had learned to kill on the battlefield, might give "bottled" courage. Dark whispers of bolshevism stirred uneasy consciences. There are always those who can see the pimple but have little idea or interest in what caused it. They love nothing better than to monitor other people's thinking and acting. "A Prohibitionist is a man or woman, who is so self satisfied that he presents himself with a Medal, called the 'CROIX DE PERFECT HE' . . . He gives himself this Medal because he is going to start to *meddle* in everybody's business but his own . . .

The first six ice-cream sodas served to six pinockle players mean six more Bolsheviks..."

Will predicted some dire results from Prohibition. For one thing, "getting bit by a snake" would become a lost art because "no man is going to let a snake bite him after liquor goes out." Also the woman who used to faint and be revived by a nip of brandy would have to "struggle along without fainting." But the saddest of all "will be the loss of the Kentucky Colonal industry. They received their title through owning the widest brimmed black hat and having the largest Bourbon capacity of any man in the country, Sah:

> When they go to dig up his Mint bed, He will say, 'just dig it a little deeper and I will get in myself, we are both non-essential.' "

Will's arguments, thanks to the writers of the Old and New Testaments, were based on solid facts which the Prohibitionist had overlooked, in much the same way as Christians "resemble" Christ. "Of course the only way we have to prove anything is by the Bible... I find in Genesis 9th Chapter 20 verse, 'Noah began to be an Husbandman and planted a vineyard.'... The minute he got to be a husband he started in right away to raise the necessary ingredients to make what goes into family life... Why don't they pick on Marrying, that's in the same verse, why single out the poor old vineyard?... Next verse, 'And he drank of the wine and was drunken and was within his tent.'... Now Noah was a chosen man... If the Lord dident punish him, where do the prohibitionists come in to tell somebody what to do?... Now Noah knew more about water than all of them put together... He was the Water Commissioner of his time... He was the first man to discover a use for it, that was to float a boat on... But as a beverage he knew it was a total failure... Now everything happens for the best.... Through Noah partaking of too much wine and going on this little spree is why the Lord picked him to gather those Animals into the Ark... If Noah had not drank we would today be without menageries . . . Other men of later generations have claimed to have seen animals that Noah dident take on the Ark . . . Perhaps their Vineyards were of a different variety . . . Noah was told to collect two of every variety of animals and take them on board . . . I defy any man to show me where he took a prohibitionist and his mate aboard . . . In the next verse we find 'Ham saw his father and told his brethern' . . . There was the foundation of the first prohibitionist, butting in where he had no business . . . *He made such a bad job out of it, that's why all bad actors are called hams.* . . . This wine had such ill effects on Noah's health that it was all he could do to live 950 years. . . . Just 19 years short of Methusalah who held the long distance age record of his and all times . . . Now in the 14th chapter when Abram was returning from victorious battle it says Melzhizedek king of Salem met them with bread and wine . . . What did we meet our victorious troops with? . . . Huylers Chocolate and Spearmint gum."

Nor did Will rely on the Bible alone for his arguments. There was Omar Khayám, "the pickled philosopher of Persia . . . In that verse about 'a loaf of bread, a jug of Wine and Thou,' look how they have jagged those three things on him . . . Bread—they voted wheat so high nobody can eat bread . . . Wine will soon be gone and the wine they have got, if it had ever been handed to Omar, I would hate to have read his book . . . Thou—I guess he meant a woman . . . Well, she has the vote and she ain't the same Thou any more . . ." There were other authorities. "Caesar carried a canteen of Chianti that would make an Italian Restaurant proprietor envious . . . History says that Nero fiddled while Rome burned . . . Now any man has got to drink to fiddle, and whoever listens to him fiddle has to drink more. . . . The Romans were the first people to discover after Noah any other reason for water . . . They put it in those beautiful Roman Baths . . . then built marble slabs to lay on and watch it . . . You never saw a picture of a Roman in the water in your life."

Politics, of course, would be affected. There was the case of women. "They could once drink but not vote . . . now they could vote but not drink . . . It will take them just as long to make up their minds who to vote for as it did to tell what to drink . . . Most of them will vote for some guy named Martiny just through force of habit . . . But if these women think they are going to get as much of a thrill around a voting booth as they did around the old punch bowl, they are going to be fooled . . . Who wants to vote if there's no place to stop on the way home? . . . Besides one has to be about half drunk to vote for most of the candidates they run nowadays . . . For a while it will feel kinder embarrassing to sell your vote while sober . . . On the other hand, the voter should ask more for his vote, as he will not be able to sell them as often as he used to . . . In the old days, if you could keep the politician drinking with you, you could sometimes sell several times to him alone . . . And it would make a difference in the counting . . . *More men have lost office through bad counting than through bad political policies* . . . A man with nothing on his hip but a patch ain't liable to mistake one hundred for one thousand . . . And if he is sober, he ain't near as liable to be asked to make said mistake . . . *A quart of Old Crow in the counting-room at night has put more men in office than voters ever did.*"

Instead of stopping divorce, as the Prohibitionists claimed, Will predicted that Prohibition would affect marriage. "They lay all the divorces on to liquor when it's only bad judgment in picking 'em . . . Some men have to drink to live with a woman, some women have to drink to live with a man, most generally though they both have to drink to live with each other . . .The drys, as usual, have it just wrong . . . It won't stop divorce, it will stop marriages . . . A couple sitting opposite at a table don't look near so good to each other over a water decanter as they do over two just emptied Champagne bottles."

Actually, Will admitted, "it don't make any difference to me which side I am on. I get paid for getting laughs and I found out that the majority of the people would laugh more if I kidded the drys. But lots of people *laugh one way* and *vote another*. Look at Congress, it *voted dry* and *drinks wet.*"

12

"The House that Jokes Built"

IN THE SUMMER OF 1918, WHILE STILL LIVING ON LONG Island, a new career opened for Will that was vitally to affect his and his family's way of life. Sam Goldwyn was making a motion picture out of Rex Beach's *Laughing Bill Hyde,* and Rex insisted that Will play the part of the hero, an easygoing tramp. Will agreed, after much argument, provided he did not have to give up his work in the *Follies* and the *Midnight Frolic.*[1] On completion of the picture, Goldwyn offered Will a contract for two years at twice his salary from Ziegfeld for the first year, and three times as much for the second year.

"You're waving that paper at the wrong boy, Mr. Goldwyn," Will said, shaking his head. "Why, if I was to take up your proposition, you'd be the maddest man in the world before you got through with me. I'm no actor."

Goldwyn got up and motioned for Will to follow him into his projection room where *Laughing Bill Hyde* was run off.

"Now, what do you say, Mr. Rogers?" Goldwyn asked. "Are you an actor?"

"Yep, you're right," Will replied. "I'm an actor all right. The worst in the world. Leave the acting business to them that can act. All I know how to do is to throw a lariat and crack jokes."

"Think it over," Goldwyn told him, "and we'll talk it over later."

It was something to be thought over and given serious considera-

[1] See *Autobiography,* for Will's description of his early motion-picture experiences.

tion. Life on Long Island had been good for the family, but it lacked permanence. Will seemed well entrenched in the *Follies* and on the Roof but no one knew better than he the uncertainty of theater business. A star today and a tramp tomorrow described it all too accurately. Then there was always the chance that something might happen to Ziegfeld himself. On the other hand, the motion picture business was fraught with the same uncertainties. Furthermore, if he accepted Goldwyn's offer it would mean moving to Hollywood where most of the production was concentrating.

A letter that Will wrote to Oklahoma on learning that a niece was to marry gives interesting information on the family as the argument waxed hot on whether to move to California or not. It informed:

William (that's the oldest boy) is a bit like your Herbert (who seems to like the Horses and Poetry better than Women), well, William seems more of a mechanical nature than affectionate. He is continually working on some scheme to make a Toy Train run. His task seems hopeless with the opposition he encounters from the nearest of kin.

Now there's Mary, that's our only Female of the specie, kinder takes after your Helen. She can't seem to keep her mind on any particular fellow any longer than the Candy lasts. We fear she is a bit frivolous, all of which I lay to breeding on the Arkansaw side. She is very patriotic, however, and is now keeping company with a Boy Scout. I haven't met the family yet, although they have lived next door for years, and must be people in moderate circumstances. They have had no new car this year.

Now James Rogers, named rightly after the James Boys, is a regular Lounge Lizard. He is to the Ladies of our town what your Pauline is to the younger Male Set of Rogers County. He has kicked up more disturbances and circulated more inside Propaganda concerning the inner working of people both in and out of his set than Count Von Bernsteins. And as for family affairs, he has the key to the Skeleton Closet.

I personally am hoping he don't marry till after he gets out of Jail. Now Freddy, our youngest, he only made his Debut into Society last Summer. He is such a ladies man that he never goes out alone and really receives more attention from the opposite sex than any of the older ones. But my Wife and I feel that they are all young yet and that a Son or Daughter-in-law would be rather an incumbrance on us as we are not permanently fixed for them as you all are there.

Well, will close by offering our best wishes to both parties. And congratulate them on the fact that they both have the worst of their first year's troubles over, as they have already seen Niagara Falls, Grant's Tomb, Statue of Liberty, Bush's Sunken Garden and the Cliff House.

Will added that he had left "a standing order with Marshall Fields for several sets of Haviland China and a gross of Baby Buggies and you all just wire them direct which to send."

The more Will and Betty talked over the offer from Goldwyn the more it appealed to them. True, Betty, who had brought her sister, Miss Theda Blake, from Arkansas to live with them, had accompanied Will on most of his *Follies* tours out of New York. They had even taken their horses along. But California had a particular lure for them. They were an outdoor family and life there could be more relaxed and informal. Furthermore, the children were delighted with the proposed move. In the end the decision was to accept Goldwyn's offer.

The chief opponent to the move had been Ziegfeld, who had long since realized Will's value to him.

"Watch out for those movie cuties," he advised.

"Shucks!" Will retorted, "if your gals couldn't break me down in all these years, what chance has those in Hollywood got?"

Loath to give up his forum for expressing his viewpoint, before leaving for California Will contracted to do a series of shorts to be flashed on the screen as "The Illiterate Digest," a humorous take-off on "The Literary Digest Topics of the Day."

In the spring of 1919 Will journeyed to California ahead of the family to arrange for living quarters. This was not a simple matter, as in addition to a house suitable for the family, there were half a dozen horses to be properly stabled. For days Will scoured Hollywood unsuccessfully for the right combination. The problem was settled temporarily when Goldwyn permitted Will to keep the horses at the studio stables where there was a fenced-in space in which the children could take their daily rides in safety. A roomy house for the family was rented on Van Ness Avenue, the family moved in, and Will went to work at the studio.

It was here that tragedy struck. While Will was on location away from Hollywood, the three boys, Bill, Jimmy and Freddie became sick. The ailment was first diagnosed as tonsillitis instead of diphtheria, which it was. Although Will drove all night with antitoxin, which could not be had in Hollywood, he was too late to save Freddie. After this tragic loss, it was somewhat a relief to move into a house Will had bought in Beverly Hills ("the House that Jokes built"), a newly developed residential district west of Hollywood. It was to be their home until they moved to the ranch house (now a part of the Will Rogers State Park) in Santa Monica in the early 1930's. Now they could have their horses close at hand as Will had added a stable and barns, a tanbark riding ring, and a swimming pool.

Will had some troubles with architects and landscape artists. One architect committed the unpardonable sin of trying to tell him how to build a barn. After telling him to run along and play with his "Looey Quince" and "velvet saddle blankets," he ended the talk by saying, "I sure got ideas of my own on how these barns are going to be built." When the landscape artist announced that he was going to pretty up the yard so it would be the pride of the neighborhood, Will dispelled all such ideas by announcing that he was going to build a seven-foot brick wall around it so "the boys could come up Sunday mornings and have a little fun roping goats and bull-dogging steers." He made the poor, befuddled man have some "groupings and spacings" of shrubbery dug up and real trees planted . . . cottonwoods and eucalyptus—trees he was "acquainted with personally." In a few months he proudly announced "you could conduct a real nice hanging in my front yard now."

The crowning insult to him was a "little fountain in the middle, one of them statues that *expectorates* continuously." He admitted to having been in the *Follies* and protested against being an Anthony Comstock, "but I felt right sorry for that little thing out there without even a bandana, playing September Morn in December." It had cost $350 to put in the fountain and Will paid $500 to have it taken out. "I didn't begrudge the money a bit. I wouldent a dared to ask my old friends to come to the house with that thing in the yard."

Betty told about that seven-foot brick wall. There was a city ordinance against such a construction, but Will got around it some way.

Then, a bit conscience-stricken that it was unsightly, he ordered a landscape artist to plant ivy around it. When he came home from the studio and saw the small slips that had been set out he blew up.

"When I want ivy," he stormed, "I want ivy I can see."

"But this will soon grow to where you can see it," the man protested.

"Get me some I can see now."

At a fantastic cost the entire wall was covered with ivy plants.

Life became very pleasant for the Rogers family in their new home. Will enjoyed his work at the studio, as it left him time to spend with his family and friends. A good description was given of Will on the set by a fellow actor and polo player, Guinn ("Big Boy") Williams: "Bill was slouched easily in the saddle of a little black nag, paying no attention to those around him. He was twirling a rope and tossing it at a nearby fence post. My idea of a leading man at that time was a cross between an Arrow Collar ad and an Olympic Swimming champion. My heroes had to have firm chins, pearly teeth and barrel chests. I took one look at Rogers. I decided that if that guy could be a star, I would be one myself inside of six months . . . Six months later I knew I was all wrong. By that time, Will Rogers to me was the handsomest and finest fellow—inside and out—that I had ever known." Part of this worship came because Will gave Big Boy, who had run away from home, enough money to go see his mother.

One of Will's favorite silent movies was *Jubilo,* made from a short story by Ben Ames Williams published in the *Saturday Evening Post.* The script writer (one of Goldwyn's "eminent authors" he had brought to Hollywood) changed the story so drastically that Will refused to do it. "We shot the scenes from the various paragraphs in the Story in the *Post,*" Will said. "When we took a Scene we just marked it off and went on to the next. It was the only story ever made that was filmed as it was written."

As if changing the story had not been enough, Goldwyn decided to change the title. Will wired him on October 17, 1919:

Thought I was supposed to be a comedian but when you suggest changing the title of "Jubilo" you are funnier than I ever was. I don't see how Lorimer of the *Post* ever let it be published under that title. That song ("In the Land of Jubilo") is better known through the South by older people than Geraldine Farrar's husband. We have used it all through the business in the picture but of course we can change it to "Everybody Shimmie Now." Suppose if you had produced "The Miracle Man" you would have called it "A Queer Old Guy." But if you really want a title for this picture I would suggest "Jubilo." Also the following: "A Poor But Honest Tramp"; "He Lies But He Don't Mean it"; "A Farmer's Virtious Daughter"; "The Great Train Robbery Mystery"; "A Spotted Horse but He is Only Painted"; "A Hungry Tramp's Revenge"; "The Vagabond with a Heart as Big as His Appetite"; "He Loses in the First Reel but Wins in the Last"; "The Old Man Left but the Tramp Protected Her." What would you have called "The Birth of a Nation?"

Will Rogers

P.S. They will film the Lord's Supper and when it is made, figure out that it is not a good release Title and not catchy enough, so it will be released under the heading, "A Red Hot Meal," or "The Gastronomical Orgy."

In the movie, *Jes' Call Me Jim,* little Jimmy Rogers, aged four, had a part. Betty was asked if she would go on location with them to look after him.

"Of course," she replied, "his father would take care of him, no doubt, but in reality I have three boys to look after—my sons and Billy."

Now that he was a motion picture star, Will was asked in an interview for his viewpoint on clothes. "Clothes don't bother me much," he confessed. "I just wear what is most convenient to get around in. Generally speaking, an old pair of pants and a flannel shirt and cap suit me from the ground up. As for women—a pretty, sensible woman looks just as good to me in a gingham or calico dress as she does in a hundred dollar evening gown, all mixed up with flum doodles and what nots."

"Do you agree, Mrs. Rogers?"

Betty nodded emphatically.

"What don't you like about the picture business, Mr. Rogers?"

"Close-ups," Will growled. "I just naturally hate 'em. I ain't never going to get used to standing quiverin' all over with a camera three inches from my nose. Don't you think it distracting, when you see a picture, for the camera to suddenly switch from a whole scene to the hero's beaded eyelashes magnified so that they look like Zeppelins?"

The easier, relaxed life in California had not blunted Will's interest in politics. Many of his political comments, as well as some on other subjects, were flashed on the screen in "Illiterate Digest," but somehow they lost the "pricking" pertinency of the personal deliverance. In the summer of 1920, as in 1916, work kept Will from attending the presidential nominating conventions. This time, though, he decided to give them "the absence treatment" by reporting them through a newspaper syndicate. "You don't have to hear somebody say a thing to know it," he said. "Why, I'll bet the typewriter—the machine, not the blond that runs it—which has lived through a convention or two just automatically runs off all the speeches including the 'applause' and 'wild cheering' for twenty minutes."

The Republicans met amid an atmosphere of hope and optimism, buoyed up by the Congressional successes of 1918 and with opposition to the League of Nations as the chief issue. "A professional 'Pray-er' was called in to get the Convention going as none of the politicians present knew how," Will reported. "Of course Bill Hays told him what to pray for. A number of leading Republicans were opposed to the prayer as they don't think it is necessary this year but they kept it in for variety sake." The keynote speaker was Henry Cabot Lodge, who devoted most of his efforts to damning Wilson.

The convention was deadlocked for some time and ended up by nominating a dark horse, Senator Warren G. Harding of Ohio, and as his running mate Governor Calvin Coolidge of Massachusetts, who had moved into the national spotlight by his settlement of a police strike. "Only two detrimental things have come out since the nomination in Harding's whole record," Will wrote. "One was his middle name, Gamaliel, and the other he used to play a slide trombone in a country band. Musical circles in Washington are now looking towards a big revival."

Although the cause of the Democrats seemed hopeless, as usual they put on a livelier show. Will reported this convention as a simulated conversation between himself and President Wilson at the White House, and commented on the noise.

"Yes, Will," Wilson says, "there is more noise. But it don't mean anything. A noisy vote don't count any more than a quiet one."

"It's too bad you can't handle the Senate on the League of Nations thing like you do those fellows at the Convention," Will said.

"I could," Wilson said, "if it hadn't been for a lot of Republicans buying in there."

"But you Democrats during the war must have made Government jobs look so good that the Republicans figured they could make money out of them even after paying big prices for them," Will said. "I would just like to have what one Republican would have made out of those jobs McAdoo had."

The Democratic Convention ended a deadlock by nominating Governor James Cox of Ohio, with Assistant Secretary of the Navy Franklin D. Roosevelt to run with him.[2]

The campaign of the Republicans crystallized around Harding's slogan of a "return to normalcy"—which untangled meant a return to *laissez faire* in economics: for the government to keep hands off in industry unless a labor union "got out of hand"; government subsidies to favored industries; and isolationism in international affairs maintained chiefly through high tariffs that kept foreign competition out. This meant, of course, that the League of Nations must not be a part of American policy. This program received a landslide endorsement at the polls.

Early in November, 1920, Will received a letter from an attorney representing the magazine *Literary Digest*, complaining that the prestige of "The Literary Digest Topics of the Day" was being lowered by his "Illiterate Digest," and to stop it. He replied:

Los Angeles, Cal.,
Nov. 15, 1920

Mr. Wm. Beverly Winslow,
Dear Sir:

Your letter in regard to my competition with the Literary Digest received and I never felt as swelled up in my life, And am glad you wrote directly instead of communicating with my Lawyers, As I have not yet reached that stage of Prominence where I was committing unlawful acts and requiring a Lawyer, Now if the Literary Digest feels that the competition is too keen for them—to show you my good

[2] Will's reporting of both conventions is in his *How We Elect Our Presidents* (Boston: Little, Brown and Co., 1952), pp. 5-12.

sportsmanship I will withdraw. In fact I had already quit as the gentlemen who put it out were behind in their payments and my humor kinder waned, in fact after a few weeks of no payments I couldent think of a single joke. And now I want to inform you truly that this is the first that I knew my Title of the "Illiterate Digest" was an infringement on yours as they mean the direct opposite, If a magazine was published called Yes and another Bird put one out called No I suppose he would be infringing. But you are a lawyer and its your business to change the meaning of words, so I lose before I start.

Now I have not written for these people in months and they havent put any gags out unless it is some of the old ones still playing. If they are using gags that I wrote on topical things 6 months ago then I must admit that they would be in competition with the ones the Literary Digest Screen uses now. I will gladly furnish you with their address, in case you want to enter suit. And as I have no Lawyer you can take my case too and whatever we get out of them we will split at the usual Lawyer rates of 80-20, the client of course getting the 20.

Now you inform your Editors at once that their most dangerous rival has withdrawn, and that they can go ahead and resume publication, But you inform Your clients that if they ever take up Rope Throwing or chewing gum that I will consider it a direct infringement of my rights and will protect it with one of the best Kosher Lawyers in Oklahoma.

Your letter to me telling me I was in competition with the Digest would be just like Harding writing Cox and telling him he took some of his votes.

So long, Beverly, if you ever come to California, come out to Beverly where I live and see me.

Illiterately yours,
Will Rogers

After writing this letter Will let a number of people on the Goldwyn lot read it. For the next few weeks they kept asking if he had received a reply.

"Nope," Will replied, "I just wasted a letter on some High Brow lawyer without a sense of humor. I'm sore at myself for having written it." [3]

[3] Copies of the letter written to Will and of his reply are in his *Illiterate Digest* (New York: Albert & Charles Boni, 1924), pp. 5-10.

When Will's two-year contract with Goldwyn terminated, he expected it to be renewed with a substantial raise. Instead, to his embarrassment and chagrin, it was dropped. Goldwyn had sold out and his operations became a part of the newly formed Metro-Goldwyn-Mayer corporation. "It stunned me for several days," Will confessed, "then I went home, as usual, and talked it over with Betty."

"No use blaming the producers," she told him frankly. "If you were going good they would want to keep you. There's something wrong with your pictures. Let's find out what it is and if possible correct it. Then they will want you again."

This was exactly the advice Will needed. He was not satisfied with what he had done. He had made a dozen pictures for Goldwyn, all of them fairly successful at the box office, but none of them outstanding.

They tried to discover the trouble, but exactly in the wrong manner. The motion-picture business was going through a reorganization, and many of the top stars began producing their own pictures. Forgetting his experience in London in 1907 and in New York in 1910, Will decided to do so himself. Pretty soon all the members of the Rogers family were up to their necks reading and discussing books and scripts and planning for the time when dad would be another Douglas Fairbanks. In the end, Will produced three one-reel pictures: *Fruits of Faith, One Day in 365* (a pictorial history of a day in the life of the Rogers family), and *The Roping Fool.* The last was the only one with real merit. By using a white rope and the little black pony, Dopey, Will had all his roping tricks photographed so that they could be shown as he did them and in slow motion. "I don't think you might consider it Art," he said in a personal appearance, "but there is 30 years of hard practice in it."

Something went wrong with a release agreement that Will had made, and as a result he found himself so deeply in debt that he had to mortgage his home, borrow on his life insurance and sell his Liberty Bonds to keep going. Even after doing this the films of his movies had to be left with the bank as further security. "If the loan is made for a Moving Picture," he groaned, "the President of the bank wants to write the story for you. The Directors want to know who the Leading Lady is, and if they could, they would keep her as collateral."

The unvarnished truth was that Will's abilities did not run in the direction of business. Nor had his and Betty's studying his acting in the rerun of his pictures made for Goldwyn uncovered his weakness. This came to him later after he had returned to the stage. "One night when I was out on the stage, twirling my rope and looking silly, nobody in the house thinking I had a serious thought, it all came to me," he said. *"I was being myself on the stage."* Every time Will was himself he succeeded beyond his wildest dreams; when he tried to get out of character he failed. Furthermore, the contrast between his success and his failure was so great that his failure in his silent movies done for Goldwyn would have been success for an ordinary person. Will had to be on a lone peak.

At this crucial time Betty was a tower of strength, as she had been in the production attempt of 1910. It was she who assured him he eventually would make it in motion pictures, and for the moment to return to New York. "We will keep our home here for the time being, and with Theda here to take care of the children, I will spend as much time with you as possible."

13

"A Return to Normalcy"

WILL'S RETURN TO THE "NORMALCY" OF BEING HIMSELF coincided with the country's doing so under President Harding. On his way to New York Will stopped off at "the national fun factory" for "fresh-laid jokes" to enliven his routine for the stage. It was an excellent time to be in Washington as the jubilant Republicans were once again in control of the government and were speedily converting it into an instrumentality for a particular segment of society. The first and most important consideration indicates quite clearly where the interest lay. Even before Harding took over the White House on March 4, 1921, an emergency tariff measure was rushed through Congress. Foreign competition must be strangled. "If there ever was a time when America had anything to fear from foreign competition that time has passed," President Wilson said in vetoing it. "If we wish to have Europe settle her debts—governmental or commercial—we must be prepared to buy from her. Clearly this is no time for the erection of high tariff barriers." The answer came after Harding's inauguration in the Fordney-McCumber Tariff Act, which established the highest duties so far in American history. When the country should have pushed boldly out into its obvious leadership of the world it cringed behind a wall to protect its rich and powerful. Profits to the few surmounted the welfare of the many. "The tariff is an instrument for the protection of a minority," Will lashed out, "but what a minority!"

The act added billions of dollars to living costs, encouraged the growth of monopoly, impaired trade and political relations with the rest of the world, and ensured that the League of Nations would become impotent.

In addition, Prohibition, now firmly entrenched in the Constitution, provided a smoke screen behind which gangsterism, racketeering and nationwide bootlegging flourished. Even more destructive, though often overlooked, its flagrant violation created a cynical attitude toward law enforcement from the lowest levels of society on up into the ranks of big business and governmental operation. The old Mark Hanna-ish concept of the "robber barons" of "what is the Constitution between friends" spread to all phases of law enforcement. The gate was wide open, particularly for big business, and Mr. Dooley's statement that "what is a stone wall to a layman is a triumphal arch to a corporation lawyer" offered lush grazing for "the rugged individualist."

In the fall of 1921 when Will arrived in Washington another interesting event was in the making. As a *coup de grâce* for the League of Nations, one of its implacable foes, Senator William E. Borah of Idaho, had suggested a Disarmament Conference as a means of preventing war and Secretary of State Charles E. Hughes had approved. The advance guard of the delegates were arriving in Washington at the time Will came and, remembering the Versailles Conference, he appraised them caustically. The announced purpose of the conference was to reduce naval armament.

On his arrival in Washington, Will was drafted to make a speech to the National Press Club. He assured the members that he was not "deeply touched" by the honor, as some of the foreign dignitaries who arrived for the conference had assured them, and as a matter of fact before the conference was over it would be the United States that was "deeply touched." Nevertheless, he had missed Washington while in California. "Getting thrown off a cliff in a movie, I would think of Washington. Thinking of a city where you couldent get a place to sleep and the hotel Clerks would insult you for asking, I would think of Washington. Prohibition, be in towns where nobody could get a drink, I would always think of Washington." The city would be one of the greatest in the country, he assured them, if it weren't for "the drawback of the Capitol with the people it brings here. Congress meets twice a year and brings you a class of citizens whose own people don't want." He reminded them that President Harding in his campaign had promised the vote to everyone except the citizens of the District. "The Esquimos will be voting before you do," he warned them.

Will kidded Congress, the Vice-President, and then he got around to President Harding. "I went up to the White House today to see if I could see the dog, Laddie Boy. While I was being moved on by a Policeman, why, out comes Will Hays. He spied me and says, 'Have you met the President yet?' I said, 'No.' So he dragged me right through three rooms filled with Ohio office seekers. Didn't even knock. Just busted right on in. I thought we would both get thrown out on our ears. But he didn't even get started to introduce me before the President said, 'Hello, where's your Chewing Gum?' So instead of me telling him anything funny, he started repeating things I had said in the *Midnight Frolic* for years. So the fellow who tells you he come right from a farm in Ohio to the White House is Cuckoo.

" 'Do you want me to tell you the latest political jokes, Mr. President?' I asked him.

" 'You don't have to, Will,' he said, 'I know 'em already. I appointed most of them.' "

In New York Will played at Shubert's Winter Garden for three weeks, and then went back into the *Follies*. "It's a great thing to get the old brain workin' again after loafin' on the movie lots," he said. "You know, you've got to exercise your brain just like your muscles. I found when I came back that I wasn't as good as I used to be. I was all out of practice."

Prohibition was a "staple" subject for his gibes, as was its impact on the nation. "Would ask you-all in the back to come up to the front, too, but I havent got room . . . This gang in the front row is here every night . . . They haven't missed a show or a drink for a year . . . They bring their present wives to see their old ones act . . . This is Bootlegger's Exchange . . . You can just look at their faces and tell how the market is today . . . Scotch was 4 points off today and Gin was steady to weak . . . a tendency to weakness. . . . These men have Diluted themselves into a Fortune . . . They have parlayed Water and Wood Alcohol into our national drink."

Taxes was another subject that came in for satire. "U.S. to spend a million dollars to try and collect income tax from corporations... What do they spend on individuals that don't pay?... Just carfare to jail is all... Those corporations pay for smartness... Stockholders of big corporations take out their Dividends in extra stock on which they have to pay no tax... Still a married salaried man that takes out his Dividends in groceries to put into his family 'corporation' has to pay just the same... The income tax has made more Liars out of the American people than Golf has... Even when you make one out on the level, you don't know when it's through if you are a crook or a martyr... Of course, people are getting smarter nowadays... they are letting Lawyers, instead of their conscience, be their guide."

The chief subject for Will's X-raying was "the Disagreement Conference" at Washington. "It's the No. 2 Company of the Peace Conference... Only a few nations have been invited, but it don't make any difference... The United States, England, France and Japan will decide what the rest will do... Japan has the largest delegation, 150... They didn't get started good in the war but they are going to swamp us in the Peace Conference... They arrived here on a Warship.... China, up to the opening of the Conference, did not know how many delegates they would send as Japan hadn't told her ... Most nations are coming to see what they can get at the Conference, but China is coming to see what *they give*... The only thing agreed on at the opening of the Conference was that Japan was agreed on what she wanted.... The Conference was opened by a speech by Secretary Hughes setting forth its purposes.... When Japan and England get through offering Reservations there won't be anything left but the 'Gentlemen and Delegates.'... Mr. Hughes got an awful lot of applause but no signatures... Japan agreed to two-thirds of Hughes's plan, that she is in favor of England and America disarming, but the other third, herself disarming, she couldent seem to derive much nourishment out of that.... France is getting uneasy ... She wants them to kinder speak about Armies if they are going to prevent war."

A couple of weeks later Will made another report. "Japan is still holding out for a larger navy.... You know you can't patrol a big coast like China has without a big Navy... You never saw such disarmament in your life as is going on... Japan has disarmed from 60 to 70% ... France has asked permission to disarm from a half to a million standing army... Italy wants to disarm their Navy until it is 'down' to Japan's.... They are secretely disarming China now.... Japan disarmed her in Mongolia... England disarmed her of Shanghai and France of Indo-China.... Well, it looks like 'Open Covenants Secretly arrived at.' "

As the conference progressed, Will took cracks at President Harding, as he had at President Wilson. In a skit Will presented a Cabinet meeting in which most of the talk was about golf and Harding bragged about a hole-in-one and other feats on the links. "See where Senator Freylinghuysen was renominated in New Jersey... That shows the great esteem the people of New Jersey have for the President.... The Senator is the only man in Washington the President can beat playing golf... The fire at the Treasury Department started on the roof and burned down until it got to the place where the money ought to be and there it stopped... The Harding Administration had beat the fire to it... A fire in the Treasury Building is nothing to get excited about during a Republican Administration."

In the spring of 1922 the *Follies* played in Washington and in his routine Will had an act on "the Disagreement Conference." Tickets were sent to President Harding inviting him and party to attend. In case this was impossible, Will offered to bring the act to the White House. The tickets came back and Gene Buck, in charge of the tour, received a phone call from Will Hays that the President was angry over Will's comments about him.

"I took the story to Rogers," Gene Buck recalled, "and he cried. He told me, 'Why, you remember, Gene, when Wilson come all the way to Baltimore to hear me in the Friars show, and came backstage afterwards and said how he enjoyed my jokes.' "

Will's tears were not of defeat or compliance. The next night he not only continued the skit but added another statement. "I have just read the President's treaty message," he said. "I thought it was the best speech Secretary Hughes ever wrote." Then in a curtain speech he told the audience that "I joked at Wilson and he liked it. A really big man will laugh at a joke on himself." He followed this by sending a wire to the President's secretary: "From now on I'm a Democrat."

At the end of the conference Will reported that it had been "like a Poker game, everybody claims they won five dollars." His comments admirably sum up the accomplishments. "We just signed up to go to Japan's aid in case China jumps on her . . . This Conference is to make war cheaper . . . All these Nations brought Experts and they can tell how much of a War you can put on with a given amount of Armament . . . If we could only get rid of Congress and our Profiteers we could put on a war cheaper than anybody, for the minute our war is over we don't have to pay our soldiers . . . We don't pay for rehearsals between wars . . . *Battleships cost a lot and will be no good during the next war* . . . They will go the same way the old-fashioned General on the Gray Horse on the hill that used to shout, 'Go on, Boys!' . . ."

Will reported sadly that this was to be the beginning of a series of conferences. "They are laying them out like a Circuit now . . . Most of these Delegates jump from here direct to Genoa . . . America hasn't decided yet whether to go or not . . . We have to take stock to see if we have enough to get to the next one on . . . They call it an 'economic' Conference and it will be if Americans don't attend."

Will predicted truly that China would be the "chief patient operated on" territorially, and the United States would do most of the sinking. A series of treaties came out of the conference; they brought some disarmament, set forth the status of China and the limitation of island fortifications in the Pacific. Although the United States was relieved of expenditures for keeping peace in the Pacific, Japan was left as the strongest naval power there—and the road to Pearl Harbor was paved.

"I can picture Balfour as I saw him at the Conference," Will wrote on March 21, 1930. "It was the professional diplomat, the trained Statesman, just coasting along with a lot of amateurs. He could sink a blueprint with more emotion than he could a battleship. He knew on account of England's numerous coaling stations all over the world that it was fast, light cruisers that were needed, so he with 'real reluctance' agreed to limit battleships. He thought it was up to us to make it a success if we had to sink the Robert E. Lee—and did. . . .

Balfour was made 'Lord' when he returned home for what he did here. I always thought he should have been made king." As a result of the conference the Atlantic remained England's ocean and the Pacific went to Japan.

"When some nation really wants to fight you," Will summed up this and other conferences, *"they don't tell you to put up your hands. They just pop you in the jaw before you know it.* Peace meetings are held after every war since Adam first swung on Eve for not having his breakfast apple there on time. When she come to, they held a peace meeting to stop wars between husbands and wives."

A few weeks after Will's return to the *Follies,* "the nicest old gentleman I ever met, especially in the law profession" came to his dressing room to see him. It was William Beverly Winslow to whom Will had written his letter about the "Illiterate Digest." Winslow had photostated Will's letter and passed copies around to the officials of Funk & Wagnalls, publishers of the *Literary Digest,* to its staff, and to his attorney friends. So Will's letter had not been wasted, after all.

By now, as a movie star and the top star of the *Follies,* Will had become a sort of father confessor to the show girls. When asked what the girls had done to him, his reply had been, "They've made me love 'em. Most of them are working for their living and working darned hard, too. You ought to see 'em at rehearsals. They know how to work and there's no nonsense about it either. There's not half of this stage-door johnny evil you hear about. I'd rather have my daughter working in the *Follies* than trooping around Hollywood, with her mother at her heels. These movie mothers! Gosh, they're the ones that cause all the troubles! If my girl ever goes in, she'll go alone. I think everything in this world of my wife, but I don't believe in this mother business on the stage or screen."

True to her word, Betty came east as often as she could to be with Will, and particularly when the *Follies* were on the road. She was just as fond of the girls as Will and was always ready to listen to their troubles. "When one of the girls is sick or in trouble," Will said, "they go to her and she fixes 'em up and takes care of them."

While in New York on this *Follies* stint Will made his first radio appearance. The only person with him in the studio was the famous announcer Graham McNamee. Thinking it might be easier on Will,

McNamee stood behind him. Then he noticed that Will kept glancing around and grinning. It finally occurred to him that Will needed an audience, so he moved around in front. Almost immediately Will's embarrassment dropped away.

In addition to radio, this period was one of growth and accomplishment in two other, different fields. One was forced on Will, so that he could earn more money to pay off his debts. It consisted of after-dinner appearances before various groups—he called it "barkin' for my dinner"—for a fee, usually $1,000. The other was the beginning of his weekly newspaper column that was to give him an infinitely wider "rostrum" from which to comment on men and affairs.

For over a year, in addition to his work in the *Follies,* Will averaged three to four speeches a week. "I encountered every breed of organized Graft in the world," he said. "I faced men that made every known and unknown commodity that the American people could very well get along without. I even got so low one time that I talked to Real Estate men. If this keeps on I will be speaking at a Kiwanis Luncheon next." No other man alive could have told the various organizations what he did.

The Advertising Men were "the Robbing Hoods of America" and when "the Thief of Bagdad quit business the Advertising Clubs of America took over his incorporation papers." The Automobile Show was just an alibi to get to New York without the men bringing their wives. The Automobile Dealers were "the old time Horse trading Gyps with white collars on" and instead of "operating a livery stable" they were in "a glass-fronted building . . . The only real difference is the glass front and the smell . . ." Their organization constituted the "mother lodge of liars" but they came by it naturally as "the old Biblical Ananias sold Chariots . . ." Even worse were the Automobile Accessory Manufacturers whom he called "the Lenins and Trotzkys of the business." They made the "brittle parts, sell 'em to the manufacturer, and he has to be the goat and try and peddle them to the public." Topping it all were the paint manufacturers. The manufacturers "put out those Cornshellers and call 'em Automobiles. You sell 'em the paint to cover 'em over with so they will deceive the people. If they have a thing they want to pass off as steel, they just put 4 more Coats of paint on it."

The Rug Manufacturers were described as "the Supreme Council of High Binders of the financial world." Their victims were girls. "A leading trade paper says that 42% of all rugs are bought by Girls and Women between the ages of 18 and 30 . . . That is the boob age . . . She will either buy a Rug or get married, and if she is doubly crazy she will do both . . . Over in Armenia, Rugs are made by the Wives and Lady Friends . . . Over there they sometimes take 4 to 5 years to make a rug . . . Over here they are bought by Wives and Lady Friends and it sometimes takes ten years to pay for one." It had been a pleasure to address the "24 Karat Klub" as a bunch "who have sold more Nickle for platinum, more alloy for Gold, than anyone in the world." On the other hand, Will had doubts about talking to the Association of Woolen Men because they should know "what a Cowboy thinks of a sheepherder." But on investigation he had found there would be very little wool there as their competitors had assured him the organization was "about 65% shoddy." In case of rain he warned them to stay inside or there would be "about 500 men choked to death by their own suits." The Fur Industry men were told that to become a member of their organization all that was necessary was "to buy $50 worth of Diamond Dye and move next to the dog pound."

Will told the National Association of Manufacturers, after reading a booklet describing the purposes and accomplishments of the organization, that the only other organization equal to them in effectiveness had been "six Irishmen that met in a saloon in Chicago and passed a resolution that King Edward should not be crowned." He called the National Chamber of Commerce "the resolution-passing end of the United States" and compared the local units to "the Old Ladies' sewing circles in towns years ago that knew everybody's business and were into everything." The local Chamber of Commerce "is the Male end of that same organization . . . They fix everything from the local Marble Championship to the next War . . . The minute a fellow gets into a Chamber of Commerce he quits mowing his own lawn."

After a year and a half of the "banquet routine," Will gave it up as a regular activity. "A great many will think that it is Dispepsia that is driving me away from behind the old banquet table . . . But it is not so . . . There is only one way that a person can survive a year of banquets and not wind up with a burlesque stomach—that is not eat there at all . . . And a better plan still—not only don't eat there, but try to get there late enough to miss the speeches, too. If you follow those two plans you will never have a spoiled banquet." Will followed the first one by fortifying himself at "a little Chili Joint on Broadway and 47th Street" where there was just a counter and a few stools. "Well, on any night I had to go to a banquet, I would go there and play about two rounds of Enchiladas, and a few encores of Chili," and he was "fortified" not only to refuse "anything that might be offered at dinner, but to set through almost any kind of speeches."

14

"Leave 'Em Lay as I Write 'Em"

A SPEECH OF WILL'S TRIGGERED THE NEXT GIANT STEP IN his career. "One of the Roosevelt boys" asked him as a favor to speak in support of the candidacy of Ogden Mills, who was seeking re-election to Congress from "the silk stocking" district of New York City. Will agreed because "nobody can refuse a Roosevelt," but he did not agree on what he would say. It was a hilarious performance. "I have spoken in all kinds of Joints from the homes of the rich on 5th Avenue to telling Jokes in Sing Sing . . . But this is my first crack at a Political speech and I hope it flops . . . I don't want it to get over . . . If it did, it might lead me into Politics, and up to now I have tried to live honest . . . Some of you might think I am speaking for my candidate's opponent but such is not the case . . . I don't know him, but he must be a scoundrel and a tool of the interests. . . . On the other hand, I don't know or have never met my Candidate, and for that reason I am more apt to say something good of him than any one else. . . . There is one thing, though, I do not understand . . . Most people take up Politics through necessity, or as a last resort, but I find this Guy was wealthy before he went in . . . Not as wealthy as now but rich . . . Perhaps he went in to protect what he had as they say there is honor among 'em. . . . His handicap is that he was educated at Harvard . . . But I understand he has forgotten most of it, so that brings him back to earth. . . . Before serving one term in Congress, he spent 4 terms slumming in the State Assembly at Albany . . . He is the only Politician outside Henry Cabot Lodge that can get into the front door of a 5th Avenue Home without delivering something... He favors a living wage for the bootleggers and a free examination for those who drink their products... He is 100 per cent for ticket speculators and everything in his district... He is the only candidate you can accept a cigar from without worrying about smoking it."

Will continued in this manner for fifteen minutes. An examination of the speech shows that it was merely an elaborated *Follies* routine, tailored for a special occasion and a special subject, as all of his speeches had been. He was being himself, as he had not been himself in his silent motion pictures. "The poor fellow doesn't know yet," Will recalled of Ogden Mills, who sat through the speech without cracking a smile, "whether I was for him or against him." In that Will was also being himself. On most subjects and on most men Will was a commentator rather than a propagandist or publicity agent.

This speech was reported verbatim in the *New York Times* for October 27, 1922, and widely read, chuckled over and commented on. One man in particular read it, V. V. McNitt, founder and owner of the McNaught Syndicate, who sensed in it the germ of a successful newspaper column.

Up to now Will's writing had been sporadic and more or less an imitation of the run-of-the-mill humor with wild exaggeration, outlandish puns, and slangy gibberish—something he would never have done on the stage. His books on the Peace Conference and Prohibition had been merely collections of what he had said on the stage, as his reportings of the political conventions for 1920 were what he might have said if he had been in the *Follies*—but with much less pertinency and "fresh-laid" quality. In addition he had done a number of things for the humor magazine *Life,* though not too successfully as a letter to the editor indicates:

Dear Mr. Shipmann:

Enclosed find some Volstead or Near Jokes. Now I read the ones you used last week (both of them). And you have *some* man on your Paper whose Genius I don't believe you fully appreciate. The way he can take 48 Jokes and pick out the absolute poorest is positively uncanny. You see I try them on the Stage, so I am in a better position to appreciate his flawless picking than you are. Now this time I am *fooling* him. I am not sending *any* bad ones. So this means that none of these will see the advantages of *Life*. Kindly have them return to me the list I sent with the ones marked off which they used. Also the Banker's Speech as I have no Copy of either.

What will *Life* take for their Waste Paper basket? I want to buy it. There is a field for a humorous Magazine.

Yours in the Follies Unedited,
Will Rogers

P.S. If Benchley and Sherwood have had the same Experience I have, we can take that Basket and Start a Humorous Magazine. If a theatrical Manager had him as a Picker and he Worked on the direct opposite from you, it would make Producing an Absolute Cinch.

Will's humor was not the sort that filled the pages of the humor magazines of the time. That was the old standardized joke with a straight man asking a question, akin to the sort used in most vaudeville skits. Will's "fresh-laid jokes" without his own delivery were buried in such a melange.

At the same time Will was negotiating with the New York *Herald* on doing a weekly column around a horse-sense spokesman, "Powder River" Powell, which would have been squarely in the tradition of American humor. It was to consist of conversations between Powder River and his barber, "Soapy" when he rode in once a week for a shave. A sample sketch did not meet the approval of the managing editor of the *Herald*. At this time McNitt entered the picture. Powder River was not Will Rogers to him either. After some scouting around, negotiating and thinking, McNitt suggested to Will that the *New York Times* might be induced to use a weekly column if Will would comment on men and affairs as he did on the stage in the *Follies*. This appealed to Will and he did several columns, finally doing one that was what McNitt and the *Times* wanted. In it, writing as he spoke, Will managed to get himself into words and onto paper.

In the *New York Times* and in other newspapers over the country, on December 30, 1922, Will's first column appeared (the first *Times* columnist who was not on its staff). It was titled "Settling the Affairs of the World as They Should be" and had this introductory comment: "The famous cowboy monologist, Will Rogers, has undertaken to write for this paper a weekly article of humorous comment on contemporary affairs. The *Literary Digest* recently quoted an editorial from the *New York Times* thus: 'Not unworthily is Will Rogers carrying on the tradition of Aristophanes on our comic stage.' " Will's justification for writing the column was that his connection with the *Follies* "has given me an inside track on some of our biggest men in this country who I meet nightly at the stage door." He would and could tell the truth about them because he had never "mixed up in Politics." Now the people across the United States were to get a weekly diet of what the *Follies* audiences laughed at, and by reading it were to have more time to mull over it.

It might be on politics. "The more you read and observe about Politics, you got to admit that each party is worse than the other... The one that's out always looks the best... They've had a Governor's Conference in Washington where they discussed but did not try Prohibition... It was the consensus that there was a lot of drinking going on and that if it wasn't stopped by January that they would hold another meeting and get rid of some more of the stuff."

Or it might be on a man. "We can always depend on Judge Elbert Gary for a weekly laugh in his speeches... But last week he pulled the prize wheeze of his career... He had his accomplices make an investigation of the Steel Industry, and they turned in a report that it was more beneficial to a man to work 12 hours a day than 8... They made this report so alluring that it is apt to make people who read it decide to stay the extra four hours on their jobs, just through the Health and enjoyment they get out of it... Judge Gary got up to read this report before the stockholders... He read for one hour in favor of a 12 hour day... Then he was so exhausted they had to carry him out and Charlie Schwab had to go on reading the sheet ... After Schwab read for two hours, the audience was carried out."

It might be on Washington. "See the Senate has a filibuster... There is no other Body of Lawmakers in the world that has a thing like that.... Why, if a distinguished Foreigner was to be taken around to see our Institutions and was taken into the Senate and not told what the Institution was, and heard a man ramble on, talking that had gone on for 10 or 12 hours, he would probably say, 'You have lovely quarters here for your insane, but have you no Warden to look after their health... to see that they don't talk themselves to death.' . . . One Senator threatened to read the Bible into the record as a part of his speech and I guess he would have done it if somebody in the Capitol had had a Bible."

The very next week a distinguished foreigner, Sir Percy Baldwin, came to this country and criticized Congress. "Now I resent that . . ." Will wrote ". . . President Harding and I can get vexed at Congress and say things, but we are all of the same family . . . The worst thing was, Sir Percy said our Congress was Rural and Pastoral . . . I would interpret it to say he meant HICK . . . Sir Percy says all they know is how to raise Hogs and wheat and sell them . . . He is wrong . . . They don't even know how to raise hogs and wheat."

Then it might be on borrowing money. "If you think it ain't a Sucker Game, why is your Banker the richest man in your Town? . . . Why is your Bank the biggest and finest building in your town? . . . Now I'm not going to put these Bankers out of Business right away . . . I'm kinder *warning* them . . . Of course the Ali Baba of this gang is J.P. Now, I give John credit. It's no small job, when you have to handle the finances of the world in addition to your own country, to be suddenly deprived of his livelihood . . . Then there is Otto Kahn, one of the most pleasant men I ever saw . . . And Charlie Schwab, who has the greatest personality of any man in America . . . Of course Charlie don't hardly come under the heading of Banker . . . He only owns just the ones in Pennsylvania. . . . You see it's not from a personal view that I am abolishing Banks. *It's just that I don't think these Boys realize really what a menace they are.*"

In his column for April 21, 1923, Will wrote his first letter to a president. At the time there were reports that Colonel George Harvey, ambassador to England, was about to resign, and Will applied for his job. His letter was addressed to

Mr. Warren Gamaliel Harding
President of these United States and
Viceroy of the District of Columbia
Chevy Chase Golf Club, Washington, D.C.

My dear Mr. President:

I can tell by observation that it [the job] does not come under Civil Service or competitive examination . . . Now I want to enumerate a few of my qualifications for the Position of Ambassador to the Court of James (I don't know whether it's St. or Jesse). But, anyway, it's some of the James Family.

My principal qualification would be my experience in Speechmaking. That is 90 percent of the duties of a Diplomat. Now I can't make as many speeches as my predecessor, unless I trained for it. But I would figure on making up in quality any shortcomings I might have in endurance. . . . The way I figure it out, what one has to do is to make his speeches so that they will sound one way to the English, and the direct opposite to the Hearst readers back over here. Now George (Col. and not the King) was rather unfortunate in that respect. He made them so they would sound two ways, but both Nations took the wrong meaning. . . .

Another qualification is my Moving Picture experience. We must pay more attention to how our public men screen if we are going to have to look at them every day in the news films. We must not only get men with screen personality, but who know Camera angles and when they are getting the worst of it. If you don't watch, you are liable to be photographed with the Mob instead of the Principals. The thing to do is some little thing during the taking of the picture that will draw the attention to you. For instance, during the Court Ceremony, I would just playfully kick the King. Now you don't know how a little thing like that would get over with the public. Or, at one of the big weddings in the Abbey, I could just sorter nonchalantly step on the bride's train, perhaps ripping it off, or any little Diplomatic move like that . . .

Now, another thing, I ride horseback, so the Prince of Wales and I could ride together and, on account of my experiences with the rope, I could catch his horse for him. . . .

Now the feature that I feel rather modest about referring to, but which is really my principal asset, is my being able to wear Silk Knee Breeches—not only wear them, but what I mean, look like something in them. The Lord instead of distributing my very few good points around as he does on most homely men, why, he just placed all of mine from the knee down . . . Say, I can put on those Silk Rompers and clean up. Now I don't like to grab off a Guy's job by knocking him, but you know we haven't had a decent looking leg over there in years. . . .

That brings us down to Golf. Now I will have to admit that my political education has been sadly neglected as I have never walked over many green pastures. Horses are too cheap for a man to spend half his life walking over the country looking for holes in the ground. But as I understand this lack of Golf will not handicap me in England as it would over here, as Mr. Volstead has not percolated into that land and the game is still fought out at the 19th hole. And, if I do say it myself, I do talk a corking Game of Golf....

I should like to get the appointment at once, as I want to get over there before all the King's Children are married. If one can't attend a royal marriage, why, their ambassadorship has been a failure as far as publicity is concerned for that event is the World's Series of England.

Now, as to Salary, I will do just the same as the rest of the Politicians—accept a small salary as Pin Money, AND TAKE A CHANCE ON WHAT I CAN GET.

Awaiting an early reply, I remain
Yours faithfully,
Will Rogers

P.S. If you don't want me, Turkey wants me to represent them in Washington. So where would you rather have me—in England or Washington?

Although Will could satirize a man like Harding, who could not take joshing, he could praise him for his good work. "Our public men are speaking every day on something, but they ain't saying nothing... But when Mr. Harding said that, in case of another war, that capital would be drafted the same as men, he put over a thought that, if carried out, would do more to stop wars than all the International Courts and Leagues of Nations in the world.... When that Wall Street Millionaire knows that you are not only going to take his Secretary and Clerks but his Dough, say, Boy, there would be the end of war.... You will hear the question, 'Yes, but how could you do it?' Say, you take a Boy's life, don't you? When you take a Boy you take everything they have in the World... You send them to war and what part of that life you don't use, you let him come back with it... Perhaps you may use all of it... Well, that's the way to do with Wealth... Take all he has, give him a bare living the same as you do the Soldier... Give him the same allowance as the Soldier, all of us that stay home . . . The Government should own everything we have, use what it needs to conduct the whole expenses of the war, and give back what is left, if there is any . . . There can be no Profiteering . . . Every man, woman and child, from Henry Ford and John D. down, get their Dollar and a quarter a day the same as the Soldier . . . The only way a man could profiteer would be to raise more Children."

President Harding made his statement as a "political" utterance on Memorial Day, and it meant no more than a preacher's prayer over the Unknown Soldier means. Will meant his.

By the summer of 1923 Will could gleefully boast, "I'm getting to be one of the writing fellers. The *Times* has already objected to some of my stuff, but I ain't the first comedian to write for them. The Kaiser wrote for them long before I did, and all he had to do to be funny was to tell the truth." More important, Will also announced that "Mr. Harding wants to see the *Follies,* but, on account of the humorous relations between the White House and myself being rather strained, he naturally feels a kind of hesitancy about coming, for at the present time you can't see the American Girl being glorified without being annoyed by a jarring presence among them which I am free to admit is myself. So I am leaving, not because I want to, but even though you wouldn't judge it by my writing or Grammar, I have some politeness and courtesy, and being a fair American Citizen (I won't say "good" as I think I have heard that used before), I certainly have a high regard for the Chief Executive of this Great Commonwealth and I won't do a thing to stand in the way of any pleasure that he may wish to enjoy, no matter how small."

A contract at $3,000 a week to do a series of two-reel comedies for Hal Roach and to be able to live at home unquestionably influenced Will more than the idea of accommodating President Harding. This time when he went to Hollywood he could take his forum with him through his newspaper column. "Don't think I am letting these prominent men get away scot free," he wrote. "I will continue to give you the lowdown on them. There are just two towns in the United States where everybody goes. One is New York so's to get where you can act different from what you vote, and the other is Los Angeles to have a test made to see how you screen. You can't find out anything in

New York. Everybody comes there but, on account of the Volstead Law not applying in that State, why, they are never sober enough to tell you anything. So I really think I can give you more details from Los Angeles on the Great American People, their habits, manners and customs."

15

"To Rescue the Country from the Politicians"

WILL WAS HAPPY TO BE WITH HIS FAMILY AND IN HIS HOME again. If he could only do something to keep him there? He went at motion-picture making with his usual zest, but in a short time Betty realized something was wrong. After he had completed a couple of two-reelers she knew why.

"They aren't letting you be yourself, Billy," she said.

"I know it," he growled. "I keep telling them so but nobody will do anything about it."

A couple of nights later at Irene Rich's house both of them were voicing this complaint. A friend, Rob Wagner, who had directed a number of pictures, was there.

"What is the trouble, Will?" he asked.

"All I do is run around barns and lose my pants," Will growled. "I've lost my pants in every big scene."

"If they would only let Billy play himself," Betty put in.

Wagner nodded his assent.

On the way home Betty suggested to Will that he ask Roach to give him Wagner as a director, and a few days later the studio manager called Rob.

"Have you any ideas on what you would do with him?" the manager asked.

"Goldwyn played Will as a character actor, which he isn't, and you have been playing him as a red-nosed comic, which is profane.

How would it do to get on the screen what the *Follies* paid him $3,000 a week for doing?"

"Might work," the manager said. "Come to the studio and we'll arrange the details."

Rob cornered Will at the first opportunity. "Do you have any ideas on what you want to do?"

"Let's do a take-off on *The Covered Wagon,*" Will suggested. "It's a box-office success and we could play on the name. I don't mean a burlesque, but to use characters and incidents satirizing it. We'll have two wagons, an ox-team from Hoboken, and a swell horse-drawn coach from Palm Beach. The two parties join and go west to found an empire, which in itself would be unpatriotic in a Republic. We could load up on Mayflower furniture, and then for stock to start our Empire, take just one bull and a crate of roosters."

While Will was finishing his current picture, they worked on a script—"the first complete working script the Roach lot had ever had." It had been a harrowing task. "Will's mind works in quick, brilliant flashes, but it lacks continuity," Wagner wrote in his *Script.* "It was my job to prepare a stout cord upon which to hang his pearls. Finally, we managed to get a straightforward story that carried the two wagons to a point in California where they parted, one going north to Sacramento and the other south to Los Angeles. Will as Torrence, in charge of the ox-team, said good-by to Will as Kerrigan, in charge of the Horse Team—he played both parts—and we stuck to the ox-team headed for Los Angeles. Will never quite got over the fun he missed by not going to Sacramento."

The various studio employees on location could not understand what was being done. There was none of the obvious, knockabout comedy, clowning or pie throwing of the usual Roach production. Then when the picture was finished ahead of schedule and under its budget, the studio officials sat through it in glum silence.

"They don't like it, Will," Rob said.

"I am going to offer to buy it," Will said, "I still think it will go."

A release date had already been set, and this prevented the sale of the picture to Will, or the studio would have accepted his offer. Wagner was told his services would no longer be needed.

In its preview a George Ade feature came on first, a tough competition to follow. But from the moment *Two Wagons—Both Covered* came on, the audience began to laugh. Then, as the story unfolded, "the laughter grew and grew" until Rob thought the people were going to tear up their seats. At the end came a tremendous cheer, something unusual in a movie house. Wagner walked out, leaving Will and a tearful Betty to their triumph, as the audience did not know they were there. In the lobby Wagner ran into a conference of studio officials.

"You never can tell," the manager said. "Rob, come over and see us tomorrow."

Although Wagner directed Will in his next picture, studio officials had decided the success of *Two Wagons* had been a fluke. They began to muscle in to be "sure" about the next picture. "If Will had been allowed to have his say," Wagner said, about the next picture, "it would have been the first great Hollywood satire. Instead, it followed the formula. So fearful was the studio that we couldn't be funny enough, that they began to hand us first one gagman, then two, and finally a supervisor! As help was added, each picture grew less and less funny. Finally, the supervisor suggested certain gaucheries and vulgarities to which we objected. When he ordered us to cut out England, in one picture, and make it a musical-comedy kingdom, we blew up. 'I'll walk through this stuff until my contract's ended,' Will said. 'Then back to the Follies.' "

While Will was suffering through the two-reelers, he kept his promise to inform the people on the antics of their prominent men and on the waywardness of affairs. He kept them up to date on President Harding's swing through the country in the late summer of 1923, in his effort to gain support for the entrance of the country into the World Court. "The show opened in St. Louis . . . I never heard of a good show playing St. Louis in the summer time . . . Only circuses . . . In Hutchinson, Kansas, Harding met a childhood sweetheart he had not heard of for forty years . . . If she had wanted to be truthful, she could have said, 'Well, Warren, up to 2 and a half years ago, I had not heard of you in 40 years either.' . . . Harding told the Farmers they been put on 'a business basis,' that as a consequence they can borrow more and carry on their operations like any other good business man . . . I don't know what kick the farmers have coming . . . When could they ever owe that much money before?"

In California he met Dr. House, the discover of scopolamin, the truth serum. "See they conducted experiments on convicts . . . I don't know on what grounds they reason a man in jail is a bigger liar than one out of jail . . . The chances are telling the truth is what got him there . . . It would be a big aid to humanity, but it will never be, for already the politicians are up in arms against it . . . It would wreck the very foundation on which our political government is run . . . If you ever injected truth into politics you'd have no politics . . . Even the ministers are denouncing it now . . . Humanity is not yet ready for either real truth or real harmony. . . .

"See where Mr. Edward Bok of the *Ladies' Home Journal* has offered a hundred thousand dollars for the best plan to stop war . . . People that praise his idea laughed at Henry Ford for trying to stop just one war . . . The very terms of the offer are ridiculous . . . He is to give half when the Trustees accept the plan, and the other half when the Senate approves it . . . Now, I am no Philanthropist . . . I am hard to separate from money . . . If I killed two Birds with one stone, I'd want the stone back . . . But I hereby make a Bona Fide offer of 200 thousand dollars to any man in the World who can draw up any kind of Bill or Suggestion, I don't care on what subject, no matter how meritorious, and send it to the Senate and send this paper a copy of the Bill submitted, and if the Senate passed the Bill as you sent it in, you get the 200 Thousand. . . . Talk about stopping War, there ain't a man in this Country that can draw up a Bill that the Senate themselves won't go to war over while they are arguing it. . . . I am only an ignorant Cowpuncher but there ain't nobody on earth, I don't care how smart they are, *ever going to make me believe they will ever stop wars.* . . . We ain't as smart as the generations behind us and they tried to stop them and havent been able to . . . The only way to do is just stay out of them as long as you can and the best way to stay out of them for quite a while, instead of teaching a Boy to run an Automobile, teach him to fly, *because the Nation in the Next War that ain't up in the Air, is just going to get something dropped on its Bean.*"

On August 18, 1923, while still on his swing around the country

President Harding suddenly died, supposedly of apoplexy but under mysterious circumstances. At the moment, Will laid it to the "Boneheadedness of Reception Committees" that had overtaxed the President. "If Jack Dempsey had left Washington and undertaken this same strain, when he got back Uncle Joe Cannon could have licked him."

A few weeks later, when the oil scandals broke, the idea dawned that the President's death might have had some connection with them. He, like Ulysses S. Grant, may have been a victim of those who ask, "What is a Government trust between friends, especially if there is a little black bag with enough money in it?" "I am going to devote my life's work to rescue the Country from the hands of the Politicans, and also rescue the Politicians to a life of Christianity," Will decided as he contemplated this.

As Will looked about over the land, two grave injustices appalled him. One was the refusal of Congress to pass a bill paying a bonus to the soldiers. "You promised them everything but the Kitchen Stove if they would go to War, and all they got was $1.25 a day and some knitted sox and Sweaters which after examining them they wore the sox for sweaters and the sweaters for sox. . . . The way to pay it is for the rich men who chiefly oppose it to submit to a tax on their tax-exempt bonds . . . These boys helped their Country in time of need . . . Tax-exempt Bond Buyers knowingly hindered it by cheating it out of Taxes . . . In 1916 there was 1296 men whose income was over $300,000 and they paid a Billion in Taxes . . . This year there was only 246 whose income was *supposed* to be over 3 hundred thousand, and they only paid 153 million. . . . You mean to tell me that there are only 246 men in this Country who only make $300,000? . . . Why, say, I have spoken at Dinners in New York where there was that many in one Dining Room, much less the United States . . . Tax-exempt Securities will drive us to the Poor House, not Soldier's Bonus. . . . Now, if a man is against it why don't he tell the real truth? . . . 'I don't want to spare the Money to pay you Boys. . . . I think the best insurance in the world against another War is to take care of the Boys who fought in the last one . . . YOU MAY WANT TO USE THEM AGAIN."

Actually, "a return to normalcy" had come full circle, and most social progress was braked to a full stop. Will's column, properly designated "The Weekly Exposure," as it began its second year never lacked for "gas" although the "bearings" of the vehicle often grated and groaned at the cargo carried. "We are staking the Reputation of our Periodical that nothing in Public Life (or out of it) is any good. It's no trouble to pick out the Bad but I tell you Readers, when you sit down to pick out the Worst, you have set Some Task for yourself."

In announcing that he was not going to run for the Presidency, Henry Ford said publicly that 90 per cent of the people of the United States were satisfied. "It ain't so . . . It's just got so 90 per cent of the people Don't Give a Damn . . . Politics ain't worrying this Country one tenth as much as parking space. . . . There is millions of people in this country that know the color of Mary Pickford's hair but think the Presidential office is hereditary. . . . There is more Mortgages in this country than there is votes . . . The country is operating on a dollar down and a dollar a week . . . Mr. Ford says, 'America is on Wheels today.' . . . He means 'America is on Tick today . . .' It is not politics that is worrying this country . . . It's the Second Payment."

When a revolution broke out in Mexico Will became furious. "I see where we have the exclusive Contract to furnish all the Ammunition for this and the next five wars, with an option on another five . . . If you can't match a war yourself, why, get the Contract to furnish the material for some other war . . . I tell you there is nothing as disheartening to a Country as to want to go to War and can't . . . So I think we are to be heartily commended for obliging suffering humanity."

Actually, it would be a good idea, Will thought, to concentrate on some "local" wars first. One of them was "the rash of husband killings" that with the connivance of criminal lawyers, a publicity craze, and the automatic pistol had broken out all over the country. If this would have improved "the character of Husbandry" some good might have resulted, but all the good that Will could see in "this rattle of Musketry in the homes" was "more Dead Husbands" but "not better ones."

The other war was among the various churches and groups within churches as to the truth of various creeds. "How the Lord got here on earth, whether by Virgin Birth or Via the Familiar Stork has nothing to do with it . . . He must have been a pretty good man after he did get here ... If they would spend less time arguing over the how, and more in following His example, they would come nearer getting the Confidence of their Church ... There is no argument in the World carries the hatred that a Religious belief one does ... Personally I do not believe the story about Noah and his Ark ... I have seen Men, since Prohibition changed their drink, claim that they saw Animals that Noah never heard of ... I don't believe Noah could round up all the Animals in one Herd without the Skunk causing a Stampede ... But if they want to argue religion, no wonder you see more people at a Circus than in a church."

As the investigation of the Teapot Dome and Elk Hill oil scandals following the arrest of Albert Fall, Harding's Secretary of the Interior, came into the Senate, Will lost hope. "Statistics have proved that the surest way to get anything out of the public mind and never hear of it again is to have a Senate Committee appointed to look into it ... If it had been turned over to some Justice of Peace, with the power to act with no Appeal, why, we would be reading this morning that Millionaire so-and-so had been served breakfast from the outside in his Cell." As a partial solution for the ills of the oil industry, Will suggested a "wet nurse" like the one the motion-picture business had. "The great criticism of the Movies is that people are suddenly thrown into the possession of Money who were never accustomed to handle it before and they lose their heads ... Why, the Oil People are rich so quick they don't have time to get the grease off their hands ... They jump from a Ford to a Rolls-Royce so fast that they try to crank the Rolls through force of habit. ... Scandal for Scandal, Oil has blackened the reputation of 99 per cent more people than the movies."

On the same day that pictures were shown in the newspapers about witnesses testifying before the Senate Committee, another picture showed a Negro with a truth machine strapped to his wrist. He had been sentenced to 99 years for manslaughter. "Now if he admitted that he killed the party he would get life ... It meant either life or 99 years for him. ... That very day in Washington there were Guys testifying *with nothing on their Wrists but Silk Shirts*. If they had taken one of those Truth Machines to the investigation, there would have been more Americans sailing for Europe than went during the War. ... What's become of the old-fashioned Felon that used to be arrested for perjury? . . . *God Bless America for a Sense of Humor."*

Will knew that a "wet nurse" would not be appointed for the oil industry and that the rich oilmen behind the scandal would not be sent to the penitentiary as Albert Fall had been. And the answer was in "lawyers," to whom he turned his attention when the investigation was transferred to Los Angeles. The "lawyers" and "the evidence" came in three private railroad cars and Will went down to see them unload:

Well, they unloaded the first Car just at daybreak . . . They were just little ones . . . Chances are there was not one in that Car whose fee run any higher than maybe 40 thousand a Case. In fact they were kinder engaged to carry the Brief Cases. . . . It was at the Second Car load that we commenced to prick up our Ears, for we were now getting into the Big Money. Lawyers come out of that car who wouldn't argue a speeding case in Traffic Court for less than a hundred thousand . . . And then maybe you would have to give 'em a retainer in case you got pinched again . . . There were men in there who had procured Divorces for every one of the 400. . . . Well, when they had unpacked this second car and got them safely away to Individual Private Suites at our Home Talent Biltmore, why, then come the real headliners. Just a few big ones that were in real touch with Mr. Doheny personally . . . Real Lawyers! Men who, on a Case like this which involved perhaps 400 Million Dollars, why, they consider themselves slumming . . . Well, I will tell you how high Mr. Doheny went for legal talent . . . He had Jack Dempsey's lawyer!

It might appear from Will's description that Doheny had hired all the important lawyers in the country. But this was not the case. "The Teapot Dome Gang went to Cheyenne . . . Mr. Sinclair unloaded at least 4 cars there."

After seeing this magnificent pageantry of lawyers, Will went to the station the next day to see Uncle Sam's "legal talent" arrive. A special with five private cars pulled in as he reached the station, but he soon learned that this was a *Follies'* private train with a special compartment for each girl. A local wheezed in on another track. "Who do you think Emerged? . . . Why Atlee Pomerene and a Mr. Roberts . . . They came crawling out of a Day Coach where they had been sleeping on the back of their Necks from Cheyenne. They didn't even have a

Caddy to carry their legal papers." Will felt let down. "Uncle Sam, no wonder you don't get anywhere. . . . Of course there is one Silvery lining for the Navy's fuel . . . That is the other side has so many lawyers, they may get fighting amongst themselves . . . and we might win Accidentally . . . But they are well fortified for that . . . They have Expert Technicality Lawyers . . . Lawyers who could take W. J. Bryan and show you on Technicalities how he is entitled to be President . . . Then there are Postponement Lawyers who could have the Falls of Niagara put back on account of the Water not being ready to come over and who on the last Judgment Day will be arguing that it should be postponed on account of Lack of Evidence." Will's prophecy proved correct. The defendants were acquitted in 1926 on a technicality, although few, including their own lawyers, doubted their guilt.

Sick and tired of the silly work he was doing at the Roach studios and pining for "the national joke factory," Will went back to New York in May, 1924, in order to be for the first time at the National Political Conventions. He described it as "that City from which no weary Traveler returns without drawing on the Home Town Bank, that City of Skyscrapers, where they are endeavoring to make the height of their Buildings keep pace with their prices, where the Babbitts from Butte and Buffalo can pay speculators fantastic prices for a cheap Show, view the Electric Signs until 12 o'clock and then write home of Bacchanalian Revels." Will was changing one "California Flea for a Billion Long Island Mosquitoes" and leaving the land where "the Movies are made to return to the land where the bills are paid." He had survived for a year on "Culls and Seconds" of oranges and wanted to return where he could get "No. 1 good California Oranges and Fruits."

16

"Presidential Follies of 1924"

BEFORE THE 1924 EDITION OF THE FOLLIES OPENED WILL had time to go to "the national joke factory" for new material for his act. "Congress has been writing my material for years and I am not ashamed of what I have had. Why should I pay some famous Author, or even myself, to sit down all day trying to dope out something funny to say on the Stage? . . . No, sir, I have found that there is nothing as funny as things that have happened . . . Nothing is so funny as something done in all seriousness . . . Each state elects the most serious man it has in the District . . . He is impressed with the fact that he is leaving Home with the idea that he is to rescue his District from Certain Destruction, and to see that it receives its just amount of Rivers and Harbors, Postoffices and Pumpkin Seeds. Naturally, you have put a pretty big load on that man . . . It's no joking matter to be grabbed up bodily from the Leading Lawyer's Office of Main Street and have the entire populace tell you what is depending on you when you get to Washington."

On the other hand, Will pointed out, "they wouldn't be so serious and particular if they only had to vote on what they thought was the good of the majority of the people of the United States." But a thousand minor interests kept them from doing so.

Outside the Halls of Congress Will found the politicians "all full of humor and regular fellows. That is when you catch them when they havent got Politics on their minds. But the minute they get in that immense Hall they begin to get Serious, and it's then that they do such

Amusing things. *If we could just send the same bunch of men to Washington for the Good of the Nation, and not for Political Reasons, we could have the most perfect Government in the World."*

Will made his first personal appearance at the Republican Convention held at Cleveland, Ohio. "At first I was going to say 'the Republican Follies' but it's not so. Mr. Coolidge could have been nominated by post card. Those misled Delegates will have just as much chance to really nominate him as a bow-legged girl would have at our Stage Door." His disappointment matched that of "a sick man who had been promised a trip to the World Series, and then when he was able to get up they take him to Grant's Tomb. The most exciting thing about the Convention when it opened was an array of badges that was deafening." Will's big thrill came when he entered the Convention Hall press stands with William Jennings Bryan. "Everybody thought I was a plainclothes man sent along to protect Bryan from the Republicans."

"You write a humorous column, don't you?" Bryan asked.

"Yes," Will admitted.

"I write serious articles and if I think of anything of a comical or funny nature, I will give it to you," Bryan offered.

"Thank you, and if I happen to think of anything of a serious nature, I will give it to you."

Will smiled as it occurred to him that *both* of them might be wrong.

With everything cut and dried, the prayers turned out to be about the most exciting thing. One of them was a "keynote prayer" in which Republican party unity was its principal plea. The only reference to anything pertaining to the Bible was the "Amen" at the end. A woman delegate received Will's highest praise. In introducing the permanent chairman she walked down front and said, "Convention, I submit to you Mr. Mondell." If it had been a man "he would have had to drag in the glory of every past Republican President back to Lincoln."

An amusing moment in the convention came when Keynoter Burton, in referring to the oil and other scandals in the Harding Administration, said, "we must condemn exaggeration and protect the innocent," the applause "like to have torn the House down." But when Burton stated that "we must amidst all these rumors of iniquity punish the Guilty," the applause was a "ripple." Burton rushed over the oil scandal "so quick you would have thought his speech was greased. He dident even have a sentence; he had only a semicolon in which he laid the scandal onto the war," which was, of course, "under the Democrats."

Will left the convention before it closed. "I love Cleveland because I knew her before this catastrophe struck . . . She will arise from her badges and some day be greater than ever. But I had to leave . . . I simply couldn't stand the incessant din, the roar, the popping of corks, and the newness and brightness of the speeches, and the 'fairness to other political parties' uttered from the platform. I just had to have rest and return to the solitude and quiet of a Ziegfeld rehearsal where everything will be as still and orderly as a prayer meeting."

After Coolidge had been nominated, he was called on the telephone several times for approval of So-and-so as a running mate. His answer was "Yes" in every case. Later, Will asked him why he had not expressed a preference.

"Nobody told them whom to nominate for vice-president in 1920," he replied, "and they did all right."

"Cleveland is negotiating with Billy Sunday to hold a revival there," Will summed up, "so the Town can get some excitement and their money back that they lost on this."

The 1924 *Follies* opened in New York at the same time as the Democratic Convention. "The Democrats go to Madison Square Garden, where Ringling Brothers Circus always plays, and we go to the Amsterdam, a beautiful theatre consecrated solely to Art. . . . It's the first time in the theatrical history of New York where two shows of equal magnitude both open on the same night . . . It means 'Man versus woman.' . . . They are featuring Men, and we are featuring Women . . . I don't mean to be partisan, just because I am with the Woman show, but I think women will outdraw Men as an attraction every time . . . Can you imagine any one going into a big barn of a place to see Al Smith when they can go into a comfortable theatre and see 100 of the most beautiful creatures on earth? . . . And Bill McAdoo, he is a dandy, nice fellow, but do you think I would go into a place to look at him when I could see Ann Pennington's knees? . . . And the costuming . . . to compare that is a joke . . . Can you imagine my old friend William J. Bryan's old alpaca coat stacked up against the creations Evelyn Law and Martha Lauber will have on? . . . Now these politicians' suits are all right in the Chautauquas . . . they know they are, for they have tried them for years . . . but not for New York. . . . The only thing they have on us is the badges . . . We are simply outbadged . . . Of course we could put badges on our girls, but who wants to see a *Follies* girl overdressed?"

Alfred E. Smith, political leader in New York City and perennial governor of the state, and William G. McAdoo, son-in-law of Woodrow Wilson, were the leading candidates. As a Catholic and antiprohibitionist, Smith was not popular in the South. McAdoo not only was a prohibitionist, he practiced its precepts. Although a strong partisan fight was in store and chances for success in the election were slim, the convention met in a carnival atmosphere. "It was a beautiful Sunday in New York . . . The New York churches were crowded with New Yorkers . . . Coney Island was crowded with delegates . . . It may have been a coincidence, but every preacher in town preached on 'Honesty in Government.' . . . The Democrats can adjourn right now and they will have had a better Convention than the Republicans had . . . In fact, I suggested to them that if I was them *I would adjourn before they nominated somebody and spoiled it.* . . . Excitement? . . . Why, there are more bands playing in this town than there were delegates at Cleveland . . . If they had had that many bands and delegations parading all in different directions out in Cleveland, why, they would have had to borrow some streets from Toledo or Youngstown. . . . Al Smith copped off Fifth Avenue for his parade and it took five hours for his followers to stagger by a given point."

At first Will had great fun reporting the convention and commenting on it in his *Follies* routines. "The Keynote speaker, Pat Harrison, told things on the Republicans that would have made anybody but Republicans ashamed of themselves . . . When he mentioned old Andy Jackson, he just knocked those Democrats off their seats . . . Then, as he saw they were recovering, he hit 'em with the name of Thomas Jefferson, and that rocked them back . . . Then he mentioned Woodrow Wilson, and that sent 'em daffy . . . The delegates would raise up and start singing, 'Hail, Hail, the Gang's All Here, What the Hell Do We Care.' . . . Even my old Side-Kick Bryan was prancing around the hall shouting . . . Now he has been brought up different . . . He has read the Bible, even if to just get quotations from, but he knows, even if those other delegates dident, that that was no way to pay tribute to a martyred President. . . . As poor as the Republican Convention was, they dident sing 'Hail, Hail, the Gang's All Here,' when the speaker mentioned the name of Lincoln."

As the convention continued in deadlock day after day, to engender some excitement Will offered himself as "a sacrifice" for the Vice-Presidency. His qualification as he gave them to the *Follies* audience were "being a farmer" he understood "the farmers' conditions" and "owning two farms, both mortgaged," he appreciated the farmer's predicament. It was conceded that the vice-presidential candidate must be from the West, and "if a man came from 25 feet further West than I lived last year, he would have to be a fish in the Pacific Ocean." His best qualification, though, was that he did not belong to either party. "I am just progressive enough to suit the dissatisfied and lazy enough to be a Standpatter." Furthermore, oil has "never touched me as I drilled a well on my farm and it was oilless" nor "have I ever worked for a big corporation." As a good after-dinner speaker, "I could learn two stories, one for dinners where ladies were present, and one for where they were not." There was, of course, the question of what would happen if the President died. "Well, I would do just like Mr. Coolidge—I would go in there and keep still and say nothing. He is the first President to discover that what the American people want is to be left alone."

After more harrowing days of recriminations and feuds, Will announced to his *Follies* audience and in his newspaper column that he was going to make a nomination that would solve all the problems. When it came into his column it was in the form of a nominating speech, "The man I am about to name," and then a listing of his "peerless" qualifications. It ended up in this way:

The man I am about to name is the only man in these grand and glorious United States who, if we nominate, we can go home and have no worry as to the outcome. Don't, oh, my Democratic Colleagues, listen to my friend Bryan . . . He named ten candidates; ten men can't win! . . . Only one man can win. . . . Oh, my newly made friends, have confidence in me . . . Trust me just this once and I will lead you out of this darkened wilderness into the gates of the White House. Oh, my tired and worn friends, there is only one man.

The man I am about to name to you is Calvin Coolidge!

A few days after this, a delegate from Arizona with only a half-vote cast it for Will. On the next ballot another delegate cast his half-vote for Will also. A reporter for the *New York Times* interviewed the new candidate in his dressing room at the New Amsterdam Theatre. "I cannot talk statesmanship clothed in the habiliments of the art of Thespis," Will said, getting up and putting on a necktie. "This is a very serious moment in the destinies of the nation. The Democratic Party is locked in a strangle-hold and can make no progress My candidacy represents nothing more than the efforts of the plain people—of which I am one—to remedy this disastrous condition of affairs. It is my duty to go directly to the scene of the conflict and marshal the forces of right and justice. I did not seek this office, but respond to public demand in the spirit in which Spartacus left his plow in the furrow. The hour demands a leader. The voice of the people calls. Who am I to hesitate?"

Will confided to the reporter that his plan of campaign was to go along with the others until about Labor Day, and "then throw in my reserves. My vote has doubled without me turning a hand, and when we throw in the reserves that will make three of us. What I need is a good campaign manager. You might announce that any retired business man looking for a safe place to invest about $25,000 with a partnership in the concern, references exchanged, will be welcome in this capacity. His work will be very light . . . He wouldent have more to do than to sign the check. I'll take the labor of spending it off his hands. And I'd like to have the word passed around quietly that I can be bought. But let them know, to save time, that I don't intend to sell out the delegates who have flocked to my support cheap. I'm not naming figures, but my Rolls-Royce needs a new tire on the left hind foot."

As the convention moved into a "Seven Years Hitch," Will told his *Follies* audience some things that had happened. "Women Delegates started with Bobbed hair and wound up by being able to sit on it . . . The Arkansas Delegation started in whittling up the Board floor and whittled their way from the Back of the Hall up to the Speaker's platform ... There was so many shavings under their Chairs that if a fire had ever broken out, between these Shavings and the long Whiskers, there would have been no way in the world to put it out ... Delegates who brought their Wives along have spent more time with them than in years ... If they don't hurry, they will be the only Party that nominated a Candidate and got him defeated the same day."

The deadlock was broken by the nomination of a dark-horse candidate, John W. Davis. His selection was "a personal triumph" for William J. Bryan, Will contended. "He is the greatest character we have in the country. Most of us attract attention twice on Earth. One when we are born and the other is when we die ... But Mr. Bryan improves on a bear ... He hibernates for four years, and then emerges, and has a celebration at every Democratic Convention. In the meantime, he lectures in tents, shooting galleries, grain elevators, snow sheds or any place he can find a bunch of people that havent got a radio. No one has ever been able to understand the unique and uncanny power that he seems to hold over the Democratic Party ... Since 1896 he has either run himself or named the man that would run ... He could take a Dictionary and sink an enemy with words at 40 paces ... His speeches have been the only thing to look forward to at a Democratic Convention for years ... He has sent more Presidential Candidates home without a Reception Committee meeting them than any Monologist living ... He can take a batch of words and scramble them together and leaven them properly with a hunk of Oratory and knock the White House door knob right out of a Candidate's hand.... Well, this time it seemed different ... All during the Convention you could hear the expression, 'Well, poor old man Bryan! He has lost his grip on the delegates. Here is once where he won't be able to name the man!' But not me ... I never wavered. When he *came out against Davis,* Davis was a nominated man.... Next to Bryan, *the New York Newspapers* have killed off more deserving candidates by supporting them than anyone or anything."

Will wired Al Smith: "I told you, Al, you would be the lucky one, that they would nominate Davis. I tried to see you during the day, and all that prevented me was the New York and Albany Police Force combined. Well, Al, that shows them, you and I, that a couple of New Yorkers are good losers. We will go back to our respective Follies, me to the Amsterdam and you to Albany. I am glad you wasent selected. It would have taken a couple of years to sweep up the paper. We will make a Joint Campaign in '28, Al, and I will take you away out West as far as Pittsburgh."

To John W. Davis Will wired: "Would have congratulated you sooner, but was afraid somebody would call for a poll of the delegates, and they never polled like they had voted. So I was in mortal fear for you until they got out of town. Hear one of the Bryan Brothers is to be associated with you indirectly. For God sake pick the right one." Davis wired back assuring Will that his vice-presidential running mate was Charlie, not W. J. Bryan. "If elected I will appoint you Ambassador to England," he added, "and I have the knee breeches."

In his wire to Charlie Bryan Will advised him to go through the birth records and if possible to show that he was a cousin and not a brother of W.J. to do so. "Thanks for the wire," Charlie Bryan answered. "Will do as you suggest about the records. In the meantime I have bought him a one way Ticket to Florida."

The slate was set for the 1924 "Presidential Election Follies."

17

"The Return to Wall Street"

THE COLORLESS 1924 PRESIDENTIAL "SWEEPSTAKES" were relegated to the want ads by the news that the Prince of Wales, then at the height of his popularity, was to visit the United States. "Everybody is making preparations for the visit of the Prince of Wales . . . He has been offered every private home to live in East of Altoona . . . I don't know his address over there or I would write him and tell him what I had to contribute . . . So I will just do so publicly. . . . He wants to avoid the crowds and be off by himself so I think I have just what he wants . . . Now in offering this, I have no Ulterior motive . . . I have no Daughter of marriageable age that I have visions of occupying Windsor Castle . . . What I have to offer is not as elaborate as some he has been offered but it might be just what he wants . . . I have a nice large dressing room at the *Follies* and I can have a cot put in and he can use it as long as he cares to stay . . . I have heard he loves dancing . . . Now where can you get Girls and dancing right at your door like I am offering him?"

The Prince of Wales may have read Will's offer and yearned to accept it. Anyhow, he said on arrival in the United States, "I say, I should like to meet Will Rogers."

In compliance with his request, the Prince's equerry, Major Metcalf, came to Will's dressing room and invited him to a dinner in the Prince's honor to be given at the Piping Rock Country Club. Ziegfeld, sensing the publicity value, moved Will's routine up early in the show so he could attend. He arrived at the dinner as the Prince was finishing his speech. The audience "was composed of 150 of the most prominent men in the U.S. A man with only 5 millions at that dinner would have been a waiter . . . I stumbled over the feet of 10 of the heads of the oldest Families of New York trying to arrive at the Speaker's Table." Here is a part of what Will said as taken from his prepared speech:

Gentlemen and Polo Players, and Guest of Honor . . . You see I am stuck already . . . It's terrible to get stuck this soon in a speech, but I am . . . I don't know what to call our Distinguished Guest . . . In the mornings he is the Prince of Wales . . . in the afternoon he is Lord Renfrow . . . and as I have not read the last edition of the papers, I don't know what he is here tonight . . . He travels under so many Aliases. . . . Well, anyhow he is a Prince in his own Country, he is Lord Renfrow on his trip over here, but with us here he is just a Regular Guy. . . .

Now I know a lot of you thought I would be all nervous up here appearing before Royalty but I am not because it is not the first time. . . . One time Sir Harry Lauder was in the audience where I was playing . . . somebody had given him a pass to get in . . . Well, of course, I was all swelled up over appearing before a Sir, and later on I got to reading some English Book and found that Sir was about the lowest form of Royalty there is . . . It's the Ford of titles . . . But I am broadminded . . . If a man can get out and make himself popular in spite of his birth, I am for him . . . I admire any man that can rise above his surroundings . . . I didn't know he was here until just by accident I happened to see a little squib down in one corner of the paper, in a kinder out of the way place. . . .

Now if you think I am coming here to tell you a lot of jokes about the Prince falling off his horse, you're mistaken. I fall just as much as he does . . . Of course my falls don't attract as much attention, but they hurt just as bad. . . .

We can't kid Englishmen about their Horsemanship. If I can't find something funny in an Englishman besides his riding I won't consider myself much of a Comedian . . . Besides if we want to see some funny riding go to Central Park . . . We don't have to wait for the Prince.

Will continued in this vein for an hour and a half. Every time he tried to stop, the Prince urged him on, even whispering in his ear something to say. A couple of days later Will played polo with him, and went to a party given in the Prince's honor by Josh Cosden, Oklahoma millionaire oilman who had been snubbed by the Newport set. "The Prince, his entourage in attendance, was graciously pleased to favour Lord Josh Cosden, Gusher in Extraordinary to the Oklahoma Oil Wells, and Lady Cosden, at a Sunrise party at the Castle Petroleum," kidded the Syracuse *Telegram* on September 5, 1924. "Viscount Will Rogers, Knight of the Lariat, Master of the Follies Garter and Commander of the Bucking Broncho, didst make Hys Royale Highness Laughe full sore with Quips of Chorus and Cactus."

It helped Will's humor "to have a Prince up his sleeve," and he made full use of it both on the stage and in his column. "The Boy went down to see Mr. Coolidge the other day . . . Some combination . . . A Mr. Young live 'go-get-'em' and just Cal settin' there . . . Wonder what they talked about? . . . Just like to know . . . It would be like me spendin' an evening with the Pope . . . At that the Pope probably has a sense of humor and he and I could swop jokes . . . But can you imagine the Prince telling Cal an English joke? . . . We can't even tell him an American one yet. . . . Up there at the club I just told the Prince that if none of the jokes got across down there before 'Silent' Cal not to worry at all."

The report got around that Will had bought one of the Prince's polo ponies. "Now that was a mistake . . . I bought one but it was for Mr. Flo Ziegfeld's little daughter . . . I have some alleged Polo Ponies of my own . . . In fact I have the best string of $40 Polo Ponies in the world, so you would hardly get me giving $2100 for some old Pony just because he belonged to the Prince . . . I wouldent give $2100 for the Crown, much less a horse . . . But anyway he was a very nice, gentle, real kid's Pony, and little Patricia Burke Ziegfeld was tickled to death with him . . . She had him following her all around, even into the house, and that made a big hit with Mr. Ziegfeld . . . I told him, 'Why, the barns that Pony has been used to, you're lucky to get him to go into your house.' . . . That's the reason I did not get one . . . I knew I could not support one in the manner in which it had been accustomed."

On October 4 Will reported that "the Prince has left us. You often hear the expression that a person has left the country flat, but in this case the Prince left the country asleep. Long Island went to bed the night after he left and has not woke up yet . . . A lot of men got their Wives back much shopworn from dancing."

Lord Louis Montbatten, the cousin of the Prince who accompanied him on the trip, termed Will "the most intelligent and delightful man in America." Some newspapers were not so kind. Will knew exactly what he was doing. "The publicity that accrued from the Prince was the means of my using it for weeks in the *Follies* and in my newspaper columns. Later, I used it when I went out on my lecture tour. I could not have bought it for a million dollars." Will looked for "the real follies" elsewhere. A few weeks after the Prince left, J. P. Morgan sailed for Europe. "They made all the photographers and reporters get off the boat, and they put in a special gangway for him to go on the boat . . . He had dozens of Policemen and Officers to see that no one molested him by even looking at him . . . Then you will hear some Bonehead say we have no classes in America like they have in England . . . Why, if J. P. Morgan was as democratic in just one day as the Prince of Wales is every day, Morgan would feel like he was slumming."

Late in October a bit of excitement was stirred up in the presidential campaign when a troupe of actors were entertained at breakfast by President and Mrs. Coolidge. This brought on a senatorial investigation at which a witness testified that for $50,000 he could have bought jokes on the stage in favor of any candidate. "Gosh, I wish I had known that . . . I would have been rich by now . . . If I had collected for every favorable joke I have told about each one of the Candidates, and if I had been paid for all I have told against each one of them, I would be a Millionaire . . . I generally give the Party in Power more digs because they are generally doing the Country the most damage, and besides I don't think it is fair to jump too much on the fellow who is down."

Will had his rules for what an actor should say. "An Actor has as much right as any one else to have his Political beliefs . . . He pays his taxes and is usually a good Citizen . . . But I don't think he should carry any Campaign propaganda into his stage work, either for or against any Candidate . . . He has no right to use his privilege as an Actor to drive home his Political beliefs . . . We are paid by an Audience to entertain them, not to instruct them politically . . . Distribute your compliments and knocks so when the audience go out they don't know where you are politically . . . Then if you want to, as a Citizen, go hire you a Hall and tell 'em what you want to . . . You are a Citizen and not an Actor then . . . I knock 'em all, and occasionally boost, when they do something meritorious, which is rare . . . So here is hoping that the stage will not, as some papers seem to think, pollute Politics . . . The worse we could do for it would be to help it . . . Besides this contamination of Actors dining in the White House won't happen again soon, as there is no Campaign until 1928."

Will insisted there were no real issues in the elections. The Democrats dusted off the League of Nations, but the Republicans countered with the World Court. The Ku Klux Klan bobbed up but just as the Republicans were "having their Campaign literature printed to denounce, somebody shipped some sheets north to Indiana, New Jersey, Maine and a few other places. So that Issue was chased up the same tree." Of course lower taxes were promised but that had been promised by every president "since Washington crossed the Delaware in a rowboat. But taxes have gotten bigger and their boats have gotten larger until now the President crosses the Delaware in his Private Yacht." Prohibition was no longer an issue but a commodity. In desperation, Coolidge announced "his policy will be Common Sense. Well, don't you know the Democrats will claim that too? Besides, Common Sense is not an Issue in Politics; *it's* an affliction. . . . Davis announces that his Policy will be Honesty . . . Neither is that an issue in Politics . . . *It's a miracle* . . . and can he get enough people that believe in Miracles to elect him? . . . The only thing I see now that they are divided on is the question, 'Who will have the Postoffices?' . . . No matter how many parties you have, they are all fighting for the same thing—SALARY . . . You abolish salaries and you will abolish Politics and Taxes."

On the eve of the election Will announced that "the fellow who don't know how it is going to come out should not be allowed to read a paper and probably hasent. Some of the County Offices, Sheriffs and Road Commissioners may be in doubt up to election time but Coolidge don't even have to stay up to hear the returns." When it was over he said, "The Republicans mopped up, the Democrats gummed up, and I will try to sum up." It happened because Davis foolishly ran on honesty. "It was too radical for Politics. Mr. Coolidge ran on Common Sense and the returns showed that there was 8 million people more in the United States who had Common Sense enough not to believe that there was honesty in politics." Will was able to report "much jubiliation on the part of the disgracefully rich, or Republican, element of the entire country . . . *They are celebrating the country's return to Wall Street.* It never had such a two weeks in the history of that ancient and honorable institution as she is going through now . . . They had to keep open 20 minutes longer and all the papers made headline stories of the fact . . . Just think of the inconvenience of the Brokers having to wait for 20 minutes after 3 P.M. in raking in more dough . . . It is one of the worst personal hardships that the Exchange has gone through in years . . . And stocks, why, anything that looked like a stock would sell . . . People would wire in, 'Buy me some stocks' . . . The Broker would answer, 'What kind?' The buyer would wire back, 'Any kind; the Republicans are in, ain't they all supposed to go up?' "

The stampede was on that ended in the debacle of October, 1929, and there was nothing to interfere with it. The business of government was to keep the government out of business—that is, unless business needed government aid! This was the absolute "norm" of "the return to normalcy" and Coolidge was its high priest.

Will was at his peak as a *Follies* performer and had perfected his technique in his newspaper column so that it would as nearly as possible resemble his verbal humor. In December, 1924, when a collection of his columns came out in book form as *The Illiterate Digest* (dedicated to William Beverly Winslow), Don Herrold, in the *Herald Tribune* of March 1, 1925, stated that Will "has no important people complexes. The President of the United States is a feller, and the Senate is just a bunch of guys. Not even the 'Follies' girls get his goat. He weaves, first of all, a spell of comfort. His chewing gum is comforting. His rope is comforting. His grammar is comforting. His rambling is comforting. He turns the New Amsterdam Theater into a grocery store, and for $5.50 a throw we sit once more around the cracker barrel. . . . He employs the same method in his newspaper writing." John Crawford in the *New York Times* added: "Those seemingly offhand remarks of his are neatly timed to coincide with some spectacular stunt with the ropes. It is not until afterward, when you try to tell it to some one who has not been to the *Follies* that you realize two things: he puts it over in the only language and intonation possible and he said something keen and penetrating and true."

According to Crawford, Will's newspaper columns and *The Illiterate Digest* were "goods off the same bolt. He is down in black and white where you can watch him closely and go back and see how he did it. He is just as unsophisticated in doing his work as a Russian toe dancer, and one job is as intricate as the other. He gives the impression of being simply the crossroads general merchandise store talkers of a continent rolled into one man. . . . He knows just what he wants to do, just how he wants to do it, and he does it. He is an expert satirist masquerading as a helpless, inoffensive zany."

In the *Herald Tribune* for January 5, 1925, Frederick F. Van de Water warned that "when censorship, having finished with books and newspapers, starts on him [Rogers], we shall sell our liberty bonds convinced that the time of national dissolution is at hand. Congress should endow him. He is its greatest guaranty of safety. . . . He says things about Congress that the rank and file of the populace would say if they only knew how. The nation has to thank Mr. Rogers for the fact that, so far, no one has launched a royalist party in America."

18

"Follies, Follies Everywhere"

WILL WAS INCENSED AT THE FLAGRANT LACK OF PREparedness in the country for no better reason than to lower taxes. "When I tell you that if I was running the Government and would raise rather than cut taxes, you know now a Comedian was crazy." Will would do this both to pay off part of the national debt and to spend more on our national defense. He screamed in anger when "80,000 people paid 800 thousand dollars to see twelve rounds of 'wrestling' between two alleged fighters, Wills and Firpo. . . . On the same day they received 150 thousand Dollars cash for 36 minutes embracing while we released on half salary General Pershing who had spent 42 years fighting for his country. . . . So if you are thinking of taking up fighting as a career, why, be sure and FIGHT FOR YOURSELF INSTEAD OF FOR YOUR COUNTRY. He was retired on half salary and a Coolidge speech. My Lord, can't our Government do something for a man who is not a Politician?"

Will's anger at this was as nothing compared to what happened when our newest and finest battleship, the *Washington,* was sunk by the navy in compliance with the Washington Disarmament Conference agreement. "All the ammunition left over from the war was shot into it, and those big guns on the *Texas* they were using, they only are good for so many shots during their lifetime . . . So we spoiled the Guns of our next best boat trying to sink the best one . . . The Secretary of the Navy said that the treaty required this vessel be sunk or broken up but permitted us the privilege of using it as a target before sinking. . . .

This was one of the advantages accorded us by the Treaty! . . . If I thought a year I could not think of anything as ridiculous as that . . . ONE OF THE ADVANTAGES GAINED WAS TO USE OUR OWN BOATS AS A TARGET . . . Maybe that is why we are going to hold another conference, so we can get permission to shoot at the rest of them. . . . The Secretary says he don't want the other Nations to find out how we did it . . . Don't worry, they are not going to sink any of theirs . . . Sinking your own Boats is a military strategy that will always remain the sole possession of America . . . The other countries sank blueprints. . . . Anyhow, if there were to be no more wars, why did the navy need practice in sinking ships?"

On December 27, 1924, Will recalled that it was the twenty-first anniversary of the Wright Brothers' historic flight. "People wouldent believe that a Man could fly, *And Congress don't believe it yet.* America celebrated the occasion by letting one aviator out, and deciding to keep the other three . . . Our Air Service is waiting for Congress to make an appropriation to have the Valves ground and the Carbon removed from the Engines."

Will was equally derisive of the farmer who expected relief from a Republican administration. He had a good laugh when Coolidge went to Chicago to speak on the problems of the farmer before the Saddle and Sirloin Club. "If a farmer ever come in there to that Club, they would arrest him for poaching . . . I bet you that it is a lot of Commission men at the stockyards and Doctors, and Lawyers that maybe have an old horse . . . They put on their Breeches and ride every Sunday Morning . . . They ride a Pan Cake Saddle, then come in and eat a Sirloin Steak . . . that has been shipped by a Rancher 15 hundred miles . . . then invite the President to deliver a message to the Farmer. . . . Coolidge said that the future of Agriculture looks to be exceedingly secure . . . It is, most of it by at least two mortgages."

Another chuckle came in February, 1925, when Judge Elbert Gary, chairman of the board of United States Steel, and John D. Rockefeller, Jr., journeyed to Washington to offer Coolidge advice on the enforcement of the Prohibition laws. "You remember a few years back and this country had to pass a special law called the Anti-Trust law aimed primarily at those two Trusts, the Oil and the Steel . . . Now if they have to pass a law to curb men like that, they are not exactly the men to give confidence to the rest of our Nation in regard to keeping the law . . . Getting them to arrange our Morals would be like appointing me to teach English at Harvard."

In addition to the Ku Klux Klan, other "special privilege" organizations and movements were springing up over the country. The one that irritated Will the most was composed of members calling themselves One Hundred Percent Americans. Will decided to rope one of this "breed" and pick his "brand." He was startled. "The first thing I find out there ain't any such animal . . . This American Animal I thought I had here, you might find in any Country . . . He is not a politician . . . He is not a 100 Percent American . . . He is not any organization, either uplift or downfall . . . He has no decided faith or religion . . . From his earmarks he has never made a speech, and announced he was an American. He hasent denounced anything . . . It looks to me like he is just an Animal that has been going along, believing in right, doing right, tending to his own business, letting the other fellow alone."

Will rode around on his horse and found "hundreds and hundreds of exactly the same marks and brands." Those that claimed special status were "a lot of Mavericks and strays." One particular group, "a bunch of Bobbed Haired men gathered in Madison Square Garden," a few days before had denounced everything on earth. "A Kid 14 years old delivered such a tribute on Lenin that he made it look like George Washington or Abe Lincoln couldent have caddied for him." At the same time millions of other "kids of the same age were playing and leading a normal life."

Will's advice was to give to the "Mavericks a hall or a box to stand on and say 'Sic 'em; knock everything in sight and when they have denounced everything from Bunions to Capitalistic Bath Tubs, then they will go home, write all week on another speech for the following Sunday. It's just like an exhaust on an Automobile . . . No matter how high priced the Car, you have to have an exit for its bad Air, and Gasses. It don't do any particular harm, *unless you just stand around behind smelling it all the time,* but who would want to follow a Car to smell its exhaust when you could just as well be in the car Riding?"

Anyway, Will was not worried about such manifestations. "No Element, no Party, not even Congress or the Senate can hurt this country now except for temporary setbacks . . . But they don't mean a thing in the general result . . . Nobody is making history . . . Everybody is just drifting along with the tide . . . If any office holder feels he is carrying a burden of responsibility, some Fly will light on his back and scratch it off for him some day. . . . Congress can pass a bad law and as soon as the old normal majority find it out they have it scratched off the books." It would be the same for the big men, on up to John D. Rockefeller. "When he is gone and Gasoline raises 2 cents, and all expenses paid and the Estate settled we will kick along. . . . *Even when our next War comes we will through our shortsightedness not be prepared, but that won't be anything fatal. The real energy and minds of the Normal Majority will step in and handle it and fight it through to a successful conclusion."*

Will's writings were attracting so much attention five of his articles had been read into the Congressional Record by March, 1925, as representing a typical American view on important public affairs. When he was quoted once more another member arose and objected "to the remarks of a Professional Joke Maker going into the Congressional Record." Will's hackles came to instant attention. "Now can you beat that for jealousy among people in the same line? . . . Calling me a Professional Joke Maker? . . . He is right about everything but the Professional . . . *They* are the Professional Joke Makers . . . Read some of the Bills that they have passed, if you think they ain't Joke Makers. . . . I could study all my life and not think up half the amount of funny things they can think of in one Session of Congress . . . Besides my jokes don't do anybody any harm . . . You don't have to pay any attention to them . . . But every one of the Jokes those Birds make is a LAW and hurts somebody, generally everybody . . . 'Joke Maker!' . . . He couldent have coined a better term for Congress if he had been inspired . . . If I had that Guy's unconscious Humor, Ziegfeld couldent afford to pay me I would be so funny. . . . Of course I can understand what he was objecting to was any common sense creeping into the Record . . . It was such a Novelty, I guess it did sound funny . . . I have engaged counsel and if they ever put any more of my material in that 'Record of Inefficiency' I will start suit for 'deformation' of Character . . . I don't want my stuff buried away where Nobody ever reads it."

In April, 1925, Will journeyed to Washington to be the guest speaker at the Gridiron Dinner along with President Coolidge. Speaker of the House Nicholas Longworth took him to the White House to meet the President. "Well, the way Mr. Sanders rushed us in to the President's private office you would have thought we were going to swing Alabama and Mississippi to the Republican column. . . . Of course I don't lay all the credit to Nick for a prompt entrance, because the President knew I was not looking for an appointment to a post-office, nor did I want a friend transferred in the Army, nor a wife pardoned out of jail."

Before going to the President's office, Longworth had made Will a bet he could not make Coolidge laugh.

"I beg your pardon," Will said, as he was presented, "I did not catch the name."

Coolidge burst out laughing. They chatted for a moment. Back in his office Longworth paid his loss.

"I never heard him so talkative," Longworth commented.

"Why, he was just as agreeable as an insurance agent," Will replied.

In his speech Will did a simulated dialogue between himself and someone else on an imagined visit to Coolidge and his report on it. "Did he ask you to eat with him? . . . You bet your life. . . . Did he charge you? . . . No, he dident. I took him down some Maple Syrup and homemade Sausage. . . . Does he still like Flap Jacks in the morning? . . . Better than ever, he has gained 10 pounds. . . . I've been reading about them Breakfasts he has Down there, where he invited people to eat Breakfast with him. . . . Yes, every time he wants to get even with some one he invited them to eat Breakfast with him . . . It's at eight o'clock and they have to stay up all night, he is a Slicker, he is. . . . Do you think this Government Business is worrying him, you know it has killed more than one President? . . . What's Cal worrying at on 75 thousand a year? . . . How about this Hobby Horse with a Ford Engine in it that he Gallops around the bathroom on every day? . . . He showed it to me, it's the funniest thing I ever saw, it ain't got any head or tail. . . . He must have got it from the Democratic Party . . . I guess he did, he got about everything they had . . . Is it on account of giving more exercise that he uses it instead of a real Horse? . . . No, it's on account of Oats, You give him a real Horse that wont eat and he will take it. . . . So you don't think he is worrying too much? . . . No New Englander ever died of Worry at 75 thousand a year. . . . Do you think all these Tales they tell about him being so close will hurt him? . . . They are the greatest thing ever happened to him, and he knows it. . . . Ford dident try to stop Ford Stories, did he? . . . Is them Politicians kinder scared of him? . . . Why, he is getting 'em so he can stand on the banks of the Potomac and throw sticks in and have them Senators swimming out and bring 'em back."

Gene Buck sat next to General Billy Mitchell. "I'd like to take him up in my plane tomorrow," Mitchell said. "Do you think you can arrange it?"

"I think so," Gene said.

It was this flight that sold Will on aviation. Perhaps it was the drama in it. "You have been with me on the last flight I will make as a Brigadier General," Mitchell told him after they had landed. "Tonight at twelve o'clock I am to be demoted to a Colonel and sent to a far away Post where, instead of having the entire air force at my command, there will be seven planes." [1] This was the reward for General Mitchell's valiant fight to convince the "brass" of the army that aviation would be the backbone of the fighting in the next war. "We ought to have the greatest air defense in the world," Will told his *Follies* audience, "we got more air. The Army and Navy are like a couple of old Hens fighting over one Chicken. . . . France gave Mitchell the Croix de Guerre, England the Order of the King, and the Republican Administration gave him the Order of the Tin Can. . . . He is the only man ever connected with the high up Aviation in Washington that used the Air for anything but Exhaling purposes."

A few months later, still carrying on his fight, Mitchell accused the army and navy of incompetence, negligence and conduct approaching treason in their contempt for aviation. He was court-martialed and suspended from the service for five years. Will was at the trial. "In the stillness of shocked dismay Will Rogers ran to Bill and threw his arm over his shoulder," General Mitchell's sister, Ruth, wrote. " 'The people are with you, Bill,' he cried. 'Keep punching.' Years later Bill

[1] Will's account of this historic flight may be found in the *Autobiography*, pp. 112-114.

said, "That was a moment of tenderness—the one moment of that nightmare which I shall never forget." [2]

In May, 1925, Will journeyed to Oklahoma for the funeral services of his sister, Maude, who had joined May in death. "I am out in Oklahoma, among my People, my Cherokee people, who don't expect a laugh for everything I say. . . . Death dident scare her. It was only an episode in her life. If you live right, death is a Joke to you as far as fear is concerned. I have today witnessed a Funeral that for real sorrow and real affection I don't think will ever be surpassed anywhere. They came on foot, in Buggies, Horseback, Wagons, Cars and Train, and there wasent a Soul that come that she hadent helped or favored at one time or another. Some uninformed Newspapers printed: 'Mrs. C. L. Lane, sister of the famous Comedian, Will Rogers.' It's the other way around. I am the brother of Mrs. C. L. Lane, 'The Friend of Humanity.' And all the honors that I could ever in my wildest dreams hope to reach would never equal the honor paid on a little Western Prairie hilltop, among her people, to Maude Lane. *If they will love me like that at the finish, my life will not have been in vain."* This is the Cherokee in Will speaking.

Saddened by the death of Maude and homesick for his family he had been away from for nearly a year, he longed to leave the *Follies* and spend the summer in California. There was an extra inducement in addition to his family. He had bought acreage in the Santa Monica Mountains, enough for a small ranching operation, and was considering building there. Some of his activities and plans were outlined in a letter to his son, Jim, then eleven years old:

Say I went over yesterday to the Palace Vaudeville house to see two Kids, a Boy and a Girl about Sixteen and seventeen, the Blatherwick Children, the Boy said he rode your Pony in a Beverly Hills Horse show and got a Prize. I guess it was Billy. They do a dancing and Roping turn and sure are good, they do some fine dancing, taps, and the Girl is a Contortionist and Dancer. They have an awful keen

[2] Ruth Mitchell, "My Brother Bill," *Reader's Digest,* May 1954. Shortly before he died, in 1936, General Mitchell predicted an air attack on Pearl Harbor "some fine Sunday morning." After Pearl Harbor, he was voted the Medal of Honor and, posthumously, given the rank of major general.

act, *so you all get to practicing.* We will have a lot of roping this summer, Fancy and Calf and Goats. We will get us some Goats and keep 'em up in a small pen all the time then turn 'em loose in the round corral and rope 'em on a horse in there. The old Show is going on fine, we have standing room every night. . . .

Jim, I wish you would look after some things down there at the Ranch for me. Get 'em to build the back part on the big barn, Uncle Lee will know what we had talked of. Get those Logs put around the outside of the east hill. Then if they have time move the old Stables, and fix up a Bunk House out of part of the old one. Now see what luck you can have on this. Did you do anything about the Tennis Court at home, and I want one of those Polo Racks with a Saddle on it out in the Riding ring to hit a ball off of, like Tommy Hitchcock had on Long Island. There is nothing to do only put a high carpenter's bench Horse there with a Saddle on. . . .

You tell your Mammy she better be rolling out of there. Old Dad is getting lonesome. Tell Bill they opened another Midnight Frolic up at Ziegfeld's last night. The first one dident go over so big (what with Prohibition on) so they opened another one. He has been trying to get me to go up there. But I don't want any of it. He has got Whiteman's Band and the Duncan Sisters this time.

Well, how's Mary and her Pack of Hounds? We will get us three or four old Curs this summer at the Ranch, shepherds, and hounds. Well, so long. Love to all. Sure will be glad to get home.

Dad

Although Will's newspaper column was bringing in more and more income, it was not enough to take care of his obligations, nor did its writing use up his boundless energy. Besides, much was taking place in the summer of 1925 that needed verbal lambasting. The most ridiculous of all was the famous Scopes evolution trial in Dayton, Tennessee. "If I was either of those men," Will commented on Bryan and Darrow, "I wouldent spend the best years of my Chautauqua life trying to prove or disprove my ancestry. . . . The Lord put all these millions of people over the earth . . . They don't all agree on how they got here, and 90% don't care . . . But He was pretty wise when He did see to it that they all do agree on one thing, and that is the better lives you live the better you will finish. . . . Coolidge is a better example of evolution than either Bryan or Darrow, for he knows when not to talk, which is the biggest asset the monkey possesses over the human."

During the summer a move got underway to draft Will as governor of Oklahoma. "Are you people getting jealous of Dayton, Tennessee?" he wired. "Even with me as Governor we can't compete with them in humor. But if you are serious, and want a Governor, I will come home where I belong anyway. However, I must have election guaranteed before I give up my present job. Wire best offer at once. Yours for Honesty in Politics." He followed this a few days later with another wire. "I havent voted in Oklahoma for years because you never had the right men up for me to vote for. Put me up for Governor and see how quick I'll come home and vote for myself. That's what Bryan used to do and look where he is today. If a campaign fund has been raised, kindly send some on now. I have two Democrats here I can bring out with me. Yours for a better Governor's mansion."

Bryan won the jury's verdict in the Scopes trial and lost it in the regard of the people of the country. He had put so much of himself into it that the strain proved fatal. Shortly after returning to his home in Florida he died. In his habitual manner Will rushed to his defense. "This country has hundreds of thousands of people who feel that they havent a soul now who will conscientiously fight for them, the plain people . . . Bryan had no Vice-President to carry on . . . So here's good luck to you, W.J., you were a novelty among politicians . . . You were sincere . . . You might have missed the White House, but you dident miss the hearts of the plain people."

A good picture of Will, who was about to leave the *Follies* to go far afield among the "plain people," was painted by the columnist George Matthews Adams:

Today I sat a few feet from Will Rogers and saw him chew his gum and spread his jokes and "gags" so thick that they blew up the room with laughter—the kind of laughter that covers your face with tears. If anybody else had said the things he said in a serious mood they would have sent for the police. But Will Rogers never hurts people. But he packs wisdom there just the same. He is one of the wisest thinkers in America. He is tremendously much of all that America is.

I studied the face of this man. It is set in rough cast like Lincoln's. His eyes are unusually keen. He has a fine nose and a splendid chin.

His mouth is rather large so that he is able to get great smiles from it to permeate into the great crowds that roar from his jibes and also to facilitate his ability to throw his gum in unison with his cowboy rope. Will Rogers' hands are big, bold and brown. His forehead is very striking in its suggestion of intelligence. *But the biggest thing about this American product is his heart.* Will Rogers is loyalty and squareness to the core.

I grow several inches in stature every time I hear Will Rogers and my food digests perfectly for weeks afterwards. Will Rogers is one of the big institutions in America.

Will was now ready to go out and meet "the regular bird" in the far-flung spaces of the United States.

19

"Meetin' the Regular Bird"

FOR A LONG TIME WILL HAD CHERISHED THE IDEA OF DOING his act all over the United States. "I kinda like the idea of an' ol' ignerant cowboy goin' out an' talkin' to the college professors an' all," he said. "An' another thing, these big shows that I been in right along they don't never get down to Oklahomy because they're too darned expensive, so the boys down home they've never seen me on the stage." An offer to do this came from Charles Wagner, one of the most successful lecture and concert managers, after the singer Mary Garden assured him Will would be a great success.

Shortly before Will signed a contract he agreed to speak at the second annual Radio Industries Banquet, on September 1, 1925, over a 26-station hookup. At four o'clock that afternoon Paul B. Klung, executive chairman of the National Broadcasters' Association, was handed a note while presiding over a meeting. "Rogers has run out on us," it read. "What shall we do?" Covers were laid for 1,500 guests at the Commodore Hotel, publicity had been sent across the country, and the banquet was to start two hours later. A hurried conference was called and a delegation sent to interview Will, some of them maintaining he had pulled out because he wasn't to be paid. He was coming off the stage at a *Follies* matinee when they arrived.

"We'll pay you anything you want," the spokesman for the group said.

"It isn't the money," Will explained. "Before agreeing to do the broadcast, I signed a contract without reading it to go on a lecture tour and there is a clause in it forbidding me from doing this sort of a show. My manager has ordered me not to do it."

This, of course, was an entirely different situation. Will sensed the predicament of those concerned. "I'm a showman," he said, "and I'll figure a way out of this. I'll be there as I agreed."

Will handled it in his usual dramatic fashion. "I have been forbidden to make a speech to you over the radio by my manager for whom I am going out on a lecture tour. . . . He figures if you ever hear me once, you would never want to hear me again . . . But I wanted to explain to you in person that it is a bigger disappointment to me than to you because when you make an Actor keep his mouth shut he is in pain . . . It's like an after-dinner speaker going to a Banquet and not being called upon. . . . I am sorry, my Radio friends, you can't see me as those here at the Tables are privileged to do . . . Hearing me is nothing in comparison to seeing me . . . Well, I will try and describe myself to you . . . I am six foot five and a half inches horizontal, weigh 195, all brawn, color of eyes, azure blue, hair jet black and wavy, features strong, complexion perfect, hands two, waist before meals, 34, home, Hollywood, politics, highest bidder, religion—wait till I look around here before announcing, oh, yes, Jewish."

Will told them he did not know what the dinner was for unless "somebody stung some Sucker with a new Radio set and said 'let's have a dinner.' . . . It would have been more useful if they would get rid of the static. . . . A dinner is all right for those of you here, but how about the millions that tune in and all they hear is . . . whistle—ooooooooooo—whistle. . . . Another reason for my not appearing is the Presence of a Senator and my contract says I am not allowed to go outside and appear in inferior company . . . There is a Moral Clause where we are judged by our Associates. . . . I see where the French are coming over to pare down the debt . . . They are bringing their own Champagne . . . My Lord, if they will just put in half a dozen extra cases they can auction them off and pay the debt at once . . . They want to see about funding the debt . . . Funding is called over here 'renewing the note.' . . . See where the dirigible Shenandoah fell . . . As usual the blame will be layed on someone who perished on it . . . That's why they can never fix a blame in any accident where no one lost their lives, there is no one to lay it on. . . . Parachutes were the first thing invented and they seem to be the only thing they don't use ... Parachute jumps from Balloons were done at every Country Fair even when I was a kid ... I was a big old Rube kid ... am yet ... and was standing around a Balloon ascension in Vinita, Oklahoma, when they asked all to help hold her, and of course if there was a rope around I had a hold of it, and they cut her loose. Uncle Clem's Boy, Willie, come offul near becoming an aviator at the early age of 14 ... At that it jerked me high enough that my feet caught in a House of David Disciple's beard."

Will concluded by saying, "I will be in every town, I don't care where you live, I will be there. Talk about seeing America first, I may not see it first but if I live I will see it, this winter, all of it."

This appearance, contrary to Charles Wagner's fears, gave Will thousands of dollars' worth of publicity. He also used his newspaper column to let the people know he was coming among them. "I am making what the politician calls a swing around the circuit ... But I am not like the politician who wants to 'meet the voter' ... I want to meet the taxpayer, and that is very seldom the voter ... I am going to give to you the real inside dope on our hired help in Washington." Will also warned the men that there would be no *Follies* girls in the show so they would not be able to use him as an alibi. Will had a personal reason. "A man only learns in two ways, one is by reading, the other by association with smarter people ... I don't like to read, and one can't find that kind of associates in New York ... I am going out among the people whom New Yorkers call Rubes ... But these people I am going out among are the people that just look at New Yorkers and laugh. I am going to be able to tell my readers something besides 'Who Ann Pennington is going with this season' and 'What millionaire has been in the front row four nights running.' I am out to see how America is living, I mean the ones that don't go home and brag on what everything cost 'em ... I am meeting the regular bird ... the one that lives in his town; stays in his town; is proud of his town; he offers no apology for not having seen last year's *Follies,* or any other year's. ... I want to find out what he was thinking about; what he was reading about."

Sociologically, he explained that he was going from a "tax exempt audience to Tax Payers," from "footlights to rostrum," "from bootleggers to boot wearers," from "National Follys to State Capitol Follys," "from Town Topics to Town Halls," in his graduation from the "Follies" to the "Concert" and from 'legs to lectures.' "

Will opened at Elmira, New York, in a church, and from there went from city to city, doing a modified *Follies* routine tailored to local conditions. He talked to all kinds of people—editors, reporters, barbers, bootblacks, members of all professions, read the local papers, and from all this gleaned bits of interesting material to add to his comments on national men and affairs. "Never look at a town with one of its prominent citizens and think you have seen the place," he soon learned. "You have seen just what he wants you to see. I always get me a Taxi and go prowling." Many of the cities, also, Will had known intimately in his vaudeville days. His newspaper columns helped bring out people to his lectures and his personal appearance in cities helped bring new newspapers for his column. It was a two-bladed ax.

As Will approached Oklahoma on his tour his pulse began to beat faster. "Everyone has deep in their hearts the old town or community where they first went barefooted, got their first licking, traded the first pocket knife, grew up finally and went away thinking they were too big for the Burgh . . . But that's where your old heart is . . . There is a million towns in the United States, and a million communities. Pick out a million people and ask 'em where they would rather be thought of well, and they will say, 'Back Home.' "

This came to Will in full measure as he brought his act into his home state. He played five towns in the state on this tour—Bartlesville, Ponca City, Enid, Oklahoma City and Tulsa—and "they laughed at me MORE than New York or London or Omaha. I was never as happy and independent in my life. I have been over 20 years trying to kid the great American Public out of a few loose giggles . . . Somebody had to act the fool, and I happened to be one of the many that picked out *that unfunny business of trying to be funny* . . . After acting the Fool all over the World and part of Iowa, I have been home, and they seemed glad to see me, and they laughed at me . . . My HOME FOLKS thought I was good. . . . I know lots of Theatre goers that will disagree with them . . . But what do I care for them? . . . What do I care for anything? . . . The old home State and old home Town and the old ranch people I was born and raised with, I got by with them . . . Twenty years of doubt and expectation of just what they would think of you . . ."

At Tulsa, closest to his home range, Will had "such an audience" as he had never before encountered. The local manager asked him if he minded if people were seated on the stage. They did not even leave him a chair for his dressing room. "They were packed in, standing at the back, and sitting in the aisles and over three hundred seated behind me on the stage . . . Two little girls come up and gave me a great floral piece . . . Well, I had never received flowers before in my life, and that did stick me . . . Well, after it seemed like ages, I got started, and they laughed, and they would laugh so long it would give me time to think of another one . . . Well, they kept on seeming to want more till I did two hours and fifteen minutes . . . That's a minor league record for a Monologist."

The next day Will went to Claremore. "They had asked me to get there by noon. . . . These Folks, after driving home from Tulsa after the show away late that night, got up the next morning and the Ladies cooked everything in the World good that was ever put before anybody at a meal, and stacked tables and tables full of it in the American Legion Hall. When I drove over and got there at twelve o'clock they had the band out and everybody in Town was there to welcome me, and we went in and had this wonderful meal that if Peggy Joyce had to pay for it, she would have had to send out and get a new husband."

Will's first lecture tour, eleven weeks in all, ended in Boston on December 14, 1925, at Symphony Hall. "Can you imagine me appearing at Symphony Hall in Boston? . . . Me, with my Repertoire of 150 words (most of them wrong) trying to enlighten the descendants of the Cod." Everybody seemed to like it "except one old boy there that thought we were 'desecrating' their Temple of Art by causing laughter in it.[1] We had been out 75 nights all over the country and hadn't received an adverse notice. Well, this old Soul is a Musical Critic and having a trained musical ear, why, naturally my jokes were 'Off Key' most of the time. 'My diction was poor' and my 'selections of jokes were extremely bad.' " In general, Parker thought Will's jokes had

[1] H. T. Parker who wrote as H.T.P.

lost their sting and that he would do well to return to the *Follies*. "In short, Parker, when you looked me over you were 'slumming.' The old Tradition got to working ... But you unconsciously paid me a *Bear* of a compliment when you said, 'Will is a small town Actor.' You bet your life I am small town ... I am smaller than that ... I am NO town at all, and that is what I am going to stay is Small Town." Will ended by saying that next time he came to Boston "you are the first man I am going to look up, and I bet you we have a good dinner and we will kill off that old Indijestion of yours, and I will have a lot of good Jokes against Yale, and maybe Harvard will have won a football game and you all will be feeling good ... But give me credit for one thing, Parker, *wasent that English of mine the Worst that was ever spoken in that Hall?"*

The critic for the Boston *Globe* was kinder to Will. "He came on stage dressed in a blue, double-breasted suit, soft shirt, knitted tie and black shoes. Nothing on the stage but a piano. He slid over behind it, putting his hands over his face, grinned at the audience as much as to say, 'Is it all right for me to come out here to try to entertain you?' " A wave of sympathetic understanding flashed over the faces in the audience.

"Aw, say, cut down some of the lights, will you?" Will asked someone backstage, and they were immediately dimmed. He threw back the lock of hair over his face. "You know, this isn't put on. Imagine me in Symphony Hall. O Lawdy, how did I ever get in here?"

A smile flashed out, appealing, ingratiating. "It just got you," the critic said, "and you smiled back. Great guy, this Rogers."

Although Charles Wagner had sent a male quartet, the De Reszke Singers, along, believing that a monologist could not entertain an audience for an evening, Will certainly could have done so. He was good enough to earn over $82,000 in eleven weeks, more than twice as much as he would have been paid in the *Follies*. Equally important, he enjoyed his lecture tours immensely.

Will spent Christmas with his family in California, and in February, 1926, began his second series in Florida, this time taking Betty along. He opened at Miami at the height of the season with a celebrity-studded audience that rivaled any *Follies* first night. It included ex-Governor James M. Cox, George Ade, Kin Hubbard, Senator Borah,

Gene Tunney, O. O. McIntyre, Carl Fisher, Gene Buck, Bernard Baruch, John Golden, and scores of others. "For two hours and twenty minutes, save for a fifteen-minute intermission, he held that audience completely spellbound and sent it away exhausted from laughter," O. O. McIntyre wrote. "The ovation at the finish was the longest I have ever heard, and someone began yelling for Mrs. Rogers, knowing she was in town. Finally, Rogers came to the edge of the stage, held up his hand for silence and whined, 'Mrs. Rogers won't come out in public. You know she has never cut her hair'—an anti-climax that catapulted another convulsion." [2]

A definite part of Will's routine in his lecture appearances at this time was the treatment Mexico was receiving from the Administration in Washington in the worst throes of "dollar diplomacy." "We come nearer running Mexico than we do New York State . . . If they pass a law they have to send it up to Washington to have it O.K.'d by our State Department . . . If they want to say an American can own land down there but not the mineral rights, why we say its unconstitutional . . . For the love of Mike, why don't we let Mexico alone and let them run their country the way they want to? . . . Americans go there only to make money . . . Not one in a million ever becomes a citizen . . . If a country is good enough to make money in, it's good enough for you to become a citizen of . . . So if you go down there, don't start yapping for America to protect you . . . If you ain't man enough to protect yourself, they better put you in a crate and keep you in the kitchen. . . . See where we demand that Tia Juana and Mexicali, in Mexico, should be cleaned up . . . It seems that they sell drinks down there right over the bar . . . You just pay for it by the drink, and not by the bottle, and they Gamble right there before your eyes . . . They claim this is ruining the Youth and the Manhood of this country . . . The Americans *don't* want to drink and gamble . . . They just go over there to see the mountains, and make these scheming Mexicans grab 'em and make 'em drink, and make 'em make bets, and make 'em watch the race Horses run for money."

Early in April, as Will's second tour drew to a close, he received a wire from Wagner that he had booked him into Carnegie Hall. In

[2] O. O. McIntyre, "Our Will," *Cosmopolitan,* October, 1931.

spite of his successes elsewhere and Betty's assurances, Will was doubtful of this appearance. "My goodness! I commenced to get scared," he admitted. "I wired Wagner, 'Don't take a chance on New York. We been doing pretty good and we better let well enough alone.' " Wagner, who later stated that Will offered him $1,000 to cancel the engagement, wired that it was too late.

Once again Will had an audience studded with celebrities. "I never thought we would meet in Carnegie Hall, and I am just as out of place as you are . . . Ziegfeld don't even know where it is . . . The *Follies* audience think it and the Museum of Art and the Library are secret Fraternity buildings . . . Ziegfeld would look for me to do a joke on Ann Pennington's knees . . . It's a different environment altogether . . . I don't know how I ever remained among all that smoke and uncovered flesh. . . . I once thought Carnegie Hall was one of those things Uncle Andy Carnegie imposed on every good-natured town, but by calling it a 'Hall' New Yorkers might think there was some sort of dancing, or something worthwhile, and go in . . . I learned later it was a tremendous building with three or four rings of Boxes around it like the Pictures of a Spanish Bull Ring . . . I also learned it was for singers and piano players, chiefly foreign. . . . Well, this art thing kinder worried me . . . I had never by any stretch of imagination been associated with it . . . I thought I ought to be playing the Columbia Theatre on 47th street, instead of Carnegie Hall . . . I was explaining my predicament to Walter C. Kelly, 'the Virginia Judge,' who you all know as America's best story teller. . . . Walter says, 'Well, Will, you have one novelty to recommend you up in that Hall . . . You will be the only short-haired Guy that ever played that joint.' "

It was time now to comment on notables. "See since I left New York, Jimmy Walker has become Mayor . . . That's good news to me . . . Jimmy always sits next to me at the Speaker's Table and gets my Cocktail . . . He is the most versatile man I ever met in my life . . . No matter what the Dinner, whether it be Jew, Catholic, Ku Klux, Negro, or just plain Ticket Speculators, why, Jimmy always brought them to their feet with the announcement that he was one of their race and that up at Albany the whole Legislature had been against them, and if it hadn't been for him, they would have been sent out of the country as undesirable Aliens . . . Jimmy is truly a Cosmopolitan . . . I have seen him weep at the plight of the Hebrews in Russia, meet him at a Friendly Sons of St. Patrick—apparently friendly—and he proposed a toast 'Down with the Jews, they are seeking their own political machine in New York.'... I predict Jimmy will be the best Mayor New York ever had... He can promise the drys enough that he won't be thought out of place among New York's other 90 percent... He believes in the political machine—that is, 'always leave the victim enough to get home on.'... Tammany never took a man's last Dollar ... They always figured with that he would earn another stake and soon be ready for them again."

Other celebrities came in for a ribbing. "Al Smith's the most popular man the Democrats have... Some have suggested that he would be elected if he changed his religion and turned Protestant... I think it would do more good if he would keep his religion and turn Republican.... Been reading about the marriage of Ellen Mackay to Irving Berlin... Her father opposed it... It would be a good joke on her Father if he made her a living, wouldn't it?" [3]

On the evidence of Fannie Hurst, Will took no chances on those he would kid that evening. "I received an invitation to attend," she wrote. "Enclosed were seven or eight box seats. I assembled a party of friends, and attended. After 15 minutes of delightful rambling, Mr. Rogers abruptly announced that he was going to introduce to the audience some of its members. He began his work around the horseshoe, beginning, as I remember, with Minnie Maddern Fiske, on to Theodore Roosevelt, Jr., until he approached my party. In my group there happened to be a beautiful young girl. When he called out my name in introduction, I pushed the bewildered young thing to her feet to take the bow for the applause that followed. 'Well, Fannie,' he said, 'I like your Benda mask.' " [4] Fannie forgot something else that Will said: "There's Fannie Hurst... Her and I write... We both write the 'Worst Stories I Have Heard Today.' She got 50 thousand for hers. She is writing for the Movies. Thank goodness I have never got that commercial."

It was reported at the time that Will's appearance in Carnegie Hall

[3] Irving Berlin not only made her a living but bailed out her father when the depression came.

[4] New York *Journal*, November 8, 1935.

brought so many tremendous rounds of applause that shortly thereafter contractors began work on the rear wall to strengthen its foundation.

In Will's newspaper column for April 24, 1926, appeared this interesting statement: "Well, I have seen America from bottom to top. I had lunch yesterday at Philadelphia with Mr. George Horace Lorimer, Editor of the Saturday Evening Post, and I am going over to Europe for the Post. I am really going to represent President Coolidge. You see, he hasent a Col. House to run over and fix things, so that is what I am to be. I want to get away about the middle of May. I want to catch Mussolini while he is going good, and before some better shot gets in their work. I am also going to Ireland and see what's keeping them so quiet, and if they are really happy, and also go into Germany and Russia and Spain."

Will and the entire Rogers family were to have a busy and interesting summer.

20

"Coolidge's Colonel House"

MARK TWAIN'S *Innocents Abroad,* PUBLISHED IN 1879, colored the thinking of Americans concerning Europe for half a century. It was the most publicized trip to Europe until Colonel E. M. House went during World War I as President Wilson's confidential adviser. Now Will Rogers was to give the lowdown on that Continent with the humor of Mark Twain and the high seriousness of Colonel House. The audacity of his going as "The Self-Appointed, Unofficial Ambassador of President Coolidge"—in short, to be his "Colonel House"—caught the fancy of the American people at once. It was to have a fantastic coverage with his weekly articles in the *Saturday Evening Post,* then at the height of its success, in his weekly columns in newspapers, and in his Daily Wire which he began while there. In addition, he was to do a series of travelogues that would be flashed on the screens of motion-picture theaters with his titles and comments. For these, an army of cameramen trailed him around to the various countries he visited.

Before leaving on his trip, Will journeyed to Washington to secure letters from various government officials and influential people (Vice-President Dawes, Senator Borah, Alice and Nicholas Longworth, congressmen, and officials in the State Department). He did not bother to call on President Coolidge, "I was very busy," but their understanding was "so antiseptic that I knew there was no use in talking over personally what I am to accomplish on this trip. I would have come up to your house, but I dident know whether you had any help or not, and keeping up a big house when you have always lived in a small one is quite a problem. Then I dident know but what you might charge me." Instead, he had lunch with Vice-President Dawes. "He was asking anxiously about your health. I had to disappoint him by telling him you were never better in your life. He just sighed and we went on talking about something possible." Will told Coolidge he was to sail on the *Leviathan* and not to bother Congress about another appropriation. "Will do as you say and draw on Mellon if necessary."

In his next letter Will informed Coolidge about the trouble he had getting a passport when he was asked for a birth certificate. "In the early days of the Indian Territory, there were no such things as birth certificates. You being there was certificate enough. While you were going through the trouble of getting a birth certificate, you could be raising another child." He was then asked if he was in Who's Who. "My Lord, I am not even in the New York Telephone Directory, and that is the most ordinary collection of humans ever assembled in America." His problems were solved when the general manager of the *Follies* vouched for him. "Why, sure, I knew your Father well," Will has him saying, "and I know that he was an American. Not 100 percent ones like the Rotarray's and Kiawanians and Lions, but enough to pay taxes."

On the *Leviathan,* accompanied by Will Jr., now fourteen, Will never let the fun stop. "Everybody received Flowers and Fruit and Candy . . . If you sent anything it hasent been sent to my stateroom yet. But there is a lot of Bundles and Baskets up there yet that havent been delivered, and I will give you the benefit of the doubt till I find out otherwise." It was signed "Col. William Rogers." "Certain news is so urgent that it is necessary for me to cable you, so from time to time you may get something, 'Collect.' I hope there is an appropriation to cover this, look under the heading, 'Ways and Means.'" One of the urgent ones was for Coolidge to "kindly find out for me through our intelligence Department who is the fellow that said a big Boat dident rock. Hold him till I return. Wilrog. That's code name for Will Rogers." A couple of days later he reported that the ocean was "as meek and docile as a Republican Convention."

Another source for comedy on the boat was a commission headed for a Disarmament Conference in Geneva. "They don't suspicion that I am going for you too . . . and I never let on . . . I just sit tight and listen." Since the commission was composed of army and navy personnel, Will was relieved. All that the army would give up was their "spurs" and the navy wouldent sink the boats from under them. "Just take your case, Calvin . . . Can you see yourself attending a Conference to cut down Presidents? . . . You might attend for propaganda purposes, but you can bet your last maple tree you wouldn't cut yourself down any or abolish the office. . . . It's all right to send Deligates and do a million and one things that the Public thinks amounts to something, but between us we know the whole thing is a lot of Apple Sauce . . . It's like, for instance, you meeting a Democrat and saying, 'I am glad to meet you.' Well, that has to be done . . . It is a custom . . . But, of course, get right down to it, you are not glad to meet him at all . . . You are just human and wish there wasent such a thing. . . . Well, I am going to Geneva and see this thing . . . There will be 21 nations there, and outside of England and France and America, the others will take it serious." Will also confided that he had made our delegates promise not to scrap "the old Republican tugboat," the presidential yacht, *Mayflower*. "So don't worry about it this summer. We will keep it till just before the Democrats get in next time and scrap it then. Be a good joke on them." [1]

Before the *Leviathan* reached Southampton the passengers were warned of an impending general strike in England and given the choice of going on to Cherbourg, which most of them did. "I am on a mission . . ." the President's Colonel House insisted ". . . and I want to show I am a soldier in the service of my country just as much as if I had on a uniform . . . I am going on to London regardless of danger, because when one devotes themselves to a cause, why, what is danger? Your devoted accomplice, Col. William Rogers."

Among his "gripful of letters" Will had one from Lady Astor's "Sister and Brother-in-Law in New York, Mrs. Chas. Dana Gibson." He had tried to assist Mrs. Gibson in getting more people to adopt babies, but it had been a failure for him. "I offered three little heathens if anyone would take them, and didn't get rid of a one of them. You can always get rid of children easier if the people don't know who

[1] So it proved. President Hoover decommissioned it.

the Parents are." Lady Astor gave a dinner for Will at which he sat next to Sir James Barrie. "I think he is a Syndicate writer, or Strip Cartoonist, or Paragrapher, or something like that . . . I think he had a Cartoon running called Peter Pan, and a little Comedy Character called the Little Minister. They were afterwards made into books . . . We broke even, for neither one of us had read anything the other had written." Will Jr. later told him about Sir James's books.

Sir James was so impressed with Will that he invited him for a talk after dinner. The apartment overlooked the Thames embankment and from a stone balustrade Sir James pointed out where Dr. Johnson had once lived and a place where Boswell stood while prying tidbits out of the recalcitrant doctor. During the war Sir James had watched the air raids from the balustrade as the German pilots had followed the course of the Thames. Bernard Shaw lived right across "the alley," and Sir James promised to introduce Will to him when Shaw returned from a trip.

"He is a great personality," Will commented on Barrie, "so quiet and soft spoken you are afraid you will scare him away if you speak. For once I knew enough to keep my mouth shut and let him talk."

It was not the general strike that upset Will; it was coffee. "Personally, I will be willing to sign over my share of the debt settlement for just one good cup of Coffee . . . Dam it, we give 'em good tea, and all we demand is reciprocity . . . Look into this, Calvin, will you? . . . Next to Farmer's relief, it's one of the big problems that is confronting us today . . . For every Fool American is coming over here this summer, and it's the fool vote that we have got to watch out for . . . I would even drink New Orleans Coffee if I had it now."

Will of course visited the House of Commons and the House of Lords. "The members of the House of Common are just as rude as Congressmen . . . They holler at each other and interrupt and yell . . . They are just like a bunch of old Nesters elected to congregate at Oklahoma City, or Austin, or Bismarck every year . . . The welfare of their country generally felt a little heavier around their November Fourth." As to the House of Lords, nothing excited them except "a raise on the tax on liquor or land."

In addition to helping Will meet prominent people in England, Lady Astor triggered off the next giant step in his career. On May 18,

1926, he sent this cable to the *New York Times:* CALCOOL, *Washhousewhite:*

> London, May 18—Nancy Astor (which is the non de plume of Lady Astor) is arriving on your side soon. She is the best friend America has here. Please take care of her. She is the only one over here that dont throw rocks at American tourists.
>
> WILLROG

This was the first of Will's Daily Wires ("Will Rogers Says") that became an integral part with the bacon or ham and eggs for breakfast of millions of Americans. It appeared on the first page of the second section of the *New York Times,* and on the front page of most other newspapers.

A few days after his arrival in London Will and Will Jr. were sitting in their hotel room reading when the telephone rang. Will Jr. answered it.

"It's for you, Dad."

"Who is it?"

"It's General Trotter, the equerry to the Prince of Wales."

Will got on the phone.

"The Prince would like to see you," General Trotter said. "Can it be arranged?"

"When?"

"Right away."

"Where does he live?"

"The York House. Come on over."

Will was ushered into a house that "looked about like an Oil Millionaire's home in Oklahoma, only more simple and in better taste . . . The whole place would have got lost in what Long Islanders humorously call their Main Saloon."

The Prince came out to greet Will and shook hands with him "like a Rotary Club President that has been coached in the best way to make friends." He had on a very plain brown suit which was like most others only it fitted.

"Hello, old-timer," Will greeted. "How are you falling these days?"

"All over the place," the Prince replied, grinning. "I got my shoulder broken since I saw you last."

"We will have to get you better jumping horses," Will said.

"Oh, they were splendid horses," the Prince protested. "They were just unfortunate in falling, that's all."

They moved into the Prince's living room where there was a fire in the fireplace, a table with a lot of books on it, and pictures of the royal family. For an hour they talked on various subjects, ranching in Canada, polo, Mussolini, and various people they both knew.

"Well, boy," Will said, as he was leaving, "the old latchstring will sho' be hanging out for you anywhere you want to light in America. If you feel that you are not appreciated over here, come on over. The President will give you a room in the White House and you can be a sort of Social accomplice of his."

In a full report to "his President," Will ended his comment prophetically: "Just between you and I, Calvin, he don't care any more about being King than you would going back to Vice President again."

On June 5 Will and Will Jr. took a plane from London to Paris. The flight was smooth over the Channel but they hit France "and somebody hadn't paid their taxes" for they hit so many "airpockets, or Chug holes" it reminded Will of motoring in Virginia. He attempted to keep his stomach under control and did so until they arrived over the airfield, when the pilot "just dropped the last 500 feet" and with it went Will's "original cargo of food."

Will passed on to Coolidge his analysis of what was wrong with France. "They won't pay their taxes . . . They have what they call an income tax, but it's practically voluntary . . . You turn in what you want to, and they never investigate it to see if it is right or not . . . Doctors or Lawyers who are earning millions of francs a year turn in their earnings as fifty or a hundred thousand francs . . . It looks to me like the only way you will ever get any money for taxes out of them is to deduct it at the source some way . . . If you ever let them lay their hands on it themselves they will never pay it . . . And, oh, Boy, how they are hating us! . . . If somebody gets a bad cold it is laid to the grasping nature of Money-Loving America . . . It's the old Gag (and nations are no different from individuals) you loan a man money and you lose his friendship . . . And the funny part about the whole thing is you go anywhere like the races, or the Opera, or any place where the prices are high, and you will see it packed and people spending more money than they do over home . . . I have dodged more big Rolls Royces and Fiats over here than I ever saw big Cars at home . . . There is lots of them over here got plenty of dough, but they are not giving any of it to their Government to pay their taxes. . . . The whole debt problem in all these Countries reverts back to one thing, and that is our coming into the war . . . They say we come in for one thing and we say and know that we come in for another . . . In other words, *what we did has never been appreciated* . . . They think we should have declared war on Germany two days before they started to march into Belgium . . . So I hope these people that are always trying to fix the world will learn something out of this, STAY AT HOME AND TEND TO OUR OWN BUSINESS! DON'T ATTEND A CONFERENCE, NOT EVEN A LUNCHEON!"

On the lighter side, one day while in Paris Will encountered Dr. Nicholas Murray Butler on the street.

"Oh, hello, Will," Dr. Butler said. "What are you doing over here?"

"The same as you, Doc," Will replied. "Let's have another."

In Rome, after much diplomatic maneuvering, an interview was set up with Mussolini. In his report to Coolidge Will said he had made up his mind "to go in a-grinning" and to treat Mussolini "like he was no more than Hiram Johnson." Accompanied by a man from the embassy dressed according to protocol, Will wore his old blue serge suit. Mussolini met them "at about the 4th green, shook hands smiling, and asked in English 'Interview?' I said, 'No Interview.' " Will informed him through an interpreter that he was not interested in how the dictator ran Italy, but he wanted to find out if Mussolini was "a Regular Guy." Mussolini conceded that he was and then asked Will what had impressed him the most in Italy. "It's the amount of automobiles meeting and neither one ever knowing which side the other was going to go on and yet nobody ever gets hit, and the amount of Bicycles ridden, and I never see anyone fixing a puncture."

This seemed to take the wind out of Mussolini's sails as he had expected the usual stock answer: the great improvements that had taken place in Italy under his dictatorship. "We have very good bicycle tires," he finally salvaged out of it.

Will talked over the atrocious "castor oil" treatment Mussolini and the Black Shirts had used on political prisoners, and kiddingly offered to buy the recipe to use on the United States Senate. When this was translated for Mussolini, he nodded his assent.

"I am going to Russia," Will said.

"Oh, Russia. You take recipe to Russia, very good for Russia. I give you free for Russia."

"What do you think about disarmament?" Will asked.

"Why, do you want me to laugh?" Mussolini answered, winking at Will. "We disarm when England disarm on sea and when France in the air and on the land. So you see we never have to disarm."

Will came away from the interview feeling, as many did this early in Mussolini's career, that the dictator might be of some help to Italy. "I was surprised as much as I was the first time I run into you, Calvin, and I come out thinking you wasn't as sober as you make yourself look. . . . It's a wonderful thing to meet people and see about how they all are about the same when you can get their minds off their Life's work. . . . Now, You, Mr. President, with your last year's suit, your speech on Economy while stepping off the *Mayflower,* your little quiet yet just as effective way of getting what you want done . . . Well, that and you would be just as funny to Italy as Mussolini is to us . . . He gets up in Public and tells Austria and Germany what to do . . . You have Kellogg send Mexico a note telling them what time to quit work that day . . . He comes into the House of Deputies and tells them the measures that shall be put through . . . You have five or six Senators for breakfast and the same thing happens. . . . You see, everyone of us in the world have our audience to play to . . . We study them and we try to do it so it will appeal to what we think is the great majority."

From Italy, Will and Will Jr. went to Monaco, where everything appeared in apple-pie order. "There is no Government, there is nothing to interfere with anything or anybody—just that little old wheel rolling for them all the time . . . I will keep looking, Calvin, but this is going to be hard to beat."

From there it was on to Spain, where Will interviewed its dictator, Primo de Rivera. As the largest neutral during the war, Rivera was incensed that Spain was not permitted to become a member of the League of Nations. "They won't let you in because you are not ready for war," Will told him. He informed Coolidge that "they all feel the same about this League and Disarming and World Courts and all that stuff . . . They feel like England and France runs the whole thing and they don't want anything to do with it . . . There ain't any of them got any use for the other one, and you can't blame 'em for looking out after themselves. . . . Say, you give them as much ocean on each side of them as we have, and then on the two ends a Mexico and a Canada, they might start disarming with you too. . . . There is a lot of things talk good in a speech, but you come to working it out when you are up against hundreds of years of previous wars and hatreds, they don't pan out."

In Madrid Will and Will Jr. attended a polo game and met the King of Spain, who was one of the players. "They rode him off the Ball, they run into him, they jumped him, and he was giving as well as taking. . . . There was times, Calvin, when it dident look like there was going to be any more Royalty left than a Rabbit . . . What I don't understand is why he has such poor horses. . . . Say, listen, if I was King of some Country, and we was having a polo game, I want to tell the world that William would prance out astride the best steeds that entered the Arena that day."

Back in London, Will Jr. decided he had had enough of it and wanted to return to California. Will cabled Betty, who decided to bring over the other two children, so they could keep Will company, and for Will Jr. to return home. The evening before he sailed, Betty wrote, "the two of them divided their neckties and trophies, and he packed his bag. Later, they went to a café for dinner. Will, who was feeling low over the loss of his traveling companion, suddenly felt a boyish arm steal around him and it remained there during the meal." These moments meant more to him than meeting kings, princes and dictators.

As soon as the rest of the family arrived, Will joined them for a vacation in Switzerland. They then returned to England, where they set up headquarters, and a few days later Will flew to Russia. The first lap was to Berlin by a regular airline and there he took a Soviet plane for Moscow. "I constituted Russia's sole aerial immigration that day . . . As I got in the plane, I commenced to think of all the jokes I had told about Russia, and then I remembered that people had remarked to me they didn't know why I had been given a passport when it was so hard to get one. . . . Then I thought, maybe they know about some of the jokes and this Aerial Cossack is about heading off to Siberia with me." However, the plane landed in Moscow right on the minute. Everybody had advised Will not to take anything with him as everything would be carefully inspected. "I tore up a handful of cards people had given me of people in Russia to look up for them . . . I took in only one suit and four extra shirts, as I was told if I had too much I would be suspected of capitalistic tendencies . . . I even dident get a shave for a few days, figuring I might pass as a native . . . I dident even have my Shriner pin or my Elk Tooth Fob on. . . . I went into a little customs office . . . They took my passport, give it a peek, and shoved it back to me . . . I opened my grip . . . He got one peek . . . dident even feel in there . . . As for looking to see what you had in your pocket or on your person, why, I could have had a bass drum in each hip pocket, a Saxophone down each leg and two years' collection of Congressional Records in my coat pockets."

Except for a guide in the Kremlin, Will was allowed to prowl where he pleased—to nearby villages, to Leningrad, and to talk with anyone he met. The *New York Times* man, Walter Duranty, arranged interviews with minor officials, but not with Leon Trotsky, whom Will particularly wanted to meet. "I told the official the nature of the visit was to find out just what kind of Guy Trotsky was personally, and that I did not want any state secrets . . . I just wanted to see did he drink, eat, sleep, laugh and act human, or was his whole life taken up for the betterment of mankind." The official shook his head. "We are a very serious people," he explained. "We do not go in for fun and laughter. In running a large Country like this we have no time for appearing frivolous. We have a great work to perform. We are sober."

Although Will insisted that his humor had a sober side, that he did not "expect Trotsky to make faces for him, or tell him the day's latest joke," he did believe the "man must have some very good human qualities, and on account of being in America at one time, he had always been of special interest to us." The answer was still "nyet." "I wanted to tell him, Calvin, that what they needed in their Government was more of a sense of humor and less of a sense of revenge. I saw this old boy wasent strong for me X-raying Trotsky . . . But I bet you if I had met him and had a chat with him, I would have found him a very interesting and human fellow, *for I have never yet met a man I dident like.* When you meet people, no matter what opinion you might have formed about them beforehand, why, after you meet them and see their angle and their personality, why, you can see a lot of good in all of them."

This is the first appearance in Will's writing of this expression, "I never met a man I didn't like," and in its context here, as in his comments on Mussolini, it takes on an entirely different meaning from that usually accepted.

Will left Russia with a contempt for those who, in their wishful thinking, marked off "the Russian experiment" as a fantasy which, like the walls of Jericho, would come tumbling down when the High Priests of Capitalism blew their trumpets. Although the Red army was "without a doubt the seediest-looking layout I ever saw in my life," somewhat resembling "a Chamber of Commerce in Evening clothes lined up to meet Queen Marie," he warned "you take those ignorant old Boys and give them some real training and they are going to be kinder hard to clean."

By this time Will was a confirmed air voyager. "If I don't have an Airship to travel in, I think I am walking."

In London Will found a full schedule awaiting him. He made a motion picture, *Tip Toes,* with Dorothy Gish and Nelson Keith. This finished, Charles Cochran begged Will to go into his *Review,* which was sagging much as the 1916 *Follies* had done. Both he and Betty had grave doubts, as Americans had never before been so unpopular in England. "Will was fond of his old friend," Betty wrote, "he couldn't refuse. He did his usual stunt and spoke frankly about the war debts, French finance and the British general strike, as well as about America's big problem, prohibition." A critic in *Everybody's Weekly,* under the heading "Go Home, Will Rogers," blasted:

Naturally, we of the audience assumed we would see this quaint Yankee in some of his inimitable drollery. Nothing of the sort. To the amazement and, I may truthfully say, consternation of the bulk of the audience, we were compelled to listen to a diatribe which mainly consisted of gratuitous insults aimed at Great Britain, France and

Belgium. . . . It seems incredible that a man like Cochran, whose sympathies should be with this country and with France because he has earned much bread and butter from each, should let his platform be used for foolish American propaganda of this sort. . . . His remarks on the present European crisis are insulting, insolent, presumptuous and in the worst of taste.

Other critics, in fact most of them, had different reactions. James Agate in the *Sunday Times,* July 25, 1926, commented that "our visitor got at once on such magnificent terms with his audience that to leave the stage was out of the question. For the better part of an hour the older generation of this revue knocked at the wings in vain. The house wanted Mr. Rogers and got Mr. Rogers, not the actor and comedian, but Mr. Rogers the American citizen and unofficial ambassador. No actor accustomed to feeling the pulse of an audience could have remained unconscious of so spontaneous and genuine a success. . . . Mr. Rogers frankly and generously accepted our recognition of him as an exceptional person belonging to an exceptional race. . . . A superior power had seen fit to fling into the world, for once a truly fine specimen, fine in body, fine in soul, fine in intellect. . . . As a piece of comic improvisation, his forty minutes' harangue was a feat of something approaching genius." After reading this over, Mr. Agate added another touch: "Probably I am doing the comedian in Mr. Rogers an injustice by suggesting that he did act. On reflection I am convinced that he did act, and act very well. . . . The experimental zest which will not accept tradition, or what other people have done, the approachableness masquerading as antipathy to race or joy of mongrelism, that Frankness which only the stupid will mistake for bad manners, the charm which seeks to disguise itself under a show of impudence, the obvious sincerity of the belief in world salvation through 'boost' and 'pep'—I am not persuaded that this clever presentation of the whole American pose can be accomplished with less of the actor's art than goes to make up, say, the canny *camaraderies* of Sir Harry Lauder. . . . America's Prime Minister of Mirth—to borrow Mr. Robey—enchanted both in matter and manner."

Instead of sending Will home, as the one critic had suggested, if nothing else a "standing room only" house caused Cochran to keep Will on as long as possible. When after four weeks Cochran handed him a blank check, and told him to write his own figure, Will tore it up. "The fun I had doing it is enough pay," he said.

Betty enjoyed his performance too. "It was such fun sitting out in front watching the reaction of the audience while Will was talking," she wrote. "Sometimes it was a bit slow, but his ribbing was almost always accepted good-naturedly. Several times I noticed groups of Americans sitting up stiffly, as if fearful that their countryman was going too far."

Will eventually met George Bernard Shaw at a stag dinner given at the Pinafore Room of the Savoy Hotel. Among other guests were G. K. Chesterton, Sir James Barrie, Lord Dewar of Scotch whiskey fame, Lord Derby, Sir Harry Lauder, Sir Thomas Lipton, and Michael Arlen, who had come from Paris for the affair.

Will and Shaw took to each other at once. "Why, they told me you were an Indian," Shaw greeted him. "I don't see any feathers." Later Shaw commented, "I had no suspicion of how important the man is. Really, he is as important as I am." Of Shaw, Will said, "We've got a good deal in common. We both know the world is wrong, but we don't know what's the matter with it."

Early in September Will and Betty went to Ireland. In Dublin, before a capacity house that included Eamon de Valera, Will played a benefit for the victims of a devastating theater fire at Dromcolliher. Before leaving Ireland Will stated in his Daily Wire: "Am bringing family greetings from Dublin to every man on the force." Later, in his travelogue on Ireland he commented that "it keeps a small nation busy raising the police force of the world." [2]

Late in September the Rogerses sailed for "Cuckooland" on the *Leviathan*. Secretary of State Charles E. Hughes was on board, and remembering his skit in the *Follies* of 1922, Will ducked his head shyly when introduced to him. "I dident know whether to hold out my hand to shake or cover up and protect myself," he confessed.

[2] This travelogue was entitled, "Roaming the Emeral Isle." The one on Holland was called "The Windmills of Holland" and the country was labeled "the lowest country in the world and it comes nearer being on the level than any other country." In "getting the dirt in Paris," he said, "they call it the Latin Quarter because nobody speaks Latin and nobody has a quarter." Rome was "the cradle of civilization" but it "looks like the rockers have been lost." Its "decline" was due to its having senators!

But in Hughes he was dealing with a different man from President Harding. They played a benefit on board the ship for the victims of a Florida tornado in which Hughes was the comedian and Will the diplomat. Over $40,000 was raised, a tidy little sum, as Will told the audience, "that would give the French heartburn when they learned it had escaped their clutches."

As the *Leviathan* approached New York City, crack reporters in special launches came down the bay to interview Will. "The United States looks perfect," were his first words, "and this Guy Hughes, he's the funniest man I ever listened to. He became so human on this trip he was almost common. Two more trips and we'd have made a Democrat of him—that's how common he is getting. We settled Russia last night and are now planning a Washington conference."

The consensus of the reporters was that after returning from the most publicized trip in history, despite hobnobbing with kings, princes, dictators and other notables, Will was the same unspoiled Oklahoma cowboy who had come to Madison Square Garden in 1905.

Will had returned from his famous trip but as yet had not made his reports to the President. Nor did he know if he would have a chance to do that. "Who knows what Mr. Coolidge reads or does for that matter?" he said later in answer to the question as to whether the President had read his "Letters." But Will was not the one to cavil. He immediately wired the President that he had arrived and asked for an appointment to make the report. By return wire came an invitation to come immediately. "Mr. Sanders, the President's secretary, met me at the train himself and we drove in a White House Limousine. We got to the White House and there sit Mr. and Mrs. Coolidge. Now there was the President of a country a third as big as Russia and more than half as big as China. He and the Leading Lady of our land waiting dinner on a Lowbrow Comedian. I had heard so much in Politics about them going to do something for the common people and this was the first practical demonstration I had ever witnessed of it."

"Well, what sort of crooks and horse thiefs did you meet today, Mr. President?" Will asked.

"The Cabinet," Coolidge replied.

There is no record of what Will and the President talked about.

He had fish hash for dinner ("and when you get to fish hash that's about the most in economy in food") and his room in the White House "was so big you could have roped a steer in it. Great big bedstead—the biggest, widest bed I ever saw—a regular Brigham Young affair."

Will unquestionably discussed Europe's attitude toward the United States. "You know of course, or perhaps have had it insinuated to you, that we stand in Europe about like a Horse Thief. . . . Now I want to report to you, Mr. President, that that is not so. It is what you call at Amherst 'erroneous.' We don't stand like a Horse Thief abroad . . . Whoever told you we did is flattering us. We don't stand as good as a Horse Thief . . . They knew what you were sore at them for." On the other hand, none of the European countries loved each other either. "I would just casually admit that we were a band of highbinders, and were just waiting to get England or France up a back alley and knock 'em in the head and get what little they had left. . . . Then as the discussion waxed warm about Uncle Shylock, I would say, 'Will you enumerate to me, in their natural order, the number of nations that you people call bosom friends?' " He found that the chief misunderstanding came over the contribution of the United States to winning the war. "If we thought that they really at heart and conscientiously appreciated what we did in the war, I think there would be no trouble getting the debt cancelled in full . . . It has been quite a while since they were saved, and they are not willing to admit they were saved . . . *The only way we could be in worse with them was to help them out in another war.*"

Will's conclusion—certainly colored by his Cherokee blood—was that the action of nations should be the same as that of "real" individuals. "Let 'em go through life and do and act as they want to, and if they can't gain friends on their own account, don't let's go out and try and buy them."

As to a war threat from Mussolini, Will told Coolidge that at the moment he was not going to start fighting, but would when he had to "to get more territory for his people . . . He is not going to plunge for the next couple or four years, for he knows the plunging is not good . . . But he has got something that all Europe is jealous of, and that is the breeding system. They are raising 500,000 boys a year.

. . . You can have all the advanced war methods you want, but nobody has ever invented a war that you dident have to have somebody in the guises of soldiers to stop the bullets. . . . If he lives long enough and Italy's marksmanship don't improve, he will have to go out hunting and bring in some more land where his people will have room to live."

In October, 1926, when his *Letters of a Self-Made Diplomat to His President* appeared, John Carter wrote in the *New York Times,* October 31, 1926: "America has never produced anybody quite like him, and there has rarely been an American humorist whose words produced less empty laughter or more sober thought. . . . His interviews with Mussolini and Primo de Rivera help to bear out his contention that European disarmament is a farce, and that the League of Nations is a piece of eyewash designed by some of the big powers to manipulate affairs to their own advantage. Perhaps Will Rogers has done more to educate the American public in world affairs than all the professors who have been elucidating the continental chaos since the Treaty of Versailles."

Woodrow Wilson's summation of Will as being "both humorous and illuminating" is borne out by this judgment. Another man was reading Will's reports with astonishment. "In addition to my deep appreciation of his humor," Franklin D. Roosevelt commented, "the first time that I fully realized Will Rogers' exceptional and deep understanding of political and social problems was when he came home from his European trip in 1926. While I had discussed European matters with many others, both American and foreign, Will Rogers' analysis of affairs abroad was not only more interesting but proved to be more accurate than any other I had heard."

Will was not content to rest on his accomplishments. The day after his report to his President he began another lecture tour.

21

His Honor, the Mayor

WILL'S EUROPEAN TRIP ENRICHED HIS MATERIAL FOR BOTH his lecture routines and his newspaper writing, both his weekly column and Daily Wire. He could speak with the authority of one who had observed on the spot and not merely from newspaper reports, which of course he continued to read. "I can tell you this will be a dignified Lecture . . . It is not going to be one of those Jazz and Apple Sauce affairs that I had last year. . . . I have watched the effects of President Coolidge being serious, and how they always think if a thing is serious it must be so . . . So me for the Deep Wrinkled Brow stuff from now on. . . . See where England is holding their fleet maneuvers in Italy's front yard . . . That is what you call courtesy among nations . . . If individuals did that kind of thing to show how strong they were in front of someone they dident like somebody would shoot 'em and everybody else would cheer. . . . Suppose Tunney exercised in front of your window every morning for no reason at all? . . . Our gunboats are all in the Chinese war, our Marines have all landed in Nicaragua, Kellogg is sending daily ultimatums to Mexico and Coolidge is dedicating memorials to eternal peace. . . . What right have the Marines got settling an election in Nicaragua? . . . I thought our Army and Navy was supposed to never enter politics . . . Evidently they have to go to South America to get into politics. . . . Lord, if it wasent for writing letters to Mexico, we wouldent need any Secretary of State. . . . I bet if they'd have an egg-laying Convention in Czecho-Slovakia, and if we could find out where it was, we'd have more delegates and lay less eggs than anybody else there."

Nor were local affairs neglected. "The Farmers won't get any relief until Wednesday—maybe late Wednesday. . . . *Every official in the Government and every prominent manufacturer is forever bragging about our 'high standard of living.' . . . Why, we could always have lived this high if we had wanted to live on the installment plan.*"

Betty had gone on to California to help get the children enrolled in school, and Will Jr., now approaching his fifteenth birthday, was enrolled at Culver Military Academy. On October 8, 1926, Will wrote him there that he had got a big laugh out of the one Will Jr. had pulled in Venice about "No cats in the alleys." At another place they had got a tremendous laugh when "old Bruce [Bruce Quisenberry, Will's nephew and manager on the road] come on to move the Piano for the roping and as he was pushing it off, why, the whole thing fell apart, and there was Piano scattered all over the stage. You know how scared Old Bruce can look, well, you should have seen his eyes. He thought he had ruined the whole show. Well, I wish it would happen every night. I got a dozen laughs out of it." The old showman even knew how to take advantage of accidents.

In a Canadian appearance, John McCormack came to see Will perform. Afterward he came backstage. "He liked the act very much but thought the quartette was Rotten and that they should be shot for not singing popular songs," Will confided to Will Jr. "That if he could afford to go out and sing Popular songs, why, he dident see why they should object. He told the manager about it and I hope it does them some good. They can pick out the poorest songs there is, it looks like." The next night Will went to hear McCormack sing, "to help make a crowd. If I hadent there would have been one more standing room."

Will gave some advice to Will Jr. on a boil the boy had which he probably picked up on his travels or back in the Indian Territory. "Eat a nickle's worth of raisins every day and you won't have any boils. If you do have any, get 'em on the outside where you can get at 'em."

By October 26, 1926, with cold weather coming on, Will had worked his way to Spartanburg, South Carolina, where he again wrote to Will Jr. This letter, he hoped, would get to him "about on your birthday . . . Now you are fifteen years old, that's getting pretty old. But you got a long way to go yet and the way you prepare for it now will help you out a whole lot in how you will be fixed for it all through the trip." Will enclosed $15. "That's a dollar for each year. Just look what you will get when you get to be 75 or 80." There was advice for the boy also:

You just stay with it there and work hard and do everything you can to improve yourself and do all you can to help out your health and make you strong. You are now slender and not very husky but that will come if you will just work on something that will develop you all the time. . . . Mama was crazy about the school and the way you are doing there. . . .

I am fixing so I can go home with you Xmas. Just what day do you get out? . . . We will break in the Polo field with a big game and a Barbecue and Roping. . . . I will be back in Oklahoma next week. I am going to get a lot more land and fix up the old ranch place. There is the place you will like when we get it going good. We will make a big stock farm out of it. I have quite a few cattle now and some sheep, and 250 Goats. We are going into the goat raising business. . . .

Now you want to get set for that Cavalry after Xmas. Find out all you can about it. I think you ride bareback a good deal. Find out just what they use and we will fix one out home. Old Rowdy, the good gentle Polo Pony, would be big like the horses you have there and you could start in on him and that would give you some confidence by the time you started. . . .

We are mighty proud of you sticking it out there when a lot of the big rough ones couldent stand it. Good night, son, merry Birthday. In a couple more years you will be riding the first string and I will have to take the old easy ones like Dopey and Dodo. You will be up on Rooster, and Scout, and Fleetfoot. Jim will have Penny and Bootlegger and Cheyenne. Lots of Love, from Old Dad.

In the fall of 1926 Queen Marie of Rumania paid a state visit to the United States for "the usual purpose" and furnished grist for Will's satirical mill. The country went into a tailspin as individuals, groups and cities vied for the honor of entertaining her. "Don't ever say America ain't Cuckoo over Titles and Royalty," Will commented. "There are dented marks on the iron fence in front of Buckingham Palace where American noses have pushed, watching to get a glimpse of the King if he happened to drive out."

The description of the various functions given in the Queen's honor, particularly a dinner given by the President, offered ripe pickings. "Just listen to what the Queen had on [taking a newspaper from his pocket] . . . 'a regal diadem circled the shingled locks of this modern Monarch, inherited from Grand Duchess Maria of Russia' . . . That's one the Bolsheviks dident get their paws on . . . 'The Crown dripped great pear shaped pearls' . . . Boy, get that . . . the Crown dripped Pearls . . . Say, I bet it dident drip them long around in front of Calvin . . . He would run and get an old wash pan or something to catch 'em in . . . Either that or he was the first one down there looking around in the morning. . . . 'These harmonized with the ropes of Pearls she had around her neck' . . . Holy suffering Cats! . . . Are they roping with Pearls now?. . . I roped with everything, but I never tried a Pearl rope . . . 'Her White Gown glittered with Sequins' . . . Watch the Society Dames dive for the Dictionary . . . America will all be trying to trade Fords for Sequins now. . . . 'Its decolletage was round in front' . . . I think this reporter must be speaking of the dress and not the Sequins . . . 'It ended in a low V at the back from which hung a train! . . .' My Goodness, I haven't seen a train on a Woman's dress since Mrs. Rogers got married in one . . . She will be digging hers out now. . . . I guess the Queen sat near Calvin during the chuck hour . . . I jest wonder what Cal said to her? . . . He must about asked her, 'What do you do in your country, Maria, to satisfy the farmer? If you can give me the recipe for that, I will see that you get the loan.' "

Will was upset when the mayor of Kansas City, in presenting the Queen to an audience, said, "This is the greatest day in the history of Kansas City." He was not, he protested, complaining because Marie "was the Queen in some minor league Balkan War trap nation" for "it would be the same if the Queen of the Biggest nation was there. . . . Last week seventeen hundred young boys and girls were in Kansas City . . . Future Farmers of America . . . to see the kings and queens of cattle, sheep, hogs and horses, real kings and queens that produced something . . . . real thoroughbreds . . . If there had been a scrawny one and an outcast in the breeding, he was discarded at home and not allowed to enter the arena . . . It was not like human royalty where they use them whether they are fit or not . . . These not only have to have the breeding but they got to face the judges and be marked on their merit."

At the finish of this lecture tour Will met Betty and the children in New York, where they had a couple of days of shopping and shows. Then they entrained for California to spend Christmas at home. Forty-seven now, Will had come a long way from that day he uttered his first Cherokee yell on November 4, 1879. He had the wife of his choice and three fine children, Will Jr., 15, Mary, 13, and Jim, 11. It was a fitting end to a tremendously successful year as they sat together on the train, but there was more to come.

As the train pulled into the Los Angeles station, it was obvious something special was going on. On the platform, as a welcoming committee, were the leading citizens of Beverly Hills, city officials, businessmen, motion-picture actors, actresses, directors and producers, a couple of brass bands, and hundreds of "just ordinary folks." Banners proclaimed a welcome to "The Hon. Will Rogers, Mayor of Beverly Hills." Others called him "The Kiddies' Pal" and "The Dog's Best Friend." A parade moved out Wilshire Boulevard to Beverely Hills in a steady downpour of rain that did not dampen the enthusiasm of the crowd one whit. "The Mayor's family," Betty wrote, "abandoned an open car in favor of drier accommodations."

On a raised platform in the park opposite the Beverly Hills Hotel, the president of the City Trustees, Sil Spaulding, after a laudatory speech presented Will with "an elegant illuminated scroll five feet high" on which was inscribed in red and gold letters his commission of office. Will's speech as "mayor" was probably unique. Notes he made for it indicate approximately what he said:

It don't speak well for your town when this many of you havent got anything to do but come to meet me . . . What's the matter with business? . . . Real estate men are always between sales . . . They must be between sales, but I don't want anybody ringing me up while here telling me they got a good buy on Wilshire . . . I am Mayor, not Santa Claus to some Real Estate firm. . . .

I am by no means the first Comedian Mayor . . . That seems to be the one requirement of a Mayor . . . I have never seen a Mayor that wasent funny, and the minute he puts on a Silk Hat he becomes Screamingly Funny . . . I may make a good Mayor . . . I have tried everything else . . . I am what you call "Groping in the Dark," and I am reaching for everything. . . .

Groping! . . . That's the only thing that has held this Joint back . . . It has everything to make a good town—burglars, poor parking regulations, shortage of water in the summer, poor telephone service, luncheon clubs, Chamber of Commerce, and everything that goes to handicap 99 per cent of the towns . . . But what you have really needed is a Good Mayor . . . Too many Mayors have been elected on Honesty . . . That don't get you anywhere . . . Now I don't say I will give the old burg an honest administration, but I will split 50-50 with you. . . .

I know you will ask, "Well, Will, how are you going to run the town if you are away so much?" . . . Say, I can run this town by telegraph, and Los Angeles, I could run it by radio even with the static on . . . There is going to be no keys given out to the city . . . Even Mark Hellinger and Doug Fairbanks have got to know when they come in . . . I am bringing over a few of the systems of Mussolini, particularly the "castor oil" treatment . . . I want to warn you, the real estate men have got to go to work . . . I don't care who you work but it's got to be somebody . . . I want to introduce a law to make Real Estate men and Moving Picture people as good as any other Citizens . . . There shall be no discrimination against them. . . .

I am sorry somebody referred to Movies as an art . . . For since then everybody connected with them stopped doing something to make them better and they commenced getting worse . . . The success of the Movies have been the animal trainers more than the directors . . . The minute directors can train actors to act as natural as a dog or a horse then they will have accomplished something. . . .

We have more swimming pools and less Bibles in Beverly Hills than any town in the world . . . We imitate Duke Kohanimoku more than we do Moses . . . We love to bathe collectively but individually we are pretty dirty . . . Really, though, the old City has done great . . . I can remember it when there wasent over 25 mortgages in the whole town . . . Why, there wasent a manicurist or beauty parlor here. . . .

I have been thinking over that reform thing and, like all smart men, I have changed my mind . . . There is nothing to it . . . Everybody is going in for that . . . Hollywood went in for it and everybody that amounted to anything moved out. . . I don't know of a single Feature Length Inhabitant of Hollywood . . . Name me anybody that is packing 'em in today and I will show you where he is only two more payments behind in Beverly Hills! . . . So come to think of it, I am for scandal . . . If Silver King pulls a party for the Wild Horse Gang, why, let it be known . . . If Rin Tin Tin gets mixed up with some two-reel comedy dog that is doing nothing but rescuing babies, why, let him have his fling . . . Life is short. . . .

So here I am, your new Mayor, God's gift to the People who dident see Queen Marie.

Will was now His Honor, Mayor of Beverly Hills. More important, he was at home with his family for a few days. "When he enters the house, either after a long or brief time away from it, we are all happy," Betty wrote at the time. "We all rush to him and greet him and circle about him, and everything is gay and joyous. This is largely due to his buoyant personality, his gift for cheerfulness. We all know we are going to have some fun. But it is also due to the fact that the head of the house is back, the family circle is again intact. We have a sense of completeness again."

22

"Congressman-at-Large of Cuckooland"

EARLY IN JANUARY WILL HAD TO TEAR HIMSELF AWAY from home to go on another lecture tour. "I bet you hated to leave home," he wrote Will Jr. "I know I did." But now his comments on Europe had lost some of their pertinence and he concentrated more on local affairs and America's place in the scheme of things as an "inside" observer. Particularly on the lack of preparedness in building an air defense. "For the 322 Pursuit Squadron with a complement of five hundred men that it has cost millions to train there were six old time Army planes of the type we trained the boys in before we went into the war . . . Only enough gasoline is allotted so that their flying time is 2/34 minutes a month. . . . Mr. Coolidge, on account of his economy plan, has suggested that they fly as high as they can on as little gas as they have, and then coast down . . . In that way they get twice the distance out of the same gas . . . This old 'Economy' is a good slogan . . . It's a great horse to ride . . . But look you don't ride it in the wrong direction. . . . We are not going to be lucky enough to fight Nicaragua forever . . . Build all we can, and then take care of nothing but our own business, and we will never have to use it . . . Tunney hasent been insulted since September. . . . If you think preparedness don't give you prestige, look at Japan. . . . We are afraid to look at hem crosseyed now for fear we will hurt their 'Honor'. . . Before they got a Navy neither them, nor us, knew they had any honor . . . It ain't your Honor that is respected among Nations . . . It's your strength. . . . Japan or England either would have just as much honor without any

Navy at all, but the Navy helps to remind you of it." What Will probably understood but did not state was that the only nations that build up big armaments are those in which the men who pay taxes, the men in power, the vested interests, expect to use it for some purpose that will result in accretions, of whatever sort, to them. In the United States, with a board of directors for industry, finance and business running the government, an expanded armed service beyond that needed for "dollar diplomacy," a protection of their interests abroad, meant only increased taxes, not gain. It was only when they became frightened enough over losing their possessions that they took a saner view.

The way in which China was treated by the rest of the world, including the United States, disturbed Will deeply. Perhaps his feeling for the way this country's affairs were mangled by the great powers was enhanced by the treatment of his own people, the Cherokees, by the whites. "China! those poor people! . . . I never felt as sorry for anyone in my life as I do for them . . . Here they are, they have never bothered anyone in their whole lives . . . They have lived within their own boundaries, never invaded anyone's domains, worked hard, got little pay for it, and few pleasures in life, learned us about two thirds of the useful things we do, and now they want to have a Civil War." This on February 5, 1927. "We had one and nobody butted in . . . China dident send Gunboats up our Mississippi River to protect their laundries at Memphis or St. Louis . . . If a package of dirty shirts got pierced by a bullet, and it made a button hole in the wrong place, the poor Chinaman had to make it good himself . . . I bet you there have been more people of the Chinese race killed innocently, and have stood for more insults and property damage in all foreign countries than any other race . . . Yet every other Nation in the World has took upon themselves some particular claim to help run China . . . Every Nation in the World have their own Land, and every other Nation recognizes it . . . But China, everybody looks on theirs as public domain . . . England holds one of their towns . . . *Now what right has England to hold one of their Towns any more than China has to make a Laundry out of Buckingham Palace?"*

The last straw for Will was the sending of missionaries to China. *"Japan is civilized now. They have a navy.* We don't send any more missionaries there now.... Any nation is heathen that ain't strong enough to punch you in the Jaw.... Why, the Chinese as a race have forgotten more honesty and gentlemanness than we will know if we live another Century... When we started in with our missionaries, that was the last straw.... Imagine with all our crime, and all of our immorality, sending missionaries to them... Imagine our going over there and telling them how to live... Here we have about as much contentment and repose as a fresh-caged Hyena... Then we go to tell some calm, contented people how to live... Why, they forgot more about living than we will ever know.... I suppose that Aimee McPherson's new religion will be sending Missionaries over to teach them how to live... She will be showing up Confucius next."

The epitome of the absurdity came in politics. "We have Disarmament Conferences to persuade Nations to disarm... Then we pick on China, the only big one that is disarmed.... *Us and England are going to get a kick in the pants some day if we don't come home and start tending to our own business and let other people live as they want to*... What they meant by the open door is everybody could come in and do what they wanted but China... The real reason they want to stop the Civil War there, it would interfere with British and our trade... We can't allow them to do anything that would interfere in any way with our commerce."

Instead of worrying too much about what happened to trade on the foreign scene, Will thought it might be a good idea to take stock at home. "This country *is not prosperous*... We got poor people in this country, only they are not the kind that asks for anything, and they are not on the street where you see 'em.... Never mind reading Bank Deposits... We got a million poor people that live in the Country that never saw a bank.... The rich are getting richer and the poor are getting poorer... That's what we better regulate instead of Nicaragua, Tacna-Arica, Mexico and China... What we ought to do is import some Chinese Missionaries to show us... Not how to be saved but how to raise something every year on the land... We just got the missionary business turned around... We are the ones that need converting more than they do."

Certainly the year 1927 was one in which the country needed to take stock. Although the "norm" in "the return to normalcy" was inflated to its uttermost, nothing was done about the chief sore spots in the economy of the country. The farmers were sinking into bankruptcy. President Harding had boasted that the farmer had been placed on "a sound business basis," but his operation had not then, nor ever had been one in which this was possible. Its very basis is a gamble with nature and when the connivances of "the middleman" are added the farmer is protected about as much as the trapper was protected by a fur association. The McNary-Haugen bill, somewhat more flexible than Harding's boasted relief, was defeated in the House of Representatives in 1924. Two years later, with the Republicans solidly in control of the government, it was snowed under in both houses of Congress. Now, in 1927, with a presidential election year in the offing, both houses of Congress passed it content in the knowledge that their "safety valve," President Coolidge, would veto it. "Put him on a farm," Will scoffed, "with the understanding he has to make his own living off it, and I bet you he will give the farmers relief the next year. I offer mine as an experiment, and if he makes a go of it he is not a President, he is a magician."

On the other hand, a Republican administration under the energetic leadership of its efficient Secretary of Commerce, Herbert Hoover, had probed deep into the world's recesses to expand American trade. As a definite and positive aid to his efforts, the armed services were kept up to the demand. "Captured boat from China . . . landed more marines in Nicaragua . . . sent new demands to Mexico . . . It looks like Mr. Coolidge will run on his war record. . . . China owes us two millions and we take over their customs . . . France owes us four billions and we are afraid to send 'em a bill for it . . . Looks like we're going to break off diplomatic relations with Mexico and ship arms to the revolutionists . . . Instead of giving them the means to shed more blood . . . all for the protection of our oil interests . . . we should either go down and lick President Calles, if there is enough cause, or get out. . . . Here we are the nation that is always hollering for disarmament, and peace and just because we are not smart enough to settle our difference by diplomacy (because we have none), why, we are going to make it possible for somebody else to exterminate the ones we don't like. . . . Suppose they don't like Coolidge down there and allowed arms to be shipped into this country to start a revolution against our Government in power? . . . *Boy! What a howl we would put up!* . . . But it's us doing it . . . So that's all right . . . Here is the greatest humanitarian nation of the world (supposedly) fixing it so more people can get shot. . . What right have we got to kick against Calles? . . . They give America 50 years to get the oil out from under the land . . . Then they want to divide it up among the Natives . . . We say it's against our laws . . . Our laws! . . . What's our laws got to do with Mexico? . . . Personally, I don't think Doheny and Sinclair, and the Standard Oil and all those are undergoing any great hardships and starvation. . . We got more out of Mexico than we put in . . . We passed a Prohibition law whereby we confiscated millions and millions of dollars worthy of property . . . We put out of business thousands and thousands of people . . . It was a business that had always been legal and legitimate and the owners werent given 50 years warning as Mexico gave the oil people." Will recommended that our relations with Mexico be taken out of the hands of a man "that knows phrases for a diplomat," whether right or wrong, and placed in the control of someone who knows people, particularly the Mexican people. He was to have a chance to help in this.

In the winter of 1927 Will made two important decisions. One was to dispense with the quartet and go it alone. He did not like the songs they chose but, more important, he wanted more mobility. The other decision was to sell the Beverly Hills house and build on the ranch. "There is no more fun at home now," he wrote to Bill Jr. "Everything is finished. I am anxious to get to work on something new."

While touring through California Will helped the legislature pass "a bill to form a lawyer's association to regulate their conduct." He expected no results. In the first place, any time anything was turned over to an association, it ended right there; and, in the second place, "a lawyer cannot be made honest by an act of the Legislature. You've got to work on his conscience, and his lack of conscience is what makes him a Lawyer."

Now that he was free of the quartet, Will used airplanes more and more for the longer hops between his lecture dates, and as he did so, he pounded on the necessity for the development of air power in the national defense. "See where Secretary of War Wilbur says there is no danger from Europe from airplanes . . . When we nearly lose the next war, as we probably will, we can lay it onto one thing and that will be the jealousy of the Army and Navy toward aviation . . . They have belittled it ever since it started and will keep on doing so till they have something dropped on them from one . . . And even then they will say it wasent a success." Not even the half dozen plans of various aviators to fly the Atlantic caused a business-buttressed administration to be able to see over its piled-high moneybags.

In the spring of 1927 the worst floods in its history inundated the Mississippi Valley. Will immediately turned his attention from everything else to the necessity for relief of the poor people caught in this disaster. He was furious. Publicity about the flood was pushed off the front pages of newspapers by lurid stories and accounts of the trial of Ruth Snyder who, with the collusion of a corset fitter, Judd Gray, had killed her husband. "There's hundred of thousands of people being driven from their homes—homes that won't be there when they come back, and they are people who never harmed a soul in their lives . . . Yet Mrs. Snyder's pictures have occupied more space in some of the papers than the whole State of Mississippi fighting for its life . . . There are ten reporters and photographers at the trial to one at the flood. . . . Just think of the amount of money that could be raised if that array of special writers, with their various talents for describing dramatic scenes, could be sent to the flood instead of the trial. . . . There is more heart interest in one housetop with its little family floating down the river on it than in all the corset salesmen in the world."

On April 30, 1927, Will and John McCormack gave a benefit at the *Ziegfeld,* his old boss's new theater, for the flood sufferers. "It will be McCormack and Rogers, those two nifty boys in funny songs and sentimental jokes." Will told the audience that "you hear a good deal about what Congress is going to do for the Mississippi Valley . . . I don't want to discourage the Valley but I would advise them to put more confidence in a boat builder . . . One rowboat will do more for you in a flood than all the Senators in Washington talking about you . . . I got more faith in high ground than in any Senator I ever saw . . . It's the Democrats that are under water, so it's going to be hard to get New England Republicans and Oregon and Washington interested." Will knew from experience what a flood meant. "If your house burns out in the country, you can run over to some one elses' and stay, but with this when yours goes your neighbors go too . . . Then the worst thing is their crops have been planted and they'll have to wait another year . . . People complain about giving them a lump sum to go and squander on a fellow that hasent lost anything but his house and barn and stock and all his seed he has already planted." This benefit raised $17,950 that was turned over to the Red Cross. Another benefit played at New Orleans raised over $40,000. Many others raised smaller sums—all of which were turned over to the Red Cross. "Lord, what a blessing an organization like the Red Cross is," Will said. "I would rather have originated it than to have written the Constitution."

A few days after playing the benefit in New York Will was "speeding along the old Hudson River . . . I was thinking how many millions and millions of dollars would be raised overnight if it was out of its banks and doing the same amount of damage the old Mississippi is. Means a lot of difference where a thing Happens. . . . But those poor share croppers, most of them Negroes, you don't want to forget that water is just as high on them as it is if they were white. . . . The Lord so constituted everybody that no matter what color you are, you require about the same amount of nourishment."

Today it seems inconceivable that a catastrophe like the Mississippi floods of 1927 could have taken place in a civilized and humanitarian country, and its government would practically ignore it. True, Secretary Hoover helped, but more as a private citizen than a government official. The "business of America is business" went right down to the very existence of the people. It would take a greater catastrophe than this—one that reached up into the ranks of the privileged and faced them with the same alternatives—to dent the national thinking.

On May 21, 1927, Will momentarily ceased to think about the plight of the flood sufferers and turned his thoughts and prayers to "an old slim, tall, bashful, smiling American boy who is somewhere out over the middle of the Atlantic Ocean, where no lone human being has ever ventured before. Lindbergh is being prayed for to every kind of Supreme Being that has a following. If he is lost, it will be the most universally regretted single loss we ever had. But that kid ain't going to fail."

Instead, Lindbergh landed in Paris to receive a more tumultuous welcome than that accorded General Pershing in World War I. He found himself a world hero. Will instantly sensed the value of this event to the lagging development of aviation in the United States and determined to help as much as possible to keep it from being lost. "There is a hundred and twenty million people in America all ready to tell Lindbergh what to do ... The first thing we want to get into our heads is that this boy is not our usual type of hero that we are used to dealing with. ... He is all the others rolled into one and then multiplied by ten, and his case must be treated in a more dignified way ... At his age and with his mechanical knowledge, why, he is just starting to be of value to us ... He is at the top of a profession that is just starting to get somewhere ... He might be the means of saving us in the next war. *Because right up there in his territory is where it is to be held.* His inspiration will do more for American aviation than anything that has happened since the Wrights invented them ... The other day at our air maneuvers in San Antonio we had over a hundred ... But we ought to have had ten thousand ... It's not only Army and Navy Aviation but it's commercial Aviation also that we want to develop." Later, when Lindbergh opened his transcontinental airline, Will bought the first ticket and accompanied Lindbergh on the inaugural flight.

On June 17, 1927, Will headed for a vacation at home but it was not to be a pleasant one. He had a gnawing, persistent pain in the region of his stomach that had begun to bother him at Bluefield, West Virginia. "Now ordinarily when a pain hits you in the Stomach in Bluefield, you would take it for a gunshot wound... But the old town has quieted down now and the sharpshooters have all joined the Kiwanis and Rotary Clubs. So I knew it wasent wounds. Then the pain struck me before the nightly lecture and I knew no one would shoot me before the lecture unless he had heard it over in another town. Well, the next time it hit me was out at my old ranch on the Verdigris River, in the same house where I was born. My niece, who was living there, she gave me some asafetida. The only thing it tastes like is spoiled onions and overripe garlic mixed. And the longer after you have taken it, the worse it tastes." On the train coming home "to check up on the moral conditions of Beverly and Hollywood, the

Sodom and Gomorrah of the West," the pain struck again. As soon as he reached home Will was examined, and rushed to a hospital.

A couple of days later one of the most famous operations in history was performed when Will underwent surgery for gall bladder trouble. For several days he was at the point of death with everything that happened reported in the press of the world as if he had been a king, president or potentate. Telegrams flooded in from everybody from President Coolidge down to hundreds who had known him only by sight or word. He reported his experiences in a book, *Ether and Me,* that still has a lively sale.

Before going into the hospital Will wrote enough Daily Wires and weekly columns to cover the time he expected to be there. The moment he was able to do so he resumed them. "They have sewed me up with so much cat I am having a back fence built at home and will use that instead of a bed. . . . Just saw the scar . . . If they charge by the inch, that operation will be a serious one. . . . Oh, Lord! Here she comes with the castor oil again."

While convalescing at home, instead of taking this chance to rest, he promoted a nonstop Ford race between Beverly Hills and Claremore, Oklahoma, the "flight" to be in either direction with a prize of $500 for the winner. "Remember, no stops for gas, oil, red lights, trains or long-armed traffic cops . . . You can come alone like Lindy, or have a passenger just so you could keep coming. This is for scientific purposes."

"Actually, Will meant this for a joke," said Betty, who was doing her best to keep him quiet, "but secretly he hoped to stir up some activity. It was impossible for him not to be building something, starting something or doing something. The nurses at the hospital had to watch him constantly to keep him from getting out of bed."

Anyway, Will's offer was not taken as a joke. A stream of Fords began the trip in both directions. At four o'clock in the morning, on July 13, 1927, Mr. and Mrs. J. Collins of Tulsa, Oklahoma, aroused the Rogers household to claim the money. They had made the 1,800 miles in three days and nights. The occupants of the car that came in second had changed a tire en route without stopping. For days thereafter Will was called upon to bail out stranded Fords between the two places. "I will be careful with my jokes after this," he sighed.

"It's costing me more to joke than I get for them. So if there are more Fords coming, please turn back." But stopping Will would have been like telling Niagara Falls "to cease and desist."

In addition to the pleasure of being with his family, Will was heartened by a couple of things while convalescing. For one thing, the Red Cross organization sent him a scroll making him a life member. "Well, sir, I am just crazy about it for two reasons . . . One, of course, is that it is the greatest organization in the United States . . . I think it's greater than the Republican Party (including governmental salaries) . . . But my real reason is it looks like a diploma. I waited all these years to get something to frame." The other event was that the United States emerged from the Disarmament Conference at Geneva without sinking the rest of its fighting ships.

Early in August, when President Coolidge issued his famous statement about the 1928 election, "I do not choose to run," Will called it "the best-worded acceptance of a nomination ever uttered by a candidate . . . He spent a long time in the dictionary looking for that word 'choose' instead of 'I will not.' The newspapers reported that he was serious and pale. When a New England Yankee gives up seventy-five thousand a year the surprise is not that he was pale but that he dident faint."

As Will was recovering from his operation in August, 1927, he received the news that he was to be ousted as mayor of Bevery Hills. "The State Legislature of California passed a law saying that no one not a politician could hold office. . . . I hereby notify the world that Beverly Hills has left my bed and board and I will not be responsible for any debts contracted by said municipality . . . I don't want to knock but the town never was so dead . . . There hasent been a Beverly date line about a divorce since I got out, not a shooting, not even a swimming pool built . . . I dident choose to be Mayor in the first place but they drafted me . . . Just a good man looking for something better."

Will did not have to wait long. The National Press Club in Washington, D.C., promptly "elected" him congressman-at-large and invited him to a dinner for his formal induction. On the way to Washington the Ex-Mayors Association, holding a meeting in Kansas City, intercepted him at Union Station and elected him president of that organization. He termed it "an earnest body of men trying to come back, all placed where they are by the good judgment of the voters and honesty of the ballot. . . . My Lord, look what the towns have escaped from . . . Sometimes we lose confidence in the American form of government, and think that our system of voting is wrong . . . But I want to tell you that after looking at you and the position you occupy today, there is Justice in the ballot . . . The American voters are like the Canadian Northwest Mounted Police, they gradually get their men, and I see you have all been got. . . . Everybody is always talking about what the country needs . . . What the country needs is more Ex-Mayors . . . If I am handed a key to a City by any of this gang, I know beforehand that the key will be rusty . . . Good luck and God help you to get into a honest occupation."

Will proceeded to Washington for the dinner of the National Press Club. He was presented with his commission by Senator Ashurst of Arizona. In his acceptance speech he said in part:

More Congressmen have talked themselves out of a job than ever talked themselves into one. . . . I certainly regret the disgrace that's been thrust on me here tonight . . . When a Boss wishes to fire a man, or lower his position, he calls him in privately and does it . . . When a man is to be hung it is done practically without flurry . . . They don't hire a hall to publicly acclaim his downfall . . . So I am sorry you have made this a public festivity. . . .

I certainly have lived, or tried to live my life so that I would never become a Congressman, and I am just as ashamed of the fact I have failed as you are . . . And to have the commission presented by a Senator is adding insult to injury . . . It's like a Second Lieutenant reprimanding a General. . . . Why, in private life a man from the great State of Oklahoma wouldent associate on the same stage with a man from Arizona, much less a Senator . . . Why, we got a thousand bushels of Wheat to every cactus in his State, a million barrels of oil to every rattlesnake he's got . . . Why, he was elected because the Gila monsters voted Democratic. . . .

When I used to read about Walter Johnson I thought, if this happened to me, I would get a bag of money, like he did. And here it is a sheepskin. . . . There is millions of men in America that have a sheepskin that havent even got a sheep, and in ten years working for the skin it hasent told them how to get the sheep . . . It looks like at least, being a cowboy, it would have been a cowskin. . . .

Will's "sheepskin" bore this citation:

Know all ye presents:

Whereas, Mr. Rogers has served with distinction as unofficial ambassador, without portfolio, and

Whereas, his service as Mayor of Beverly Hills, California, has added another scintillating page of American History, and

Whereas, Mr. Rogers, being at present without official connection, is in the status, as he has carefully explained, of "a good man looking for something better," now, therefore

Be it resolved, that the National Press Club, recognizing superlative statesmanship when it sees it and believing that the country's greatest need is not a good five-cent cigar but a Congressman Will Rogers, hereby appoints the said Hon. Will Rogers Congressman-At-Large for the United States of America, effective immediately, his tenure to continue during good behavior.

Done at the Club's Headquarters under its official seal this, the Twenty Seventh Day of August in the year of our Lord, Nineteen Hundred and Twenty Seven.

(Signed)

Louis Ludlow, President
W. H. Atkins, Secretary
Emmet Daugherty, chairman,
Board of Governors

Will contributed one notable service as congressman-at-large. Early in 1928 he was called before the House Flood Control Committee as a taxpayer and in his "unofficial" capacity to give testimony on the 1927 Mississippi River floods. His testimony is interesting:

What is your postoffice address?

Well, I am waiting for the best offer from California and Oklahoma. Beverly Hills, California, is the latest one.

What is your business?

Everybody's.

You have heard of the floods of 1927, I take it?

Yes, sir, I am one of the few Congressmen that have heard of it.

Tell us your views on what should be done.

It was a terrible thing . . . I do not want to give advice so soon after being a Congressman-at-Large, but it does look like that we ought to give some relief to people like that. They could use it to very good advantage . . . From the looks of the people and the looks of the condition of their land and their home, I do not know how they would be able to pay any part of the relief . . . It is a tremendous need . . . It is the biggest thing we have got, the biggest thing we have before us now. . . .

What is the sentiment of the country in regard to it?

The sentiment of the country is in favor of it. . . . Regardless of any political idea that some men might have linking it up with his particular scheme, the sentiment of the country, as I have found it in every state, is for relief. . . . I think if it were left to a vote of the people tomorrow they would do anything they could to help in regard to it, because, regardless of what we say, *when anything is put right before the people and they know that there is a real need for it, they are for it every time.*

It's the "chairman" of and "a board of directors" for a "business" government that puts balancing a financial budget against balancing a people's budget. Nobody knew or practiced the opposite more than Will Rogers, as his next step as an "unofficial" representative of the United States would prove.

23

"Unofficial Ambassador to Mexico"

ON THE MORNING OF SEPTEMBER 20, 1927, WHEN LINDbergh flew into Los Angeles, Will was at work on a motion picture, *The Texas Steer,* and could not be at the airport. But he and Betty attended a reception that afternoon at the Ambassador Hotel for the famous flyer. Will was incensed at the proceedings. "From the time he sat down between Mary Pickford and Marion Davies, the autographing started . . . They dident let him eat . . . They dident let him say a word . . . They dident let him do a thing but sign his name . . . He signed on the back of old Movie contracts, on old back number marriage certificates, on recent and long forgotten divorce papers . . . Louis B. Mayer wanted him to autograph the Metro-Goldwyn-Lion . . . The writing was supervised by Thalberg, ink by Carter, pen by Waterman . . ."

There was one ceremony Will refused to miss, work or no work. He and Betty flew to San Diego (where Lindy's plane had been built) and watched Lindbergh arrive the next day. "Here he was coming back to the very starting point. . . . When he taxied up to the hangar, and got out there was workmen and helpers that had built the plane . . . Men who had known him for the two months while it was being built, and maybe you think he dident sorter hurriedly pass us old reception Committee by to grab those old boys by the hand and tell 'em what the old boat had done. . . . You never saw such beams of happiness as was on their faces when they each felt that Slim had remembered them. . . . 'Boys,' he told 'em, 'my real trip is finished now.' "

At a banquet that evening, when Will sat next to him, Lindbergh was presented with a silver model of his plane and a parachute.

"I guess they will expect you to even demonstrate the parachute," Will said.

"Gee, I would like to!" Lindbergh's face gleamed in anticipation.

The next day Will and Betty flew back to Los Angeles in a tri-motored Ford plane piloted by Lindbergh. Will sat up by the flyer in the copilot's seat and talked with him about the future of aviation.

While Will was "resting" from his operation he finished the work on *The Texas Steer* at a studio in Burbank and made lecture appearances in nearby cities. After that the cast went to Washington to shoot some scenes there. A number of politicians visited the set. One day a man came in wearing a top hat and cutaway coat. "How're you, Senator," Will greeted him.

"I'm an extra," the man said, grinning.

"I'm sorry I called you Senator," Will said. "You ain't sore at me, are you?"

Someone asked Will if he had read the script of *The Texas Steer.*

"Nope," he drawled; "what's the fun of making pictures if you know how they're goin' to come out?"

But Will had his suspicions. "It was the stage play of a Texas cow-man elected to Congress on bought votes . . . We brought it up to date by not changing it at all . . . In the stage version he dident know what to do when he got to Congress . . . That part is allowed to remain as it was . . . The Cattleman-Congressman used to play poker more than legislate, and that's left in the movie. . . . There was a little drinking among the members at the time . . . For correct detail in our modern version that has been allowed to remain in, increased a little in fact . . . Of course, I'm the cowman who's elected to play dumb in Washington . . . I was told all I had to do was to act natural . . ."

A *Saturday Evening Post* article for October 29, 1927, "Duck, Al! Here's Another Open Letter," has in it political knowledge that belies the "dumbness": He advised Al Smith to write this letter to all state and the National Democratic Committees:

I, Al Smith, of my own free will and accord, do this day relinquish any claim or promise that I might have of any support or Deligates at the next Democratic Convention. I don't want to hinder what little harmony there is left in the party; I not only do not choose to run, but I refuse to run. But will give all of my time and talents to work faithfully for whoever is nominated by the party.

This, Will said, would sound as though Smith was sacrificing himself, "and in '32 they will nominate you by radio, and you will have a united Party. A half-wit knew you-all couldent win in '24. Well, it's the same this year... You couldent put on a revival of Thomas Jefferson and get away with it." Will cautioned Al not to let the New Yorkers kid him. "You got no Platform, you got no Issue, you can't ask people to throw somebody out just because somebody else wants in. You meet too many Democratic Leaders—that's what's the matter with the Party—these same leaders not knowing any more about Public Opinion than they do.... Then, you New Yorkers get a wrong prospectus of things... The outsiders don't care nothing about New York, and if you think Tammany Hall is an asset, you just run and try to carry them with you and you will find you have been over-handicapped."

Will admitted that Smith was "the strongest thing the Democrats have had in years... But it's not a Democrat you meet in the finals; it's a Republican. You can't lick this Prosperity thing; even the fellow that hasent got any is all excited over the idea. You politicians have got to look further ahead; you always got a Putter in your hands when you ought to have a Driver. Now, Al, *I am trying to tell you how to be President, not how to be a Candidate.*"

In the 1920's, as in all periods pregnant with change, there were those who gathered groups around their prejudices with the purpose of maintaining special status or propagandizing. Will was particularly incensed at such movements as America First or One Hundred Percent Americans. During the war a lot of the "boys had gotten to know and understand each other, and find out each other's viewpoints." But after the fighting was over, "on investigation it was found a lot of these boys were not 100% Americans at all... Why, a lot of them couldent even speak English... a lot of them dident even go to churches, and worse than all, a lot of them went to the wrong churches

... So these societies commenced to be formed and they grabbed our little civilization just when it was going over the brink and hauled it back to normalcy." Will suggested that the only thing to do was to "form an America Only Club ... I figure the patriotism should run around 165 to 170% American ... It will make a sucker out of these 100% organizations."

After *The Texas Steer* and Will's lecture commitments were finished, in November he intended to take off a few weeks for rest and relaxation with nothing to do except his newspaper and magazine writings, and a few odds and ends that would have kept most people busy. He and Betty roamed around Arizona and New Mexico, sightseeing, and then made their way via the old ranch in Oklahoma to Detroit, Michigan, where Henry Ford unveiled for them the new Model A that the country had been waiting a year to learn about. "Here is the biggest news I have ever gathered," Will announced on November 14, 1927. "It's a real beat on the rest of the press ... I have spent the whole day with Henry Ford, saw and drove in the new car. And here is what you have been waiting for for years—get ready—HE HAS CHANGED THE RADIATOR!" Before leaving Detroit, Henry Ford promised Will the first Model A off the assembly line.

Will's plans to relax were interrupted in an interesting manner. Under the ineptness of "dollar diplomacy" the relations between the United States and Mexico had worsened by the month. "Up to now our calling card to Mexico or Central America had been a gunboat or violets shaped like Marines ... We could never understand why Mexico wasent just crazy about us ... For we always had their goodwill and oil and coffee and minerals at heart ... So when the punitive smoke had cleared away we couldent figure out why they dident appreciate the fact that they had been shot in the most cordial manner possible, that we were only doing it for their own good ... We couldent realize their attitude in not falling on our necks and blessing us for giving them the *assistance of our superior knowledge of government.* ... Well, to show you that they couldent take a joke and were utterly lacking in humor, they resented it instead of thanking us ... We got to counting up and taking censuses, and we found that our last Southern friends geographically were located at Brownsville, Texas, and Key West, Florida."

As later Secretary of State John Foster Dulles expressed it under similar political climatic conditions, "the purpose of the State Department is not to make friends" but "to look after the interests of the United States"—primarily the business interests. "The first thing we knew these people were buying things, and we looked close and they dident have our trademark on 'em. In fact they were getting things in other countries and not from us. They was going away over to Europe to do it."

This was not only a "horse of a different color," it was a different gait. "It's all right to lose a friend, but when you lose a friend *that spends money with you* it's beginning to be serious."

Many of the imperialists in the United States such as William Randolph Hearst, the big mining and oil interests, were either publicly or privately for taking over Mexico. Will had sarcastic words on that. "Where did this country down here with no great chains of commercial clubs, and Chambers of Commerce and junior and freshmen Chambers of Commerce, and Rotarys and Kiwanis and Lions and Tigers clubs, and no golf pants, and no radio advertising programs, where did a nation like that come in to have oil anyhow? . . . It was kind of an imposition on their part to even have us to go to the trouble of going down and taking their country over . . . We should have taken the whole thing when we took the part we did."

Instead, when they started interfering with "our oils and bananas, we just got out the old typewriter, loaded it with ammunition and commenced shooting the notes to 'em. . . . We would show 'em! . . . We would keep 'em so busy reading they wouldent have time to pass laws . . . But the rascals wouldent even go to the trouble of having the notes translated. . . . We tried diplomats on 'em, but they wouldent dip . . . So we begin to realize that we better find some way to fix this up." At that moment President Coolidge had an inspiration. He appointed as ambassador his old friend and classmate at Amherst, Dwight Morrow, then with J. P. Morgan Company ("to lend it an air of respectability"). Morrow had an even greater inspiration, he asked Will and Charles Lindbergh to come to Mexico to help get him off on the right foot with the Mexican people.

Will accepted his assignment as "unofficial ambassador to Mexico" with mixed emotions. He loved Mexico and its people and would have done anything to help them. On the other hand, he looked quite naturally on a J. P. Morgan partner as an unlikely person to bring about improved relations. On his arrival in Mexico City he was somewhat heartened to learn that Morrow's first act had been to tour the country for two weeks with President Calles. This had aroused wide criticism among the aristocracy and the vested interest groups who sneered at Calles as a revolutionist. "I came here accredited to this Government to the men who are at present running it," Morrow stated bluntly, "and not to the aristocracy."

Will was plunged into the middle of the struggle when Morrow took him at once to the presidential palace at Calles's request. A tough election had just been won and a number of contestants were not able to answer roll call any more. It was a ticklish time. At the door of the reception room where President Calles was waiting to receive him, Will suddenly drew back.

"I demand an interpreter," he said, in a high-pitched voice.

A frown passed over President Calles's stern face. Nevertheless, he beckoned to his official interpreter to come forward.

"Tell this Bird . . ." Will indicated Calles ". . . Make it perfectly clear to him, that I am just down here traveling around for fun. I am not a candidate for anything."

Calles's frown deepened as this was translated, he gulped and then burst into a great roar of laughter, as he held out his hand to Will. Morrow, who had been transfixed with fright, stated later that this "impertinence" on the part of Will broke the ice and, from then on, he could deal with Calles on a personal level.

Will continued his complete disregard for diplomatic protocol. On another occasion he delayed an official dinner given by Calles while he chatted with a group of soldiers. Calles let him know through his interpreter that he was not amused.

"Well, I'm awfully sorry." Will grinned. "You tell the President I have been in Mexico only four days but I already have found out it is better to stand in good with the soldiers than the President."

"You had better be careful," Calles said, with assumed sternness. "When people begin fooling with my army, they are likely to be shot at sunrise."

"That don't worry me a bit," Will answered, grinning. "I'm never up that early."

For the first time in history the Chief Executive of Mexico came to the American Embassy in Mexico City when President Calles attended a banquet given in his and Will's honor. He heard a speech from Will that was as impertinent as Will's approach had been and, although it must have lost much in translation, he led the laughter. A couple of days later he went with the party that took Will out to see where the fighting bulls were raised, although Will steadfastly refused to go to a bull fight. "My life has been saved too many times by a horse to watch what happens there," he said.

As a gesture of good will, Lindbergh was to fly nonstop from Washington to Mexico City. He lost his way and instead of landing on schedule at eight o'clock in the morning he did not arrive until three o'clock in the afternoon. "I saw over 200,000 people, including the President and his cabinet, wait eight hours to welcome him," Will marveled. "Any other aviator in the world would have come down to see where he was, but that determination made him stay up there till he found the name of a hotel, one building, and he found the city on the map and laid his course from there. . . . In France and America, they like to have tore up the plane to get souvenirs . . . Here hundreds took it up on their shoulders and carried it into the hangar. . . . Instead of being bombarded with ticker tape, the streets were two inches deep with flowers. . . . Morrow and I have resigned as Ambassadors to Mexico."

On the evening of Lindbergh's arrival Will had an engagement to speak at University City at a dinner given in his honor. "All Mexico waited for Lindbergh in intense anxiety," Mrs. Dwight Morrow recalled. "The crowds on the street as he was conducted to the chancery and the delirium of delight in the city is indescribable. In the excitement, I forgot until my secretary reminded me of Will's speech and that we were to go hear him. Many of the guests were late." Mrs. Morrow felt sorry that Will had to make a speech under such circumstances. "When he arose to speak, I was distinctly nervous for him. It was a waste of my pity. From the first sentence he held the whole room in the hollow of his hand. I had entirely underestimated his power and his understanding of an audience. He shocked, flattered, cajoled, teased, tormented and enchanted the guests. He began by reminding us that we were in a University Club and said he questioned the qualifications of many present for membership in the college group. 'Where is your sheepskin?' he asked suddenly pointing to a well-known golfer near him. 'You brought your score card at the Churubusco Club and they let you in. And where is yours?' His finger singling out a marvelous bridge player. 'I know you can play bridge, but you never learned that at College.' He went up and down a long table calling man after man by name and giving credit for something he could do—horse racing, polo, dancing—but scoffing at his education."

During this time Mrs. Morrow wondered what Will would say about her husband, the ambassador. Not once did Will look at him or address him. "There's Mrs. Morrow," he finally said, "up there at the head of the table—Well, I guess I'll have to admit that she got a degree at Smith, but good heavens! What did she do with it? She went slumming one day in Amherst and got herself a husband." The roar of laughter shook the club. "It was the hit of the evening," Mrs. Morrow stated, "and nobody was more amused than my husband. To have left him unscratched, would have been a confession of weakness on Will Rogers' part. The cleverness of the attack through me delighted the audience." [1]

Later Will concluded his appraisal of Morrow by saying that he was not in Mexico "to bat any .300 in the Dinner League. He figured that the men running the Government may not have known a demitasse from a hors d'oeuvre and they might have scabbards on their knives to keep from cutting their mouths, but they was the people that he had to deal with." Morrow was in Mexico to do business with them and not to "lead a cotillion in a charity" fete and if he got away with it, "it's liable to change the business of Embassying. He is just liable to change it into a human job." Whether he did or not he was *"Wall Street's sole contribution to public life."*

Will had promised his family to be home for Christmas and to make certain he flew out. "Left Mexico City at 3 o'clock, spent the night in Tampico, lunch in Brownsville and on to Kelly Field, San

[1] Tulsa *World,* Nov. 10, 1935.

Antonio, for dinner. Flew over the Rio Grande Valley, which is wonderful. The only thing the matter with it, they say, the Republicans are about to take it." Will made it home in time for Christmas and found a present for himself. It was the first Model A that Ford had promised him. "I sure am using it. Nobody is looking at these Rolls-Royces here in Beverly."

The following year would bring the next giant step in Will's career.

24

"Unofficial President of the United States"

IN JANUARY, 1928, WILL BEGAN TO ASSUME "UNOFFICIAL" presidential duties when he gave a "message" on the State of the Union. It came when he acted as master of ceremonies on the first completely national radio hookup from his home in Beverly Hills. On the program with him were Paul Whiteman in New York, Al Jolson in New Orleans, and Fred Stone in Chicago. After getting the routine under way, Will announced he had a great surprise for the millions of listeners. Over the air came what sounded like the voice of President Coolidge:

Ladies and Gentlemen: It's the duty of the President to deliver a message to the people on the condition of the country . . . I am proud to report that the condition of the country as a whole is prosperous . . . That is, it's prosperous for a Hole . . . There is not a "hole" lot of doubt about that . . . Everybody that I come in contact with is doing well—Hoover, Dawes, Lowden, Curtis and Al Smith are doing well . . . But not as well as they would like to be doing this time next year . . . Mellon has saved some money, for the country, and done very well for himself . . . He is the only Treasurer that has saved faster than Congress could divide it up . . . Congress is here now though to grab what he has got . . . It would have been cheaper to have sent each Congressman and Senator his pro rata share and saved the expense of holding this Congress. . . .

Just a few words on the public issues of the day . . . They won't seat two Republican Senators . . . The Democrats dident mind them buying their seats but it was the price they paid . . . It would establish a price that would have made it prohibitive for a Democrat to even get standing room much less a seat in the Senate. . . .

I sent Dwight Morrow to Mexico . . . Smart Boy, Dwight, one of the two smartest boys in our class at Amherst where we were preparing for College . . . Lindbergh is busy in Central America . . . We seem to get in wrong faster than he can get us out . . . I wish he was twins. . . .

I made a statement last summer in which I said I dident choose to run . . . It seems to have been misunderstood . . . So months ago I clarified it by saying, "I still don't choose to run." If they misunderstood "Choose" in the first place, I don't very well see how they could do it again. . . .

On farm relief, I give 'em rain and a good crop . . . That beats all the McHaugen bills for relief . . . Fill a Farmer up, that will stop him from hollering quicker'n anything. . . .

On our Foreign Debts, I am sorry to state that they are just as Foreign as ever, if not more so . . . Cuba and South America, I am going there at once to try and show them that we are not as bad as we've been . . . Nicaragua, we are still having a little trouble down there, but I think we will gradually get it all Buried. . . .

Prohibition, prohibition is going down about as well as usual. . . .

Radio audience, I thank you.

By the end of this incredible speech—although if examined carefully it has magnificent kernels of truth in it—wires were humming all over the country. It seemed impossible that President Coolidge had made such a speech but, on the other hand, it seemed impossible that Will would have imitated the President in such a manner. And the imitation had been perfect! Will had some explaining to do and he hurried to Washington. "I found on my arrival that some people had censured me severely for leaving the impression the other night that Mr. Coolidge was on the radio. . . . Well, the idea that any one could imagine it was him uttering the nonsense that I was uttering! . . . It struck me that it would be an insult to any one's sense of humor to announce that it was not him . . . So I wrote Mr. Coolidge a note explaining, and received a two-page letter within thirty minutes from him, written all in his own longhand, saying that he had been told about it, but knew that anything that I did was done in good-natured amusement, and not to give it a moment's worry . . . I knew my man before I joked about him." Nevertheless, Will's imitation offended Coolidge deeply and it took the tact of Mrs. Coolidge to smooth it over.

"Will Rogers can imitate President Coolidge and get away with it," a wag commented, "and the President was rather funny, too, when he put on the cowboy pants out in the Black Hills."

After a quick trip to the Pan American Conference in Havana, on January 15, 1928 ("For goodness sake, get an international anthem that goes for everybody when it's played, and make it short"), Will began another lecture tour. "Hoover was in the Presidential race from the old days of 'Save a lump of sugar a day and it will keep the Kaiser away' . . . He was the first 'Food Dictator' . . . He took us off beefsteak and put us on calories . . . He grabbed the Catholic Vote by making Baptists eat fish on Friday . . . Fed wheat to hogs and made the Jewish soldiers eat pork . . . He put a fixed price on wheat and sold steel and iron to the highest bidder . . . He had us sweetening our coffee with a slogan, 'Drink it black and give the enemy a whack' . . . He buttered our bread with a slogan, 'Spread it thin and we are bound to win' . . . He won the war, but he ruined our stomachs."

While swinging through Old Kentucky, Will was made a colonel. "I thought I would get out of Kentucky without being made a Colonel . . . The Governor's name is Sampson . . . a very strong man . . . He slayed the Democrats with 'the jawbone of an ass' . . . His Democratic opponent ran on a 'no horse racing in Kentucky' . . . He not only supplied Sampson with the jawbone, but made himself the whole animal by thinking that Kentucky would vote against horse racing . . . It's Colonel Rogers, suh . . . Boy, put another sprig of mint in the julep."

In March, 1928, a curious thing happened to Will when he spoke to three thousand Cherokees who still lived in the ancient territory of the tribe. They listened stoically to his performance, showing no emotion and not cracking a smile. He gave them a thrilling performance with his rope and still no response. "Then, suddenly," reported Ben Dixon MacNeil, "he became furious. His transformation was terrifying, and for three minutes his astonished audience was treated to a demonstration of what primitive, instinctive hatred could be.

Some long-forgotten, in-bred memory welled up in his heart and he ripped into Andrew Jackson. To the Cherokees, Jackson is known as 'the betrayer' and their removal to Oklahoma is 'the betrayal.' No enemy of Jackson was ever more bitter than was Rogers. The Indians listened, and then the quiet was ripped by the screaming war cry of the tribe, while Rogers stood, white, trembling, and aghast."

On this same tour Will kept four thousand people at Raleigh, North Carolina, waiting for half an hour while he did a private show in an alley. When he came to the theater, some twenty boys were waiting for a glimpse of the famous cowboy-comedian. One of them held a dingy rope in his hand.

"Hi, boys," Will called, "lemme see that rope."

The wide-eyed audience formed a ring around him as he performed his magic with the rope. Although his performance was billed at 8:30, it was 8:55 when he neatly spun a noose over the boy who owned the rope and told them to leave.

"Take us to the show," the kids clamored.

"Naw," Will drawled, taking some money from his pocket. "You get this fixed," he said to the rope owner, "that'll be eighty-five cents apiece and fifty cents extra for you. Get along to a movie."

Ten minutes later he was on the stage going through his routine.

On May 26, 1928, Will made his own report to a country that was rapidly approaching that "hole" in its false prosperity. He warned them:

The Lord has sure been good to us . . . Now what are we doing to warrant that good luck any more than any other Nation? . . . Now just how long is it going to last? . . . The way we are acting the Lord is liable to turn on us any minute . . . It just ain't in the book for us to have the best of everything all the time . . . We got too big an over-balance of everything and *we better kinder start looking ahead and taking stock and see where we are headed for. . . .*

You know, I think we put too much emphasis and importance and advertising on our so-called High Standard of Living. . . . *I think that the "high" is the only word in that phrase that is really correct. . . .*

We sure are a-living high . . . There hasent been a Thomas Jefferson produced in this country since we formed our first Trust . . . Rail-splitting produced an Immortal President in Abraham Lincoln, but

Golf with 29 thousand courses, hasent produced even a good a-Number-1 Congressman... There hasent been a Patrick Henry showed up since business men quit eating lunch with their families, joined a club and have indigestion from amateur Oratory... Suppose Teddy had took up putting instead of horseback riding... It's also a question what we can convert these 4 billion filling Stations into in years to come... I am only tipping you off, and you all are supposed to act on it.

The summer of 1928 was cluttered up with the "national follies" of the presidential nominating conventions. The Republicans met in Kansas City, Missouri, and the Democrats in Houston, Texas. "It will be great to meet all the old Newspaper boys who grind out dope for the home papers trying to keep the Conventions interesting... Political Conventions would die standing up if it wasent for the inventive genius of the Boys that make the Actors look colorful... It's when you leave and take one of these conventions apart, and just see what was really inside it, then is when our sense of humor asserts itself... But then it is too late.... The country just smiles and waits four more years and here they are back again... The ones that failed to save the Country the last time are Patriotic... they are back again for another trial.... Lower taxes and all the old Gags are dusted off, and away they go again... The same old Leaders are there, just rarin' for something to lead."

On his way to Kansas City for the Republican Convention Will's plane broke a wheel when it landed at Las Vegas, Nevada, and turned over. "Am the first candidate to land on my head, and being a candidate, it dident hurt the head." He grabbed another plane, and at Cheyenne, Wyoming, had another crash. Not deterred, he crawled onto a third plane and flew into Kansas City.

Will's report on what the Republicans had accomplished, as set forth in the keynote speech, is illuminating. "Here are just a few things that Republicans were responsible for: Radio, Telephone, Baths, Automobiles, Saving Accounts, Prohibition Enforcement, workmen living in houses, and a living wage for Senators.... The Democrats had brought War, pestilence, debts, disease, Boll Weevil, need for Farm Relief, gold teeth, suspenders, floods, famines and Tom Heflin. ... Once I thought he [the speaker] was referring to 'Our Savior,' till they told me, 'No, it was Coolidge.' . . . When he told how many million we saved, his voice raised . . . But when our savings had reached the billions, why, his voice reached a crescendo . . . All expenditures was spoken of in an undertone."

Once again the Republican Convention was as orderly as a well-run board of directors meeting rubber-stamping prearranged business. This, however, was not as Will had predicted. It was Herbert Hoover and not Calvin Coolidge who was to be chairman of the board. Certainly he who had made a tremendous fortune of his own was more symbolic of "rugged individualism" or the "norm" in "the return to normalcy" at its "ripest" perfection.

"They havent even got Hot Dogs to sell in the Convention Building," Will stated in a satire that has in it much wisdom if properly understood.

Stock speculation and hot dogs!

What a contrast in understanding the "norm" in "the return to normalcy," the "rugged individualism" of Herbert Hoover. And who understood better than Will Rogers the conditions that existed or predicted more accurately what was to come. The United States that had returned to the dominance of Wall Street with the election of Coolidge in 1924 was to continue that dominance for another four years.

Will advised Jesse Jones, the Houstonian who had brought the Democratic Convention to his city, to have "hot dogs." He went there for fun and not to see a potential president nominated, as he had warned Al Smith. "There is nowhere for the Democrats to go . . . Their only course of action was to go wet, but this they would not do as they did not know if there were enough votes there to make it all the way to the White House. . . . 'We want Smith, for he is the only man we got a chance with . . . We wish he was Dry instead of Wet, but as he is not we got to make the most of it . . . We got to dress him up so he will look WET in the Cities and DRY in the country . . . We got to hold our Wets, but for God's sake, don't turn loose of the Drys. . . . It's like Coolidge, 'I am for Labor, but not against Capital.' "

Will knew quite well that the claims of the Republicans to have brought "Properity, Peace and Plenty" could not be successfully countered. In spite of Will's advice, Smith sought and received the nomination "as candidate" for the Presidency, and to counteract his stand on Prohibition, a dry, Senator Joseph Robinson, of Arkansas, was chosen as his running mate. The contestants in the "official National Political Follies" were set for the race, with the outcome as certain as a footrace between Nurmi and Einstein.

More revealing of the conditions of the country was an "unofficial" campaign conducted by the humorous weekly *Life,* with Will as the candidate of the Anti-Bunk party. This was the brain child of Robert Sherwood. Will was termed "the invincible candidate of the dissatisfied voters of both parties," and had been selected after a search was made, "in a quiet way, for a bunkless candidate who would run on an honest, courageous and reasonably intelligent platform." Further reasons were his "supply of genuine Indian blood," which made him closer to "a 100% American than a lot who bragged about it"; that as a humorist he would be "the first President in 62 years who was funny intentionally" (although this might be fatal, as "the American voters like to laugh at their politicians and not with them"); his experience as a "Public Servant" in being unofficial diplomat, mayor of Beverly Hills, congressman-at-large, and veteran of thirteen campaigns with the *Follies;* his knowledge of the world that exceeded that of "all the 18 august members of the Senatorial Foreign Relations Committee"; and he "was a good scout, which in itself was reason enough." Before accepting the nomination, Will was assured that there would be "no baby kissing, passing out of cigars, laying cornerstones, dodging issues" or disguising "himself as a farmer with a rake in one hand and a sap bucket in the other." After thinking it over Will announced that "I chews to run," and in his "acceptance speech" he said:

Your offer struck me like what the better fed English Authors call "a bolt from the Blue." It leaves me dazed, and if I can stay dazed I ought to make a splendid candidate. . . . Now I know after being nominated for anything, it's customary after first buying a drink, to register modesty . . . In fact, the modesty lasts no longer than the drink . . . Every Candidate always says, "Why, there is dozens of men that is more competent to fill this office than I am." . . . Well, I don't feel that way about it at all . . . It looks like you Boys was inspired when you made your choice . . . For after all, it's only the office of

Candidate that I am accepting . . . *You know it don't take near as good a man to be a Candidate as it does to hold the office* . . . That's why we wisely defeat more than we elect . . . Now you might have found "a dozen better men than me," but I doubt it . . . I think I can accept defeat in as poor English, and with as well hidden "Sour Grapes" as anyone you could have chosen . . . In fact, I have already got in my mind the message of congratulation to the winner, and am really anxious to hurry up and lose, just to see how it will look in print. . . .

I am in hearty accord with the Anti-Bunk Party, but by its very name it means that we will have no political support. . . . I admit I can make a living outside politics . . . Now when you admit that, you lose right there the support of all politicians, *for if there is one thing that a politician hates worse than a recount, it's somebody that is not in their business.*

Will conceded that his nomination without expense to the taxpayer would be against him; hotels would oppose him for not being able to furnish "the Back Room" for the nomination; and every city except Kansas City and Houston would be angry for not holding a convention there. There would be no Party Leaders ("that's what hurts our two big Political Parties worse than getting caught, is Party Leaders"), Slogans ("slogans have been more harmful to the country than Luncheon Clubs, Sand Fleas, Detours and Conventions"), or Sex Appeal ("of course if it unconsciously manifests itself, why, we can't help it"). His platform would be short and simple: "WHATEVER THE OTHER FELLOW DON'T DO, WE WILL." As to voters, since he could not pay anything he would not get a Republican vote, and if the Democrats had to vote for nothing they would stay with their own party. His one political promise was that "If elected I absolutely and positively agree to resign."

As keynote speaker for the Anti-Bunk party, Judge Ben Lindsey, after pointing out that the two big parties were alike ("the candidates vie with each other to shout the loudest 'for Heaven, Home and Mother,' 'the Sanctity of the home,' 'the virtues of our Christian Peepul,' 'the Constitution and the flag' and 'Law Enforcement' "), warned that the new party offered the only hope. "I have seen the politicians laughing their fool heads off at Will's jokes, but all the time they were anxious because they know that everything Will says is true, and the truth hurts, especially in politics. And if there is any issue, personality or question, national or international, that he does not know more about than most of the statesmen, in or out of Congress, I want somebody to tell me what it is. Will Rogers will make the people laugh, but what is more important, he will make them think. *And it takes a real man to do that in these days when the real joke seems to be about oil, and Sinclair and Fall and Teapot Dome. It is high time that we quit taking such serious matters as jokes."* This conclusion takes on a deeper meaning when it is realized that Will wrote it himself, as he did all the material for the "campaign" with some assistance from Robert Sherwood.

Will hedged, as did the other candidates, on his Cabinet. "Peggy Joyce is kinder crowding me on wanting to be Secretary of the Treasury . . . I may have to marry her to get rid of her . . . She feels that in four years she could pull off enough marriages to put this country on its financial feet. . . . Been asked who will be my Vice President . . . Won't have one . . . All he does is draw $15,000 and break gavels trying to make that Senate behave. . . . Mencken's been kinder nosing around to get in our party . . . Claims he can give us a Literary standing that would read like a Eugene O'Neill first night . . . He's got some smart people reading him . . . I told him what's worrying me is do they know anything? . . . He said he dident know that they did, but they're a harmless bunch, and if we landed them like he had, they'd never know enough to leave us . . . Henry's a nice boy and would make a good man for a Keynote speech . . . He'd have so many big words in there that the people would think we at least stood for Webster. . . . Then we could get Jim Tully to interpret it for Hollywood. . . . Then we'd get Will Hays to clean up the Tully interpretation so it could be published outside of jails."

In the July 12 issue of *Life* there was a cartoon by Low, from the London *Evening Standard,* entitled "The Great American Circus." It showed Hoover as a fat little clown standing on one foot on an elephant juggling a bottle of bootleg whiskey, a can of oil, and a wisp of wheat straw, symbolizing his efforts to justify the party in its handling of bootlegging, the oil scandals, and the failure to grapple with the problems of agriculture. Al Smith was trying to drag in a reluctant donkey. Back of it all Will was coming out on a prancing horse labeled as the Anti-Bunk party.

The Republican campaign, according to Secretary of the Interior Work, was to be "instructive," and such minor matters as Prohibition were not to be discussed. "Why, my Lord, Doc, there is nothing more instructive than to tell a man where to get a drink . . . Now it's mighty noble of you, Dr. Work, to not want liquor dragged into a perfectly high classed soul-inspiring Campaign . . . But what's on your Hips is bound to sooner or later percolate to your mind . . . And what's on your mind is bound to break out in talk . . . And when you speak or talk, you just about have spoken all of Politics, for that's all it is. . . . There is not enough words in old man Webster's Dictionary to hide behind . . . It's fine of them to want to run a Campaign on a high plane, but it would be just like me wanting to conduct my campaign on a strictly Grammatical basis . . . I would like to but I just ain't equipped for it, and that's the way they are . . . The whole campaign won't be a month old till everybody in it will revert to type . . . *So that gives you a rough idea of how low it will fall.* . . . They got their minds on the tail end of Pennsylvania Avenue, and they will promise anything short of perpetual motion to have Senators eat breakfast with 'em."

In the August 9 issue of *Life* Will challenged Hoover to "a joint debate" in any "joint you name." "Now you are a man, and so is Al, that has got by without a lot of Bunk . . . And the debate might be that you both by rights ought to be in my Party, 'The Anti-Bunks.' . . . But what the debate could be, that you have let yourself be hitched to a Platform that is nothing but Bunk. . . . As a man is known by the company he keeps, I will show you, now you have entered Politics, that you will be mixed up with more Bunk than you ever thought existed. . . . *You may say the Issue is 'Prosperity.' You will try to show that we are prosperous because we* HAVE MORE. *I will show where we are* NOT *prosperous because we havent* PAID *for it* YET. . . . You say that 'Prohibition is a Noble Experiment.' I would say that it was an 'Amusing' or 'Exciting experiment,' but it has hardly reached the 'Noble' stage up to now. Then there is Farm Relief, Tariff, and all the Usual Bunks, and I will debate you on those too."

Will offered to debate Al Smith also, but more out of sadness. It would make very little difference, after the election, what they talked about. He did state though what he would do. "The first thing I would do would be to paint the White House green, so they can't call it the White House any more."

On August 4, 1928, Fred Stone, who was to open on Broadway with his daughter, Dorothy, in October in *Three Cheers,* was critically injured in the crash of his airplane. Although Will had a full lecture tour lined up, he went to his friend's rescue. "If you don't want Dorothy to wait until you are entirely recovered," he wired, "I will go into the show with her, just to sort of plug along till you are able to rejoin, and I will do the best I can with the part. Dorothy can keep telling me how you would have played it. Dorothy, of course, would be the star, and I don't want any billing. Anything you, Dorothy and Dillingham says goes with me." Fred forwarded the telegram to the producer with the comment that he would hesitate to accept a gift so generous from anyone except so whole-souled and true a friend as Rogers. Dillingham gratefully accepted Will's offer, which meant giving up half a million dollars in earnings, although Will kept up his newspaper writing and his Anti-Bunk campaign.

The voter came in for X-raying in the September 21 issue of *Life.* "I see where my friend, Mr. Franklin Roosevelt (blood but no political relation to THE Roosevelts), says this is the 'silly' season for Politics . . . He calls it the 'Bunk' period. Franklin seems to be stealing our stuff . . . He claims that the last weeks in August and the first ones in September are the time for the Bunk to percolate. . . . Well, our claim is that the Bunk period extends from Jan. 1 to December 31 inclusive." Will also took issue with Roosevelt on the statement "that conditions have changed, that the old idea that the Republican party is the party of prosperity is no longer held to . . . He says that people nowadays are smarter and they know the facts, and won't be misled like they used to. . . . Now Franklin Roosevelt is a very fine man, he is one of the highest type men that we have in the Business of make-believe, or Politics, if you like the old name . . . But while we are exposing Bunk that statement of his gives us our cue for today. OF ALL THE BUNK handed out during a campaign the biggest one of all is *to try and compliment the knowledge of the voter and tell him he can't be fooled like he used to be. . . .* Franklin Roosevelt, or any other man that knows anything, knows that the Voter is no smarter than he ever was. How are the voters going to be any smarter when the Candidates themselves are no smarter? . . . *No, we are more 'smart Alec' than we were, but we are no smarter.* We have bathtubs, airships, four-wheel brakes, reducing pills, manicurists, men's corsets, *and* Prohibition . . . But I doubt if at any time during the history of the world were we ever as down right *Dumb* as we are today."

Will added his over-all endorsement of this belief when he warned: "No nation in history was ever sitting so pretty. If we want anything, all we have to do is go buy it on credit. *So that leaves us without any economic problem whatever, except perhaps some day to have to pay for them."* That day was soon to come and Wall Street had used its particular brand of "gambling vacuum cleaner" to suck up all the "wherewithal."

The November 2 issue of *Life* had on the cover a telegram to go to the winner: "Heartiest congratulation on your great victory. As for me I would rather be right." Will summarized the entire campaign by saying, "It'll take two generations to sweep up the dirt."

The editors of *Life* sent this telegram to Will at 1:28 A.M. on election night:

All you know is what you read in the papers, so you probably haven't heard that *you were elected President by the Great Silent Vote of this nation.* No one except us knew that this vote existed—even the voters themselves were ignorant of it; no one except us knew that it went unanimously for you. The newspapers may say that the other candidates piled up millions of votes, but don't let that worry you. *You're in.*

For the rest of his life Will was to be the "unofficial" President of the United States.

25

"As Millions Cheered"

PROBABLY NOTHING IN WILL'S CAREER CAUGHT THE heartstrings of the United States more than his going into *Three Cheers* to help out his friend Fred Stone. "In the fifteen years that I've covered the Broadway Beat," one reporter wrote, "I have never heard a mean syllable said about Will Rogers. Imagine that! In the Broadway Arena where the code is 'Get the gravy while you can, and to hell with the fellow who comes in second.' Now Will does this for Fred Stone!"

This was a unique experience for Will. "Rehearsing! Think of it! . . . Twenty-three years on the stage and I never rehearsed before . . . This is a kind of a part and I'll have to learn the lines so the other Actors will know when their cue comes . . . I feel like a Kid at his first school entertainment. It wouldent be my luck for your father to be a dramatic actor," he complained to Dorothy. "He had to be a dancer. That's tough, because I would like to take a crack at that Barrymore stuff. I know I could ruin a good drama, but taking dancing lessons at my age is like an old man taking up football."

The show opened on the road after a couple of weeks of rehearsals and then moved into New York on October 15, 1928. "Putting on a Fred Stone show without Fred is about like Ringling bringing in his circus and announcing that the elephants, clowns and horses were not with it." The telegrams poured in on Will by the hundreds on opening night. "Three Cheers to you, Bill," Ziegfeld wired. "There is still some sentiment left in the theatres . . . We are not all governed and controlled yet. You are doing a nice thing tonight for our dear friend, Fred, who could always be depended upon when God could be depended upon. But remember you are only pinch hitting. You still belong to me. Sorry I cannot be there tonight but I am sending the boss, Billie. Love, Flo." Billie Burke added to this: "You are going to break our hearts for being such a darling, but we certainly are proud of belonging to the theatre tonight."

Although Will had a part in the show, as King Pompanola of Itza, wearing a crown and red leggings, he carried the script in his back pocket and consulted it shamelessly. Soon he was right back in his old routines. "My little dancing goes over great, the little stunt with Dorothy and me is the biggest hit in the show," he wrote Bill Jr. "I have two comedy songs that go fine. One with Andy Tombes (he used to do Gallagher and Shean with me in the *Follies*), we have on dress suits and are barefooted, and it's a scream. We never look at our feet or let on that we are not fully dressed." It was Will Jr.'s birthday and Will sent him $17.

Will never received as high critical acclaim as for his performance in *Three Cheers*. Perhaps the knowledge that he was doing it for a friend brought more out of him. "Although I apologize for what may seem to be bad manners," George Jean Nathan wrote in *Judge,* "I hate to think what 'Three Cheers' would have been like if Fred Stone hadn't had that accident and been able to play the lead in it. . . . Rogers single-handed takes one of the poorest librettos ever written . . . sticks it peremptorily into his back pants-pocket, manufactures a whole evening of wheezes in its stead and converts the session into a rib-tickling affair. If Stone had been on the job in his stead, all that we should have got in the place of the excellent jocosity would have been the same old routine Y.M.C.A. flipflops, vaudeville hoofing and theoretically humorous little squeaks—to say nothing of the lines concocted by Anne Caldwell and R. H. Burnside. Rogers' informal drooleries send these lines scooting shamefacedly back into the wings. He fingers his nose at them, rends the Caldwell-Burnside plot until it turns pale in the face, and converts the occasion into something eminently worth the money. A toothsome clown, this Wilhem; an observation, true enough, that hardly comes under the head of news."

St. John Ervine added more depth to the criticism in the New York

World, October 17, 1928: "I think I could be cruel to Mr. Rogers. I think I could clench my teeth and insist that he should perform without a moment's break for the whole evening. . . . Not every day does one meet a comedian who can keep our interest incessantly engaged. To hear him discoursing on current politics is *both illuminating and intensely funny. I now announce to the world that I have learned more about American politics from Mr. Rogers in one evening than I have learnt from all the editorial and textbooks that I have read since I landed in New York. . . .*

"This man knows . . . He is the most richly endowed comedian I have seen in America, for his stuff, which I understand he makes for himself, is always funny and is frequently witty, and is nearly always wise. If Mr. Rogers can make me, a foreigner, feel intimately and humorously acquainted with the domestic policies of the United States how immensely influential his effects on the natives must be. I am afraid he disorganized the show, but so far as I am concerned, he can continue to disorganize shows for the rest of his life."

Another approach to Will's performance came from Robert Littell in the New York *Evening Post,* for October 20, 1928: "I think a study of Will Rogers should be made by all other inferior comedians. His stuff is his own, and quite inimitable, but there are certain ways of getting it over which could profitably be examined. Will Rogers makes a statement, then another, then a third. All together they make perfectly good sense, and are often funny, so that your mouth widens toward a smile. Then, after the briefest pause, comes a sudden final thrust which explodes the whole business as if it were gunpowder. Will Rogers is master of this slow-fuse business. There is a *public platform manner* among comedians as well as politicians. *Will Rogers always talks to us privately and confidentially.* Even before he opens his mouth to speak, the barrier of the footlights is down and we are in the same room with him. . . . If he didn't have supreme command of this informal mood, some of the things he says, the cracks he gets off at big people all the way up to the President, would sound fresh and in poor taste. But his drawling tact always saves him from that."

Robert Sherwood best described Will's triumph in *Three Cheers:* "I'll never forget 'Three Cheers' . . . you sang, and danced and tumbled, and told about a million jokes, all good, and you put on a different performance every night. A person could see 'Three Cheers' at the Wednesday matinee and then come back and see it again in the evening and not know it was the same show. Between performances you'd read something in the papers that caused you to rewrite the entire part. The doorman at the Globe Theatre used to complain about you because it was his job to tell chauffeurs of private cars what time they should come back after the show. He never knew what to say, because some nights you'd ring down the final curtain at ten past eleven, and other times, when you were really in a talkative mood, you'd keep the audience in their seats and hollering for more until midnight." [1]

Will's "partner," Dorothy Stone (of whom Littell commented that Will "could not have had a better partner than Dorothy Stone") told an interesting anecdote on how he handled unusual situations. During Christmas, Betty brought the children to New York to be with Will. After Christmas, at a performance, Dorothy noticed that Will was nervous and upset—missed his cues—and was not himself.

"What is the matter, Bill?" she asked when they went off.

"Well, Dotty, Betty and the children came down to the show to say good-by. They're in my dressing room, but we've lost Jimmy somewhere, and they've got to catch a train in a few moments."

The call came and they returned to the stage together. As they did so, Will happened to glance up at a box and there sat Jimmy all alone, his chin cupped in his hands, watching the show. A loveable grin spread across Will's face.

"There you are, young'un," he shouted, "hurry up and come down or you'll miss the train."

Will turned to the audience, grinned sheepishly, and explained what had happened. Then as Jimmy came down from the box, he went over and kissed him good-by, sending him scooting backstage with a slap on his bottom.

While Will played in *Three Cheers* the Rothstein murder case was much in the news, and he made some comments on the way it was being handled. Among them was that Mayor Walker was so busy with his other activities that he did not have time to pay any attention

[1] From a letter to Will quoted in the Providence (Rhode Island) *Bulletin,* June 14, 1930.

to such trifles. Jimmy sent word for Will to lay off him. That evening Will came out, peered around the audience, and said: "If the man who killed Rothstein is in the audience, I want to give him a last chance to give up." The audience howled, knowing this was about all that Walker was doing. The publisher, Paul Block, a friend of Jimmy's, lambasted Will in a paid advertisement in the New York papers. That evening Will went for him. "Mr. Block is mad at me . . . He's printing pieces in the papers about how awful it is for me to make cracks about our prominent men . . . Of course, I've never said anything about Mr. Block . . . not a word until tonight . . . But I would if I had known how bad he wanted it . . . And I promise to say something about him the first time he comes to this theater . . . That ought to put him back in good humor again . . . He asks what right do I have to make light of the names of the mighty? . . . Course he's talking about Jimmy Walker . . . There ain't nobody but me and Jimmy should be slower to get mad at each other . . . We both make our living by kidding the public."

As the country waited for March 4, 1929, when President-Elect Hoover's hand would grasp the throttle of our national affairs, political news was scarce. "Mr. Hoover lands at Old Point Comfort tomorrow . . . That's about the last comfort he will get for the next four years. . . . Certainly a great business opportunity showed up in the papers today . . . No training, no conscience necessary . . . All you need is six hundred thousand dollars [the cost of a seat on the New York Stock Exchange], but you get it back the first good day . . . *Wall Street is dividing the kitty with 275 more members* . . . The farmers ought to go together and buy one seat . . . That would relieve the whole bunch . . . Dident we used to have a word during the war called 'nonessential?' . . . Our new Chief of Police here has just about quit raiding the 'Speakeasies' . . . His squads were just exhausted . . . It was just like trying to keep dry with nothing but a Lamp Shade over you . . . About the best he can do now is to try and do what he can to keep 'em from opening 'em up right in the Police Stations . . . The Juries they have here in New York on all the Night Club cases have refused to convict . . . They have just brought in a series of verdicts of 'Poor business judgment on the part of the accused for entering a business that is already overcrowded' . . . In some cases, they have opened 'em up right in the Jury rooms for accommodation of the Juries."

In April, 1929, *Three Cheers* closed in New York and went on the road, playing first in Boston. It was there that Will claimed to have received the biggest laugh of his career. From the stage he introduced Babe Ruth and his new bride to Charles Francis Adams, the only living descendant of two presidents and the new Secretary of the Navy under Hoover. Babe shook hands with Adams. "Now, folks, you wouldent think after having these two men, one a descendant of two Presidents and the other the greatest Sport favorite we ever produced, that we possibly could have a bigger man here tonight than either of them . . . In fact, bigger than both of them put together . . . Well, we have . . . I want to introduce him . . ." All eyes turned the way Will was pointing, perhaps expecting President Hoover to be there ". . . the giant of the Ringling Brothers Circus." Will had planted him in a box.

Three Cheers closed in Pittsburgh on June 1, 1929, and the next day Will flew to California to begin another career, acting in talking pictures.

Burns Mantle, in the New York *Sunday News* for October 28, 1928, best summed up the gallant gesture Will had made for a friend. It was not the money he had given up, for Will already had more "than is good for his children, if not for himself. If that were all his sacrifices meant, it would be nothing. No, it isn't the money that means anything in this sacrifice. It is the prompting of one man's affection for another that is the big thing. It is the urge of Will Rogers' friendship for his injured pal that counts. It is his willingness to give up something that he'd rather do to save the Stone show that makes it an unusual event on Broadway. And so Rogers emerges again as a big man in show business and in fact, an impulsive, generous, clean-souled sentimentalist. Let them who will grow mushy over the incident. Fred and Will know what it means and what it stands for. They do that sort of thing, make that kind of sacrifice, in the Western ranch country from which these boys came, every day in the week and never think anything of it. There is never any question of money involved, nor any mention of it." Somehow, it is deeply suspected, there was a lot of Cherokee in it also.

The Museum of Modern Art

A cadet at Kemper School, Boonville, Missouri, 1897

On arrival he created a sensation with his ten-gallon cowboy hat, flaming red flannel shirt, fancy vest, and a red bandanna handkerchief knotted at the throat. His trousers were stuffed into high-heeled red-top boots with jingling spurs on them.

Betty Blake of Rogers, Arkansas, in 1900

The Visiting Girl

"I was such a sport it took me eight years to talk her into marrying me . . ."

The Museum of Modern Art

Will showing off his rope tricks to a crowd of boys "down under" in Australia in 1903. He was billed as "The Mexican Rope Artist" and was dressed in a tight-fitting red velvet suit, crisscrossed with gold braid and with broad, gold stripes down the trouser legs. Later, he wore this suit in a special performance at a rodeo for Betty's benefit, much to her embarrassment.

The Museum of Modern Art

Will and Irvin Cobb

The two had been friends since Will's vaudeville days when Irvin discovered that Will wasn't a phony cowboy. Will once turned down a lucrative writing assignment because he couldn't take time off from roping goats and talking to Irvin Cobb. The other cowboy is little Jimmie Rogers. From his look he would like to get the picture-taking over and start twirling his lariat.

The Museum of Modern Art

The Rogers children loved horseback riding better than any other sport. But they took to other kinds as well. Here is Jim about to take off for a fast trip on his bicycle.

The Museum of Modern Art

The Rogers children began learning to ride on their second birthday. Here is Will, Jr., riding hell-for-leather soon thereafter.

The Museum of Modern Art

Will in his first moving picture, *Laughing Bill Hyde,* based on a novel by Rex Beach of the same name. This was made by Samuel Goldwyn at the old Ft. Lee, New Jersey, studios, in the summer of 1918 while Will was still in the *Ziegfeld Follies.*

The Museum of Modern Art

In 1921 Will went into moving-picture production for himself. He produced three one-reel pictures. Among them was *One Day in 365,* a pictorial story of a day in the life of the Rogers family. Here they are at breakfast.

The Museum of Modern Art

The goat is roped! Will is off his horse with the piggin' string in his mouth, and down goes the goat . . .

The Museum of Modern Art

Better tie him good . . . That goat may look as if he is finished but he is just 'possoming . . . If that piggin' string isn't tied right, he'll be up and away like an antelope . . .

The Museum of Modern Art

In Dublin, Ireland, in 1926. Will loved the Emerald Isle and the Irish took him to their hearts. "It keeps a small nation busy," he told them, "raising the police force of the world."

Wide World Photo

The 1932 Presidential Campaign

In introducing Franklin D. Roosevelt at the Hollywood Bowl Will said, "This speech may have lacked . . . floweriness . . . Come back when you are President and I will do better . . . I am wasting no oratory on a mere prospect."

Left to right: F.D.R., Jimmy Roosevelt, W. G. McAdoo and Will.

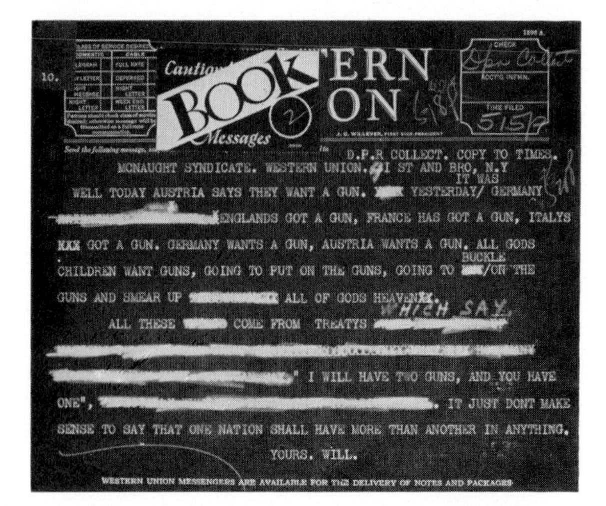

D.P.R COLLECT. COPY TO TIMES.
MCNAUGHT SYNDICATE. WESTERN UNION. 41 ST AND BRO, N.Y
WELL TODAY AUSTRIA SAYS THEY WANT A GUN. IT WAS YESTERDAY/ GERMANY
ENGLANDS GOT A GUN, FRANCE HAS GOT A GUN, ITALYS GOT A GUN. GERMANY WANTS A GUN, AUSTRIA WANTS A GUN. ALL GODS CHILDREN WANT GUNS, GOING TO PUT ON THE GUNS, GOING TO BUCKLE/ON THE GUNS AND SMEAR UP ALL OF GODS HEAVEN.
ALL THESE COME FROM TREATYS WHICH SAY, " I WILL HAVE TWO GUNS, AND YOU HAVE ONE", . IT JUST DONT MAKE SENSE TO SAY THAT ONE NATION SHALL HAVE MORE THAN ANOTHER IN ANYTHING.
YOURS. WILL.

WESTERN UNION MESSENGERS ARE AVAILABLE FOR THE DELIVERY OF NOTES AND PACKAGES

Will's Daily Wires were usually typed on telegram blanks. He crossed out his errors with x's, then wrote over them with a heavy black pencil.

The Museum of Modern Art

"All I know is what I read in the Newspaper . . ."
"They never could tell whether I was reading or sleeping . . ."

Curtis Studios

"When I roped Betty I did the star performance of my life . . ."

Written on Will's and Betty's twenty-fifth wedding anniversary on November 25, 1933.

The Museum of Modern Art

Will Typing One of His Daily Wires

"When Will beat out those pieces of his," Irvin Cobb said, "it sounded like a brewery wagon running away across a covered bridge."

Wide World Photo

Will and Wiley Post at Seattle, Washington, August 8, 1935, before taking off for Juneau, Alaska, in "the little red bus" in which they crashed to their deaths near Pt. Barrow, Alaska, on August 15, 1935.

The Museum of Modern Art

America's "Unofficial" First Family
Standing: left to right, Will, Will, Jr., Mary, Jim
Seated: Betty Blake Rogers

The Museum of Modern Art

The Rogers's ranch house at Santa Monica, California, now a State Park.

"What I shall remember of it was that I felt perfectly at home. I ate four times as much as I usually do. Chicken and ham on the same platter . . . hot biscuits . . . coffee that a spoon would stand up in . . ."

26

"The Crash Heard 'Round the World"

IN THE SAME DAILY WIRE IN WHICH WILL BADE THE Coolidges farewell, on March 4, 1929, he stated that "we got Hoover all set now for four years. After that he will have to hustle for himself. There is an option clause in his contract, but *we will look him over carefully before we exercise it.*" This prediction had two elements in it. One was the condition of the country and the other was the capacity of the man selected to lead it.

The United States was faced with the accumulations of eight revolutionary years in which the social and economic structure of the country had changed radically without a corresponding evolution in its political machinery and methods. "The business of the United States is business," said President Coolidge, and under his benign rule, as far as business was concerned, the greatest consolidation of companies in history had taken place. In 1919 only 22 mergers of public utility companies ("the arch of the Republican Party") took place. By 1926 over 3,500 concerns had gone into holding companies. More than half of all the electric power generated was by three companies and 15 companies controlled over 90 per cent of all power produced. From 1919 to 1929 over 1,200 combinations in mining and manufacturing involving the merging of 4,000 and the disappearance of 6,000 firms were manipulated. The number of banks in the country had shrunk to half. Chain stores in the retail trade were rapidly replacing independent concerns. In communication and transportation the same thing had happened. By 1933 less than 600 corporations owned over 50 per cent of the nation's corporate wealth. In manufacturing, 1/10 of 1 per cent of the corporations owned 46 per cent of the assets. In mining 2/10 of 1 per cent owned 35 per cent of the assets. One and 2/10 of the utilities companies owned 84 per cent of the assets. Three automobile companies manufactured 90 per cent of the cars. Four tobacco companies made 90 per cent of the cigarettes. Four typewriter companies produced 95 per cent of all typewriters. The chief natural resources were owned or controlled by a few concerns. Fifty per cent of all copper was controlled by four companies; United States Steel owned over half the iron ore deposits; and the Aluminum Company of America had a practical monopoly of that metal. On the other hand, while other phases of the economy were booming, agriculture had sunk to an all-time low.

Although the country had turned to Hoover with wild enthusiasm, the doubt implied in Will's prediction was of how well he could handle the skeleton of reality on which had been imposed the padded prosperity of an overstuffed and "overfatted goose." Prophetically Franklin D. Roosevelt had given the answer before the 1928 election. In comparing the fitness of Governor Al Smith and Secretary of Commerce Herbert Hoover for the Presidency he wrote:

I want to lay down the hypothesis which I believe to be true that an executive post such as that of Governor or President *calls for more than mere executive ability*. For instance, I know dozens of supremely successful corporation executives—Presidents of great railroad systems, of nationwide industrial corporations, of huge banks, and I can frankly say that very few of them would have successful careers as State Governors or in the Presidency. The administration of a government chief executive calls for an added quality, or to be more correct, two qualities. . . .

First, the rare ability to coordinate an executive branch of government with the legislation thereof. Secondly, equally rare ability to present great public issues in such simple terms to the voting public that without heat or passion, that voting public can act fairly and honestly on those issues. . . .

I have long been a friend of Sec. Hoover. I have tried to picture to myself what kind of President he would make. I am proud as an American citizen of the fine and able way in which Sec. Hoover has carried out his relief work . . . his aid to industry through the Dept. of Commerce . . . But Mr. Hoover as President would have a very different task to perform. His previous tasks have been directed, first one then the other, toward one definite aim. He has been sole dictator of each of these tasks. . . . In a sense each has been an amplification of a specific engineering job. . . .

The task of the Presidency is far different. . . . The President of the United States must have a mind not single-tracked, but like a great railroad yard. . . . Though I admire Hoover greatly as an administrator for a single task, I cannot picture a President Hoover successful in jumping at half hour intervals from problem to problem, from point to point, in the administration of the vast array of business affairs of the Federal Government and keeping his equilibrium.[1]

This was written before the end of the time "when betting on the Republicans was like being a Broker—you couldn't possibly lose." At that time another quality would be needed, a realization that "the people's budget" must be balanced before the financial one of a businessman's government.

The condition of agriculture was so deplorable that President Hoover called Congress into session to consider its problems. The moment Congress convened, the lobbyists for big business were waiting to remind those who had accepted its aid in campaign contributions that "a little competition from foreign markets was looming on the horizon, and it would be appreciated if it was knocked in the head by higher tariffs before it became larger." Will saw what was coming. "The tariff is an instrument for the benefit of those who make to be used against those who buy . . . As there is more 'buys' than 'makes,' it is an instrument of the minority . . . But what a minority! . . . It's good-by to any relief for the dear old farmer . . . Hoover is going to have to pay his election debts . . . But he pulled a bad one when he ever let them kid him into monkeying with that tariff thing . . . All he had to promise was to get some sort of legislation to help the farmer . . . He dident have to have a grab bag for the Pennsylvania manufacturers."

[1] *Franklin D. Roosevelt's Own Story* (Boston: Little, Brown & Company, 1951), pp. 105-106.

One of Will's prime targets in the tariff fight was lobbyist Joseph Grundy from Pennsylvania. "Mr. Grundy is kinder the Federal Reserve of the Standpat Republican Party . . . When the boys need a little more nourishment in the way of some financial fodder for the forthcoming election, why, Mr. Grundy is the Lad that O.K.'s the shipment out to the needy Senator, and his benefactions have been known to reach as far down as a mere Representative in Congress. . . . Politics is advertised under the heading of idealism, but it is carried out under the heading of business, and the bigger the business, the bigger the Politics."

While the tariff fight was going on, the fruits of an overstuffed and undercontrolled economy were ripening in the wild orgy of speculation and manipulation on the stock exchanges. President Hoover, in good Republican tradition, did not think it a proper function of government to interfere directly or that controls were necessary. Will's voice was one of the few that warned about what would happen. "The whole financial structure of Wall Street seemed to fall the other day on the mere fact that the Federal Reserve Bank raised the interest rate from 5 to 6 percent . . . Any business that can't survive 1 percent raise must be skating on mighty thin ice. . . . Why, even the poor farmers took a raise from 6 to 10 percent, with another 10 percent to get the loan from the banks. . . . It took all of that to completely break 'em, and nobody connected with the government paid any attention . . . But let Wall Street have a nightmare and the whole country had to help get them back in bed again."

Foreign relations and the state of preparedness of the country had proceeded along normal Republican lines. In 1928, following a suggestion of French Foreign Minister Aristide Briand, Secretary of State Frank B. Kellogg took the lead in negotiating a series of treaties renouncing war as an instrument of national policy. This is not to sneer at an honest, sincere effort, but as a means strong enough it was on a par with the idea that the stock market could be kept in bounds by the consciences of individuals, particularly those of "rugged individualists," if consciences came into the thinking at all.

In the spring of 1929 a bill came up in Congress to build some cruisers, to replace some of the strength lost in the sinkings following the Washington Disarmament Conference, and Will commented: "Mr.

Coolidge will be getting out in a couple of weeks, and he wants as much to happen as possible under his Czarship. *Course there is a lot of things that he hopes don't happen till he is out of sight of the White House.* He wants the cruisers voted under his coaching, but he kinder wants Congress to stall along and not vote the money till after Hoover is in . . . He *is more set on going out of office having his Budget balanced than any one thing.*"

It was absolutely necessary to have the cruisers, Will argued, otherwise we would have nothing to sink at the next disarmament conference. "You see people kinder work this way, that is, their minds do . . . One year they are warlike, they get to thinking, why shouldent we have the biggest Army and the biggest Navy in the World? . . . Then along come some taxes and bust 'em in the face and they seem all at once to get the Peace fever. . . . England sees us building these Ships . . . They will gradually start spreading a little talk about what a shame it is to build against each other, and the first thing you know we have fell for it and are just dying to get to a Conference and sink something. . . . Then we go to the other extreme, we sink everything except the Deligates that went, the very things we should sink . . . Why don't we either go and build a great Navy, or have none at all, *for running second don't get you anywhere in anybody's war* . . . People are not going to quit fighting any more than Individuals are going to quit fighting . . . A Nation is nothing but a boy grown up, and he hasent any too good education in growing up."

Will had planned to go to China in the summer of 1929 but his work in *Three Cheers* prevented it. He was particularly sorry in July when it looked as though war might break out between Russia and China. England had recognized Russia, and was getting "all set for the old war contracts. . . . You know there is nothing makes a disreputable nation look respectable so quick as to have it give you a fat war contract. . . . All our highly civilized nations are great humanitarians but if two countries are going to kill each other off, neutrals at least would like the privilege of furnishing the ammunition. . . . When the Judgment Day comes, civilization will have an alabi, 'I never took a human life, I only sold the fellow the gun to take it with.' "

The situation in China also brought some comments on the relations of the United States with that unhappy country. "China has been awful nice to us . . . They have let us use their home grounds to send our Marines when we dident have any other war on for them at the time . . . Why, there has been times that if it hadent been for China allowing us to go in and shoot at them, why, we wouldent have had a soul in the world to shoot at . . . We have made 'em keep what we call the 'Open Door.' That means they wasent allowed to charge too much tariff on our stuff coming in, or they wasent to keep us out of any family feuds they might have . . . *We send Missionaries there. They go through Chicago on the way out* . . . Missionaries teach 'em not only how to serve the Lord but run a Ford Car . . . Then the American Agents sells 'em one . . . *You take religion backed up by Commerce and its awful hard for a heathen to overcome.*"

In October, 1929, Will was invited by Henry Ford to attend a birthday party for Thomas A. Edison in Detroit. He flew from Los Angeles to Chicago, where he was informed that the flight to Detroit had been canceled on account of bad weather. Irritated at the delay, he found a pilot who was willing to try to get through. Headwinds slowed them down and it was dark by the time they reached Detroit, where the field was not lit for night landing. The pilot passed a note back saying they would have to return to Chicago. When over the city, he passed back another note that they were out of gas and he would have to make a crash landing. Flares were dropped which showed a vacant lot. As the wheels of the plane touched the ground in an apparently safe landing, Will, who had braced himself for the crash, heaved a sigh of relief and relaxed. As he did so the plane turned over, slamming him against the side. The pilot helped load him into a taxi.

"Where do you want to go, buddy?" the driver asked.

"Chicago," Will mumbled, half-conscious.

"Well, buddy, you're in Chicago now."

Will spent the night at the Sherman Hotel, where a doctor strapped up his sides and chest to ease the pain. Early the next morning he flew to Detroit, refusing to wait for an X ray of his chest. After the celebration he flew to New York, where an X ray showed that all his ribs had been cracked. He flew back home with yards of adhesive tape strapped around him. It was very uncomfortable, so on the advice of

Betty's chauffeur he stripped it off, split an old inner tube and strapped that around his chest.

"When he came home at night," Betty wrote, "it would have slipped in a loose roll around his waist. But he was still cheerful and he did not let it interfere with his calf roping."

Will's crash in Chicago was minor when compared to the one "heard 'round the world" that started on October 28, 1929. "I have been in Washington on Inauguration day, Claremore on Fourth of July, Dearborn on Edison Day . . . But to have been in New York on 'Wailing Day' . . . You had to stand in line to get a window to jump out of, and speculators were selling space for bodies in the East River. . . . If England is supposed by International Treaty to protect the Wailing Wall, they will have to come here to do it . . . The wall runs from the Battery to the Bronx . . . You know there is nothing that hollers as quick and loud as a gambler . . . Now they know what the farmer has been up against for eight years."

Will had a scoffing laugh when it was reported that "Mr. Morgan, Lamont, Charley Mitchell and Mr. George Baker held a meeting and let everybody see 'em in this huddle . . . Then the market perks up . . . I was just thinking what a great idea it would be if we could get these boys to room together for six months . . . There is no telling to what heights the market might go . . . Just think what a calamity if they forgot where they were to meet some day to inspire confidence."

Will gibed even more loudly a couple of days later. "Sure must be a great consolation to the poor people who lost their stock in the late crash to know that it has fallen in the hands of Mr. Rockefeller who will take care of it and see that it has a good home and never be allowed to wander around unprotected again. There is one rule that works in every calamity, be it pestilence, war or famine, the rich get richer, and the poor get poorer . . . *The poor even help arrange it. . . .* But just as Mr. Brisbane and I have been constantly telling you, Don't gamble; take all your savings and buy some good stock, and hold it till it goes up, then sell it. *If it don't go up, don't buy it!"*

Will gave a vivid description of Wall Street. "I dident have anything particular against Wall Street, but knowing the geographical and physical attributes of it, I knew that it was crooked . . . You can stand at the head of it, and you can only see the bend . . . It just won't let you see all of it at once as short as it is." From Wall Street and from Washington came a new note. "America already holds the record for freak movements . . . Now we have a new one . . . It's called, 'Restoring Confidence.' Rich men who never had a mission in life outside of watching a stock ticker are working day and night 'restoring Confidence.' Railroad men met yesterday with Mr. Hoover and agreed to lower the fares on prominent delegates rushing to conference to Restore (Confidence. . . .) Writers are working night shifts, speakers' tables are littered up . . . Ministers are preaching statistics, all on 'Restoring Confidence'!"

Will was asked by President Hoover to help in the movement. "Now I am not unpatriotic, and I want to do my bit, so I hereby offer my services to the President, my Country, and my friends around Old Trinity Church, New York, to do anything (outside of serving on a Commission) that I can, in this great movement . . . But you will have to give me some idea where 'Confidence' is, and just who you want it restored to."

Since no one properly enlightened him, Will made his own analysis. "Confidence hasent left this country . . . Confidence has just got wise, and the guys that it got wise to are wondering where it has gone . . . You take confidence, it's one of the hardest things in the World to get restored once it gets out of bounds . . . I have helped restore a lot of things in my time, such as cattle to the home range . . . Herded *Follies* Girls toward the stage door at stage time . . . Helped revive interest in National Political Conventions . . . Even assisted the Democrats in every forlorn pilgrimage, and a host of other worthy charities . . . But I tell you this 'Restoring Confidence' is the toughest drive I ever assisted in . . . The trouble is the market has taken the joy out of gambling."

Will promised to help with words. "Course I havent been buying anything myself . . . I want to give the other folks a chance to have confidence first . . . There is none of the Greedy Pig about me . . . This Confidence was *'for sale,'* and I wanted them to have the very first chance of buying it." Will admitted that he went over to the side of the stock market group for "vanity, *for I could see all the big men over there,* and I felt flattered when I saw that I was to join in this great work of getting people back to contributing to Wall Street again."

It would take some time to accomplish it, he warned. "Some of them not only lost confidence but they lost money, some of them all of their money . . . And it wasent 'Paper Money' they lost. So we will have to wait till they get some money in some other business, perhaps in some business in which they really have confidence. *Then they will be able to get back into the market not only with new confidence but new money.*"

As Will made this damning judgment on the final crash of "the return to normalcy," he wondered "what a little gentleman in a rented frame house in Northhampton was thinking." On the other hand, he knew what President Hoover was doing. Faced with the inability to handle that "railroad yard of tracks," he was appointing commissions right and left to search for answers for him. One of the commissions had as its task to discover "what has brought the social changes in our lives here lately." Will answered this one: "Buying on credit, waiting for relief, Ford cars, too many Republicans, Notre Dame coaching methods, and two-thirds of the Americans, both old and young, thinking they possessed 'It.' "

The best evidence Will saw throughout the country for "restoring confidence" came from Henry Ford, who raised wages at his plants and attempted to shame other employers into doing the same. "Some of those old babies are pretty hard to shame . . . They offered to help prosperity but they dident want to hardly go to that means to do it." Earlier in the summer Will had passed a different kind of judgment on Ford—an over-all evaluation of his contribution to American life. "Henry Ford is 66 years old today . . . He has had more influence on the lives and habits of this nation than any man ever produced in it . . . Great educators try to teach people, great preachers try to change people, but no man produced through the accepted channels has moved the world like Henry Ford . . . He put wheels on our homes . . . A man's castle is his sedan . . . It will take a hundred years to tell whether he has helped us or hurt us, but he certainly dident leave us like he found us."

On Christmas Day, 1929, Will passed a terrible judgment on the Terrible Twenties, a decade of "a return to normalcy." "Passed the Potter's field yesterday and they was burying two stanch old Republicans, both of whom died of starvation, and the man in charge told me their last words were, 'I still think America is fundamentally sound.' And today they are burying hundreds all over our free land whose intention of celebrating Christmas was splendid, but whose judgment in bootleggers was bad."

27

"There Ain't No Civilization Where There Ain't No Satisfaction"

IN 1929 THE LABOR PARTY CAME TO POWER IN ENGLAND and in October Prime Minister Ramsay MacDonald visited the United States to make arrangements for a disarmament conference to be held in London after the first of the year. "Peace is like a beautiful woman," Will warned, "it's wonderful, but has been known to bear watching. So when we are having tea with Ramsay, let's hold out a rowboat."

Soon after the first of the year the delegates began to assemble in London "to disarm themselves of the things they figure won't be used in the next war, which will leave them more money to develop the things they will use . . . *It's an economic, more than a humanitarian affair* . . . It's like holding a traffic conference and just discussing the limiting of horses and buggies . . . I wonder if we ever will get so civilized that one will be held to limit submarines, airplanes and chemicals? . . . *You can't say civilization don't advance,* however, *for in every war they kill you in a new way.*"

In New York, between motion-picture commitments, Will had a sudden idea. "When I was a little boy out in the old Indian Territory I remember seeing a sheriff disarm some men one time and it always fascinated me . . . But I had never seen it since so when I got to New York and they told me they was going to disarm whole nations over in London next week I wanted to see how it is done."

The American delegation had already sailed, and Will feared they might get "the disarming done before I got there," so he scurried around and found that the *Bremen* would sail that night and, being a faster boat, would arrive in London ahead of the delegation. Winfield Sheehan, Will's boss at Twentieth Century-Fox, described how it was managed: "I was at the Savoy-Plaza Hotel when a telephone call came from Rogers. I didn't even know he was in New York. He needed a passport in a hurry. I put through a call to some friends in Washington and got him a temporary passport. Will told me he was going to do some shopping as he had not brought any clothes from the coast. That evening he came to my hotel, wearing a new, hand-me-down blue serge suit he had bought. Under his arms, he carried several paper parcels containing some changes of underclothes, a half-dozen shirts, six red bandanna handkerchiefs, a five-cent comb and a nickel cake of soap. He refused a bag I offered him and that midnight boarded the *Bremen* with his wardrobe under his arm."

On Will's arrival in London he cabled that the conference was a success. "The American delegation just arrived and went into a conference at the American bar and sunk a fleet of schooners without warning . . . They brought eighteen young typewriters—not the machines but the ones that run them . . . That's four and a half blondes to the delegate, and I can write in longhand everything that will be done here in the next month . . . They even brought some Marines on the boat to show it was a peace conference."

The big feature was a speech by King George officially opening the conference. "It was nothing but a Democratic Convention with a silk hat on . . . The King made the best speech and then showed his real intelligence by leaving . . . When speaking, he was facing the American delegation . . . When he went out he happened to think, so he sent four men back and they carried the gold throne chair out . . . That will go on record as the first lack of confidence shown."

At a dinner given by Ambassador Dawes, Will met Admiral Takahira, one of Japan's delegates. "Admiral, I am going right home to America and I want to say that I shook hands with the winner." As to the conference itself, France and Italy did most of the talking, but "the Japs never say a word or miss a word." In his summation of expectations of what would be accomplished, Will stated: "I see where Coolidge is going to print the history of the United States on a single rock . . . Well, I could print the history of the results of this disarmament conference on the head of a pin and have room enough left over for the chorus of 'Yes, We Have No Bananas.' "

While in London Will had tea with Lloyd George, spent two hours with Bernard Shaw ("once in my life I knew enough to keep still and he was going great") and invited him to visit the United States ("he is coming as soon as I come home and civilize 'em")—so he did not feel his trip was wasted.

After a chat with Ambassador Dawes Will reported on the struggle of "old ambitious Mothers to get their daughters presented at the Court of St. James . . . They use every ruse known to scheming science . . . They have letters from their Postmasters, Congressmen, Senators, Young Voters League, and do everything that they can to blackjack the Ambassador into thinking that if 'Our Millie' is not one of the favored, that they will see he is recalled from London and sent to Peru . . . They take Houses in London, and start their Campaigns early . . . They use dinners as bribes, and would use money if they could."

On his return home Will signed a contract for fourteen radio talks of fifteen minutes each for the unprecedented sum of $72,000. There was a great outcry at his being paid $350 a minute just to get up and "blather." An editorial in *World's Work* defended him. "Under the guise of genial raillery," it said, "his mission is to tell us the hard, blunt truths about ourselves—truths about our politics, our civic standards, and our social habits. They are the sort of truths we do not always like to hear, but we will take them with a contagious chuckle and a piece of chewing gum—Confession is good for the soul, and he supplies it." What was not generally known then was the fact that Will donated the money to charity.

One of the "hard, blunt truths" concerned England directly but the Western world in general. "They got Gandhi in Jail in India . . ." this on May 5, 1930 . . . "He preached 'Liberty without Violence.' He swore all his followers 'to truth and constant poverty.' He wanted nothing for himself not even the ordinary comforts . . . He believed in 'prayer and renunciation.' Well, naturally, a man that bold couldent run at large these days. They figured a crazy man like that was liable to get other people to wanting those fanatical things . . . *The whole thing gives you a pretty fair idea of what would happen to our Saviour if he would come on earth today* . . . Why, say, he wouldent last near as long as he did then . . . Civilization has got past 'truth and poverty and renunciation' and all that old junk! *Throw those nuts in jail!*"

On Memorial Day, 1930, Will visited the incapacitated veterans of World War I at Sawtelle Hospital in Los Angeles. It brought him thoughts of then and now. "Flags flying, and old men and young marching . . . Free room and board and a day's speeches a year ain't hardly all we promised 'em at recruiting time, but they are good sports and take it good-naturedly . . . They know we will have the same old 'bologna' to hand out to the next bunch, to keep our investments intact . . . only we don't call it investments, we say it's democracy."

He had the same disappointing story to tell when he read the list of the girls picked "to bend a knee before Royalty. I kinder thought Dawes would pick out a bunch of Girls in our land who had accomplished something . . . But, no, it was the same old racket . . . The bank book got you in . . . Achievement couldent hurdle a flock of Credit slips . . . The whole thing is the prize 'Hooey' of all time . . . They don't say a word . . . The Queen don't say a word to them . . . They just come by, do a little bum courtesy and then they are through for the day."

On the other hand, Will was getting more satisfaction out of life than ever before. He had hesitated, partly because he was away so much, to give up "the house that jokes built." He even started to remodel it and out of this came his decision. "You see," he explained to his friend Rob Wagner, "when they got to tearin' out things, they found what the architect called a 'condition,' then they found another 'condition,' so out came another room, and another and *another*. Finally, they tore the whole thing down and took it away. But . . ." he flashed his grin ". . . the joke's on the architect, for I'm not goin' to rebuild."

The chief reason, however, was that a house had been built on the ranch, and Will and his family moved there.

The famous sports writer, O. B. Keeler, of the Atlanta *Journal*, gives an on-the-spot impression of the house at the ranch. "When you walk into the Rogers' ranch house, you're at home. You know what that means. I have been in a lot of houses, here and there, about the world. Some very fine houses. Some were not so fine. Some were not fine at all. And not all of them made you feel at home. Will Rogers' ranch house is different from any home I have been in, as a home. But what I shall remember of it, beyond anything and everything else, was that I felt perfectly and absolutely at home." Betty had a talent for inducing this feeling.

The main ranch house was divided by a patio, built around two great live oaks. This patio, with a luxuriance of ivy and potted plants, served as an outdoor living and dining room. The only roof was a pergola of rambler roses at one end. The rest was left exposed to the sky except that on cool nights an awning could be drawn over it and a log fire built in the stone fireplace.

"That's where we eat," Will told Keeler. "Come on in the washroom and clean up."

"It seems a bit odd," Keeler wrote, "to sit at a long table covered with blue-checked cloth, and be served by perfectly trained servants. But homelike! I ate four times as much as I usually do when out to dinner. Chicken and ham, on the same platter; beautiful vegetables; hot biscuits—no better were composed south of the Smith & Wesson line. Coffee that a spoon would stand up in, good hot bracing coffee. And Mr. Rogers advising the girls in a stage whisper, 'Here, Girls, eat up, there's plenty more.' " Uncle Clem, for all the world.

Indoors, the enormous living room centered around another rough-hewn fireplace. On the mantel was a model of a covered wagon, a memento from Will's *Two Wagons—Both Covered* days. Over the mile-wide fireplace stretched a set of Texas longhorns. The walls of the room were stained redwood and bristled with a hodgepodge of spurs, riding quirts from Argentina to Canada, and mounted brass- and silver-bossed saddles from all over. Hung on them also were four of Charlie Russell's best Westerns. The floor checkered a "bright mosaic of Navajo rugs" and the chandeliers were a doubletree and neck-yoke of pioneer days "more charming in their '49 rusticity than a glittering Delmonico drop."

At one end of the room was a plate-glass picture window that looked out toward the ocean and part of the city below.

"That's Flo Ziegfeld's idea," Will told Keeler. "He liked the view but he had to go out on the porch. So he got his chauffer to make some measurements when I wasent looking and one day here come a big truck with a load of glass about eight feet high, and some men who began knocking out the end of my house without asking me anything about it. And there you are."

Outside there were barns and stables, a complete polo field, dogs, cattle, goats, poultry, and horses—at least a hundred of them, more or less, depending on whether Will had seen another one he liked or some old stray that did not have a home. "From the size of our feed bill," Betty said, "you would have thought we were an orphanage for all the stray horses in the United States." Yes, the Rogers family was a good one for a horse to live with. Will's workroom was upstairs at one end of the house where he could do his reading and writing undisturbed. For further privacy he built far up a canyon a log cabin complete for living.

Life was meant to be enjoyed here. "There ain't no civilization where there ain't no satisfaction" applied to the home as well as to the country.

"Working for Will was just like being one of the family," said Ben Petti, who drove Betty's car. "I felt I lived there and it was my real home. I guess I'd been hurt, sorta, if Will hadn't invited me to his parties. He always did, you know."

Although Will's horses were treated like members of the family, automobiles as machines were to be used. One day Will drove up in a new Dodge truck with a cloud of steam coming out of the radiator.

"Have you ever thought about putting water in it?" Petti asked.

Will scratched his head in mock bewilderment. "The darn thing had water in it when I bought it," he said.

Another time he came in with a new Buick all battered up, the running board smashed and the tail pipe completely off.

"I had to get home in a hurry," he explained to Petti, "so I took a short cut across the desert."

"But it's a new car."

"Oh, sure, it must have been a pretty tough rock I run over. But don't worry, Ben, they make new cars every day."

Will had the car repaired but never used it. He learned that a Wild West Troupe needed a car to get to their engagements and did not have the money to buy one. Apologizing tor a few scratches on it, he donated it to the troupe.

Will played as hard as he worked. He never lost his interest in roping. One reason for this was a fear that remained with him constantly that "the public was going to find him out" and he might have to make his living again by his skill with the lariat. His favorite roping partner was Fred Stone, whom he had taught to rope and who could give him stiff competition in trick roping or in calf or goat roping. Will had a stuffed calf in his living room and when guests were there he practiced on it, unable to stay still for a moment. One evening the Stone family were there. Fred Stone was wearing his hair long for a part he was to play in a motion picture.

"Get yourself a haircut, Fred," Will said, as he made a deft catch of a leg of the calf from a most difficult position. "You sure look terrible."

"Can't do it, Will," Fred replied, his rope making an equally difficult catch. "Need it for my part in the picture."

"Shucks, Fred, you can wear a wig . . ." another difficult catch ". . . and you ought to get those bushy eyebrows trimmed. They look like fetlocks."

"Can't wear a wig . . ." a catch by Fred ". . . always looks wiggish . . ."

"Aw, no, Fred, I don't think so . . ." two ropes this time, one catching the head and another the foot ". . . you sure need spruced up . . ."

Recalling dozens of such incidents later, Dorothy Stone realized that she had witnessed scenes that people would have paid anything to see.

28

"Washington Would Sue Us for Calling Him Father"

THERE HAD ALWAYS BEEN PLENTY OF "COMEDY," OF humor in the United States for Will, but a country going "to the poorhouse in an automobile" was a situation more ludicrous—hence more heart-rending—than even war. The talk was absurd. "Since the Wall Street crash, which the Republicans refer to as a 'business readjustment,' prominent men have done nothing but tell us the strength of the country . . . 'Steel was strong' . . . 'T. and T. was strong' . . . 'radio was strong' . . . 'Breath was strong' . . . We have been 'stronged' to death in speeches and statements, but last night Mr. Coolidge said, 'The heart of the American people is strong,' and here over 500 died of heart failure during the late 'Republican readjustment.' What he really meant was that 'the American public's head is strong but his heart is weak.' "

As more and more people were laid off from their jobs, Congress spent most of its time haggling over the tariff bill. A vacancy had occurred in the Senate from Pennsylvania, and lobbyist Joe Grundy had received the appointment. "Senator Joe Grundy is receiving Republican praise for not voting on the Tariff measure . . . His side was already nine ahead . . . I will withhold my applause till I see what he does when a tie comes up." Will hinted also that those spending their time on the tariff might have a second thought. "Have your stenographer compile you a list of ex-Senators and Congressmen who are still living. . . . You would be surprised, g-e-n-t-l-e-m-e-n."

If some of the members of Congress, knowing where their support came from, were not worrying, President Hoover was definitely concerned. "This is a great country . . ." Will commented ". . . We used to think that 'prosperity' was a 'condition' . . . Now we find that it is a 'commodity.' . . . Mr. Hoover has ordered it to be delivered to us in sixty days, same as you would a sack of flour or a side of bacon. . . . If 'good times' is not laying on your doorsteps in two months, we can sue the Republican party, get judgment against 'em, along with 123 previous judgments we hold against the same corporation."

Nevertheless, the tariff seemed more important than the condition of the people. "It is to a Politician about what a bone is to a dog, and a fixed Jury to a Los Angeles culprit . . . It's not only his bread and butter but it's his dessert and toothpick." According to Will, Coolidge had been too wily to get involved in it. "But when Mr. Hoover come along, the old Political Boys' mouth just watered . . . They said here is some new money in the game . . . Here is a fellow that learned his Politics feeding the Armenians . . . Now if he has fed them, why, can't he be induced to slip some sustenance to us, for no Armenian or even a Boa Constrictor can gobble up any more Pork from a Barrel than a Politician."

The result was the Smoot-Hawley tariff bill that raised duties to an all-time high. Although 1,028 leading economists of the country petitioned President Hoover not to sign it, he paid off his political debt and did so. He may have followed his "conscience" and its path of political credos, but it was a strange act to make it possible for industry to raise prices when no one was working to buy the products produced. The act produced immediate foreign retaliation and hastened the decline of world trade. Within two years twenty-five nations had raised their tariffs accordingly. There is "economic" as well as physical cannibalism.

Grundy's extrafinancial reward was to have his statue placed alongside that of William Penn as the two allotted to Pennsylvania in the Capitol Hall of Fame. "The old Keystone State put William Penn in there for what he took away from the Indians in Pennsylvania," Will commented. "Now Grundy gets the other statue for what he has taken away from the white people of Pennsylvania."

As "the Hoover flag" of an empty pocket with a hole in it continued to fly for more people, the state of Pennsylvania voted to send Grundy back to his lobbying and gave his senatorial seat to Jim Davis. "Grundy now holds the same position with the Republicans in the Senate as Knute Rockne does with the great Notre Dame Team," Will gibed. "He's back as coach. You don't see Knute crying because he is not on the team." This decision in Pennsylvania should have been a warning to the Administration.

The "prosperity" President Hoover had "ordered" did not come and that "corner we were going to turn" kept receding. The whole promise of coming prosperity and how to reach it achieved a ridiculous height for Will when Ex-President Coolidge advised "the working man to spend his money, and buy everything that he could possibly afford" so that it would put more money into circulation. It was not for "businessmen" to do so! "Here is a man that the whole basis of his popularity is based on economy and thrift, and all at once to help out a situation, why, he says 'Spend.' So it's hard to tell what to believe nowadays."

As the off-year elections in 1930 approached, with the first test of Hoover's stewardship at the polls, Will had one of his most satirical laughs. "I used to try to get what I thought would be some funny political angles over the radio, and it was awful hard... But last night along came my old friend, Nick Longworth, on the air and hit on a humorous angle that I had never thought of, and I bet none of you had either. He blamed the Democratic party for the financial depression that is enveloping the world. It's really the biggest advertisement the Democratic party ever had. Why, if they was that important, they wouldent be Democrats. They would all be Republicans, but it was a new reason at that."

Election day gave Will reason to gloat. "Democrats give me a birthday Present yesterday, November Fourth... I was 51 years old and they elected fifty-one Democrats. The Democrats nominated their President yesterday also... Franklin D. Roosevelt."

Thanksgiving Day was not so pleasant in what it indicated. "The original idea was to give thanks for a 'bountiful harvest'... Well, the 'bountiful harvest' is the very thing that's the matter with us... Too much wheat, too much corn, too much cotton, too much beef... too much production of everything... So we are going through a unique experience . . . we are the first nation to starve to death in a store house that's overfilled with everything we want." Will found further satire on this when Hoover gave his State of the Union message. The President tried to explain the causes of the depression, which irritated Will. "If a snake bites you you ain't going to stop and study out where he comes from and why he was there at the time . . . You want to figure out what to do with yourself there and then . . . Hoover went on to show that we did have a lot of assets left, and was in pretty good shape . . . *They show that there is just as much of everything as there ever was, and all that . . . But they don't tell that what's the matter with us is the unequal division of it. . . . Our rich is getting richer, and our poor is getting poorer all the time, that's the thing that these great minds ought to work on . . . Not be figuring out what the cause of this depression was, but let us fix our taxes, or our government work, and our whole system so we can kinder keep it split up a little better.*" The one thing that needed attention at the moment was "substantial unemployment" and not tariffs, world courts, and disarmament.

It is amazing how the Republicans, as F.D.R. scoffed, had claimed "paternity" for the "prosperity" of the 1920's and now tried to wiggle out of being the "daddy of the depression." They would have two more years to bridle their "offspring" and then, as Will had said, Hoover would be looked over carefully by the people.

Will had warned also that "the Lord" Himself might look us over and take away His help. He did so in a region roughly known as the Southwest, once marked on the maps as "The Great Desert." Here land was broken for agriculture that should never have been touched with a plow, natural coverage in the way of brush and trees was destroyed, and wrong uses of the land resulted in soil erosion. These sins against nature, combined with a long drought, powdered the soil, and when the wind blew there were dust storms, some five miles high and so dense that visibility was reduced to a matter of feet. Thousands of farmers were forced to abandon their lands.

Added to this, increasing unemployment came to the region, as well as the rest of the nation, from the depression, and the region Will still called home was in a desperate condition. On January 3, 1931, at a little village—England, Arkansas—there was a spontaneous uprising which should have been a warning to those who think "it can't happen here." Five hundred men, farmers whose crops had not even come up because of the drought and the dust storms, who had no food for their families, marched into the little village to a grocery store where their credit was not good and demanded food. There was no threat, no violence, just a group of grim-visaged men caught in a natural and an economic vise not of their making who were not going to see their children and wives starve to death. Will understood what this meant if our elected leaders did not. "We got a powerful government, brainy men, great organizations, many commissions, but it took a little band of five hundred simple country people (who had no idea they were doing anything historical) to come to a country town store and demand food for their wives and children. . . . They hit the heart of the American people more than all your Senatorial pleas and Government investigation. . . . Paul Revere just woke up Concord . . . These birds woke up America . . . I don't want to discourage Mr. Mellon and *his carefully balanced budget,* but you let this country get hungry and they are going to eat, no matter what happens to budgets, income taxes or Wall Street values . . . Washington mustn't forget who rules when it comes to a showdown."

Will's advice had no effect on Mellon. A man whose brother said it took a machine gun to operate a coal mine was not discouraged that easily. His business had been the accumulation of money, and, for him, it was "the life blood" of existence and the government's primary function was to protect it. And his viewpoint was shared by the President. Feeding starving Belgians and Armenians did not threaten the economy in which these men operated. It would be protected from any upsets abroad by tariff walls and a friendly government. "Those in charge of the government think it is a bad precedent to appropriate money for food . . . It's too much like the 'dole' . . . They think it would encourage hunger . . . The way things look, hunger don't need much encouragement . . . It's just coming around naturally, *and don't get a farmer who is hollering for food, mixed up with a Red, who is hollering for devilment.*"

Will blasted at a do-nothing government. "If you live under a Government and it don't provide some means of you getting work when you really want it and will do it, why, then there is something wrong . . . You just can't let people starve, so if you don't give 'em work, and you don't give 'em food or money to buy it, why, what are they going to do? . . . What is the matter with this Country anyhow? . . . With all our brains in high positions, and all our boasted organizations, thousands of our folks are starving, or on the verge of it . . . Millions of bushels of wheat are in Granaries at the lowest price in twenty years . . . Oil, there was never such an overproduction of oil in the World, and yet Gasoline was never much higher . . . But there you have a business that's in the hands of a few men, and they see that the price is kept up . . . *It's not regulated by supply and demand, its regulated by manipulation."* Harding's statement that the Republican party had made it possible for farmers to be good businessmen had been somewhat on the "rhetorical" side.

Will suggested that "every City or every State should give work of some kind, at a livable wage so that no one would be in actual want . . . Of course it would cost the Taxpayers more money . . . But if you are making it, and all your fellow men are not, why, you shouldent mind paying a good slice of it for the less fortunate . . . Course the big man's argument, and all the heavy Taxpayers' alibis, is that when you take too big a slice from a man as taxes, it takes that much more out of his investments and might cut down on money being put into an enterprise . . . But it dident work that way after the war, and during it . . . Why, income taxes run as high as 70 percent on every dollar earned, and yet there was more money being made and put into things than there is now . . . If your income taxes go to help out the less fortunate, there could be no legitimate kick against it in the world . . . *This is becoming the richest and the poorest country in the world. Why? Why, on account of an unequal distribution of money."*

The way to achieve this distribution was "by putting a higher surtax on large incomes" and for this to go into "some public work, at a livable wage . . . I don't mean a wage that is maintained in other lines . . . I mean a wage is provided for the unemployed" so they could survive. This would not constitute Charity, and would be an insurance against idleness from which might come serious upsets. "Now that we got that settled, all we have to do is get it by Congress . . ." said this *first* New Dealer . . . "and see if the Republicans will vote a higher income tax on the rich babies . . . It might not be a great plan, *but it will Dam sure beat the one we got now."* Rank heresy from a man making nearly a million dollars a year!

Will's conscience would not permit him to sit by under such circumstances. Having three weeks between pictures, he flew to New York and there persuaded the Texas Company to underwrite the chief expenses of a money-raising tour, including the services of a crack pilot, Frank Hawks; then he went to Washington, where the Red Cross approved his plan and he was allowed the use of a navy plane. While in the Capital he talked with President Hoover, who was adamant in his stand that the federal government had no responsibility for the well-being of the people of the country except as it flowed out from a free-enterprise system. "He feels it would break down the real spirit of American generosity and spoil all that our great American Red Cross had worked so hard to achieve." Said another way, President Hoover thought that the Red Cross was able to grapple with a huge segment of the upsets that resulted from the depression, perhaps the largest segment, with only a friendly nod from the government!

During the next three weeks, sometimes making as many as six appearances a day in six different places, Will raised nearly a quarter of a million dollars, all turned over to the Red Cross, half to go to the needy in the cities and the other half to those in the country. Not a cent was taken out for expenses. Will not only paid his own personal expenses but often began the contributions with a generous check.

In his appearance at Stillwater, Oklahoma, Will's old boss, Colonel Zach Mulhall, was waiting to greet Will at the airfield. "The old cowman, in red shirt, bandanna and broadbrimmed Stetson met the plane at the flying field," Walter Harrison, editor of the *Daily Oklahoman* wrote. "He was crying like a baby as he put his arms around Will, and the tears in Rogers' eyes were not caused by the biting wind that was blowing. Reaching the Hall where the show was to be held, already crowded with people, Will asked me, 'Can't you find some place where I can talk to Colonel Zach alone?' The only way I could see was to clear the fire exit and steer Colonel Mulhall down the stairs to where Rogers was waiting. I saw Will hug the old boy like a mother hugs her baby. Then he whispered in his ear, and stuck a roll of bills that would choke a horse into the old man's hands." Will had learned somehow that Mrs. Mulhall was sick and the Colonel was in desperate need of money.

The Oklahoma House of Representatives on February 17, 1931, voted a resolution designating Will "The most useful citizen of the State of Oklahoma." In appreciation Will wired the Governor: "I want you to hand this to your entire Legislature for me. It's just my thanks for their voting me as having been some use to my state in my little career . . . There is not much a comedian can do only act a fool, but if it brought any happiness to anybody then we are repaid by laughter. The world and my own stage has been mighty good to me in many ways, but to receive this added payment from my home government feels like an advanced payment that I havent yet earned but which I hope to live up to before I am planted on that hill at Oolagah."

A few days later, on Washington's Birthday, he let his mind sum up conditions in the country. "Here is what Washington missed by not living to be 199 years old . . . He would have seen our great political system of 'equal right to all and special privilege to none' working so smoothly that seven million are without a chance to earn their living . . . He would see 'em handing out rations in peace time that would have reminded him of Valley Forge . . . In fact, we have reversed the old system, *we all get fat in war and thin in peace* . . . I bet after seeing us, *he would sue us for calling him 'father.'* "

A couple of months later, another picture finished, Will went out on another relief tour. This time it was to Nicaragua, where the capital city, Managua, had been destroyed by an earthquake. In his own way, as in Mexico, he was trying to make up in neighborly friendliness for some of the harm done by our sending Marines there under "dollar diplomacy." "Am sitting in a Marine tent and am going to sleep here . . . The Doctor is coming around to shoot me for typhoid and then I am going to learn to cuss and will be a real Marine . . . I have finally found somebody poorer than a Southern cotton renter family." Will's hatred for the wrong use of the Marines did not keep him from feeling pride in these gallant "soldiers of the sea."

The situation at Managua was so desperate that the President of Nicaragua asked the American minister to challenge Will to find something humorous about it to make the people laugh. "Well, you know these little small shakes occur quite frequently . . . This morning just as the reveille bugle was blowing one come and everybody jumped out of bed . . . So now they are going to use a quake instead of reveille . . . Here is a divine spark of relief for the anti-prohibitionists . . . Everything in town was destroyed but the brewery . . . churches, schools, banks, stores, but it was an act of Providence at that, for the water works were destroyed and all they had to drink was beer . . . The commandant sent 20 Marines to protect it and with the 100 already there, why they were able to hold it . . . Even a quake has its good points, the Senate and Cabinet run out of town and havent shown up since . . . What wouldent Hoover give for that recipe!"

After Will had put on benefits to raise money for the stricken city, as well as appeal to Americans to send money, he stopped on his way back to straighten out a diplomatic mess made by Senator Brookhart of Iowa. "This Senator was asked to make a speech," said Roy T. Davis, minister to Panama. "His talk consisted solely of denunciations of the social conditions in Panama. Both the Panamanians and the Americans living there resented the speech, and the President and other officials of the country were considering asking for an apology from Washington, when Rogers arrived. The newspapers had taken up the gauntlet and were demanding satisfaction. Like most diplomatic incidents that may lead to considerable trouble, this one had a foundation on an occurrence so slight that it could be dispelled by taking the proper perspective. I talked over the situation with Rogers and he understood instantly."

That very evening Will gave a benefit at a local theater in Panama City for the earthquake victims at Managua. More than a thousand people were unable to get in. The President of Panama and other dignitaries of the country occupied boxes resplendent in gold leaf, and everyone of any consequence was in the theater. As Will shuffled to the center of the stage, the hostility of the audience could be felt.

"Well, folks," Will drawled, as he scratched his head. "All I know is what I read in the papers, you know . . . I read what our Senator said about you 'Wallowing in Sin.' . . . Just as soon as I read that, I hopped in a plane and flew to Panama . . . I thought if you was 'wallowing in sin,' why, I'd ask you to move over and I'd wallow with you."

There was a moment of silence and then a roar of laughter swept the audience, most of whom understood English. In one bold thrust Will had swept away all the resentment of the senator's crabbed speech with a good cleansing dose of laughter. Of course, he added to this when he wondered if the senator contemplated moving the Canal so that it would be between "Des Moines and Iowa City" *where no sin existed!*

As if senators creating diplomatic messes were not enough, President Hoover's vacation trip to the Virgin Islands stirred up a hornet's nest that the "unofficial" President had to correct. "In the days before America had gone 'racketeer' the Islanders made Rum, and good Rum . . . It was a legitimate business, carried on by experts, that had made it for generations." Then when Prohibition came along this industry was closed down, practically bankrupting the islands. In his remarks about the islands, Hoover had described them as "a poorhouse" and regretted that the United States had purchased them (done during World War I to keep them from falling into the hands of Germany). In addition to this, President Hoover and party "landed as though prepared for a buck dance in the slums."

Will was assured that the islands had not been a "poorhouse" when the United States purchased them, but became one after that. "We did not walk into America's arms for charity," he was told. "America has no concept of the rights of other people. Their narrowness (although the richest nation on earth) makes her the most hated Nation, even when she is doing a real good. *But may the day never dawn when the inhabitants of these islands look on her in the same manner as do the people of Mexico and Latin America.*"

Will went ashore to see what he could do to counteract this impression. "I told 'em to go ahead and make their rum, that there was no reason they should take Prohibition seriously because they belonged to the U.S. . . . So with a bunch of them we all went and had a nip of Rum Punch, and I don't mind telling you the Islands looked great to me . . . I gave them Capone's address, as I wanted to see 'em get started with the best folks we have over home, where they could get the most for their product . . . Of course, they will have to start from the bottom in regard to Competition, for the U.S. had twelve years of business start on them . . . But they will be all right now, and the next time a President visits them, their product will be making them rich just like Chicago, or any of their competing centers . . . I am going to have those Virginders so rich they will be able to have 20 thousand dollar funerals, and a President won't mean anything to 'em."

Will was not so kind with a group back home. "A couple of years ago no business seemed to be up to date unless it had its 'holding company' . . . The title 'holding' seemed like you had something so the suckers went for it . . . But now the stockholders find out that all they were holding was the bag . . . So that's what's the matter with your Wall Street . . . You can't go out now when your business ain't doing so good and merge with something else that's doing worse and form a 'holding company' and issue stock . . . What you got nowadays you got to 'hold' yourself . . . The buyers are looking in the bag now before they hold it."

Will had a good laugh when his home state wanted to confer another honor on him. "What's this mess over some degree the Oklahoma Chamber of Commerce been wiring me about? . . . They are as bad as I am . . . An honorary degree would read as foreign to any of them as a prescription . . . What are they trying to do, make a joke out of college degrees? . . . They are in bad enough repute as it is, without handing 'em around to comedians . . . The whole honorary degree thing is the 'hooey' . . . I got too much respect for people who work and earn 'em, to see 'em handed around to every notorious character . . . I will let the Oolagah kindergarten give me one, D.A. (Doctor of Applesauce)."

The world situation was worrying Will. "That Russia is kicking up an awful lot of dust, and Germany is harboring a terrible lot of dissatisfaction—That Hitler has got 'em all stirred up over there . . . Then those little Balkan Nations, they are like a mess of stray Terriers anyhow . . . Russia and Poland are always on the verge of War . . . Then Italy is ranting around down there trying to pick up some more country and outlet for their population . . . France is watching them with an Eagle eye all the time, and that's just what Mussolini wants . . . France feels she would have no trouble whipping them, but if she went down there to do it, Germany would take the opportunity to get at them . . . *There is more in the wind than just our little local condition over here . . . This old World of ours as a whole is not sitting so pretty just at the present time . . . You can't pick up a paper that from one to a hundred don't prophesy that Prosperity is just around the corner . . . But let me tell you that war is nearer around the corner than prosperity is."*

Will was particularly concerned about the Russians. By no means did he take the Soviet accomplishments as did many wishful thinkers, something that would dry up and blow away. "You know those rascals in Russia along with all their Cuckoo stuff have got some mighty good ideas . . . If just a part of 'em work they are going to be hard to get along with . . . Just think of everybody in a Country going to work . . . I don't mean just the ones that want to work, but I mean everybody . . . What they mean by work is to produce something, to be of some benefit to the whole community . . . A whole Nation of 150 million people all working, no profit, no Board of Directors, no Dividends, No Wall Street to support . . . their own Steel mills, their own Ore mines, own water power, and an unlimited supply of coal, Wood, the greatest forests in the world . . . You see they are playing with the biggest natural resource fountain in the world . . . Those folks have everything that any other Nation has, only more of it . . . Now they are buying brains, people to show 'em how to get all this organized . . . We have thousands of trained men over there, working to show them how to work with different machines . . . Now when they learn that, they won't leave us any corner on it, for no Nation has a monopoly on brains . . . No, you can't laugh 'em off, they sure got some weird ideas, and things that a people like ours would never in the world tolerate . . . *But they got some ideas that if carried out properly is bound to make the world do some changing in this unequal division of wealth. . . .*

"No Country ever had more, and no country ever had less . . . Ten men in our Country could buy the World, and ten million can't buy enough to eat." This, plus the death of the League of Nations, were the residual contributions of "the return to normalcy . . ."

On the positive side Will had something to crow about. It was the flight of Wiley Post, as pilot, and Harold Gatty, around the world in the *Winnie Mae* in eight days and fifteen hours. Post was a one-eyed Oklahoma boy and the backer of the flight was an Oklahoma oilman. The backer invited Will to come to Claremore for a special ceremony honoring the two, and since the city had no airport one was built in six days. "I came clear across the continent, our little amateur continent," Will said, "to pay in a small way my admiration and respect for these two boys . . . Post used to be a farmer . . . It wasent ambition that drove him away from the farm . . . it was the Republican Administration . . . Not all farmers took to the air but all of them have to eat it . . . These two boys knew the world was cockeyed but they wasent right sure it was round . . . They found this out . . . It seems fitting that this gathering should be in Claremore, Oklahoma. . . . Air is these boys means of transportation, and Claremore has furnished more air to the world through one native son than her share . . . There were two other folks who had a lot to do with the success of their round-the-world flight besides Post and Gatty . . . They were women . . . their wives . . . It takes a lot of nerve to let a husband make that trip."

As he said this, Will was speaking for Betty. She already had her worries. "Lately Rogers has been doing a deal of flying, across the continent and to South American Countries," O. O. McIntyre wrote. "Next to a bucking horse, he loves the air, but it worries his wife. He now tells her of his jaunts just before he starts for the airport. To several he has confided: 'I got to give it up. It worries Betty' "[1] He would give it up at the same time he'd quit writing on politics. "Mrs. Rogers is right," McIntyre said. "To lose Will Rogers would not only be a personal loss to her and to many others, it would take on the proportion of a national calamity."

Will began taking his politics even more seriously as inactivity in Washington had in it only the hope that blind economic forces would cure the troubles. The most mature answer Hoover seemed to be able to come up with was to appoint another commission to study the major problems, commissions that were freighted with men of his own economic and political thinking. More and more convinced that the national government was not going to concern itself directly with the plight of the people, Will concentrated on persuading the various communities that something be done about employment on their level. The one big problem facing the country was unemployment, men out of work and unable to buy the necessities of life for their families. While millions went hungry, hundreds worked for the government on

[1] *Cosmopolitan,* October, 1931.

a commission to determine if any drinking was going on in the country and how to stop it!

In spite of Will's valiant efforts, the winters of 1931 and 1932 were, as a tough old West Texan expressed it, "rough on rabbits."

Although Will did not attend the London Economic Conference in 1931 he kept a close eye on it through press reports. As usual he pinpointed the most interesting phase of it. "Our delegates went by special boat . . . Dressmakers worked for months before . . . But a skinny little fellow with nothing on but a breechcloth, a spinning wheel and an old she-goat comes there representing more humanity and with more authority than all the high hats in the world . . . It's sincerity versus diplomacy. . . . Jimmy Walker passed up an interview with Gandhi to go to a night club . . . Class will tell . . . 'What an extravagance!' Gandhi exclaimed when he saw Buckingham Palace all lighted up, 'for a country trying to balance its budget!' "

Will and Betty took a short vacation trip to Roswell, New Mexico, where their son, Jim, was in a military school. While in Roswell they journeyed to Carlsbad and on their wedding anniversary Will walked Betty "for seven miles through the celebrated Carlsbad Caverns . . . I thought the biggest hole in the ground was when you was drilling for oil and struck a dry hole . . . But this is bigger even than that . . . It's just the Grand Canyon with a roof over it . . . Then when you get inside it's got all the cathedrals in the world in it, with half of 'em hanging upside down." They sat in the big room with the lights turned off holding hands while "Rock of Ages" was sung. "If a 'drunk' suddenly woke up in that Great Hall in there, he would think he had died and gone to heaven."

In the fall of 1931, with politics in the Far East boiling over, Will decided to make his deferred trip there for a firsthand look.

29

Will Looks Over the Far East

ON BOARD THE S.S. *Empress of Russia* HEADED FOR THE Far East, Will encountered his old friend Floyd Gibbons, whom he had met in Warsaw, Poland, in 1926 at the time of the Pilsudski revolution. Everything was peaceful and quiet on the ship except for a couple of Chinese boys who had "lost on Notre Dame" and "some missionaries going out to make all the world good and pure like the U.S." Will expected his usual seasickness but it failed to develop. "I'd surprise myself by going down to breakfast, and then lunch, and then dinner . . . And, mind you, all this time I was packing in the Fodder." He even survived a typhoon in "the middle of Mister Balboa's Ocean," a "Chinese Typhoon, that had run into Monsoon, that was crossed with just plain Hurricane, and Oklahoma Norther . . . But I kept eating and HOW! They were always passing something and I was always not letting anything pass me."

On the trip Will read about "old Ghenghis Khan that flourished around all over this Country about 12 Hundred . . . If you enjoy Jessie James, Al Capone and the Younger Boys, you want to read about this Baby . . . Oh, Lord, the World was his Oyster, He ruled everything from all of China clear to the gates of Vienna, and from the North Pole to Africa, and did it all on horseback . . . There was a real Buckarro for you." However, he did more talking with Floyd Gibbons than reading. "Floyd is a war man, and is over here to tell you about them . . . I am a peace man . . . I havent got any use for wars and there is no more humor in 'em than there is reason for 'em . . .

Get your war news from Gibbons and your Geisha Girl news from Rogers . . . I am over here scouting for Ziegfeld *Follies,* and I want to see where they train these Japanese diplomats that go to an international conference and bring home everything but the desk the treaty is signed on."

After landing in Japan, on December 6, 1931, Will wired back his preliminary report: "After drinking at least two barrels of tea and wanting to be fair, here is about how Manchuria looks to me: China owns the lot, Japan owns the House that's on it. Now who should have the policeman? . . . China is trying to save its country, Japan is trying to save its investments, the League of Nations is trying to save its face . . . Now somebody has got to lose." Nobody analyzed the situation better—not even in book-sized reports.

Gibbons stuck it out with Will and Japanese aviation for only a few days and then took to the trains. The Japanese pilots flew too close to the top of the rice fields. They were training for more dangerous missions.

After touring Japan Will flew down the Inland Sea from Kobe to Nagasaki, and then across the Sea of Japan to Korea. "Say, I found people that have funnier hats than the Princess Eugenia kind you are wearing back home . . . It's a sort of black cab driver's derby but it's made of screen netting like the thing we used to keep over cheese in the Claremore Grocery Store." From Korea Will flew to Dairen, "the most modern city and fort you ever saw." He spent an afternoon visiting historic old Port Arthur, which featured in the Japanese-Russian War, the birthplace of modern Japan and the graveyard of old Russia. "If I can't find the present war, I can find where some of the others were fought . . . I am only two wars behind."

From Dairen Will flew to Mukden in Manchuria, where most of the war news was coming from. "The Chinese army evacuated the city and the American newsmen moved in . . . They been here so long and times are so tough that about half the banditry committed is by them . . . They got no American news until I mushed in over the snow today . . . They did not know Old General Garner, with 220 Democrats, had marched on Washington." As a result of the 1930 elections the Democrats controlled the House for the first time since 1918, and John Nance Garner was now the Speaker.

After finding no evidence of a war in Mukden, Will went on to Harbin in North Manchuria. "This is supposed to be the livest and most unique town in all the Far East . . . It's Chinese territory and Soviet railroad headquarters . . . Also the refuge of the old Czar Russians." The nearest thing to a war that he could find was a Chinese and Russian production of *Abie's Irish Rose*. "It's known as the Paris of the Far East and its night life keeps it going . . . When the shadows of evening broke over the Siberian Steppes, why, the Scandalousness did begin. . . . In our early Western civilization, every other house was a saloon, in Harbin every house was a Cabaret . . . They just sang, danced and drank themselves through two wars to prevent wars . . . The Russians are a Gay lot, when they got anything to be gay on, and even when they havent they don't just fold up and holler hard times like the New Yorker does. . . . They take it on the chin, dig up some more Vodka and stand the fiddler off for another gazottsky . . . All down through China, Shanghai, Tientsin, and everywhere there is thousands of these White Russians . . . The men, lots of them, doing Coolie work, but it's the Women that have had it tough . . . These Girls, simply to eat, have had to live under the most degrading circumstances—at the mercy of the lowest class of every race of people under the sun . . . It's not Gay in Harbin . . . there is a semblance of attempted gayety . . . but it's just sad . . . It's not lively; it's not amusing; it's just depressing . . . The suicides run higher than anywhere in the world . . . They generally hit the dope, and then to the River . . . I could tell the difference between a White Russian and a Red Russian —that is, if it's a Girl . . . If she was pretty, she was a White Russian . . . These Reds were a mighty hard looking lot. . . . There must be something about that 'everybody split up what you got with me' idea that makes 'em all look alike . . . When you get everybody alike, that should be the height of Communism."

On his return to Mukden Will reported that "the League of Nations is sending a commission here to look over the grounds . . . That's like a Sheriff examining the stall after the horse has disappeared." He then stated he was on the ground and could send the same report, only shorter, for much less cost. "There is only two things certain out here . . . The Manchurian problem wont be settled this year or next . . . The second certainty is any commission that tries it will wind up in wrong with both sides . . . We don't belong to the League . . . They are the ones that are refereeing it and we have yet to referee a fight successfully . . . But of course we will join 'em and get in wrong . . . It's too big an opportunity to lose."

Will's plans called for him to go to Peiping from Mukden by railroad, but he was warned not to as this was the line the bandits chiefly operated on. "I figured my jokes wouldent go so good out in this snow waiting for Claremore, Oklahoma, to ransom me, so I am taking roundance on 'em by boat." To reach Peiping, he "bobbed around on one of China's oceans for three days in a boat just six inches longer than a Ford." In Peiping his chief advice to those coming to the Far East was not to bring most "standard American equipment such as Scotch, cigarettes or toilet articles, or clothes," all of which could be bought in abundance, but "for mercy sakes bring a pillow, one with feathers in it . . . These out here are stuffed with rice, which wouldent be so bad if they cooked it first."

Will's doubts about the missionaries that American churches were sending over were verified. The missionaries had taught the people "not to fight but to rely on the Lord and this with the Chinese Diplomats who had relied on the League rather than fighting had also been disastrous. Now they feel that both have fallen down on 'em . . . This is a time in the history of the world when you better be pretty well prepared or you won't get anywhere." His over-all conclusion of the Manchurian affair is enlightening. "Pardon me for trying to get humor from a serious situation, but when a country bigger and more fertile than the whole state of Texas changes hands, yet war is not declared on either side and five months later the League sends a jury out to see how it was done, now there is a laugh in there somewhere."

While in Peiping Will was presented to the Chinese Emperor. His guide and interpreter was a young Chinese by the name of Tommy Lee, who had lived in the United States and had enjoyed Will's motion pictures. "Was you ever the Guest of an Emperor in his own Home? . . ." this to Senator Borah ". . . I mean a real live Emperor, with him in the House, not one of those things where there is a Guide showing you around telling you where the Emperor did live. . . . The House was not so Elaborate . . . If we had been putting on an Emperor's set in Hollywood, we would have walked right by this one without photographing it . . . He brought in some Robes . . . Mandarin Robes, they called 'em . . . beautiful things . . . He asked me to pick one out . . . all beautiful, fur-lined Kimona-Effect things . . . Had me try one on . . . I said, 'Ha! . . . This is not for me, is it? This is a Woman's Gown.' . . . They assured me it was 90 percent Male . . . I said, 'Now, won't I look cute prancing in Beverly Hills with this thing flowing and me hollering, 'Whoops, Boys, Mother Rogers is back from China?' . . . I asked Tommy Lee which was the best one, and he nodded at one . . . He had his eye on the same one I did . . . It was lined with Mink . . . not Dog Mink but Mink . . . The Young Marshal said, 'That's too small for you.' . . . I said, 'Yes, for me, but not for Mrs. Rogers.' . . . So I Glommed the best one, and Tommy grinned like a Possum, and I grinned more than the rest." It is odds on that Tommy clutched a large bill in his hand as he grinned.

Christmas Day found Will in Shanghai, one of the few that he had not spent at home. "Maybe you think I wasent lonesome . . . I just thought, 'What a Yap! Over here trooping around trying to get something to write about, when Everything Funny in the World that is happening is happening right there at home." While Will was in his room writing a letter to Betty, Mr. Abend, the *New York Times* man, called to ask him if there was anything he would like to do.

"I would like to see the famous Shanghai Bar," Will said.

After Will had finished his letter to Betty and posted it, he sat waiting for Mr. Abend, thinking, "What a day to see the Bar . . . Here it is six o'clock on Christmas day and the Bar crowded with people from all over the world who were away from home taking a cheering drink to forget their loneliness . . . I am not a Bar Connoisseur, but, naturally, in my Rambles I had seen some that for length you could stand in a row about as many friends as you wish to pay for . . . Tia Juana, Mexico, has one that if it was a hundred yards longer would reach San Diego . . . Some of New York's speakeasies are only limited by the length of the block . . . But this was to be the World's longest . . . Time and again I had pictured in my mind the crowd that would frequent such a place . . . Being in Shanghai, I naturally thought that this place must have been the origin of the Shanghai-ing of Sailors . . . I could just visualize the Swinging Doors, the Sailors from every Port in the World, the Marines of the U.S., English Tommys, Italian Marines, White Russians, Red Russian, Blue Russian."

Mr. Abend picked Will up at the hotel and drove to a structure that looked like a bank building or a city hall. They climbed a long row of steps and entered an imposing hall. A uniformed attendant took their hats and coats. Great marble pillars were before them. Will signed a guest book, after which they entered a tremendous room. There before Will's eyes stretched the bar. "Bobby Jones could have just made it in two . . . About a niblick shot apart scattered along it, was bartenders, and standing right in the center on the Purchaser's side was one lone figure, an Englishman. He had on Spats, a Cane, and was perhaps sixty, with sideburns, and of course, a glass of Scotch-and-soda sat before him." It was only then that Will realized it was a Club and not a private bar.

When he saw there was only one customer, he decided to buy him a drink, so he ambled over. "Pardon me, sir," he said, "would you be kind enough to join me and my friend in an Eggnog to the Yuletide?"

The man turned on him like he had been bit. "I beg your pardon," he said, "I don't think we have been introduced. Good day, sir."

From Shanghai Will was supposed to travel by way of the Philippines, but a delay of a boat he was to catch would have kept him from making connections with a KLM plane from Java and Sumatra near Penang. Instead, he proceeded directly to Singapore, where he made a speech to a Rotary Club. "I never did make such a fool out of myself . . . They got to laughing at my riddles and, actor like, I kept getting more pleased and longwinded as the day wore on . . . They said there were fifty nationalities belonging to the club . . . It sure lacked a lot of being the Best Rotary speech ever made, but for distance and amount of words uttered, why, it will always stand unsurpassed . . . I believe they laughed better from four to five than from one to two." Actually, Will talked so long that he missed a trip out to the Maharajah of Johore's estate.

Will spent the night in a little hotel sixty miles from Penang at a small village where KLM had a landing field. He went to see a local motion picture and the theater manager recognized him from some of his movies. The next morning the KLM plane breezed in on time but it was so heavily loaded that the pilot doubted he could take Will along. "He asked me how much I weighed . . . I sorter drew in my stomach, looked haggard-faced, and said 176 . . . Then he asked about baggage . . . I was rambling light . . . I had a little yellow-looking grip, a little zipper bag and a small typewriter . . . Well, here sit these three little orphan pieces, the pilot he picked them up, and said, 'Is this all you have?' I said, 'Yes.'. . . Well, he went off and figured up and then come back and said, 'You get on by two Kilos.' "

For the next ten days that KLM plane, with the same pilot, "a great big young fellow, but with 15 years flying," was Will's home across India, and the Middle East into Europe, ten thousand miles in all flying in the daytime with overnight stops at a string of strategic airfields on the way. It was all enjoyable for Will except that he missed his newspapers. "Honest there was times I would have given any amount of money for an American newspaper . . . Why, I would have given $100 for the *Claremore Progress* or the *Claremore Messenger,* and that's just two of the smaller papers of Claremore . . . Take my ham away, take my eggs away, even my Chili, but leave me my Newspaper."

Will was also out of touch with the world because of lack of telegraphic facilities. At Baghdad, on January 15, 1932, he was able to file his Daily Wire. "You Bible students, stockmen and hunters better note this . . . Flew low all morning between Euphrates and Tigris . . . It's all level prairie and uncultivated . . . Most animals I ever saw were there . . . Thousands of cattle, donkeys, camels, water buffaloes, deer . . . Now over Jerusalem and Holy Land and Baghdad . . . Never catch me traveling over here again unless I have read the Book first." Later, from Cairo, he was less enthusiastic. "These Pyramids, Mexico's got bigger, and the Sphinx, Coolidge's got him licked to death." One look at Corsica as he flew over it and Will had no doubts about why Napoleon left there.

When Will secured a newspaper so that he could read what was going on in "Cuckooland" he was deeply discouraged. "See where Congress passed a two-billion-dollar bill to relieve bankers' mistakes and loan to new industries . . . You can always count on us helping those who have lost part of their fortune, but our whole history records nary a case where the loan was for the man who had absolutely nothing." A couple of days later he had more disheartening news. "Got the dope on these International bankers that are crying for us to cancel the debts . . . Every American trade commissioner and business man over here tells of the flock of bankers' representatives over in Germany and Europe in the last few years . . . Hotel lobbies full of 'em offering all kinds of commissions to help put over loans for American Banks . . . The loans were forced on them . . . Now they want the Government to cancel to make up for their mistakes." Their kind of "patriotism" was quite simple. The only way they had a chance for their loans to be paid was for the government to cancel the debts.

Betty joined Will in London and, on January 27, 1932, they flew to Paris "in a big four-motored passenger plane, a bar, hot meals, two stewards and everything." European aviation was getting somewhere even if American was just plodding along. They planned to have a quiet vacation in Paris, but Will had not been there an hour when he was drafted to make a speech to the American club. He frankly told them that the sentiment in the United States was against canceling the debts and that the reason was lack of appreciation, particularly in France, of America's contribution to the war. "We loaned you the money, cut the amount to be paid in half, cut the interest in half, give you 65 years to pay . . . We was called boastful, greedy, called Uncle Shylock . . . We got no German Colonies, we got no reparations, yet we was called selfish . . . If the Americans felt in their own hearts that you nations over here really appreciated what they did for you, you would get your debt voluntarily cancelled tomorrow . . . Now you folks don't know America . . . You can take a stick of candy and lead America right into the ocean, but you can't cuss and drive 'em in there." It was, Will stated later, "the best received and most favorably commented on speech I ever made."

On February 1, 1932, Will and Betty wound up at the Geneva Disarmament Conference, the first one she had attended. "The first laugh was when the Japanese delegation arrived . . . The younger members of their delegation have been called back for military service . . . The Conference was held up for one hour while we all went to the League of Nations meeting to demand of Japan that she quit shooting while the opening session was in conference . . . That like to broke up the meeting." A couple of days later Will announced that the conference was off to a flying start and that *"there is nothing to prevent their succeeding but human nature."*

Deciding that they would be considerably older before anything important was accomplished at Geneva, Will and Betty sailed back to "Cuckooland" abroad the S.S. *Europa* and landed at New York on February 9, 1932. It was a much different kind of welcome from that which they had received in 1926. Much of the buoyancy had gone out of Will because of the conditions existing in the country. The seven million unemployed had now swelled to eight, to nine, and was eventually to reach twelve million people, and yet in the richest, supposedly most humanitarian country nothing was being done to correct it. Nevertheless, he was glad to be home. "Oh, Boy, I was glad to set my big feet on American soil even if it has got a second mortgage on it . . . Had the greatest trip I ever had and I believe if everybody made it, they might come back a little poorer, but better off in the feeling toward our country . . . I know business is off—they say 60% . . . well, that still leaves us 30% ahead of anywhere I have been."

Before going home to California, Will and Betty visited the Morrow family. Dwight Morrow had died the autumn before and, oddly enough, Will had heard about it from a peon far in the mountains of Mexico. They saw the Lindbergh baby. "It's the cutest thing you ever saw, walking and talking and has his father's blonde curly hair, even more so than his dad's . . . It's almost golden and all in little curls . . . His face is more of his mother's . . . He has her eyes exactly . . . His mother sat on the floor in the sun parlor among all of us, and played blocks with him for an hour . . . His dad was pitching a soft sofa pillow at him as he was toddling around . . . The weight of it would knock him over . . . I asked Lindy if he was rehearsing him for forced landings . . . After about the fourth time of being knocked over he did the cutest thing, he dropped of his own accord when he would see it coming . . . He crawled up in the back of the Morrow Automobile that was going to take us away, and he howled like an Indian when they dragged him out."

After reaching California, Will made another trip, though a short one. Will's friend "Big Boy" Williams told about it. Big Boy was awakened one morning with a pounding on his door. It was Will.

"Come on, Big," Will said, "we're going on a trip."

While he was dressing, Big Boy learned that there had been a blizzard across the mountains at Victorville, and that the telephone lines were down and the roads practically impassable. Will had urgent business there, so he said. They made it through when almost all the other cars were stalled. In Victorville they went to a ranch where Dopey, the pony that "helped raise the children," had been put out to pasture. Will found Dopey safe and warm in a tight barn, petted him for a few moments, then started the hazardous 150-mile trip back home. He was just taking care of an "old friend."

30

"The Bankers Are the First to Go on the Dole"

ONCE AGAIN A PRESIDENTIAL ELECTION FACED THE American people and this time there would be issues—grave issues. The Republicans' "return to normalcy," instead of guaranteeing perpetual prosperity, progress and peace, had proved a mirage both at home and abroad. The country was faced with perhaps its worst economic emergency resulting from revolutionary changes its leaders had not prepared for, taken cognizance of, or even knew existed. On the international scene, instead of active membership and participation in an effective League of Nations, an aborted one had been left an orphan on the doorsteps of European and other nations, the most powerful of which had used it as a means of aggrandizement, thereby making war more certain rather than preventing it. On the domestic scene, the Republican party had returned the country to *laissez faire* while sprinting forward into "business socialism" at a pace which if continued unchecked would have ended inevitably in some form of fascism—no matter how designated. The nearer this came to consummation the more inevitably it would be opposed by an offsetting militant communism. Desperate people adopt desperate measures. The only other course was a healthy dose of American democracy such as Woodrow Wilson's New Freedom had administered to pre-1912 Republicanism. The ringing question by 1932 was whether "the patient" might not have become "too ill" while Hoover commissions held consultations.

After a short visit at home following his trip to the Far East, Will flew to Washington to check up on "the fun-factory." He reported that the new Speaker of the House, Democrat John N. Garner, was doing "a great job handling this Congress," and that Ogden Mills, for whom he had made his first political speech, had been appointed Secretary of the Treasury to replace Andrew Mellon who had been made ambassador to the Court of St. James's. "Safeguarded and protected by the Secretary of War, Pat Hurley," he called on President Hoover "to report on Manchuria, Hollywood, Shanghai, and Claremore."

Will and President Hoover talked over the unemployment situation, and the President expressed "almost with emotion," his fear of adopting a program resembling that of the dole in England where those unable to find work were "doled" out small sums weekly. Hoover had hopes that a new agency of the government, the Reconstruction Finance Corporation, soon to get into operation, might help get people to work. Its purpose was to alleviate the financial difficulties by lending money to banks, insurance companies, railroads, states, municipalities, and other public agencies in the hope that this would reduce unemployment. Will did not share this hope. President Hoover was also concerned about hoarding and asked Will to write a joke about it. "Humor might show 'em how foolish they are," Will has Hoover saying. "Now go do that." Here he was, Will had to admit, on a Hoover commission after all his joking, "the Hoover anti-hoarding joke Commission." He agreed to accept, to complete the "joke," if Wickersham, chairman of the Commission to Study Prohibition, also was placed on it.

On February 24, 1932, Will warned that "you cant get a room in Washington . . . Every hotel is jammed to the doors with bankers from all over America to get their 'hand out' from the Reconstruction Finance Corporation . . . And I have asked the following prominent men in America this question, 'What group have been more responsible for this financial mess, the farmers? . . . Labor? . . . Manufacturers? . . . Tradesmen, or Who?' . . . And every man—Henry Ford, Garner, Newt Baker, Borah, Curtis, and a real financier, Barney Baruch—without a moment's hesitation said, 'Why, the big bankers.' . . . *Yet they have the honor of being the first group to go on the 'dole' in America!*"

On his way back to California Will stopped at the old home ranch for some good navy beans, corn dodgers, and a heartening visit. "Out on the Rogers ranch at Oolagah, where I spent yesterday . . . Herb McSpadden, my nephew, had to take a milk stool and beat an old cow over the rear end, she was hoarding her milk . . . A farmer at Claremore, named Morris Haas, hid five hundred dollars in bills in a barrel of bran, and a cow eat it up . . . He has just been able to get eighteen dollars of it back up to now . . . This hoarding don't pay." Will had performed his "commission" duties up to the level of the performance of members of others.

Late in February Will was alone in the ranch house when the telephone rang and awakened him from a sound sleep. With the other members of the family away, he grabbed it nervously thinking something had happened to one of them. The call was from William R. Hearst, Jr., in New York, who told him the Lindbergh baby had been kidnapped. The shock was even worse because he and Betty had seen the baby only a few days before. "Never since the two days and night that this same kid's father was out over the Atlantic has the attention of everybody been centered so completely on one thing." During the terrible days that followed, as best he could, Will was Lindbergh's unofficial protector. "I think the boy has used splendid judgment in this . . . Remember, it was his sober judgment that first suggested, 'Get the baby back at any cost,' and then start worrying what the punishment would be." Here, as so often, the press acted as if this case was for its own glorification. Later, when the trial of Hauptmann was in progress, the Lindberghs found refuge in the Rogers ranch house in Santa Monica.

By the end of March, 1932, Will reported that the Geneva Conference had bogged down in hopeless confusion. The enormity of the failure of the United States to enter the League of Nations and do its best to make the organization work was now evident. For the first time in history, at the suggestion of the United States, a proposal was before the body to cut armaments by one third, to outlaw chemical warfare, bombing planes, heavy artillery, and tanks. She also announced her willingness "to consult" with other nations in the event of a threat to peace.

"Unofficial observer," "to consult," this was the fantastic role of the most powerful nation in the world at a time when it should have been putting the full force of its power behind action to prevent war! To "collaborate" with this it was bogged down at home economically and socially in the bankruptcy of the same "rugged individualism" that had limited its voice abroad.

But other countries were not so hamstrung. Germany demanded arms equality. The Soviet delegation, smiling cagily behind their impassive masks, threw a smoke screen over the entire proceedings *by proposing total disarmament.* Then, as later, they had the progaganda value of a suggestion they knew would get nowhere. "A Russian gets up and proposes something and the rest of the Congregation dont know if he is 'kidding' or on the level . . . She just loves to put a thumb in the soup and let the guests see it's in there . . . The whole world's nerves are 'jumpy' anyhow right now . . . Anybody with a sheet over their head can run the world home and under the bed." France wanted an international police force that would protect her against Germany. Japan was pursuing her relentless course in Manchuria; the Nazis were preparing to take over in Germany, and, when they did, to get out of the League. All the while Mussolini was setting a pattern for Hitler, and others, to follow, In the United States the Wickersham Commission brought in a two-ton report in which "it was suspected there was a little drinking taking place." Nevertheless, it did not recommend the repeal of the Prohibition Amendment.

Will had a magnificent laugh when his comment about the bankers and the dole brought down on him a blast from the "mighty" in an editorial in the *Wall Street Journal.* He was adjured to confine his jokes "to some semblance of truth." "Now I want to be fair, even with the bankers, for they are pretty touchy now . . . I have had critics come out and say, 'As an actor old Bill is not so hot' . . . Well, I just wanted to come out and call him a liar, but in my heart and conscience I knew he was right . . . So I know how you 'boys' feel . . . Now if you will take this money and loan it out to a lot of little fellows that need it, you bankers got a chance to redeem yourselves . . . People are not 'pointing with pride' to your record in this crisis up to now . . . Will be glad to reprint any alibis." Those used to getting aid from the government, in one form or another, when they got it again thought it right. Their consciences or their guilt played no part in it.

This came out a few weeks later. "No matter what the poor old dumb government tries to do, the 'big boys' have a scheme to beat it... Now the big bankers have got a new 'racket.' Instead of them going direct to the New Finance Commission for dough, they send the folks that owe them... He gets it from the government and then pays them off... That dont leave a single soul out snipe hunting with a sack but the Government... And, Brother, when one of those 'Big Babies' transfers one of his loans over to Uncle Sam, it's not a 'frozen asset'; it's a 'petrified persimmon.'"

With the Democrats in control of Congress, a tax bill was passed that took as much as 72 per cent of incomes in the higher brackets. Will approved of this. "You got to earn big money or you dont pay it, so there should never be any holler about that... But there should be a distinction between earned and un-earned income... A man that earns every dollar by his work, then another earns the same by having enough money invested to bring him in that much... One has his principal to fall back on, and the other has nothing to fall back on when his earning capacity has diminished." The Republicans believed there should be a distinction also, but the other way around.

This high-bracket income tax was followed by an inheritance tax that was to take a huge chunk of an estate at the death of the owner. "Now you wont catch those rich old boys dying promiscuously like they did... This bill makes patriots out of everybody... You sure do die for your country, if you die from now on." Will knew when he wrote this that "the rich old boys" would keep right on dying with the knowledge that their "lawyers" had seen to it that "the dumb old government" did not profit, directly, from their demise.

The Senate, somewhat confirming Will's suspicions about Wall Street and its inhabitants, began an investigation of its activities in April, 1932. "The U.S. Senate who investigates everything after it's dead, is going to dig up the body and hold an autopsy... They will find out exactly what everyone else already knows, 'Deceased died from overgorging while the gorging was gorgeous.'" Next day he reported that very little was got out of "this fellow Whitney [who was later sent to the penitentiary] thats the head of the 'Wall Street Gang' ... There is one noble thing about our modern racketeers... They will go to the electric chair before they will give away any of the workings of their organization . . . At first, we thought we was going to get the names of our 'Big Men' who were betting the country would never amount to anything . . . Oh, Yeah! . . . All they found out is that the Street is located at the sharp end of New York City, that not only the traders but the Street itself is short, that neither don't lead anywhere . . . *It will live down everything except* that Charlie Dawes called it 'a peanut stand.' " The damning evidence came when "a little Italian Congressman (and a Republican, too, strange to say) from New York City, LaGuardia, dragged in a trunk full of cancelled checks *that brokers had given to financial writers* . . . You know, it's too bad everybody was so busy getting in on it that no one had time to investigate Wall Street before 1929 when the horse was being stolen." It does seem that "keeping government out of business" had not been too successful.

When Will turned his eyes to another kind of racketeering he had to admit that as a reporter he was a total failure. "Shows the difference between a good reporter and a punk one . . . Two weeks ago I had two hours with Al Capone . . . He told me all that I read today [in the newspaper] that he told Mr. Brisbane, and more . . . But there was absolutely *no way I could write it and not make a hero out of him,* and even as superb a writer as Mr. Brisbane couldent either . . . Everybody you talk to would rather hear about Capone than anybody you ever met . . . *What's the matter with an age when our biggest gangster is our greatest national interest?"* Will passed on one statement that Capone had made in answer to his question as to what was the matter with the country: "We got too many crooks in high places." Capone should have known.

Will's general summation of "the State of the Union" came once again on Memorial Day: "Bands playing, soldiers marching, orators orating, telling you it's your duty to 'Buy Liberty Bonds' . . . Fifteen years later, no bands, no marching, no orators, just a patriotic girl or a broken piece of human frame trying to sell a Poppy for a few cents, made by even a more unfortunate brother in one of our 55 hospitals . . . War has degenerated from the price of a Liberty Bond to the price of a poppy . . . *Six million of these boys regular customers are disabled this year too, and from the same war* . . . So those that have will have to try and make up for these by buying more . . . There is only one sure way of stopping war, that is to see that every 'Statesman' has the same chance to reflect after it is over that these Boys making the poppys have had."

Will was soon to have his own "Memorial" day and a sad one. For some time Will's old boss and friend, Flo Ziegfeld, had been ill. To complicate matters, show business had been as hard hit as any by the depression. Will saw to it that Ziegfeld lacked for nothing that could make him more comfortable. On July 24, 1932, he had the sad duty to report that Ziegfeld had died. "Our world of 'make believe' is sad ... Scores of comedians are not funny, hundreds of 'Americas most beautiful girls' are not gay ... Our benefactor has passed away ... He picked us from all walks of life ... He led us into what little fame we achieved ... He remained our friend regardless of our usefulness to him as an entertainer ... He brought beauty into the entertainment world ... The profession of acting must be necessary, for it exists in every race, and every language ... And to have been the master amusement provider of your generation surely a life's work has been accomplished ... He left something on earth that hundreds of us will treasure till our curtains fall, and that was a 'badge,' a badge of which we were proud, and never ashamed of, and wanted the world to read the lettering on it: 'I worked for Ziegfeld.'"

At the nonreligious funeral service Will was asked to say a few words to those present. He wrote his talk out on a telegram blank and repeated it from memory without changing a word:

We stand before our Lord to give back all that is mortal of our friend. I am not ordained, or have any ecclesiastical credentials. I am not an accredited witness, neither am I an innocent bystander. I am simply one of our profession paying a last and small tribute to a master of our craft.

Among us gathered here, our religious beliefs are many, but one belief is universal with all, and that is that there is some Divine higher than the earthly. We can speak to Him in many devious ways, in many languages, but He sees us all in the same light, and judges us according to our actions, as we judge the actions of our children different because we know they are each different.

Among all our earthly accomplishments, the greatest is to beautify, for beauty speaks no language, beauty appeals to every eye that is put into the human head.

Well, certainly our Divine Being above welcomes back into His fold a man who has been on earth and given to it beauty.

The next day Will turned to another duty that distressed him almost as much. In May, 1932, 15,000 unemployed veterans of World War I marched to Washington and petitioned Congress to pay at once Adjusted Compensation Certificates that had been issued by a niggardly government in lieu of paying the soldiers a bonus. For over a month this group of men lived from hand to mouth, yet in an orderly manner. After the Bonus bill was defeated in Congress in June, President Hoover ordered "the Bonus Army" to leave the city. When the men refused, on July 28, 1932, they were driven out on the President's order by troops under the command of General Douglas MacArthur. This, no doubt, brought to Will's mind "the trail of tears" over which his Cherokee ancestors had been herded by federal troops. "They have the same rights there as any other 'lobbyists'... They at least were not paid, they were doing it for themselves... which placed 'em right away about 90 percent higher in public estimation than the thousands of 'lobbyists' that are there all of the time... But no matter how you feel about the whole thing, you have got to admire the fine way that big body of hungry men acted while they were there... They were hungry, and they were seeing our government wasting thousands and millions before their very eyes, and yet they remained fair and sensible... Would 15 thousand hungry bankers have done it?... Fifteen thousand farmers, fifteen thousand preachers... And just think what fifteen thousand Club Women would have done to Washington even if they wasent hungry!... It is easy to be a gentleman when you are well fed, but these boys did it on an empty stomach... And it is too bad their fine record was marred at the finish by somebody blundering."

31

"The 'Peanut Stand' Gets a Cop and the Poor Man a Friend"

THE YEAR 1932 LOOKED MUCH ROSIER TO THE DEMOCRATS than to the Republicans. They had already secured control of the House of Representatives and the chances for taking over the Senate and capturing the White House seemed solid. Al Smith, with a consuming desire to be president, was nervously hopeful. The sanity of Will's advice to him in October, 1927, was evident. If he had followed it he probably could have had the nomination with little trouble. But as a soundly beaten candidate in 1928 and with his religious beliefs there were grave doubts. The chief opposition that loomed was from the man who had nominated him in both 1924 and 1928, and whom he had persuaded to run for the governorship of the state of New York. In handling this position, Roosevelt had attracted national attention by progressive management of the affairs of the state, putting into operation many programs which he later used as president. In addition, following the disastrous defeat of the Democrats in 1924, Roosevelt had carried on an unceasing correspondence and personal contacts with the party leaders in an effort to weld together a party that had been split wide open by sectional, religious, and Ku Klux Klan disputes, as well as by differing views on Prohibition. He had as an extremely able and acute ally that master politician James A. Farley. Of course the greatest ally of the party had been the inept and blind handling of the demands of the depression by the Republicans, with a complete lack of understanding of its implications. Power and property are always blind to the meaning of revolutions, even revolutions that would save the property and the legitimate power.

Will had a good laugh as the time for the conventions came. "The country did not realize the election was so close till we see by the papers that each political party has 'some' plan of relieving the unemployed . . . They have been unemployed for three years, and nobody paid any attention to 'em . . . But now both parties have discovered that while they are not working, there is nothing in the Constitution to prevent them from voting . . . So the idea is to dust off old campaign promises and no matter what the other side promises, see their promise and raise 'em two more."

Will considered it as foolish for the Republicans to hold a convention as the blazing lights in Buckingham Palace had seemed to Gandhi when England was trying to balance its budget. Before it met, Hoover had already announced his "campaign plan, the route, the towns, and who he would shake hands with, and what he would wear. And as for the platform, it will be the same one they have read for forty years, but have never used, and the speeches will be the same ones delivered for forty years but never listened to."

Nevertheless, Will was on hand when the convention opened in Chicago. "A newspaper man spoiled my whole Convention by asking me if I was an alternate . . . A delegate is bad enough, but an alternate is just a spare tire for a delegate . . . An alternate is the lowest form of political life there is . . . He is the parachute in a plane that never leaves the ground."

The wet lobbyists were all over the place. "They gave out a badge and a drink . . . Although a number did not know what to do with the badge, this wasent true for the rest of the gift." No doubt, also, the drink was needed, particularly by the keynote speaker. "If he 'points to accomplishments' he is sunk, and if he 'views with alarm' he is sunk . . . So we are just liable to get two solid hours of weather." Although nearly twenty thousand people in the galleries yelled for repeal, it was the one thousand on the floor that "had a vote so that question was straddled again." But not the nomination of Hoover. "Democracy and the right of free speech had a set back . . . Ex-Senator France wanted to withdraw his own name and proposed the name of Calvin Coolidge for President . . . Well, that machine just bundled him right up and threw him into the alley . . . That was the real sensation of the Convention . . . During all the ravings of the accomplishments of the Republican Party, not one mention was ever made of Coolidge, so when Snell and his strong-arm men stopped France and bodily threw him off, there is no possible cabinet job can ever be too high for them . . . See you at the Democrats where they will let anybody nominate everybody."

After the nomination President Hoover announced that he was going to remain on the job in Washington and not go out electioneering. "That's kinder like a pitcher saying, 'I don't need to even warm up against this team.' "

The Democrats also met at Chicago with "hundreds of hopefuls" backed by delegates with one idea: "Stop Roosevelt!" If this could be done, then they would try to stop each other. "At a time when they should be 'starting,' they are 'stopping.' "

Will was encouraged at the opening of the convention when Commander Evangeline Booth prayed without reading it. "That was a fine prayer . . . That's the kind of prayer I like . . . You can communicate with the Lord God Almighty without writing him a letter." The presence of the head of the Salvation Army at this convention had some significance also. Even more so was Will's being called upon to address the convention. He was introduced by Eddie Dowling, the musical comedy star, and for fifteen minutes all discord was forgotten. Here is part of what he told them:

I am not a delegate . . . I have no political affiliation in this Convention . . . No one paid my way here, so if I'm rotten I won't owe you anything . . . I'm going to stand here and act the fool until the Democratic Party agrees on Prohibition . . . I'll probably be here from now on . . . As soon as they can get enough of the platform Committee sober enough, they will turn in a platform . . . Everything you do is read . . . Even the splendid prayer we heard from the Minister this morning was read . . . They can't think offhand on their feet to impress the Lord enough to help a Democrat nowadays. . . .

As I look at these smiling, homely faces it seems like old times . . . I want to tell you I was gratified by the grand reception you gave Mr. John W. Davis yesterday . . . It showed not only splendid spirit of Democratic loyalty, but a darn good memory . . . I had breakfast with Cox this morning . . . Does your memory go back that far? . . . [a photographer started to take his picture] Get out of here with that darn thing . . . Every delegate brought his own photographer . . . Every candidate his editorial writer . . . Speaking of prohibition, you'll fight about it and argue about it . . . Then you try to get a plank that is wetter than the Republicans and one that is drier than theirs . . . Speaking of the Republicans, I was here for their uprising . . . Now I'm going to break a precedent . . . I'm going to say something good for the opposition . . . Course it will take quite a while for me to think of it . . . But I want to compliment the Republicans . . . They did the best they could with what little they had. . . .

I don't know who you're going to nominate . . . I like all of the Candidates . . . I sorta hate to see a Convention come around because some of the Candidates have to lose . . . I wish we had a system so we could nominate them all so all could have a week apiece. . . .

Now, you rascals, I want you to promise me one thing . . . No matter who is nominated, don't go home and act like Democrats . . . Go home and act like he was the man you came to see nominated . . . Don't say he is the weakest man you could have nominated . . . Don't say he can't win . . . You don't know what he can do . . . or how weak he is until next November . . . *I don't see how he could be weak enough not to win . . . If he lives until November, he is in!* . . .

Will was given an ovation that surpassed anything ever seen at a Democratic convention before. The Democrats had their wish, a prayerful one, that Hoover be nominated by the Republicans. Now all they had to do was to get a good candidate themselves. Heywood Broun had a wry and illuminating comment to make on this speech: "It seems a little ironical that the same Convention which thinks Will Rogers is a clown accepts Huey Long as a Statesman." Broun termed Will's speech "wise, adroit and witty."

On June 30 Will thundered forth big news. "Did the Democrats go Wet? . . . No, they just layed right down and wallowed in it . . . They left all their clothes on the bank and dived in without even a bathing suit . . . They are wetter than an 'organdie' dress at a rainy day picnic. Al Smith was four years ahead of his time." This was the first giant step away from "normalcy" in a "return to sanity."

In the nominations that followed, Will's name was entered as a "favorite son" by the state of Oklahoma, with its 22 votes going to him on the first ballot. "I made the mistake of going to sleep and when I awoke my votes had been stolen . . . They dident even leave me a vote to get breakfast on . . . Course I realize that I should have stayed awake and protected my interest but I had been taking opiates all night . . . No man can listen to 35 nominating speeches and hold his head up . . . Now I dont want you to think that I am belittling the importance of those 22 votes . . . They was worth something there at that time . . . Not in money, mind you, for there is not $2.80 in the whole Convention . . . But they buy 'em with the promise of office . . . I expect at that minute Roosevelt's bunch would have given me Secretary of State for that 22, and could have sold to Al Smith for maby Mayor of New York . . . And what do I do? . . . Go to sleep and wake up without even the support of Virgin Islands . . . I not only lost my 22 delegates but I woke up without even as much as an alternate."

In the final balloting the state of California, which had come to the convention pledged to John Nance Garner, swung to Roosevelt, starting the climb onto the bandwagon. As a consolation prize, the nomination for the vice-presidency went to Garner. "It was a victory of the country boys over the city slickers . . . New York and Chicago come here thinking that on account of being uninstructed, they would carry off the gravy . . . Tammany was no more for Smith than Smith was for Tammany . . . Well, they thought they would be in a position to stop Roosevelt, sell out to the highest bidder and go home driving the bandwagon . . . Great idea . . . All that went wrong with it was that the old orange squeezers from California thought of it first, sold out and was on their way West with the loot before New York and Chicago jiggilos could get their cards marked . . . It was a lesson in rural politics."

When Franklin D. Roosevelt flew out to Chicago to accept the nomination, instead of waiting to be officially notified, he broke a tradition of long standing. He made this symbolic of his campaign. "My friends, may this be the symbol of my intentions to be honest and to avoid all hypocrisy, to avoid all silly shutting of the eyes to the truth of the campaign. Let it also be symbolic that in so doing I broke traditions. Let it be from now on the task of our Party to break foolish traditions. Let us now and here highly resolve to resume the country's interrupted march along the path of real progress, of real justice, of real equality, for all of our citizens great and small. . . . Wild radicalism has made few converts, and the greatest tribute that I can pay to my countrymen is that in these days of crushing want there persists an orderly and hopeful spirit on the part of millions of our people who have suffered so much. . . . To fail to offer them a new chance is not only to betray their hopes but to misunderstand their patience . . . To meet by reaction that danger of radicalism is to invite danger. Reaction is no barrier to the radical. It is a challenge, a provocation. The way to meet that danger is to offer a workable program of reconstruction . . . The people will not forget the claim made by . . . [the Republicans] that prosperity was only a domestic product manufactured by a Republican President and a Republican Congress. If they claim paternity for the one they cannot deny it for the other [the depression] . . . I pledge you, I pledge myself, to a New Deal for the American People."

The fundamentals of the campaign to follow were evident to Will from the start. "The Democrats will be attacking and the Republicans defending . . . All the Democrats have to do is promise 'What they would do if they got in,' but the Republicans have to promise 'What they would do' and then explain why they havent done it. . . . It is more than an election of partys, or policies, but rather an election where both sides really need the work."

On September 23, 1932, when Candidate Roosevelt was in California "to shake the lemon trees to try and bring down some Republican fruit that might fall in the Democratic basket among the oranges," Will introduced him to a capacity crowd in the Hollywood Bowl. In his speech Will caused the huge stadium to reverberate with laughter. He ended with: "Governor Roosevelt, you are here tonight the guest of people who spend their lives trying to entertain . . . This great gathering is neither creed or politics, Jew or Gentile, Democrat or Republican, and as to whether they vote for you or not—and thousands of them wont, never mind what they tell you—everyone of them admires you as a man . . . Your platform, your policies, your plans may not meet with their approval, but your high type of manhood gains the admiration of every person in the audience . . . So we meet not Roosevelt the Candidate, but a neighbor from the other side of the Rocky Mountains. . . . This introduction may have lacked logic, and particularly floweriness, but you must remember, you are only a Candidate . . . Come back when you are President and I will do better . . . I am wasting no oratory on a mere prospect."

President Hoover soon realized that the campaign might not be a walk-in, as he had at first assumed, and at that moment affairs in Washington did not seem to need quite so much of his attention as he had previously thought. "He began studying timetables."

As the campaign waxed hotter and the name-calling more flagrant, Will decided that since he was between pictures he would get away from it. "I am leaving for everything south of the equator . . . Revolutions are thicker down there than Roosevelt Republicans . . . Am flying down the West Coast by Chile, then to Argentine for a week, and up the east coast by Brazil . . . I will see more in a week than a New York gossip artist can see in five years through key holes . . . South America is our coming country, so it's good to know where it's at . . . I want to get back before election."

It was another great trip for Will, in which he created good will in half a dozen countries, but he made one very bad calculation. He arrived back in the United States, as he had planned, a few days before what he thought would be election day, November 4, only to find it would be on November 7. "I would rather have made a forced landing in the Andes, or purposely stood straddle of the Equator for another week . . . From now on, you will never catch me without a calendar."

On November 1 he had blasted both candidates. "There should be a moratorium called on Candidates speeches . . . They have both called each other everything in the world they can think of . . . The high office of President of the U.S. has degenerated into two, ordinarily fine men, being goaded on by their political leeches, into saying things that if they were in their right minds they wouldent think of saying . . . Imagine Mr. Hoover last night, 'Any change of policies will bring disaster to every Fireside in America!' . . . Of all the conceit! . . . This country is a thousand times bigger than any two men in it, or any two parties in it . . . This country has gotten where it is in spite of politics not by the aid of it . . . That we have carried as much political bunk as we have and still survived shows we are a supernation . . . So you two Boys just get the weight of the world off your shoulders and go fishing

... Both of you claim you like to fish ... Now instead of calling each other names till next Tuesday, why, you can do everybody a big favor by going fishing, and you will be surprised but the old United States will keep right on running while you boys are sitting on the bank ... Then come back next Wednesday and we will let you know which one is the lesser of the two evils."

Although Will offered his condolences to President Hoover because "the country had looked him over and decided not to renew his contract" ("You was handed a balloon that was blowed up to its utmost ... You held it as carefully as anyone could, but the thing 'busted' right in your face."), on mature thought he was incensed at the tone of the Republican campaign. "Now can you tell us that ordinarily intelligent men can stand up there day after day and say, 'If the Democrats win this will bring hardship to every Fireside in America, the grass will grow in five hundred streets. It will retard Progress for 100 years'? Now a thing like that dident have to be said ... Half the streets wont grow grass even if you quit using 'em, that's why they decided to use 'em as towns was because they wouldent grow grass ... As a matter of fact, if they would grow grass they would be worth more as a Range than they would as a Town." This is what Will's cowboy friend had thought back there in Higgins, Texas, before the turn of the century. Will was lecturing to deaf ears. Someone said about the stalwarts in the Republican party: "The Old Guard may surrender, but it never gives up." Will's advice was: "Rest up for '36, mow the grass out of the street, get that disaster out of the fireside, and start another battle for those postoffices."

Will waited for several weeks until those who wanted "something got through congratulating" Roosevelt, then, as "unofficial President," he wired him. "I thought maby a wire just wishing you could do something for the country when you get in, and not wishing you could do something for me, that the novelty of it, when backed up by the facts, might be welcome." Here are some of Will's suggestions:

Your health is the main thing ... Dont worry too much ... *A smile in the White House again* (by the way when was the last one?) *why, it will look like a meal to us* ... Pick up some good men and make 'em responsible for their end ... If people are starving and your granaries are full, that's your Secretary of Agriculture's business is to feed 'em . . . If Nicaragua wants to hold an election, send 'em your wishes but no Marines . . . Disarm with the rest of the world, but not without it. . . .

And Kid Congress and the Senate, dont scold 'em . . . They are just children that's never grown up. . . . Dont send messages to 'em, send candy . . . Let your Secretary of State burn up the notes that come from Europe. . . . Dont let these State Governors get in your hair . . . A State is to the Federal Government what an ornery relation is to any of us . . . The more you do for them, the more they expect . . . Keep off the radio till you got something to say . . . Be good to the press boys in Washington, for they are getting those 'Merry Go Rounds' out every few weeks now . . . Stay off that back lawn with those photographers . . . Nothing will kill off interest in a President quicker than "Weeklys" with Chamber of Commerce and Women's political organizations. . . .

Now if some guy comes running into your office telling you what "Wall Street was doing" that day, tell him, "Wall Street? Why, there is 115 million of my subjects dont know if Wall Street is a thoroughfare, or a new mouth wash . . . Its happenings dont interest me." . . .

Why, Governor, you can go in there and have a good time . . . We want our President to have some Fun . . . Too many of our Presidents mistake the appointment as being to the Vatican and not to just another American home. . . . Just don't get panicky . . . All you have to do is manage 120 million "hoodlums" and the higher educated they are, the bigger hoodlums they are, and the harder to manage . . . The illiterate ones will all work, and you will have no trouble with them . . . But watch the ones that are smart, for they have been taught in school they are to live off the others . . . *In fact, this last paragraph is about all that is the matter with our country. . . .*

Now if you dont like these rules, I can send you some more, but you will get the next bunch collect. Yours, with all good wishes, Will Rogers.

Will had one more bit of advice to give to President Roosevelt. When President Hoover invited the President-Elect to come to Washington to confer on problems of the day, Will advised Roosevelt not to go, telling him nothing was going to come of it. Roosevelt accepted, of course, and Will's prophecy proved true. The Republican press throughout the country jumped on Will for his advice. The remark of the Grand Rapids *Record* for November 17, 1932, is typical: "Mr. Hoover has been badly beaten politically. *He didn't deserve the beating.* He has been the victim of economic misfortunes over which he nor any man in his administration had control." It is a good guess that the same newspaper, if still in existence, would make the same statement under the same circumstances. It seems almost incredible that even then it could be assumed that a government of the people could ignore the economic distress of a nation in the grip of a catastrophe like the depression, and as a government with the same political beliefs had practically ignored the Mississippi floods of 1927. As Hoover's administration ended, unemployment had reached nearly 12 million, 5,000 banks had closed, 32,000 businesses had failed, farm prices were at the lowest in decades, and the national income had dropped from $80 billion in 1929 to less than half of that. Most significant, the entire middle class was in danger of being wiped out.

From the first President Hoover and his advisers had grossly underestimated the depth of the depression, the extent of the upsets, and the fundamental causes behind them. Instead of giving relief where needed, Hoover's greatest sin was in paying a political debt and giving it in form of higher tariffs where it definitely was not needed. Actually his action more closely resembled that of the chairman of the board of a holding company shoring up the finances of the component companies, than that of President of the United States. Will had it: "Mr. Hoover is an engineer . . . He thinks gold is like water, put it on at the top and it will seep on down and water all below . . . Gold, or money, don't work that way . . . Put a bag of gold in Death's Valley on Monday morning, and by Friday night it will be home to Papa J.P. . . . Gold goes up not down like water . . . Put it at the top and it stays there."

The country had to wait four long months, through another winter, with conditions worsening by the hour, for something to happen. It was rougher than ever on the rabbits.

32

The United States Moves into the Future

ON DECEMBER 7, 1932, READERS ALL OVER THE COUNTRY chuckled over their breakfasts as Will informed them that he was "in no way responsible for the editorial or political policy of this paper. I allow them free reign as to their opinion, so long as it is within the bounds of good subscription gathering." On the other hand, he wanted it distinctly understood "that their policy may be in direct contrast to mine. Their editorials may be in purely for humor, or just to fill space. Every paper must have its various entertaining features, and their editorials are not always to be taken seriously, and never to be construed as my policy." This had come because of a tiff over an editorial in the *New York Times* commenting on some of his opinions.

But this was as nothing compared to his irritation at critics who complained about his writing on politics. "I have written on politics for years . . . talked on politics before that . . . You never heard me tell a mother-in-law joke . . . It was always our National or International affairs . . . I have been in almost every country in the last few years . . . I have talked with prominent men in those countries, our Ambassadors or Ministers, and I would have to be pretty dumb to not soak up some information . . . I was in Japan, China and Manchuria . . . I wrote one paragraph (about who owned the ground, the house and who was to police it) that was copied all over the Far East, and editorials written on it . . . Well, I couldent have done it by staying in Hollywood or in an editorial room . . . Still you will read some letter where it says, 'Why does Will Rogers butt into these International problems he knows nothing about?' . . .

"Where do these other fellows get all of their vast stores of knowledge? . . . I never hear of 'em going any place . . . Those New York writers should be compelled to get out once in their lifetime and get the 'Folks' angle. . . .

"Now I read Politics, talk Politics, know personally almost every prominent Politician, like 'em and they are my friends, but I can't help it if I have seen enough of it to know that there is some baloney in it . . . *Now I am going to be like an umpire, or referee* . . . I am going to keep on doing the same as I have in the past . . . I am going to call 'em like I see 'em . . . If I dont see things your way, well, why should I? . . . *I hope I never get so old that I cant peep behind the scenes and see the amount of politics that's mixed in this medicine before its dished out to the people as 'Pure statesmanship.'* "

When Will saw what continued to happen, "the R.F.C. loaned the railroads money, medium and small banks money, and all they did with it was pay off what they owed to New York banks," he became increasingly irate. "Every industry, every man in the United States has been hit by the depression, and before public funds were dealt out, you should have first found out, have we enough to give aid to everyone, every industry . . . If not, then don't give aid to part and leave the rest out . . . But, no, they dident do that . . . They just started right in by helping the bankers, so every man, woman and child in the U.S. thinks, and rightfully so, that they have got as much right to get some sort of Government aid as the bankers . . . Due to the lack of foresight of our lawmakers, *the bankers, the railroads, and big business got the first U.S. Dole,* and it will never be finished till the last one hundred and twenty million reach in and get theirs because they feel they got it coming." Will might have added that big business had for years been on a "dole" in the form of protective tariffs. In spite of the "dole," banks were closing by the hundreds all over the country and nothing was done about it.

As the United States was preparing to reverse its retreat into "normalcy" and move into the future, Will defined those who had really prospered in the 1920's:

Rugged individualism was a good thing for the "rugged," but it looked like we had millions that wasent so rugged. If a man is "rugged" he ought to be able to make a living under any type of government . . . The only trouble about this Rugged Individualism is that you cant tell just how much of a man's good fortune is through his ruggedness and how much through good luck . . . You must always remember that the "rugged" made it off the "unrugged." . . .

"Built by rugged individualism and good luck," natural resources that dident cost anybody anything, had a lot to do with making many a man rich and "rugged" . . . Now that the natural resources are gone, it's taken away many a "ruggedness" . . . There is nothing that will take the "ruggedness" out of a man quicker than taking away free things that made him rugged. . . .

What we mean by a "rugged individual" is one that has made something . . . "Rugged" is Latin for rich . . . The cry is "keep government out of business . . . Don't watch us so close . . . We made our money when nobody was looking . . . If you are going to watch us, we are not going to show you how we made it." . . . Some big businesses is like a burglar, they cant operate if some cop is going to keep an eye on 'em. . . .

As March 4, 1933, approached, the crisis in banking, in industry and in agriculture became more and more acute, with unemployment increasing daily. While Franklin D. Roosevelt's "the only thing we have to fear is fear itself" speech brought hope to millions, it was the action that followed that delighted Will. "President Roosevelt closed the banks before lunch and called Congress into session while he was having dessert . . . America hasent been as happy in three years as now . . . No money . . . No banks . . . No work . . . No nothing . . . But they know they got a man in there who is wise to Congress, wise to our big bankers, and wise to our so-called Big Men . . . The whole country is with him . . . Even if he does what is wrong they are with him, just so he does something . . . If he burned down the Capitol, we would cheer and say, 'Well, we at least got a fire started anyhow.' We have had years of 'Dont rock the boat' . . . Go on and sink it if you want to . . . We just as well be swimming as like we are . . . One thing you have never got a Republican Administration to do, voluntarily close a bank . . . Their theory was leave 'em open till they shut . . . For three years we have had nothing but 'America is fundamentally sound' . . . It should have been 'America is fundamentally cuckoo' . . . The worse off we get the louder we laugh, which is a great thing . . . And every American International banker ought to have printed on his office door, 'Alive today by the grace of a nation that has a sense of humor.' "

Anxious that the people should know that his act of closing the banks was an emergency measure to strengthen them, President Roosevelt explained what was being done in a "fireside chat" on March 12. Will added his endorsement. "Mr. Roosevelt stepped to the microphone last night and knocked a home run . . . His message was not only a great comfort to the people, but it pointed a lesson to all radio speakers . . . leave a big vocabulary at home in the dictionary . . . Our President took such a dry subject as banking (and when I say 'dry' I mean dry, for if it had been liquid he wouldent have had to speak on it at all) . . . Well, he made everybody understand it, even the bankers." When Will's bank opened under the Emergency Banking Act of March 9, 1933, he did not go near it. "Shows you I heard Roosevelt on the radio . . . Bankers should have over their desks this motto, 'God bless Roosevelt, God bless radio,' and then, P.S. 'God bless interest' . . . And that Congress . . . Nowadays Mr. Roosevelt just makes out a little list of things every morning that he wants them to do (kinder like a housewife's menu list) and for the first time in their lives they are acting like U.S. citizens, and not like U.S. Senators or Congressmen . . . Now we got a man to do their thinking for 'em, and the whole country is better off."

Other action came quickly. The Tennessee Valley Authority was set up for a regional control and development in the states traversed by this river—a project Presidents Coolidge and Hoover had both vetoed after Congressional approval. The outcry from the utilities lobby had been "Don't put the government in the power business." Will answered this. "They are always wanting the government to spend the taxpayers money to build something, then don't want 'em to run it . . . Why cant the Government run it, or anything else they have built? . . . They run the Post Offices . . . Too bad the dam is not closer to Washington. We could use it for our Presidents to fish in."

Preparations got under way at once to remove the Eighteenth Amendment from the Constitution. In the meantime Congress made

3.2 percent beer legal. "I dident sample this low voltage beer . . . I have always claimed America dident want a drink as bad as they wanted the right to take a drink if they did happen to want one." In his enthusiasm over a Congress that was "behaving" Will offered to buy a drink for each member.

On April 19, 1933, an executive order stopped the export of gold and thereby effectively took the country off the gold standard. "The best way to tell when each one of us went off the gold is to figure back how many years it was since we had any . . . The last I remember getting my clutches on was in Johannesburg, South Africa, some five dollar English gold pieces that we carried in a belt around our waist . . . So I went off the gold in 1902." Will frankly admitted that he could not understand the money situation, and Arthur Brisbane charged him with being worried. "I am not worried, I am confused . . . There is quite a difference; when you are worried you know what you are worried about, but when you are 'confused' it's when you dont know enough about a thing to be worried."

On April 30, 1933, Will spoke before the Gridiron Club in Washington at a dinner in honor of President Roosevelt. "We are gathered here to do homage to a man that has no precedent in accomplishments in such a short time . . . He has done more for us in seven weeks than we did for ourselves in seven years . . . We elected him because he was a Democrat; we honor him because he is a magician . . . He is the Houdini of Hyde Park . . . Maybe this Houdini can't get us out of every pair of handcuffs we have dumbly stuck our own hands into, but if he can only get one of our hands out, and leave 'em on the other, we will be a terrible lot better off . . . This Maverick has disgraced the Roosevelt Klan, and like Gandhi dared to throw his lot with the untouchables, the Democrats . . . But Gandhi did have the advantage of him, Gandhi did have a party . . . But when Roosevelt went to the Democrats, they not only had no party, but dident even have a loin cloth . . . And that's giving it the polite name . . . You know all these big companies, their officials naturally are Republicans, so knowing that I might get up here tonight and boost Mr. Roosevelt, so I said, 'Is it all right with you fellows?' And they said, 'We would naturally rather be saved by a Republican, but if we can't, why we certainly are not against being pulled out of the mud by a Democrat'

... That's one thing about a Republican, he is broadminded that way."

A week later Will attended a dinner given by the United States Chamber of Commerce. "The humorous part of it was that all the big manufacturers and producers in there had been all their life hollering, 'Keep the Government out of business'... Well, my companion was Jesse Jones of the Reconstruction Finance Corporation, who had a mortgage on every full dress suit in the house ... There is not a business that the Government hasent been asked to join ... Nothing makes a man broadminded like adversity." Most of the money had been lent under President Hoover, who considered it un-American, practically immoral, for the government to feed hungry people!

While in the East, accompanied by Betty, Will signed up to do seven coast-to-coast radio broadcasts for $50,000, with the Gulf Oil Company as his sponsor. The proceeds were to be split 50-50 between the Red Cross and the Salvation Army. "I wanted to make a contribution to a couple of good causes that had done such fine work during 'our earthquake' and I dident have the dough to do it with, so Mrs. Rogers figgered it, as she does most other things. She says, 'You got the wind to do it.' So I got nothing in the transaction to lose but my voice and I never lost it yet."

On May 21, 1933, since the Senate had been "behaving" itself, Will addressed it as a group. "The Senate will kindly come to order ... Sit down there, Mr. Garner, I'm running this Session of the Senate ... And if you be right good I wont tell 'em you are the Vice-President ... You can stay awake tonight ... This is one speech you havent heard a dozen times ... And, Mr. Garner, I got some regular business for you ... There is a little poker game going on ... Now listen, we are going to have some order here ... Huey Long, quit prowling around there and sit down ... If you got no place to rest yourself, Louisiana *will gladly dig you a place* ... And don't even look like you want to make a speech. ...

"Wait a minute! ... Here is a bill from the President ... I don't know what it's about and we will pass it with the usual procedure of not reading it ... All those in favor say—EYE—All opposed say NO—The EYES Have it. ...

"Hello, Alice, you will have to stand up there ... We havent enough seats for the Democrats ... I know he is your fifth cousin ... I am Harry Lauder's but it never got me anything. . . .

"Wait a minute ... Here is a note from the President ... He says read this ... He tells me he cant think of anything else, so to adjourn the Senate, not only now, but forever ... Wants you to go home, if you have the nerve or the fare ... There has been quite a bit of discussion between the intellectual end of our Government, representing Mr. Tugwell, Ezekiel and Moley, as to just whether they need you boys back here again."

While in Washington Will and Betty spent a night at the White House and as its "unofficial President" Will reported to the nation on the state of the President's health. "You wonder how this man, under this tremendous strain, is taking this ... I have not been in a home since 1929 where it really looked like there was joy and happiness and good spirits like that one ... I don't mean that he is unmindful of all of those out of work ... But, by golly, he is not sitting down moping over it ... He has a grin on his face ... This man absolutely believes, he knows that he is going to help these people ... It is not conceit, it is absolute confidence ... The unemployment is the thing that worries him the most; it is not Europe ... you know, this fellow, he has got some kind of feeling ... I believe that he has some kind of divine feeling ... He knows things are going to be all right ... Humor and laughs ... My goodness, I dident get anywhere with my little jokes ... At dinner, he wanted another helping of fish ... He told us (there was about 12 of us there) 'The hardest thing, the biggest hardship I have had in the White House is to get a second helping of anything.' ... I said to him, 'Well, Mr. President, why don't you put it in the platform the next time—a second helping for all Presidents?' . . .

"In the morning, Mr. Roosevelt sits in his bedroom ... I think he has breakfast in bed ... He had the awfullest sweater over his pajamas I ever saw ... He sees people that come in there ... He doesnt go to the office until about eleven o'clock ... When I came in, I said to Mrs. Roosevelt, 'Where is the President?' ... She said, 'Wherever you hear the laugh' ... So I went in there, and there he was ... He said, 'Now, Will, sit down here a minute and you will see what everybody wants as they come in and out.' I said, 'No, I can't do that. It is about ten o'clock and the Morgan investigation is on at ten o'clock . . . I have got to go . . . Lord, I can see a President any time, but I never did see Morgan in my life. I am not going to monkey . . .' So he told me, 'Will, I don't blame you. I wish I could see him too.' "

Will hoped that what J. P. Morgan told a senatorial investigating committee might be educational, not only of the Morgan investigation itself but of all business. "It's going to show us just how 'Big Business' got big . . . It got big according to law, but not according to Hoyle." He also hoped it might show the way to much-needed reform. "Carter Glass who knows more about money than any man in America, talked in the Senate today of his new bank Bill . . . It protects deposits and makes bankers responsible to each other . . . In other words, he wants to set a banker to watch a banker, instead of leaving it to the depositors to try . . . He also wants to stop banks from racketeering in trusts and holding companies . . . It really sounds too good to pass."

The bill passed on June 16, 1933. It provided that all member banks of the Federal Reserve System separate themselves from security affiliates and created the Federal Deposit Insurance Corporation guaranteeing bank deposits up to $5,000 (later raised to $10,000). It also restricted the use of Federal Reserve credit for speculative purposes, restrained the banks from dealing in foreign securities, and prohibited private banks from acting both as banks of deposit and at the same time serving as securities underwriters. In effect, this took the control of currency and banking away from Wall Street and placed it in Washington, where the interests of all the people could be served rather than that of special groups. This control was bolstered by the Securities Act passed later in the year (made effective by a supplemental act in 1934 that established the Securities and Exchange Commission) in an effort to prevent another stock market debacle. Wall Street at least had a measure of control clamped on it.

Aviation received a couple of tremendous boosts in the summer of 1933. One was when Mrs. Roosevelt made a transcontinental flight. "There is a real boost for aviation . . . But here is what she really takes the medal for . . . Out at every stop, day or night, being interviewed, talking over radio, no sleep, and yet they say she never showed one sign of weariness, or annoyance of any kind . . . No maid, no secretary, just the First Lady of the Land on a paid ticket on a regular passenger plane . . . If some of our female screen stars had made that trip they would have had one plane for secretaries, one for maids, one for chefs and chouffers, and a trailer for 'business representatives' and 'press agents.' " The other came when Wiley Post made his flight alone around the world. "I would have liked to have been in there with Post instead of that robot he used as a navigator . . . And I could have if I had known as much as it did . . . What did I tell you about that little one-eyed Oklahama boy? . . . He is a hawk, ain't he? . . . He holds the doubles and singles championship now . . . If he ever decided to make up a foursome to go round, I will take out a ticket with him."

At the end of his seven broadcasts Will, who never really liked performing over radio, seriously considered giving up the medium entirely. As the news got out, he received a petition signed by all the senators urging him not to do so. "Well, it was one of the most pleasant things I ever had happen to me . . . Here was the U.S. Senate that I am always kidding about, and here they come and do a nice thing like that . . . The next fellow that knocks the Senate will have to answer to me . . . That's my privilege and nobody else's . . . You know after all with all their arguments and time taking, they do a lot of good . . . Those old boys watch a lot of stuff that if it wasent for them would be railroaded through . . . The Senate is more of a night watchman than the House is . . . It is kinder like one of these things you have in a kitchen sink to keep the spoons and plates and stove, and all those little things from going through."

At first the idea back of the National Industrial Recovery Act appealed to Will, particularly in its intention to ensure fair competition on an industry-wide basis, prohibiting child labor and other abuses. On August 27, 1933, he went on radio, as he had on unemployment for President Hoover, and asked that it be given a fair test. "I tell you, folks, I came away from Washington last week with the idea that the little fellow has got somebody in his corner in Washington . . . I don't mean the Administration is against big business, but for the first time in years the big man comes to Washington the same as the little one . . . If this Administration ever goes under, it should have written on its tombstone, 'Perished through trying to give the little fellow a square deal.' "

One of the big questions that was causing much argument was inflation, particularly after the "Gold Repeal Joint Resolution" of June 5, 1933, which canceled the gold clause providing for the payment of public and private debts in gold. This brought a comment from Will. "We are awful weak now because Roosevelt has just operated on our heart . . . Our gold is our heart . . . And when you take out our heart and start monkeying with it, we are always kinder leery as to whether you can get it back and beating again . . . You see your gold, or your heart, has just got so many beats in it, and you go start trying to put in more, and you are fooling with life."

As fall came and the clamor increased, Will laid down a formula for those who had a right to howl. "Various forms of business has picked up, yet those very businesses are the ones that say the whole thing is all wet. The newspaper advertising pages have more space sold than in the last few years, yet the editorial page denounces the whole thing every day . . . You can't be participating in better times and then legitimately knock it . . . The only ones that can take the hide off it is the ones that have absolutely not been helped one iota in any way . . . You know, the little fellow is the best gambler . . . Life itself has been a gamble with him . . . But the rich guy, and the banker (who Roosevelt is trying to get to put out their money), they want to know in advance what is ahead . . . They want to be tipped off as to what the dollar is going to be worth . . . He has always played with marked cards, he has always known . . . Now he is where he is asked to take a chance, and he wont lay her on the line . . . He keeps the dough in his pockets till he sees the marked cards, and he criticizes the dealer for not giving him a look at the hole cards before they are dealt . . . He wont bet on his country being bigger than any system, even if it was a bad one." Will then said that, even if Roosevelt had not known what to do, he did know when the United States Chamber of Commerce passed a resolution telling him what to do. "Do what the Chamber said not to do."

In November, 1933, when the United States recognized Soviet Russia, hoping to regain some trade lost by the Smoot-Hawley tariff act, Will saw little hope. Their chief exports were caviar, "without a doubt the poorest fodder on earth," and vodka, "as harmful looking a thing as branch water, but when you start sampling it, your eyes begin expanding, and your ears begin to flopping like a mule's . . . It's the only drink where you drink and try to grit your teeth at the same time . . . By the time it reaches your Adam's apple, it has acted . . . A man stepping on a red-hot poker could show no more immediate animation . . . It's the only drink where you can hit the man that handed it to you before he can possibly get away . . . No, we havent started to realize the benefits we got from recognizing Russia till the caviar and vodka start coming in."

By the end of December Will was able to announce with conviction that "there is lots more good cheer this Xmas than last (or the last three), and it's not all out of bottles either . . . It's in the heart, in the confidence, and in the renewed hope of everybody . . . Even the most down and out, while he might not see a turkey Xmas day, he can see one in the future." He could also report that Secretary of State Cordell Hull had visited Argentina, Chile and Peru "under his own name." It would take another Republican administration before South Americans began spitting and throwing rocks at our representatives.

33

The Howls and Growls—and Cheers

EVERY MOMENT THAT WILL WAS FREE OF HIS MOTION-picture assignments he spent in Washington. This was possible, of course, only by air travel. As the "unofficial President" he had an authorization from Eugene L. Vidal, director of aeronautics in the Department of Commerce, "for any scheduled airline to carry you as a passenger in any aircraft operated on the line." On those not on a regular passenger run he had to be "equipped with a parachute." He once described flying as sitting on a can containing *The Birth of a Nation* and commented, "If it had been Garbo or Hepburn I wouldent have got so cold."

The political scene in Washington was boiling the way Will liked it. "That Roosevelt handled that Congress this morning just like a mother would a fretting baby . . . Just when any other mother would have told it to hush, and be a good baby and not cry, he dident tell 'em a single thing to do . . . Just slipped 'em a piece of candy . . . And they were all just tickled to death, rolling on the floor, with their toes in their mouths . . . And goo-gooing to each other."

This was not true for the business world. "Mr. Roosevelt proposed in his speech . . ." this was January 4, 1934, ". . . that the NRA and a lot of these other government regulated business ethics would be made permanent . . . Well, that was a terrible blow to some business men . . . They had figured they would only be required to be honest by the government till the emergency was over."

By late January, 1934, when Will journeyed to Washington to

attend a dinner that Vice-President Garner was giving for the President the atmosphere was tense. The political commentator Frank Kent described the situation: "With their sense of proportion everybody had lost their sense of humor. The Senate, the House and the Administration were saturated with sentiment, dripping with zeal, of one sort or another. One set of statesmen thrilled with holy fervor over the glories of the New Deal, visualizing the day when the Government would bear all of the burdens and everybody be happy and prosperous and good. . . . Another set believed that, with the best intentions in the world, he had launched us upon a crazy program, the end of which will be a catastrophic crash, with the nation a bankrupt, and the people plunged into misery. . . . *Into all this portentous solemnity came Mr. Rogers.* For two days he kidded Senators, Representatives and others, *until the fever of some had abated and the chill of others worn off.* . . . For example, one serious gentleman, viewing with alarm the financial uncertainty, propounded that oft-repeated question, 'What can a man put his money in these days?' 'Taxes,' said Will. 'You needent worry about what to do with your money . . . That's all been arranged for you . . . Everybody's money is to go into taxes . . . That's going to save you a lot of trouble.' "

Will was naturally puzzled over "some of the hands the New Deal dealt," but he admired the way in which, as one experiment sagged, Roosevelt would have another one ready. "You know Roosevelt's got a lot of relief boards going . . . He's got farm relief . . . mortgage relief . . . unemployed relief and a lot of others . . . But he hasent sprung the last one yet . . . RRC . . . That's the Republican Relief Corporation . . . Yes, sir, he's going to relieve the Republicans . . . Soon as he's done that, he's through . . . Then everybody will be relieved and there won't be nothing else to do."

At the Garner dinner Will wore the old blue serge suit and Roosevelt made him turn around to show the shiny seat. The dinner was "knee deep in Caviar . . . That was on account of recognizing Russia . . . I would figure a fish in Russia would lay a hard-boiled egg . . . It was a little dull there . . . If they had waited two more weeks there could have been a little vodka or Bourbon to go with the caviar . . . I dident notice real close, there could have been a little slipped in." In his speech Will bowed to Gene Buck and said: "If it hadent been for

Gene, who dug me out of a little vaudeville act, I might be working in one of your CCC camps, Mr. President, or punching cows out on Jack Garner's ranch at Uvalde, Texas."

Will and Betty had dinner at the White House on Roosevelt's birthday and remained for the reception afterward. "It was the first time I had ever seen one, and I pretty near had an argument with the President while he was changing from his tuxedo, which he had worn at dinner, to his dress suit, which he would wear to the reception... He had asked me into his room to show me all the things he had in there... I asked him if he sat down while the people were passing the receiving line and he said, no, that he stood... Well, then I blew up... I told him he ought to sit down... That was one time I was telling the President of the U.S. what to do... I have done it a lot of times but not so they could hear it, but this time I was laying the law down... Well, anyhow I dident get away with it... He went right down and stood up nearly an hour and a half."

When Will and Betty entered the ballroom a ripple of excitement went over the crowd, as all eyes surveyed his old blue serge suit. He was the only man not in full dress. Will's eyes lit on Mrs. Alice Longworth and he shambled over to her, made "a courtesy" and kissed her hand. "I wasent going to let some French Diplomat have anything on me... She had on some queer earrings... They was great long gold buckets that looked kinder like miniature coal scuttles... I think she wore 'em just for a laugh... They was gold, and she wanted to see if her fifth cousin would confiscate it."

On Lincoln's Birthday Will summed up the situation in terms of what Lincoln would have done if alive. "In the first place, he wouldent chop any wood... He would trade in his axe on a Ford... Being a Republican, he would vote the Democratic ticket... Being in sympathy for the underdog, he would be classed as a radical progressive ... Having a sense of humor, he would be called eccentric."

In addition to having a sincere regard for Will's ability, both as a humorist and as a political analyst, President Roosevelt was shrewd enough to realize the value of having his "unofficial President" on his side. He was also perceptive enough not to use him in national appeals asking concerns "voluntarily" to employ more men in a manner that would treat the revolutionary upsets the country was facing as something the National Red Cross could handle. Will would call up the White House and Mrs. Roosevelt would say, "Come on over." He described one such visit when invited to "tea." "Funny thing, that's just what it was, a tea . . . You know the last few years we come to look on tea as a sort of blind, and the cup really ought to be fortified with some liquid with a short wave frequency . . . Professor Nicholas Murray Butler, the only man that has more initials of degrees after his name than Mr. Roosevelt's plans, well, when Dr. Butler saw there was no other potent ingredient on the tray but—oolong—why, he just wouldent take anything . . . I felt sorry for the old Ph.D. . . . Here he had fought 15 years for repeal, and then be handed a handfull of tea . . . If I ever saw a dejected looking man, it was Dean Butler . . . If I had had a little flask of corn on my hip, I would have slipped the old pedagogue a nip."

As the months ticked off in 1934 it became obvious that the NRA was running into grave difficulties. "The complaint division of the N.R.A. opened . . . They come in wagons, planes, trains, dog teams and limousines . . . You wouldent think there was that much wrong with one plan, but everybody that hadent done well, maybe partly due to their own efforts, was willing to lay it onto the NRA . . . They lined up in the morning outside the Department of Commerce building, and when you line up around it, it's just like lining up on the borders of Texas . . . But it's not only the NRA . . . They come to Washington to complain on everything . . . Everybody either has a kick or a wish, and he is just as big a pest no matter which one he is there on." Will had his own criticism of the NRA. "The code could have been mailed out to everybody on a postcard . . . Any labor hired, six hours a day, no pay less than so many dollars a week, no sweatshop, no child labor . . . If we had spent as much time observing it as we have spent arguing over it, it would have worked, right or wrong . . . There is a great good in it and evidently great ills in it."

President Roosevelt made a fireside chat on it late in March, 1934. He pointed out that "ninety percent of our people live on salary or wages, ten percent on profits alone . . . People in this country whose income is less than two thousand a year, buy more than two-thirds of all goods sold . . . If these people are not assured of an income, the goods produced cannot be sold." Change the amount of income, and the same thing is still true.

Conditions on the foreign scene were shaping up so that it seemed to Will that war was edging closer and closer. "Poor old France and Japan are about in the same fix . . . France don't know whether it would be better to jump on Germany and lick 'em now while they can, or wait till Germany pounces on them . . . Japan is in the same spot . . . They feel they can lick Russia now, or will she wait till Russia is able to pounce on them? . . . The thing of living as an ambitious nation is not what it's cracked up to be . . . One day our eyes are turned to Europe . . . The next it's Japan that draws our attention . . . We are going to have a crooked neck from trying to look both ways . . . Mussolini's troops camped on the Austrian border . . . Hitler says nothing, which means he is too busy moving troops . . . England lends moral support, yes, and two battleships . . . France backs Austrian government, and sends a few hundred planes over to deliver the message . . . Chile is selling nitrates, Europe is fertilizing again . . . Japan coronated the new emperor of Manchuria . . . They would have had the coronation earlier, but they dident have any armored car to haul him to the festivities in . . . From all I can read in the papers dated from some foreign capital, the ambition of their lives seems to be to get us and Japan into war . . . Now if any nation on earth can give any excuse why we should fight Japan, any more than they should, they ought to get a prize for thinking of it . . . Besides we couldent go to war with 'em now, for we just sent our fleet around on the East Coast in case we would have trouble with Portugal, or Spain."

At the end of May, 1934, Will was able to report one improvement in our foreign affairs. "Roosevelt gave Cuba a new treaty . . . The 'Godfather' clause is taken out . . . All their revolutions are to be strictly 'home talent' . . . Porto Rico is to be 'wet nursed' by the Interior Department instead of the Army and the Philippines are rehearsing for their freedom . . . The thing to do was to give them their freedom . . . Then we would be called 'Brother' and not 'Big Brother.' "

In his last radio broadcast for the summer Will announced that "having finished two pictures, and a stage play, and finally having caught a calf that I been roping at in between time, I am thinking of taking my boys with me and go round the world . . . We're heading for Siberia by the way of Honolulu, Japan, Manchuria, and then across the Trans-Siberian Railway into Moscow and Leningrad... Then I am going to find Finland... If Finland can go to the trouble of paying us, I can certainly take the time to try and find them... Mrs. Rogers accompanies us till the traveling gets rough and we run out of luxuries... I got a daughter but she is working... *If I run onto Mr. Roosevelt over around Honolulu, maybe I can get him to go with me*... This is a secret mission I am going on... When I get back, the Senate will investigate me and see if they can find out why I went ... It's a Commission to end friendly relations between nations... All the others have been good-will tours, and they have been so successful that no two nations are speaking to each other... The reason I am going to travel all over Russia is that it's trying the greatest experiment in the world, outside of ours."

A couple of weeks before leaving on the trip Betty noticed certain familiar symptoms in Will.

"Where do you want to go?" she asked him one morning at breakfast.

"I want to see Mary," he said.

Their daughter was acting in summer stock in Maine and, after breaking the news to Betty, Will was on the next plane out of Los Angeles. He stopped at a ranch in Texas for a day's roping, and then on to the old ranch at Oolagah. "They was threshing oats, and the women folks was cooking for the threshers... I got a niece there that was raised in the city, that married my nephew, a real cowhand, and darned if she ain't the best cook in Rogers County... Get a city gal if you want a country wife... For these old country gals have had enough of it... They are headed for the pavement..... Caught the passenger line out of Tulsa for Chicago that afternoon... Then changed for Cleveland, then for Washington, and here I was in Washington at four A.M.... Well then I flew that night up to N.Y." There Will saw Dorothy Stone in *As Thousands Cheer,* Paula Stone doing a dancing act, and Carol Stone in *The Sparrow* and "Fred was walking around just beaming." They all had dinner at Dinty Moore's and Will was out at daylight and on the plane for Maine. "Lakewood where they have the theatre and summer stock company and a real one, is a great boon to the speaking stage... They all live in little cottages around the lake, put on a different show every week, and rehearse the one for the next week . . . Lord, I wouldent know which one I was doing. I tried to interest Mary in the trip to Japan, but couldent."

Back in California, Will had harrowing problems to conquer. Going on a trip with Betty was not like going on one alone. "I got one little old soft red grip that if I just tell it when I am leaving it will pack itself . . . A few old shirts with collars attached, and a little batch of underwear which can be replenished anywhere and throw the old ones away . . . You don't figure on laundry at all and it's cheaper, for when you start paying excess on these planes, brother, till then you havent seen any excess . . . So me and my little red bag and typewriter, one extra suit, and that's all." Now he was being dragged off the polo field or from calf roping to try on white shoes or a palm beach suit. "It ain't supposed to fit, if it does it's uncomfortable . . . I balked when they tried to make me take a bathrobe . . . If you follow this family around, you could pick up a lot of unworn things . . . I will come into New York harbor with the little red bag, the old blue serge and the typewriter."

34

Around the World with the Rogerses

THE FAMILY SAILED FROM SAN FRANCISCO ABOARD THE S.S. *Malolo* on July 22, 1934. "Mr. Roosevelt is out here somewhere on Japan's ocean fishing . . . awful long way to come to fish . . . I think he come away out here so he couldent hear the Republicans roar and to get away from any new scheme that his own gang might cook up." In the middle of the night, a few days out, Will was awakened and told that the notorious bandit Dillinger, termed "Public Enemy Number One," had been caught while coming out of a motion-picture theater. "Hope it was mine," he cabled of the picture shown.

The boat docked on July 27, 1934, and the passengers received the traditional Hawaiian welcome. "I got to my hotel and I had 28 of those things around my neck, and they were all of a different, and wonderful fragrant breed of flowers . . . Right up above us and kinder over to one side on a balcony apartment was the Presidents rooms . . . Had a lot of bathing suits hung out . . . Guess I am the only person ever went to Honolulu and dident take a whirl at the ocean . . . But I couldent ride one of those ironing boards with my stirrups hobbled . . . My kids tried it, but they come in a new way, they had the board riding them . . . It was standing up on end right on their necks."

On the evening of their arrival Betty and Will had dinner with the President and his party, mostly prominent men from the islands. There were ten or twelve there, and F.D.R. was in great humor, highly pleased with the spirit and prosperity of the islands, and with the way in which the various nationalities lived together in harmony. Will was taken to task for referring to the Pacific as "Japan's ocean" and of the islands as Japan's when they decided to take them over. "Don't take yourselves too seriously, folks . . . When you lose your sense of humor and let a little dig like that get under you skin, you lose the greatest thing in life . . . If I took myself serious, where would I be? . . . I'm still just an old cowhand at heart."

The President and Will were the honored guests at the Honolulu Chamber of Commerce dinner, and Will was kept speaking for over two hours, with F.D.R. leading the laughter. "The President is the only Harvard man that ever come out here that dident get something . . . He come with a fishing line, and dident even get a bite . . . The other Harvard boys, those old missionaries, the first settlers come with a Bible years ago and got an island . . . So we can't say the intelligence of the Harvard graduates has advanced any . . . Here we go and elect him President, and it looks like he is the least farsighted of any of them . . . We cant let Hawaii go . . . We got nowhere else for our army and navy to go for a vacation. . . .

"I am like Paul Revere . . . I am rushing out here to tell Mr. Roosevelt the Dam has broke and the Republicans are rushing, or washing down the valley . . . To the polls . . . to the polls . . . All good Democrats . . . Well, it dont matter whether they are good or not, we cant be too particular . . . to the polls, and keep the Democratic Congressmen and Senators in office . . . November 4th is coming. . . .

"Mr. Roosevelt is the only President that dident have to learn to fish after he got in office . . . The others thought it was in the ritual they signed when they went in . . . Coolidge used to fish, but, God, how he hated it . . . The darn fish were too talkative . . . Mr. Hoover fished because he wanted to carry out the Coolidge policy . . . None of 'em liked the sea . . . Mr. Coolidge used to get on the *Mayflower* but he saw to it that it dident get out of the Potomac. . . .

"Here is the place where tourists used to come two thousand miles to be shocked by girls dancing in buckwheat skirts . . . Now they stay home and watch 'em dance in the raw . . . Hawaii maybe first suggests nothing but sunburn, surfboard riding, ukuleles and cocoanuts, but when you get here, you really find folks working. . . . Diamond Head is just an old volcano that has seen better days, something like the Republican Party . . . Hawaii's volcanoes are like everything else nowadays, they're laying off . . . This depression has hit those volcanoes too, and if you ever saw a sad-looking sight it's a volcano that's been hit by a Republican depression . . . they just sorter sag in the middle and all sides hang loose, nothing going in and nothing coming out. . . .

"Hawaii is the only place I know where they lay flowers on you while you are alive . . . they hang 'em around your neck . . . That's better than laying them on your chest where your hands are crossed."

Quite naturally, Will visited a cattle ranch in the islands to see how it was operated and the cattle worked. He also visited the army and navy installations. "You dont have to be warlike to get a real kick out of our greatest army post, Schofield Barracks, and the Navy at Pearl Harbor . . . If war was declared with some Pacific nation, we would lose the Philippines before lunch but if we lost these, it would be our own fault."

While in Hawaii Will received a letter from the Post Office Department stating that the government planned to build a new post office building at Claremore and the site selected was owned by him. Uncle Clem's old livery stable had stood on it. He immediately wired permission to the city officials to sell the lots to the government, and to use the proceeds for some worthy civic enterprise or give it "to some old lady to buy a cow." It was used as an endowment for a public library, and a few months later, using reclaimed brick from an old schoolhouse and WPA labor, a fine new building was constructed. Set in the south side of the building was the cornerstone that had been in the old livery stable building.

On August 3, 1934, the Rogers family sailed on the S.S. *Empress of Canada* for Japan. On shipboard Will cabled that President Roosevelt's parting advice was: "Don't jump on Japan, just keep them from jumping on us." On arrival in Japan he "found everything peaceful . . . They want a bigger navy and I think I will let 'em have it, for they are going to build it anyway." The only hopeful sign was that he "saw a lot of golf courses being put in . . . They won't have their world supremacy in business long . . . That's the beginning of a nation's financial decline."

To Will's great joy ("It's better to take your wife, anyhow, than to have to explain the whole thing to 'em") Betty decided to go on around the world with them. "She was the best sport of the bunch."

Nothing much was happening in Manchuria and after sightseeing there they headed for Russia. By now robberies were taking place on the road from Mukden to Harbin, and on from there to the Siberian border. "The bandits rob it and leave nothing but their tracks . . . They sometimes hold up passengers and keep 'em for ransom . . . Now quite a few American folks asked us in Mukden if we wasent taking a chance . . . Well, I never heard of a comedian being held for ransom . . . I figured no Chinaman wanted to sit watching me for days, and listen to jokes about Huey Long and Bilbo . . . But I don't mind telling you that after being on it two nights and a day, I was mighty glad when we reached the Russian border . . . Imagine anybody feeling safe when they reached Russia . . . But that's one thing about Russia, there is no holdups and no kidnapping." Eight days later, after they arrived in Moscow, they learned that American friends in Harbin had been taken from the train, stripped of their clothes, and held for ransom.

Everyone in Harbin had told them that the food on the Russian "de luxe" train that left every seven days for Moscow was poor. "So we outfitted like we was going over the Chilkoot pass . . . I warned the family to lay in their own provisions . . . I am a bean man myself, but the youngest, Jim, beat me to it . . . He cornered the canned bean market before I got a crack at 'em . . . I got an old washbasket full of plunder . . . Everybody else did likewise . . . You couldent get in our compartments for salmon, sardines, thermos cans, coffee percolators, everything but an ice cream freezer. . . . Well, we went into the diner just as a lark . . . A waiter, before we sat down hardly, brought a dishpan full of caviar . . . I been too stingy to get used to it . . . The boys dont like it . . . But Mrs. R.—the little woman—womanlike, and knowing its price, just couldent sit there and see it get away . . . It come with the meal tickets which we had . . . Well, anyhow, they had more food on that diner than I ever saw in the whole Harvey system . . . Now we tried to give away that food, but let me tell you something about these Bolsheviki Russians—they are a mighty proud lot."

The eight days spent crossing Siberia provided ample time to see what lay beside the railroad line. On the other hand, Will had a definite disappointment. Before starting the trip he had been promised that they would be allowed to stop along the way and planes would be available to take them into various parts of Siberia. Nothing was done about this, and he was forced to remain with the train until it reached Moscow. They could get off at any of the stops, however, and look around. "Now we picture Siberia as a vast wasteland . . . Well, it might be a wasteland in the winter time (and so is any other country with snow on it), but I want to tell you old cowmen down in Texas and Oklahoma that it's exactly like the Indian Territory was when I grew up in it as a boy . . . And if you can find a finer one than that was before they plowed it up and ruined it, I dont know where . . . The whole of Siberia across the Trans-Siberian R.R. is a low, rolling prairie with the most beautiful green grass, stirrup deep. . . . Boy, what a cow country! . . . Not a fence, all you would need would be one drift line between you and the Arctic Ocean . . . And Rivers . . . the most rivers I ever saw, and the biggest ones . . . These rivers run to the Arctic Ocean instead of South . . . Looks to me like they run uphill . . . But I wouldent be surprised . . . Everything else in Russia runs backwards . . . And great tremendous log rafts floating down all of 'em . . . They sure got some timber somewhere in that country . . . But it's not along the railroad. . . . Been asked if the railroad was double-tracked . . . Well, we kept meeting trains at full speed, and if there wasent a double track, there was some awful clever railroading done."

In Moscow, in addition to the sights of the city, the family were shown a motion picture, *The Three Songs of Lenin.* It was composed of actual newsreels taken during Lenin's life and during the early days of the Bolsheviki government. The title came from the three stages in Lenin's career: first, the song of freedom of the workingman; then the song of the revolution; and, finally, the song of industrial and commercial accomplishments. Among other scenes was that of Lenin's burial in Red Square in 1924. Thousands stood in thirty-five degree below weather to witness it. "Since then the worship of Lenin had become a national religion . . . But they say that there has never been a one of those put to death that dident just before being executed say a prayer or make a sign of the cross . . . And that's what President Roosevelt was telling us all at dinner in Honolulu . . . He said he told Litvinof, 'Now, Litvinof, you were raised to be a rabbi . . . You don't tell me that just because you have had to denounce God to be a member of the Party, that if you know you were going to die right away, you wouldent remember that old religious training and pray.' Well, the President laughed and said Litvinof changed the subject."

The Moscow Will had seen in 1926 was greatly changed. "Talk about a town on a boom! . . . This is it . . . I never saw so many buildings going up in my life . . . You have heard of equality of sex in Russia . . . That's not so . . . The women are doing the work . . . They are digging a subway . . . I have talked all day with Morris Hindus, Walter Duranty and Louis Fischer . . . Here are three men that know their Russia from A to Bolsheviki."

While in Moscow Will attended a Writers' Convention. "They don't recognize you unless you are a Bolsheviki writer . . . They hold this Convention and the question is, 'What will we hand the folks this year?' . . . They have only got one line to hand 'em, and it takes a pretty smooth writer to juggle that around and make it look new . . . You talk about everybody being equal! . . . There is a guy over here named Maxim Gorky that has sold 19 million copies of his books in the last five years . . . His income last year they said was seven million rubles . . . That guy has made all of that just writing *about how terrible the rich are* . . . Certainly taught me a lesson . . . *I am going to open up and start telling what I know about you all* . . . I have been too lenient with folks."

Will went to a horse race and "when the trotters came out old David Harum wanted to come down and take over the ribbons." There were 36 races, with all the horses belonging to the government, but "raised and entered by different parts of the Army and the collective farms." Will also flew down through the Ukraine and Caucasus to the Black Sea. The oil wells "smell just like regular capitalistic ones" but the flying struck him as extra good. "We had about a 65 or 70 foot ceiling and they struck right under it." Odessa was a particularly interesting city. "Russia and Turkey been fighting over this for a thousand years . . . Do you remember the Russian picture, 'Potemkin'?—that long row of steps from the ocean to the hill . . . Well, they are right into this hotel." Will reported the chief sport of Russia to be parachute jumping. At one meet "a jazz band jumped out with every player a-tooting on a horn and blowing things and playing as they come down . . . That should be followed in this country . . . That is the future of jazz bands, jumping out of airplanes." Without parachutes?

After leaving Moscow Bill Jr. went to Germany, Jim to Paris, and Betty and Will toured the Scandinavian countries. They were to assemble in London for the crossing home.

In Helsinki, Finland ("Integrity's last stand"), Will attended a meeting of its unicameral Diet, and hoped that the United States might follow this example. The great Finnish runner, Pavo Nurmi, "run down to the plane" forty miles from where he lived to meet Will at Abo. "The greatest compliment ever paid me in all Europe," he termed it. In Norway Betty and Will flew up and down fjords in a small seaplane, landed on a mountain lake and chased reindeer in a plane. Will cabled "Skol" back to Minnesota, assuring the Norwegians there they could be proud of their homeland.

From the Scandinavian countries Will and Betty flew into Austria and the Balkans, to see how "this powder keg" of wars was behaving. Once again Betty conscripted him into going to the opera. "I will last about one act and then start hunting a vaudeville show." In Bucharest, he reported, "the king is in the Mountains and Queen Marie is at the seashore . . . This is a corn country . . . The only civilized country in Europe that knows what a roasting ear is." He called Budapest "the star city of all Europe" and reported that "Hungary is a kingdom but got no king, and they are looking for one . . . I believe the Old Kingfish will fit 'em . . . I can fix it for you, Huey." In desperation he stated that he and Betty were going "to keep flying up and down this Danube River till we find a place where it is blue." Then it was breakfast in Budapest and dinner in London.

The first thing that Will read on arriving in London was that the chief problem in the United States continued to be where the "so-called big men" would invest their money. "The whole world would give their right leg to be bothered with that problem . . . If they can't figure what to do with it, the President will figure out a way for them to invest some of it . . . taxes . . . The English have the highest tax rate in Europe, and they are the first to recover . . . They are the ones that used to give the dole to the unemployed and we said England was ruined forever . . . *But here is something you want to remember, all her big men had confidence in her all the time . . . They bet on England to win . . . Over home they are betting on ours to lose."*

On board the S.S. *Ile de France* Will had more comments. "You know the American business man or traveler from home is a queer duck . . . All over Europe and a couple of days ago on the boat all I heard was, 'I tell you I am afraid of things at home . . . It don't look good to me' . . . Well, for the last couple of days the market has picked up and today's news said the strikers went back to work . . . Now they are running around the boat grinning like a possum . . . *Imagine people who's whole idea of our country is gained from what it does every day in a stock market?"*

When Will once again set foot on American soil, September 25, 1934, he cried out: "Boy, it's great to get back into a country where something happens! . . . Talk about Japan, Russia and Europe . . . Why, even a society reporter could cover the news."

This trip around the world had been a memorable one for Will and Betty—a second honeymoon. On their first one a quarter of a century earlier they had made the Orpheum Vaudeville circuit on which Will had roped Teddy and Buck McKee on the stage, twirled his rope, and pattered a little about what he was doing. Now his "rope of words" was lassoing most of the world, but the same old "rope of love" held him and Betty together as it had then—only with deeper ties.

35

"To the Polls . . . to the Polls"

WILL'S REPORT TO THE COUNTRY ON HIS TRIP WAS MADE over a nationwide radio hookup from Radio City in New York. It was not so cheerful and enthusiastic as his joy in getting home had been. He gave to his listeners, if they had the ears and the minds to hear, some profound advice. "I find quite a dissatisfied element here . . . Now you would naturally think it was the unemployed or the fellow with a job who is afraid he will lose it, or the middle class man that generally feels that he bears the brunt of everything. . . .

"But it is not these classes at all . . . They all feel hopeful . . . *It's the rich that's worried* . . . Now the normal thing would be to pass that off and let 'em worry . . . But they are an important part of the scheme of things for us . . . *So the thing is to see what it is that they are scared of, and what they are hollering so about. . . .*

"Now you would say a man to holler he must be hurt . . . But we find that they are not hurt . . . That's the funny thing about it . . . They are hollering *because they are afraid they will be hurt. . . .*

"Well, that's pretty early for a fellow to start hollering. . . . Now I hate to see a condition like that . . . Any country where the rich are arrayed against the poor is no good . . . I have seen 'em where they bumped off the rich and made everybody poor, and when I say made 'em poor, they made 'em poor . . . We want to keep that condition from arising here."

Will thought that the best way to understand the divergence of views would be "for somebody to give a real definition of 'Liberty'. . .

Now what might be one class's 'Liberty' might be another class's 'poison'. . . Course I guess absolute 'Liberty' couldent mean anything but that anybody can do anything they want to anytime they want to . . . Well, any half-wit can tell that wouldent work . . . So the question arises, 'How much liberty can I get and get away with?'. . . *Well, you can get no more than you give . . . Thats my definition.*" Certainly, the concept of the "rugged individualists"—that those less "rugged" must have the "liberty" to go hungry, unclothed and unsheltered because it might interfere with their own profits and dividends—is not the "liberty" of a democracy.

As the 1934 off-election elections neared, the Republicans were hoping that the "Roosevelt honeymoon" was over. Instead, the number of Democrats in both houses of Congress was increased substantially. The people were not going to refuse help any more than the bankers had, and all they had to do was to look to the White House or listen to a fireside chat to know where the help had come from.

On his fifty-fifth birthday, November 4, 1934, Will said he was being accused of padding his age so that he could go on social security earlier. "That's going to be the very next thing . . . It's advocated by practically everybody and it would be the grandest thing we ever had . . . It would be a great mental relief to millions and millions of old folks . . . There is nothing more terrifying than the thought of facing the future with nothing to carry on with . . . I don't know where they will get the money . . . Take it out of increased taxes, I suppose . . . Anyhow, I sure do want to see an old age pension, if we have to print money for it." The Social Security Act was passed in 1935 and signed into law by President Roosevelt the day before Will died.

As 1934 drew to a close, Will became increasingly irritated at those who kept appealing to the President to do things for their special interest. "The American Chamber of Commerce sends about three appeals a week, 'Can you guarantee our members so and so?'. . . We have a hard time finding good stories in the movies . . . I suppose we ought to 'appeal to the President,' and the movie companies ought to appeal to him for a guarantee as to what conditions will be by the time the picture is out. . . . C. L. Bardo, Pres. of the National Association of Manufacturers, asks the President the following, 'Business must have more definite ideas as to the direction in which the Government is headed.'... I can just see Mr. Roosevelt rushing in with a guarantee reading about as follows, 'Nobody guaranteed me anything when I took over this job ... No man gambles more than a President of the U.S.... So you will pardon me if I am not able to guarantee business that it won't lose.' "

Then there were the big financial institutions, who were whining, "Mr. Roosevelt, we think you mean well, but your ideas are wrong... We are not going to play with you." To this Roosevelt should have answered, "I am sorry, gentlemen, I'd love to have you with me... It's a game called heavy, heavy, hangs over your head, and it's not an axe... It's just a printing press inflation which stops all Government interest... Dont slam the door as you go out." Will had his own answer to one of "New York's very, very leading bankers" who visited the Fox studio, "and, incidentally, his studio," and accused him of being an inflationist. "I told him I wasent an inflationist, that to be honest with him, I dident know anything about it... But the thing that I felt was *that if industrialists and business men dident start investing, and helping the President, they would force the President to do the very thing that they kept hollering and asking him not to do* ... That fellow had an economist with him... Pretty near everybody's got one, either that or a police dog, and the more wealthy have both."

If everyone with money had done as Will did at that time, things would quickly have changed for the better. Betty's last Christmas present to him was a tractor. When the time came for planting, in the gardens and fields around the ranch house, Will hired seventy-five unemployed cowboys to do it.

"But, boss, we've got the tractor," the foreman protested.

"Yes, I know," Will drawled, "but tractors don't eat."

Nevertheless, Christmas at the ranch was not as gay as it might have been. Betty and Will were paying the price of their children's growing up. Mary could not come home because she had a chance to play in a show back east. "Doggone, we are all broke up at not being able to see you Xmas... and you not being here is going to knock it into about half what it was to be ... But we are glad you have this chance... You have worked pretty hard and been pretty plucky about it, and I do hope this turns out all right for you . . . It will break the ice anyhow, and that's what's so hard . . . And it's no great disgrace if a show don't run long now . . . I guess you saw where old Pop led 'em all for box office . . . Your Garbos and Hepburns were about twentieth, and your Bennett . . . I am public enemy number one . . . I wouldent have been up there if Marie Dressler had lived . . . I was second last year, I led the men, but I never would have led her . . . It was just that I was lucky in having a pretty good average of pictures . . . Thats why I dread a real flop."

The year ended on a happy note for Will. On a special program over a national radio hookup Will was honored as "aviation's star passenger." Director of Aeronautics Eugene Vidal, of the Department of Commerce described the development of aviation in terms of Will's airsickness. "Years ago when the first air mail services were started he rode more as a stowaway than a passenger, receiving the same treatment as the air mail letters except for the actual stamping. . . . Extreme heat and cold, long and bumpy flights, nerve-racking noise and vibration, as well as cramped quarters naturally affects stomachs, and Will's stomach wasn't exactly air-minded. . . . Ten years ago he was asking for and using one airsickness receptacle for fifty miles . . . Five years ago, about one for five hundred miles . . . Lately, none!"

It is time now to have a look at Will as "public enemy number one" in the talking pictures.

36

Playing Himself in the Talkies

WILL WAS NATURALLY NERVOUS AS HE BEGAN HIS CAREER in talking pictures. He had never been satisfied with what he had done for the screen. His first vehicle was based on Homer Croy's *They Had to See Paris* and in it he played an oil millionaire from Oklahoma who took his family to Europe. It was a sort of *Innocents Abroad* in presenting the antics of this nouveau riche family in Europe. Its success meant much to Will, who was craving to spend more time at home. "If I am a success, I won't have to go around the country and speak to everybody in person . . . Instead, I can send it to them in a can . . . I can spend more time with my family." Will also wanted to expand his audience. "I am a great one to appeal to the older folks, but I can't even get my own children to read what I write . . . And when I'm on lecture tours, I notice that there is a lot of older people in the audience and comparatively few young ones . . . I made up my mind when I went into pictures this time that I would try a different plan and see if I couldent reach the young people as well. 'Let me be the only homely one in this picture,' I said. 'Let all the others be real good-looking.' I want the young folks to like it!"

They Had to See Paris was a tremendous box-office hit not only with the older people but with the young ones as well. Will was himself in it. It was followed by *So This Is London, A Connecticut Yankee at King Arthur's Court,* and *See America First,* in which a family took in the sights of the United States in a Ford (which stood still as the scenery moved past). "The way they are shifting you around the map anyone would think you were Marco Polo, or the Cohens and Kellys [*Abie's Irish Rose*] or the Notre Dame football team," Robert Sherwood warned. "Not that you aren't good in any part of the globe, but it's beginning to look to me as if this travel gag was going to get a little bit monotonous and there isn't anything so fatal as monotony, as a lot of ex-movie stars will be able to tell you . . . Don't let them make you a 'series' star—like Will Rogers in Egypt, Will Rogers among the Passionate Gorillas, Will Rogers at Yale."

Perhaps because of this criticism, Will demanded, as his contract gave him the right to, the privilege of selecting his own scripts. The next day a truck backed up to his house and a couple of hundred scenarios were dumped out. Will took one harried look and had them sent back to the studio.

On one question he was adamant. He met Don Marquis on the Fox lot. "What are you doing here, Don?" he asked.

"I'm writing a story for you."

"Oh . . ." A worried look came over Will's face as he thought, perhaps, of Mehitabel's escapades. "You ain't putting any love scenes in it for me, are you?"

"Why not?" Don asked.

Will turned and waved a hand toward the rim of mountains on the horizon. "Them hills are white with the bones of actors over fifty who thought they could still make love."

Actually, Will's talkies were so successful with children that in many towns and cities, school was let out so they could go to special matinee performances. One reason for this was that the censors' scissors were never used on them. "Will never would make a movie that parents didn't want their children to see," Will Hays stated. "I talked with him about a story a friend of his wanted him to do . . . 'I know it is a fine play by a great writer,' he said, 'but it's for grownups. Most of the story is great but there is a scene in it that people wouldn't want their children to see. You can't omit that scene without spoiling the story. It should not be left out, but I just don't want to play in any picture where folks may think they shouldn't have brought their children.' "

Will's procedure in making a picture became a legend in Hollywood.

After a story had been agreed upon, the night before shooting began he would take the script home, "just to get the general gist of the story." The next day he would arrive at the studio, "smiling that wise-sheepish grin of his—totally and blissfully unprepared in his lines." Anyone who had played with him knew this, but the newcomers did not. "So imagine the actor who's never played with Will Rogers," commented his favorite cameraman, Hal Mohr. "Innocent as a lamb, he arrives on the set, bubbling with gratitude at the opportunity to play in a picture which everyone knows beforehand will be a knock-out box-office success because Will Rogers is in it. He waits for a certain cue in a speech. The cue doesn't come. For Will ad-libs his lines. Furthermore, he improvises them differently every time he plays the scene . . . It isn't because he's too lazy to learn them; it's because each time he rehearses a scene he thinks of a better way of delivering a speech. Something spontaneous that fits the situation far better than the lines the author has written. A spicy humorous touch, like those that give his morning column such punch." In *Steamboat 'Round the Bend,* which Will played with Irvin Cobb, Director John Ford met with the two of them to talk over a scene.

"Do either of you, by any chance, happen to have the faintest idea of what the story is about?" Ford asked.

"I don't," Will confessed. "Something about a river, ain't it? Well, back at Claremore, where I was raised, we don't have any rivers to speak of, so I don't know much about 'em."

"I suppose you haven't had time to glance at the script, then?"

"Been too busy roping calves, John," Will admitted. "Tell you what, you sort of generally break the news to us what this sequence is about, and I'll think up a line for Irvin to speak, and then he'll think up a line for me to speak and that way there wont be no ill feelings or heart-burnings, and the feller that can remember what the plot was about—if there is any plot by then, gets the first prize which will be a kiss on the forehead from John Ford."

Rochelle Hudson, who played with Will in several pictures, had an amusing experience in *Life Begins at Forty.* Will "stubbed his tongue" on a scene twelve times and then, on the thirteenth try when he got it perfectly, Rochelle just stood there with her mouth open, staring at him and unable to say a word.

"Well," Will drawled, with a sly grin, "I guess I sort of gave you a precedent to go by, didn't I?"

On the set, if Will was not reading a newspaper or writing his Daily Wire (the running board of his old touring car, which he used as a dressing room, served as a seat where he pecked out his "Will Rogers Says"), he was clowning or roping. While making *Mr. Skitch* he was twirling his rope in a printshop scene where there was a shelf loaded with a dozen articles including a beer bottle, which he roped. It fell on Sterling Holloway's head but fortunately did not hurt him. The director took Will's rope away from him, "in the interest of safety." A few moments later he was attempting to rope flies with a string. His old touring car was something alive. Louise Dresser said that "one would have thought a horse was hitched to it. It was 'Get up' to start, 'Whoa' to stop, and sultry language addressed as though to an animal when the machine got contrary." The reports that Will Rogers did not swear on occasion, in fact, on most occasions, was, as Mark Twain said about reports of his death, "highly exaggerated." He was "a beautiful cusser," as one man expressed it, and no one loved a good, salty story better than he did.

Will and Shirley Temple were great chums. The two of them would sit together and talk for hours. "Will would talk Shirley's language," Jack Lait commented. "Not baby-talk and not shop. He had the heart of a child and he would make her giggle and she would call him Uncle Will. Rogers was the only actor the management allowed her to become chummy with." Perhaps his friendship with her disclosed the secret of the success of his pictures with children.

When the company for *The County Chairman* went on location in the Mojave Desert, the usual welcoming committee—the band, autograph hunters, town officials, and Chamber of Commerce glad-handers—were at a railroad station to welcome Will. As he stepped off the train, he noticed off to one side a hundred disreputable tramps waiting to say hello "to the idol whose words of wisdom they managed to read in papers salvaged, along with cigarette stubs and cigar butts, from an ashcan."

With a hurried "Howdy do" to the official party, Will sauntered over to the group of "forgotten men." Half an hour later, when he left them, he had distributed $300 among them—all the cash he had. He had to borrow money from the supervisor to get him through the trip.

While on location here a cowboy cornered Will. "One of them European princes wants to buy some of my polo ponies," he said, "but I don't know what he will use for money. What'll I tell him?"

Will scratched his head. "Tell him to give you what he's got down, and the rest when he gets married."

The studios of Hollywood are cursed with one kind or other of pests who knew celebrities "back when." Most are "name-droppers." But some claim credit for the success of the celebrities in their earlier days. One such kept bragging around the Fox Studios how he had been the brains in getting Will started. One day they happened to meet.

"Hello, Will, old fellow," the man greeted.

"Hello," Will replied, fixing him with an eye that seldom forgot a face and never a friend.

"You remember me, don't you?" the man said, glancing uneasily at those in hearing. "I used to be around New York when you were in the *Follies.*"

"Oh, yes," drawled Will, "you were the feller who used to write all my stuff for me, weren't you? I ain't been doing so well since I lost you."

The stories run into the hundreds of those whom Will helped in their motion-picture careers. When Irvin Cobb read the script for *Judge Priest,* a movie based on his stories about a wise old judge, he was surprised to find that some other actor other than Will would play most of the final scenes. "Surely Will will find a plan of shoving that other poor chap, whoever he is, into the shadows and steal the climax himself," he thought. "What happened? That splendid veteran artist, Henry Walthall, carried off the last sequence with Bill standing on the side lines throwing him the cues and practically effacing himself in order to give Walthall a better opportunity to hold the center of the stage. And another result was that Walthall, who in recent years had faded somewhat out of prominence, was given a fat contract on the strength of the performance."

While making *Steamboat 'Round the Bend* Will called the director, John Ford to one side. "John, this kid is good . . ." he inclined his head toward Anne Shirley ". . . she's swell, and she's such a sweet little thing, off and on. Makes me think of my own Mary, somehow. What say, let her dominate this scene instead of me?"

"But you are the star," Ford protested.

"I'm getting the star's billing and the star's salary," Will argued, "but the star of this picture, man or woman, is the one that can steal it. Have a heart, John, give the kid a chance . . ."

There was little else that Ford could do.

Will personally asked that Irvin Cobb be allowed to play with him in *Steamboat 'Round the Bend.* He not only thought that Cobb would make a good actor, but he liked to have him around to talk with. The studio manager told Cobb it was not much of a part.

"I am not much of an actor," Cobb said.

"You know how Bill is," the manager said. "He'll go out of his way, yes, fade into the background himself, to give you a chance. Not because he's your friend, but because he'd do that for some man he never saw before and never expects to see again. When it comes to temperament, he's one trouper that doesn't know the meaning of the word."

Oddly enough, Louise Dresser credited Will's success to an unsuspected quality. "There have been many, many articles written about Will Rogers," she said, "but in none of them have I read of what I think, next to his humor, is the cause of his great popularity on the screen. The woman like him. Friend Will has more sex appeal than Clark Gable. That's strong talk, but as proof, if it were not so, how could he have won such a wife as Betty Rogers?" It was Louise Dresser's devout wish "that every newcomer to the screen could play his first picture with Will Rogers, for with him to help that camera panic from which we have all suffered, would be nothing at all. Kindness and consideration for his cast, for everyone connected with the picture, is creed with him." When a picture was finished ahead of schedule, Will paid the salaries of the extras and the small bit players who lost out because of it.

Spencer Tracy had another explanation for Will's amazing success on the screen. "The longer and more intimately I know Will Rogers," he wrote, "the more I admire him—the more convinced I am that much of his charm lies in his boyishness. In spite of his amazingly wide contacts with world affairs and with the men who bring them about, in many ways Bill has never grown up . . . A strange paradox . . . he is, at the same time, one of the best-known, and one of the least-known, men in the world. By inclination, he is a grand mixer; by instinct, he is as retiring as a hermit . . . As long as Will was talking about someone else, he was brilliant but when it comes to himself he is shy, incurably, painfully shy, ill-at-ease, embarrassed, eager to escape. . . . I have never known a man who was more interested in finding out what makes the wheels go round. I've never known anyone who could throw more enthusiasm into everything he does, into his play and into his work."

According to Frank Borzage, who directed him a number of times, the quality that made Will the outstanding comedian in the films "was his own ability to make audiences forget that he was a comedian. This quality of his was very apparent in the scenes where Rogers was called upon to portray the simple, human emotions that touch the very soul of mankind. The sincerity and conviction with which he did them is what might be expected *of a great tragedian.* Audiences forget Rogers as a wisecracker and think of him as a human being torn with emotion." Although Will many times denied having a "mission," he was basically a crusader and his comedy was merely to make his message more palatable.

Actually, as Will often stated, he wanted to take "a crack at that drama thing" and he had a chance in the spring of 1934 when he played in Eugene O'Neill's *Ah, Wilderness,* taking the part that George Cohan made famous on Broadway. He was a smash hit when it opened in San Francisco. With him was his old sidekick, Stepin Fetchit, who had also played with Cohan.

"Mr. Gawge M. Cohan, he looks toward the audience when he says that line, Mister Rogers," Step said, in mild criticism.

"Well, I'll tell you, Step," Will grinned, "in the legitimate racket every actor faces the audience once because he wants to count the house. I don't have to bother, I'm on straight salary here."

Will's elation over his success in *Ah, Wilderness* ended when it played in Pasadena, California. "Relying on you to give the public nothing that could bring a blush of shame to the cheek of a Christian," a clergyman wrote him, "I attended your performance with my 14-year-old daughter. But, when you gave the scene in which the father visits his son in his bedroom and lectures him on the subject of relations with an immoral woman, I took my daughter by the hand and we left the theatre. I have not been able to look her in the face since."

This letter shocked Will so profoundly that he quit the play immediately. "I am through . . . I could never again say those lines—even to myself in the dark . . . If they hit one person—especially a minister—that way, I could never repeat them. I am out of the show and I will not do the moving picture version either."

The tragedy of this decision is that Will was to be lent by Fox to M-G-M to do the motion-picture version of *Ah, Wilderness.* The time set for the shooting was late summer of 1935. Instead of making the picture, Will headed out on a vacation flight to Alaska with Wiley Post!

Will's parts in talking pictures consisted of an Oklahoma oil millionaire, a small-town pharmacist, a race-track gambler, a small-town newspaper publisher and editor, a physician short on a knowledge of medicine but long on common sense, a lazy landlord, a horse trainer, a wise old judge, and the captain of a steamboat. They consisted of a "gallery of Cuckoolanders" that were all his, and yet each one was individual. At the time of his death he had a contract with Fox that called for ten pictures at $200,000 each, three of which he had completed. In the other seven he intended to round out the range of "Cuckoolanders." One had been rejected by the studio, but which he intended to do, one way or another. "It was based upon an old country philosopher who had the mind and assertion to pretty much run his whole part of the country . . . He became famous state-wide and then by his quaint philosophy to be known to every household in the nation . . . The public opinion became turbulent and as a result he was elected to the Presidency . . . He named the village postmaster as postmaster general . . . the head of the volunteer fire department as his Secretary of War . . . the township squire as Attorney General . . . and someone who had come from his community and watched a steamship dock as Secretary of State." Is it just possible that Will had plans for his old age?

Will had a more realistic view of the motion-picture business itself. "It's made up of two rows of figures, when it's time to talk about a new contract for Rogers or discuss whether that old feller should be dropped, they pull out those figures . . . If Rogers' pictures show a good profit, they want to sign Rogers again . . . They don't stop to say, 'Well, it's because Walthall was so good and Stepin Fetchit certainly made him look bad' . . . So the more work the others do and the better parts they have, the better it is for old Rogers. Why, when I ride over the range down in Santa Monica, I see many a piece that Step's acting has paid for—I even got a Canyon there that I call Fetchit Canyon . . . The more my pictures make, the more I'm worth as a talkie actor . . . I want them to be good . . . I ain't clowning all the time."

Will knew that he had succeeded in talking pictures as he never had in silent ones. "You know, Dave," he said to David Butler, one of his directors, as they discussed Marie Dressler after her death, "there is a permanent record of her on these talking pictures, and she'll always be with us. Don't worry, old Will himself will always be there, too, unless they get tired of me."

One of the last parties Will attended was at the Café de Paris on the Fox lot in honor of the fifty-seventh birthday of Bill Robinson, the greatest soft-shoe dancer of all time. Will loved Robinson as a friend, respected him as a man, and admired him as a performer. "The newspaper men told me they never saw him stay up so late," Robinson recalled. "There were a lot of old-timers there, Trixie Friganza, Walter Kelly and a lot of actors who had not done so well, and lost out when the stage went to pieces, and they couldn't get into the movies. Will was saying the boys had no place to go. 'Even Bill Robinson has got no place for his wonderful feet on the stage any more and he has had to go into the movies to use them,' he said. Then all of a sudden, he began to cry, thinking of the old days and how many artists of those times had nothing any more. At the same party he said, 'I just made a picture *with* Bill Robinson.' Nobody seemed to notice anything. Rogers said again, 'I just made a picture *with* Bill Robinson. If it was in vaudeville, everybody would get it. Wake up.' I don't like to say this because it sounds conceited, but I don't know anybody else as big as him who would have said that . . . He put me in fifteen or sixteen scenes in the picture that I wasn't written in for . . . He wouldn't let them hide my face."

At this same party Will recalled old times with Walter Kelly, the "old Virginia Judge," whom he had played with many times in vaudeville.

"Walter," Will said, "there's one thing we've found out, isn't there?"

"What's that, Will?"

"That it's a great old world, no matter what all seems to be wrong with it, and that we get along a lot better smiling than crying. Anyway, that's my story and I'm going to stick to it."

After finishing his last picture, *Steamboat 'Round the Bend,* Will was hunched up in his car outside the set when Irvin Cobb came along.

"Come on out to the ranch, Irvin," Will said. "We'll get a couple of bronks and ride up the trail to the top of the canyon." The sidewinder smile was on Will's face and the squint in his eyes. "I love to see you in the saddle—you do such humorous things on a horse."

Cobb wanted to go. More precious than anything to him had been the rides up the canyon blathering with Will, but he was afraid Will was just being courteous.

"Can't, Will," he said, "got to get home."

"Better change your mind, old-timer," Will argued. "This picture's done and I'm fixing to go my way and we may not get together again for quite a spell."

Cobb's final picture of Will alive was hunched up in the car, waving good-by and grinning. His thought as he left that day was that "Will was almost the only man I ever knew who went plumb to the top and yet never used the necks of his friends for the rungs of the ladder he climbed on."

37

"I Got to See That Alaska"

WILL WAS IN A GRIM MOOD AS 1935 MOVED ONTO THE stage of history. "We are getting two fairly well-defined schools of thought on what is one's obligation to another. . . . Mr. Roosevelt has a very liberal idea on the subject . . . He thinks that there has to be a more generous feeling toward those who are in need, and if it can't be arrived at by persuasion, he will arrange some other way of making each meet their share. . . . He has done a lot in his attitude to offset a Communistic feeling, for if he did happen to lean to the more conservative element, there would be some justification of hollering for a more equal division . . . But with his doing all he can, and still keeping within the bounds of fairness to all, why, he offsets the old Red . . . I am hoping to get back and see some of 'em down there on that ten yard line in Congress fighting to hold those seats . . . We are living in a great age, ain't we? . . . I think we are in for quite a few changes . . . *I think you will see lots of folks offering to play ball and glad of it, that now think it's their ball, so why should they furnish it.*"

This was not going to be done without a last-ditch fight, a fight that if it had been completely won would almost have ensured the coming of communism. Shellacked at the polls, the special privilege groups turned for protection to the Supreme Court, most of whose members had been appointed by Republican presidents. They were going to use "government" to protect business against "government."

In January the Court "went Republican and said, 'There is nothing you can do about the oil business by law' " when it declared the provision of NRA setting up a code for the petroleum industry as unconstitutional. A few days later, the question of the legality of the right of the government to control the currency in the Gold Act came before the Court. It was upheld in a 5 to 4 decision. A switch in one vote would have decided that a sovereign people, no matter how they voted, had no right to control their medium of exchange, and in effect would have returned the control to Wall Street.

Will had hoped that the NRA might do some good, but even before it was declared unconstitutional it had fallen by the weight of "its own complicated structure." Men in business were no more ready to adopt a nationwide code of ethics and live by it, than nations with their own selfish interests had been ready to join a strong League of Nations and follow international codes of ethics that would prevent warfare. It was unemployment that disturbed Will most and other ills should have been bypassed until this had been cut down. "The minute a thing is long and complicated it confuses . . . Whoever wrote the Ten Commandments made 'em short . . . They may not always be kept, but they can be understood . . . They are the same for all men. . . . Some Industry cant come in and say, 'Ours is a special and unique business. You cant judge it by the others.' . . . No committee come Pullman-carrying-it into Jerusalem looking for Moses and saying 'Ours is a special business.' Moses just went up on the mountain with a letter of credit and some instructions from the Lord, and he just wrote 'em out, and they applied to the steel men, the oilmen, the bankers, the farmers, and even the United States Chamber of Commerce. . . . Well, thats where Moses had it on Hugh Johnson . . . Hugh Moses Johnson went up on Capital Hill and come down with 24 truck loads full of codes . . . He just couldent come out and say, 'Thou shalt pay so much. And thou shalt work thy men only so much, and if thou canst not getteth thee some more, but payeth them likewise.' . . . Hugh should have been born B.C. (before codes) . . . Course that is not all our troubles . . . It wouldent have solved everything any more than the Commandments have solved human weaknesses, *but they did stop all arguments as to whether they were good and fair to all concerned, and they left no argument as to whether they would work if you kept them. . . .*

"But in Moses time the rich dident gang up and say, *'You change that Commandment or we won't play.'*" Perhaps Will was "historically" wrong in this assumption, but the implication of what he said is just as pointed.

In January Wiley Post, who had been experimenting with stratosphere flying, invited Will to make a transcontinental trip from Los Angeles to New York. "He's got the same old *Winnie Mae,* and he's going to try and make it in about seven hours, he's going to fly at an altitude of thirty-five thousand feet and use an oxygen suit." Will decided against going in an oxygen compartment. "If it gets a little stuffy in there, you can't stick your head out at thirty-five thousand feet . . . You got to stay in there, and that's about as long as anyone breathed one mess of oxygen."

Will went out to the airport at daybreak to see Wiley off and accompanied him for a short distance in a camera plane. After taking off, Wiley dropped his wheels. "We left him at eight thousand feet right over the mountains . . . Soon after he had trouble, and had to land . . . He brought her down on her stomach . . . That guy dont need wheels." In spite of this failure, Post, by his stratosphere flights, contributed greatly to the advancement of aviation, particularly in high-altitude flying.

Late in January, 1935, Will and Betty had a nostalgic "old-timer's night" together in New York. It was Sunday and after Will's radio talk they were to have dinner and a quiet evening. "Well, I hadent any more than walked in the place till I was booked for a benefit performance, a kind of combined broadcast by both companies, Columbia and National, for the musicians . . . It was around eleven . . . Well, then I come from my broadcasting and I hear of another show . . . It's a big benefit for the Actors Fund, a fine charity ably sponsored for all these years by the beloved Daniel Frohman . . . Well, I was tickled to death to go there . . . Here I havent been in town over 30 minutes and book myself two shows. . . . You never get so old that somebody dont want you at a benefit, and they always got audiences, too . . . I do know that N.Y. people are the most liberal of all and they always fill a house for a good cause."

As Will and Betty went from show to show they ran into old friends. First, it was Charles Winninger who played Uncle Andy in Ziegfeld's

Show Boat. "I was with Blanche Ring in *The Wall Street Girl's* twenty years ago when he and Blanche were married." After that Will talked with Charley Aldrich, who rode bucking horses in *The Roundup* in which Maclyn Arbuckle starred. They then went to "an Italian Restaurant where we used to go and get the best food in the world, 'Leones,' met the fine old Mother and four sons . . . You eat so much you cant do much but a short benefit afterwards." At the first one they talked with Lillian Shaw, 'the stage's best character singer . . . Played in vaudeville with her for years . . . Lillian looked great . . . John Bunny, the first movie comedian, played with her." To make the evening complete the Actors Fund benefit was played at the old Amsterdam Theatre, where Will had spent ten years with the *Follies.* "Some of the old stage hands were still there . . . Gee, if I had just had as good jokes as I used to have in those days! . . . Saw Blanche Ring there . . . She looked great . . . And Elsie Janis . . . What a marvel, sings, dances, and imitates like no other human in America and throws the rope better than I do . . . Saw Heywood Broun back stage . . . as fat, jolly and amiable as ever."

As Will and Betty walked out of the stage door of the Amsterdam Theatre they had tears in their eyes. "No Amsterdam Theatre, no Flo Ziegfeld . . . I would never have been as lucky, for no other manager in the world would have let me go my own way and do as I saw fit."

Later, at their hotel, Will reminisced about show business. "Isn't it a shame that not in our whole amusement business has any of those we have seen tonight had a successor . . . Everyone of them today can walk on a stage and show that when they learned their trade it was a professon and not an accident. . . . People who have spent a lifetime perfecting the art of entertaining people, then to have the whole stage profession snatched from under them, and ship your entertainment to you in a can."

In March, 1935, President Roosevelt sent a message to Congress asking for legislation for more stringent control of holding companies. It was not meant, he pointed out, to interfere with legitimate business. On the other hand, in the wrongs committed under this device before the stock market crash of October, 1929, it had constituted, in Roosevelt's words, "a corporate invention which can give a few corporate insiders unwarranted and intolerable powers over other people's money."

This was really grist for Will's grinding. "Say did you read about what Mr. Roosevelt said about those 'holding companies'? . . . I wouldent want my worst enemy to call me names like that . . . Now Huey Long, and Father Coughlin and General Hugh Johnson can call each other names, but theirs is all in good clean fun, they don't really mean it, any of 'em . . . But Mr. Roosevelt ain't kidding . . . And what makes it worse, is that it's true . . . *A Holding Company is a thing where you hand an accomplice the goods while the policeman searches you."*

This brought thunderbolts from the mighty down on his head. In desperation he composed a letter, signed by him, that could be sent from the syndicate to all newspapers in answer to complaints. When they kept pouring in, he took care of them in a weekly column. "The other day I went 'Popping Off' about holding companies . . . Now as a matter of fact I don't know a thing about a 'Holding Company' . . . I had read, naturally, that there was graft and inflated values in the forming of a lot of them . . . Then when I read Mr. Roosevelt's tirade against them, I said to myself, well, here is a man that must know what he is talking about . . . He is not given to just having it in for a legitimate enterprise . . . Well, I dident figure that little half-witted remark would upset the whole holding company business. . . .

"But I forgot that a remark hurts in proportion to its truth . . . If it's as untrue as to be ridiculous why, nobody pays any attention to it . . . Now I don't know what it is, but right or wrong, there must be some little teeny weeny bit of underground connivance connected with the idea of holding companies . . . *or is there?* . . . I'm going to stay with writing about the Senate . . . I know those guys backwards, cause thats the way they are generally going . . . So take up your holding company squabbles with Roosevelt, and lay off me."

In March, 1935, Will began to get fiddle-footed again. "I never have been to that Alaska . . . I am crazy to go up there sometime . . . I would like to go in the Winter when those old boys are all snowed in, and I could sit around and hear 'em tell some of those old tales . . . They have lied about 'em so much now that I bet they can tell some good ones . . . They do a lot of flying up there . . . There is some crack aviators . . . Wiley Post went back up there this last summer to visit one of 'em that had helped him out, and they went hunting in a plane . . . Fred Stone and Rex Beach have been up there a lot, but I never did get further north up that way than about a block north of Main Street in Seattle."

In addition to his fretting over conditions in the United States, Will's anxiety about the international situation increased daily. In March, 1935, Mussolini began moving troops into Abyssinia in an effort to gain the needed land for his calculated population explosion. Stalin's army was now over a million. "Russia is in enough devilment, but wonder what the world did for somebody to lay everything on before Russia come along? . . . Then there is Germany . . . I had my head turned and Hitler broke out on me . . . I thought I had him covered . . . He tore up the Versailles treaty . . . It wasent a good treaty, but it was the only one they had . . . They was years making it and tore it up in about a minute . . . England sent its delegation over to talk with Hitler . . . But England dident get to say a word . . . Hitler talked all day and England dident know any more when they went home than they did when they got there . . . Another man named Eden has gone to talk to Russia . . . Then France is going to talk to Russia . . . No nation likes Russia, and they don't like Communists, but they would use them in case of war . . . That's one good thing about European nations . . . They can't hate you so badly they wouldent use you . . . They've told Russia, 'it looks like we're going to have war and we would like to split it with you boys.' . . . So they're going to let Russia in on a good thing in case it shows up . . . You see, they're rushing around now trying to sign up . . . There'll be delegations come and say, 'We dident come to persuade you, or anything, but in case civilization is attacked, why, where do you boys stand?' . . . Well, we better say, 'If civilization hasent done any more than it has since the last war, why, we're against it' . . . So we'll just stay with the side that's against civilization."

In April, 1935, Will summed up the world situation in startling terms: *"Well, today Austria says they want a gun; yesterday it was Germany wanted a gun; England's got a gun; France has got a gun; Italy's got a gun . . . All God's children want guns . . . Going to put on the guns . . . Going to buckle on the guns and smear up all of God's heaven."*

A few days later he jumped down the throats of the critics who were yelping their heads off at an effort to improve conditions in the United States:

I could sit down by the hour and tell of plans that has been tried in the last couple of years that havent worked, that have maby not only looked foolish, but were foolish, but darn it all that criticism wouldent do any good . . . *It would only add to the yell of the pack . . . It would be just another howl in the wilderness* . . . I could sit down from now till morning and tell you what Roosevelt should not have done, but if you give me five minutes continuous time, I couldent tell you what he should have done, and neither can any of the rest of them. . . .

They can view with alarm by the hour, but they cant point with pride to something else for a minute . . . All they say is, *"Let business alone."* . . .

Well, that all sounds fine, and it looks like a good thing to do, and it would be a good thing to do, *but it was done. . . .*

It was already done . . . Mr. Hoover certainly let it alone, right during this same depression. There was not one sign of a handicap put on it . . . There was no hollering about usurping the rights of the Constitution. . . .

The Constitution was a-going wide open and business had the same leeway. . . .

Then what was the holler? All you have to do is to remember back . . . "Why dont the Government do something? . . . Why dont they put out five billion dollars?"

This is not the first time this sum of money has been asked for . . . *It's however the first time they ever got it. . . .*

I think this fellow Roosevelt saw there was a lot of ills connected with the way businesses were run, and he started in with idealistic plans as to how they should be remedied . . . And he has found that any business wont work with you when it's not paying . . . He has persuaded, he has coaxed, he has tried, but you cant make you or I invest our money if we are afraid, and he has kept 'em afraid.

On May 27, 1935, Will tried to console President Roosevelt. "Poor old 'New Deal,' she went to bat three times today with the Supreme

Court pitching and she struck out each time." Once was the Frazier-Lempke bill aimed to help the farmers, another was on a Republican relieved of his job, and the third was declaring the NRA unconstitutional. "We are a funny people . . . Business men have howled from every luncheon table the evils of the whole NRA, then all at once the Supreme Court says, 'The bridle is off, boys, from this day on every man for himself.' . . . Now these same men are rushing back to the banquet tables and unoccupied microphones and shouting, 'Wages must be maintained' . . . 'Cutthroat competition must be curtailed' . . . 'Child labor is wrong' . . . 'The sweat shop must not return.' . . . You cant please everybody. . . . Then the Stock Market went down six points . . . The country is free to return to Republican ways . . . Republican Presidents never went in much for plans . . . They had only *one* plan . . . It said, *'Now, boys, my head is turned, just get it while you can.'* "

In a speech before the Alfalfa Club, with President Roosevelt present, Will kidded him about giving up his "headship" to "nine old men in kimonas." "I am telling you these Democrats are just practically 'nutty.'. . . They havent been as scared since the time in 1932 when they thought somebody might run instead of Hoover . . . The President even gave the [members of the Supreme] Court a dinner the other night, and I understand he give the old boys a little nip to drink, not bribery, mind you, just a little mild persuasion . . . Well, he dident get much satisfaction out of 'em . . . They all drank and went home about half tight, and he don't know any more about their decision than Huey Long knows what his tomorrow's speech in the Senate will be about . . . He is just as ignorant of what is going on in the minds of those nine old men with kimonas on as a U.S. Senator is on what his constituents are thinking about . . . The Democrats forgot there was nine old men here that dident change after the last Administration . . . They told Farley to get rid of 'em, but he was so busy putting Democrats in Republican jobs that he plumb forgot to replace these nine old men . . . They was just a bunch of fine old men what everybody liked, but nobody paid any attention to them . . . Every once in a while a case would finally reach them and in a couple of years be decided 5 to 4 . . . Well, here is the mistake the Democrats made . . . I mean it's one of their mistakes . . . Their principal mistake was in ever learning the alphabet . . . Well, the Democrats started messing with the Constitution . . . Well, you give a Constitution to a Democrat and it's just like giving a box of tacks to a baby . . . Sooner or later he will swallow one of 'em . . . The only difference between a Democrat and the baby is the Democrat *will swallow all of 'em. . . .*

"You see, he thought he could play with the Constitution because nobody was watching it . . . But they dident know that Jouett Shouse wasent working and, with Senator Nye investigating the Duponts, it looked like they was out of a job . . . Raskob guessed wrong in 1928, and they needed some respectability as well as money . . . So they thought of Ed Hutton [1] . . . Ed wasent doing much . . . Every time you elect a Democrat, you close two things, the Red Light District and the Stock Exchange . . . So the firm of Shouse, Raskob, Hutton and a whole powder can full of Duponts started in watching the Constitution. . . . They had the money, but Shouse had the idea and the title . . . He says, get 'Liberty' in here somewhere . . . You cant go wrong with Americans if you mix the word 'Liberty' in . . . It's such a novelty to Americans that they go for it . . . So when the Democrats saw that all that was watching the Constitution was the 'Liberty League,' why, that was a cinch . . . But the Democrats figured without those nine old men in kimonas . . . So that's what makes Washington so jumpy . . . It's not the soldiers, under the auspices of the secondhand automobile dealers, who are demanding their bonus . . . It's not the voices of William Borah and Hiram Johnson making the last pleas for American independence . . . It's nine old men who Washington had forgot, not the forgotten man, but the forgotten nine men."

A week before Will flew off to Alaska he took notice of information given out by President Roosevelt ("it dident get much publicity in the press") that 58 of the richest people in the United States paid no federal income taxes on 37 per cent of their income. "This soaking of the rich has got two sides to it . . . Roosevelt gets him a pack of humorously called 'Brain Trusters' to help him devise ways and means of trying to get this extra 37 percent . . . And the rich get them some

[1] These men, representing many hundreds of millions, were the motivating "spirits" in the much-laughed-at Liberty League. Here was an organization whose activities should have erected around it a pyramid for the preservation of the *status quo* (Latin for "the hell-of-a-mess we're in").

lawyers that are just as smart as Roosevelt's tribe, and their job is to cook up an antidote . . . So, up to now, most of the soaking of the rich has been done in the papers and not at the cash register."

On Will's last night in Los Angeles he and Betty went to a rodeo and remained until time for his plane to leave. She described it in her book about him:

The California air was cool, and as we sat in the grandstand at Gilmore Stadium, I remember thinking there was something incongruous about a rodeo under floodlights. I missed the sunshine and the hot smell of cattle. But Will was having a good time. Since the old Indian Territory days when he had taken part in them himself, Will had never lost his delight in the rodeo contests—calf roping, bulldogging and bronk riding. Even tonight he could not stay away, although his bags were packed and he was taking the eleven o'clock plane to San Francisco on the first leg of his flight to Alaska. . . .

Sitting there in our box under the floodlights, I watched him grin and wave to the contestants as they rode by on the tanbark. Will knew most of the boys in the show, and one by one, as the evening wore on, the old-timers came over to shake hands with him. . . .

Someone gave Will a little wood-and-paper puzzle while we sat there. Quite unconsciously he toyed with it throughout the evening. It was a mannerism I knew so well, and which was so much a part of him. His restless hands could never stay still. Then, when the show was over, I saw him stuff the puzzle in the pocket of his coat. The printed program went there too. . . . His pockets, like those of a boy, always held trinkets or souvenirs of one kind or another.

We drove from Gilmore Stadium to the airport. The waiting room was crowded and we slipped outside to talk until the plane was ready to go. Then we said good-by, and with his overcoat over his shoulder and a roll of midnight editions under his arm, Will stepped aboard. The plane taxied down the field, turned around and came back for the take-off. As the ship nosed up, I caught a fleeting glimpse through the window—he was smiling—and I stood looking up at the red and green lights of the plane until they disappeared in the darkness.

Will stopped at San Francisco to conduct a little business and then flew to Seattle, where Wiley Post was waiting for him. A few days later, Betty went east to be with Mary, Bill Jr. signed on an oil tanker to go to the Philippines, and Jim was on a ranch in Oklahoma.

In the meantime, in "the little red bus," Will and Wiley flew to Juneau, following the inner passage. "Most marvellous trip. No danger with this guy . . . Thousand mile hop from Seattle to Juneau . . . Was going to stop at Ketchikan for lunch but mist and rain, and he just breezed through never over 100 feet off the water, and talk about navigating, there is millions of channels and islands and bays and all look alike (to me) but this old boy turns up the right alley all the time . . . You know I just been thinking about things at home . . . You know who I bet would like to be on this trip, Mr. Roosevelt."

A trip to Skagway "to see the famous Chilkoot Pass" had to be postponed, and Will and Wiley spent the day talking with Rex Beach and others in Juneau. When the weather cleared up, they made a quick flight into the Yukon country ("making the Chilkoot Pass in ten minutes and it took the pioneers two and three months"), then to Anchorage. "Had a day off and we went flying with friends, Joe Crosson and Joe Barrows, another fine pilot . . . In a Lockheed Electra we scaled Mount McKinley, the highest one on the North American continent . . . Bright sunny day and most beautiful sight I ever saw . . . Crosson landed on a glacier over half way up it in a plane and took off . . . Flew right by hundreds of mountain sheep . . . Flew low over moose and bear right down in the valley."

In his last published weekly column Will described a visit with trappers. "Well, thats one thing I dont believe I could ever be, that trapping animals . . . On the other hand I expect I do things every day that a trapper couldent do . . . Here we pass up folks every day, every hour, that we could help, but dont go to the trouble doing it, when we can well afford the time or money . . . The old trapper would mush through the winter fifty below for days to help a friend . . . We think they punish animals . . . We punish humans only we dont think so."

While in Fairbanks Will began another Weekly column but never finished it. The last page was still in his typewriter when their plane crashed. The column was about dogs and the part they played in Alaskan life. He had met the famous "musher" and dog-race winner, Seppala, who won fame in his race to take diphtheria serum to Nome at the time of an epidemic. Will learned from Seppala that the dog Balta (who has a statue in Central Park in New York) was not the real canine hero. The real leader was named Fox, but because of Balta's romantic name he was played up by the newspaper men. Will ended with an anecdote told him by a miner who had a dog named Mickey. The dog got chased by a bear and ran straight to his master, who had to shoot the bear. "They say there is more fellows been caught by a bear just that way . . . An old pet dog jumps the bear and then they hike straight to you, and the bear after 'em, and the first thing you know you got a bear in your lap, and a dog between your feet . . . So Mickey is a great bear dog . . . So there is two kinds of bear dogs, the ones that drive 'em away and the ones that bring 'em in . . . Little Mickey thought he had done it, as the miner said he chewed all the hair off the bear, after death."

The narrative ends at this point. It was time to leave for Point Barrow. The Yukon River is narrow at Fairbanks, with several bends in it, and Wiley was afraid they would have trouble getting the plane up with a full load of gas. Instead, they took off with a partial load, landed at a lake fifty miles away, where gas had been sent, then headed into the Arctic north.

38

"A Smile Has Disappeared from the Lips of America."—John McCormack

IN THE WEIRD, HALF-LIGHT OF AN ARCTIC EVENING, August 15, 1935, the silence was broken only by children playing in the streets of Barrow, Alaska, the northernmost part of the North American continent. These youngsters were taking advantage of every moment, for soon almost complete darkness would shut them indoors for a long winter. Most of the adults were inside eating their supper, or talking. At ten o'clock an Eskimo, Clare Okpeasha, came running into the village from the southwest, out of breath. He had covered fifteen miles of the rain-soaked tundra from the place where he and his family were camped for seal hunting.

"Airplane fall . . . maybe two mans die near my camp," he gasped to a couple of men who came out at his cry.

An excited buzz went up as others poured out of houses and soon filled the rain-puddled street. Within ten minutes a whaling boat was manned and filled with men and boys, among them the government schoolteacher, Mr. Daugherty, and Technical Sergeant Stanley R. Morgan, of the United States Army Signal Corps, on duty at Barrow.

There was considerable speculation in the village as to the men in the plane. It was known that Will Rogers and Wiley Post intended to come to Barrow to visit "King Charlie" Brower, the famous Arctic trader, but they were not expected for several days. No plane was due from Nome by way of Wainwright, which would be on the course where the Eskimo was camped. A plane coming from Fairbanks to

Barrow would fly from the southeast. In making the flight Joe Crosson always touched the coast southeast of Cape Halket and then followed the coastline northeast to his destination. Wiley Post would certainly have consulted Crosson on the best route to take.

On the way to the scene Sergeant Morgan questioned Clare in an effort to learn the identity of the two men.

"How do you know how many men were in the plane?" he asked.

"Me talked with mans," Clare replied.

"After they had fallen?"

"No, before they fall when they come down on water and ask me how go to Barrow, where Barrow is, how far?"

"Did they tell you their names?"

"No, mans no tell names, but big mans, two mans, one sore eye with bandage on eye. He and other man then go inside plane, and man with sore eye start engine, and go up, maybe ten fathom and then engine spit, start, then stop, start some more little, then plane fall just so [indicating with his hands a bank, and a fall on right wing, and a nose dive into water, with a complete somersault forward]."

From this description Morgan and Daugherty knew that the plane was Wiley Post's and the passenger was Will Rogers.

"Did you wade out to the plane and see if they were alive?" Sergeant Morgan asked.

"No, me stand on sandspit forty feet away and holler to mans, but no answer, and so me hurry quick to Barrow to tell people to come quick."

Hampered by strong currents and ice floes, it took three hours for the boat, powered by a small outboard motor, to reach the scene of the accident. Dense fog and partial darkness gave the place a ghostly appearance, and their hearts chilled at what they felt sure they would find there. It was obvious, as they drew near, that no human being could have survived the terrific crash. The plane was a mass of twisted and broken metal, wood, and fabric partially underwater.

By now other Eskimos from the hunting party had managed to cut into the cabin and take Will's body out, as he had been well back and partially protected by the baggage. The force of the impact had driven the engine back on Post's body, pinning it down. The plane had to be torn apart to extricate it.

Wiley Post's wristwatch had stopped at 8:15 P.M., which obviously was the time of the crash. Will's Ingersoll watch in his pocket was still running and showed 3:30 A.M., the same as the watches of those in the boat. In the few seconds it took to fall, Wiley had switched off the ignition to prevent fire. In Will's pockets there was a stub of a pencil, a picture of his daughter, Mary, clipped from a newspaper, a few coins, a knife, the program of the rodeo, and the little wood-and-paper puzzle.

The bodies of the two men were wrapped in eiderdown sleeping bags, found in the wreckage, placed in Clare's umiak, which was towed behind the whaling boat. On the return trip the Eskimos sang death hymns in their native tongue. At Barrow the umiak was drawn across a sand pit separating the ocean from a lagoon, and rowed to the door of the hospital, where the bodies were turned over to Dr. Henry R. Griest, a Presbyterian medical missionary in charge of the institution. With the help of a nurse and Charlie Brower, Dr. Griest prepared the bodies for interment. As there was no mortician and no casket in Barrow, the bodies were wrapped in clean linen and placed under lock and key in the warehouse of the hospital to await instructions from the families.

For days Barrow had eagerly awaited the arrival of the two famous men. "We have no brass bands, no banqueting halls," Dr. Griest wrote, "no professional speechmakers, but we do have the choicest reindeer roasts to be had anywhere. We are by common consent permitted to shoot fat wild geese when we can, for our own consumption, since if the game laws were observed by us we would never secure such game. And we had hoped to place before these noted travelers such a feast by way of venison and wild fowl as would prove worthy."

Savored with King Charlie's wry wit, wisdom and rich experience, nothing could have pleased Will and Wiley better. Will would have brought Charlie down laughing, and the old buccaneer's exploits would have made Will's report of arctic doings more vital. Instead, a black Friday broke over the little village. "It is doubtful if a person in Barrow slept that night," Sergeant Morgan reported. "All sat around the hospital with bowed head with little or no talking."[1] Will's Cherokees would have done the same.

The chill spread over all Alaska. "Thursday everybody in this country was smiling at Will's jokes," Rex Beach wrote. "Today there are no smiles here. This is the blackest day Alaska has known."

A wireless from Colonel Charles A. Lindbergh, acting as representative for the families of the deceased men, ordered that the bodies be turned over to Joe Crosson to be flown back to the States. Crosson flew to Barrow, the bodies were loaded into his plane, and after only a few hours of sleep and rest he took off on his sorrowful mission. He continued his flight, almost without food or rest, until at Seattle the controls were taken over by W. A. Winston, Pan-American pilot, who flew to Los Angeles. There Will's body was removed and Crosson continued on to Oklahoma with the body of Wiley.

Long before now the "black fog" that had descended upon Alaska had spread to the United States and to much of the world. As a "tear suffused the eye of America," its heart went out to the families of the dead men. Betty was in Maine, where Mary was in *Ceiling Zero,* which had as its climax a fatal airplane crash. Will Jr. was on a Standard Oil tanker at San Diego. Jim was on his way to New York in an automobile with his cousin after "playing cowboy."

"It can't be," Betty gasped when told of the accident. "I love him too much."

While waiting for Will's body to be returned, the family gathered in New York, and from there went by train to California. To escape curious crowds, they were taken off the train at Victorville by Betty's brother and driven to the ranch house in Santa Monica. There a box awaited Betty from Juneau, Alaska, addressed in Will's handwriting. Inside was a red fox fur—a mute testimonial that no matter where Will happened to be his thoughts never strayed far from her.

The linen that was wrapped around Will's body bore a note from Mrs. Griest to Betty: "I could recognize Mr. Rogers by his pictures

[1] Much of the information for the above has been taken from Sergeant Morgan's official report to the War Department, and from Dr. Griest's account in his mimeographed publication, *The Northern Star* (published "every once in a while"—this one for November, 1935), pp. 35-37.

I have seen. Both carried faint smiles on their still faces." The family went to Forest Lawn to view the body. "At first I thought I would not go," Betty wrote, "that I would just remember his cheery Goodbye at the airport, but his sister Sallie and Dr. White were convinced that I should go—that I might always regret it later if I didn't. There was not a mark on his face. I came away greatly comforted. As Mrs. Griest had said—he was smiling—and I could just imagine Will laughing down from his seat in the back of the plane—waving to the lone figure on the shore—a goodbye to his newest friend—as Wiley pointed the nose up, turned the plane around and headed off in the right direction."

Betty's first thought was that Will should be buried at Chelsea beside his father and sister. But the family lived in California and she decided in favor of interment there.

> The last scene was in the little chapel at Forest Lawn Memorial Park [wrote Will's long-time friend, Harry Carr]. The mobs of the morning had scrambled and fainted and gone away. The little church was a scene of serenity and fragrance. A gentle breeze from the ocean caressed the flowers and stirred the flag that draped the bronze casket before the altar. . . .
>
> Into the tiny church came Will's old friends. Every person in every pew was a comrade . . . an intimate . . . an old tried friend . . . men who had ridden herd in the choking dust of the range, who had dared the perils of the sky with him . . . who had shared last nickels in his struggling stage days. . . .
>
> In front of me sat an old frontiersman who had one piece of his ear shot off . . . one pew filled with Indians from Rogers' ranch in their work sweaters, stolid and immobile . . . but in many a tepee on lonely reservations the death song will be chanted with bitterness and sorrow . . .
>
> Into an almost empty church comes Will Hays and takes his seat in the rear . . . Mary Pickford in a little white dress . . . Frank Borzage . . . Bill Hart, white-haired, his face working with grief . . . a group of aviators with the wings that will continue to dare and die just the same. . . .
>
> Marching up the aisle, two navy officers in full dress, representatives of the President of the United States, to pay tribute to a gentle-hearted cowhand. . . .

The Postmaster General of the United States . . . actors from the studios . . . the last to enter the church were Fred Stone and his wife and daughters. . . .

The service was as simple as Will himself . . . the farewell of a group of comrades to one who had ridden over the horizon.

The Irish-born American tenor, John McCormack, expressed the mood of the country when he commented that "a smile has disappeared from the lips of America and her eyes are suffused with tears." The smile has not returned and the tears continue to flow.

Enough could not be said or heard. Practically all other news was pushed from the front pages of newspapers, little and big, and the radio airwaves were jammed with it. "Nowhere in the memory of the oldest newspapermen is there a record of the passing of a private citizen rating an eight-day 'follow-up' series in the national press," wrote Jack Lait. "Few Presidents who died in office held general interest so long . . . And yet of the amazing matters I have covered—crimes, war, disaster—never has any account I have written elicited such a flood of communications from the entire country . . . Only intense worship of an individual could cause people to so cherish little anecdotes, to so crave answers to little questions of fact . . . And not one dissenting word! . . . Not even the familiar constitutional cranks, carpers and hero-haters have come forward, a unique manifestation."

Messages went out to the press from President Roosevelt, Vice-President Garner, Cabinet members, former President Hoover, Senate Majority Leader Robinson ("probably the most widely known citizen of the United States, and certainly the best beloved"), Speaker of the House Sam Rayburn. Other messages came from such great industrialists as John D. Rockefeller, Owen Young, Charles Schwab, Henry Ford ("Will Rogers' death comes to me as a great personal loss"). Others came from the Prince of Wales, Lady Astor, and other notables in England, France, Italy, Mexico, Japan, China, and countries all over the world. Will's own profession added its grief in a way that would have pleased him. "When you want to get a line on a feller, don't get it from the man himself, don't get it from the feller he pals around with . . . Get it from someone who works with him." A veritable flood of messages came from these—L. B. Mayer, Will Hays,

Eddie Cantor, George M. Cohan, Chic Sales, Gene Buck ("He enjoyed a position never before attained by anyone of whom I ever heard. He could go any place, see anything, talk or write about it afterward, and in such a way that the humble and the great accepted it"), Irvin Cobb, Irene Rich, Stepin Fetchit. "I really can't believe Will is gone," Spencer Tracy said. "He was so alive and real." In unveiling a plaque in honor of Will at the Fox Studios, Shirley Temple choked up and forgot her lines. "I loved him, too," she got out. The 6,000 members of the organization Hoboes of America observed a thirty-day mourning period ["Well, they got more time to mourn than other people, ain't they?" Will might have said about this].

A movement began immediately, backed and endorsed by almost every prominent man and woman in the country, to establish a memorial to Will. Press releases skillfully handled by professionals fed stories to morning and afternoon editions. But somehow this was not the way people wanted to remember him. Congress appropriated half a million dollars for a memorial and President Roosevelt vetoed it in a message Will would have approved. Then came the action that would have warmed his heart. Betty donated the land at Claremore, where Will always said he would live someday, and the legislature of the state of Oklahoma appropriated the money for a memorial. The building was dedicated on November 4, 1938, on Will's fifty-eighth birthday.

The chief speaker at the ceremonies was Jesse Jones, who ended by saying, "We miss Rogers as we have missed no other man. We did not fully realize, while he was still with us, the tremendous service he rendered to his country. Many times since he left, I have seen situations where Will Rogers' droll comments would have been of immense help." The climax to the dedication came in a radio broadcast by President Roosevelt from Hyde Park. "This afternoon we pay grateful homage to the memory of a man who helped the nation to smile. . . . And, after all, I doubt if there is among us a more useful citizen than the one who holds the secret of banishing gloom, of making tears give way to laughter, of supplanting desolation and despair with hope and courage, for hope and courage always go with a light heart. There was something infectious about his humor. His appeal went straight to the heart of the nation. Above all things, in a time grown too solemn and somber he brought his countrymen back to a sense of proportion. . . . When he wanted people to laugh out loud he used the methods of pure fun . . . And when he wanted to make a point for the good of all mankind, he used the kind of gentle irony that left no scars behind it . . . The American nation, to whose heart he brought gladness, will hold him in everlasting remembrance."

At the end of President Roosevelt's address, Will's daughter, Mary, unveiled the heroic bronze of him done by Jo Davidson. Later, at another ceremony, a similar statue was unveiled in the Capitol, where Will took his place in the Hall of Fame.

The Memorial building, in a superb setting overlooking Claremore, Oklahoma, is a rambling, ranch-style structure. It has four main foyers grouped around a central rotunda with Will's statue in the center. In the east foyer there is a magnificent display of saddles and trappings that Will collected from all over the world. The north and west galleries contain Will's personal effects and trophies, including his credentials to the Russian government and his battered portable typewriter. In the other foyer are thirteen dioramas depicting the highlights of Will's life.

Many of Will's friends thought he would have preferred that his final resting place would be in the Will Rogers country that he loved so well. A crypt was built by private subscription at the Memorial for this purpose. It was not until Betty was on her deathbed that she consented to have his remains moved. His body was interred in the crypt, in a private ceremony, on May 22, 1944. A month later Betty died. In the autumn her body was removed to the crypt, and she now rests beside Will and their son, Fred Stone Rogers, who died in infancy.

"Will's here all right," said Joe De Yong, cowboy artist, poet and friend of Will, when he visited the Memorial. "I feel his spirit in the wind as it hits my face."

Many thousands of visitors at the Memorial feel the same way. Perhaps Debs Myers in *Holiday,* April, 1950, caught the real reason: "In the garden outside the Memorial, amidst the redbud and dogwood, an old man and a boy stand talking before Will Rogers' tomb. 'But, Grandpa,' the boy says, 'why did they bury him in Claremore, they're a lot fancier places than Claremore, ain't they?' The old man looks at the town below, dozing in the fading sun. 'Claremore and Will Rogers,' the old man says, 'they belong together, part of the prairie; and no matter how far a man goes, at the end he likes to come back to his roots.' "

Index